THE LAST MODERN

Also by James King

William Cowper: A Biography
Interior Landscapes: A Life of Paul Nash

co-editor
The Letters and Prose Writings of William Cowper
William Cowper: Selected Letters

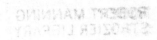

THE LAST MODERN

A Life of Herbert Read

JAMES KING

Weidenfeld and Nicolson · London

Copyright © James King 1990

First published in Great Britain in 1990 by
George Weidenfeld and Nicolson Limited
91 Clapham High Street, London sw4 7ta

isbn 0 297 81042 1

Photoset by Deltatype Ltd, Ellesmere Port, Cheshire
Printed in Great Britain by
Butler and Tanner, London, Frome.

For John Covolo

*in friendship
and gratitude*

Contents

Illustrations

Barbara Hepworth and Ben Nicholson, 1932 (Hulton-Deutsch)
Interior of the studio flat at 3 The Mall, Parkhill Road, Hampstead (Read Family)
A page layout from *Art and Industry* (Faber & Faber, 1934)
The surrealist exhibitors, 1936 (Eileen Agar)
Naum Gabo at work in 1938 on a Construction (Grant and Nina Williams)
Gabo's prototype design for the Jowett Car (Graham and Nina Williams)
André Raffalovich: drawing by Eric Gill, *c.* 1920 (*Eric Gill*, Fiona MacCarthy, Faber & Faber, 1989)
Douglas Cooper: drawing by Graham Sutherland, 1966 (William McCarty-Cooper)
John Gray: collotype of pencil drawing by Eric Gill, 1928 (*Eric Gill*, Fiona MacCarthy, Faber & Faber, 1989)
Edward Dahlberg (Bernard Gotfryd)
Read with Jung at Küsnacht (Read Family)
Madonna and Child by Henry Moore, Hornton stone, 1943–4 (St Matthew's Church, Northampton)
Crucifixion by Graham Sutherland, oil on hardboard, 1946 (St Matthew's Church, Northampton)
Read with Peggy Guggenheim and Ruth Francken in Venice, 1953 (Ruth Francken)
Read with portrait of himself by Karel Appel, oil, 1962 (Read Family)
Read asleep (Ruth Francken)
Stonegrave (Jorge Lewinski)
Read in his study at Stonegrave, *c.* 1960 (Read Family)

page 127 'Getting Ready at Burlington House: An attempted gate-crash by the Moderns is frustrated': cartoon by T. Derrick (*Punch*, 3 January 1934)
page 159 'Surrealist Exhibition, London 1936': cartoon by James Boswell (*Left Review*)
page 190 'Oh, *that's* Herbert's muse': drawing by Taylor (*New Yorker*, *c.* 1940–5)
page 217 'Snake Around the World and a Boat' from *Education through Art* (Faber & Faber, 1943)
page 243 *The Poet Reading to his Children* by Barbara Hepworth: oil and pencil on paper, 1948 (Leeds City Art Gallery)
page 302 'WHAAM!' by Heath (*Punch*, 8 March 1967)

Acknowledgements

Although this is not an 'official' biography, I stand much indebted to the kindness and thoughtfulness of Herbert Read's family. Towards the end of my research on this book, Lady Read received me at Stonegrave and answered my many questions about her late husband. Read's children, Thomas Read, Sophie Read Hare and Piers Paul Read provided me with valuable pieces of information, as did their brother, Benedict, who is his father's literary executor. William Read talked in detail about his older brother. John Read, the son of Herbert Read and his first wife, Evelyn Roff, discussed his parents' troubled marriage with great candour. More than anyone else, John was privy to many important pieces of information about his father's early life. I could not have written this book without his generous, much appreciated help and friendship.

I am grateful to the following individuals for assistance with the writing of this book: Eileen Agar, Michael Anderson, Pat Arrowsmith, Sir Martyn Beckett, Eric Bentley, Stanley Berne, John Berger, A. Betteridge, Kenneth Blackwell, Jennifer Booth, Michael Bott, J. T. Boulton, Sir Alan Bowness, Neville Braybrooke, Stanley Burnshaw, Peter Cadogan, Janet Carruthers, April Carter, Andrew Causey, Marion Helen Cobb, Giles Constable, Francis Judd Cooke, Richard Cork, David Daiches, A. C. Davis, Alexander Davis, Charles L. De Fanti, Michael De-la-Noy, T. J. Diffey, Peter du Sautoy, H. S. Ede, Caroline Elam, Valerie Eliot, Eric Fernie, Ruth Francken, Colin Franklin, Norman Franklin, Gillian Furlong, Alfreda S. Galt, Juliet Gardiner, Margaret Gardiner, Albert Gérard, Howard Gerwing, Sir Lawrence Gowing, Graham Greene, John Guenther, Nicholas Hare, Lilace Hatayama, Cathy Henderson, Patrick Heron, John V. Howard, Linda Hutcheon, Sheila Jones, Robin Kinross, William Kinsley, Dorothy Kosinski, Bruce Laughton, Edward Lavitt, Linden Lawson, Robert Lima, Edward Lobb, Christina Lodder, Sir Lesley Martin, E.

Martineau, Nigel McIsaac, Dorothy Morland, P. S. Morrish, Stephen Z. Nonack, Fiona Pearson, M. R. Perkin, C. G. Petter, J. Pimpaneau, Norman Potter, Anne Pottier, Jean F. Preston, Kathleen Raine, Michael Randle, Jennie Rathbun, Paul C. Ray, Celia Read, Louise Read, Emily Read, Flora Read, Sir James M. Richards, S. P. Rosenbaum, T. G. Rosenthal, John Russell, Nicholas B. Scheetz, Margaret Selley, Linda Shaw, Anne Sinclair, Margaret M. Sharp, C. D. W. Sheppard, Richard Shone, Robin Skelton, Lola L. Szladits, Neil Somerville, Frances Spalding, Muriel Spark, Sir Stephen Spender, Charlotte Stewart, Geoffrey Summerfield, Michael Sweeney, Meg Sweet, David Sylvester, Hans Syz, Richard Taylor, David Thistlewood, Valerie Thomas, Paula Thorne, Michael Turnbull, Jonathan Vickers, Ann Waldron, Nicholas Walter, Diane Watson, Nina Gabo Williams, Patricia Willis, S. A. Yates, Jerry Zaslove, Arlene Zekowski.

I wish to thank the staff of various institutions for access to material in their possession and for their assistance: BBC Written Archives; British Council Archives; National Sound Archive; The British Library; Calderdale District Archive; Central Library, Edinburgh; Cornell University Library; The Getty Center for the History of Art and the Humanities; Georgetown University Library; Houghton Library, Harvard University; Archive, The Institute of Contemporary Arts; The Lifwynn Foundation; The Henry Moore Foundation; Berg Collection, The New York Public Library; The Library, Princeton University; The Roland Penrose Archives; Queen's University Library; The Russell Archive, McMaster University; Scottish National Gallery of Modern Art; Tate Gallery Archive; School for Peace Studies, The University of Bradford; The Library, The University of California at Los Angeles; The University of Edinburgh, Library; Brotherton Library, The University of Leeds; The Library, University of Liverpool; The Library, University of London; Routledge Archives, The University of Reading; Harry Ransom Humanities Research Centre, The University of Texas at Austin; National Art Library, The Victoria and Albert Museum; Beinecke Library, Yale University.

The following have kindly given me permission to quote from unpublished or published material in which they own copyright: Benedict Read for permission to quote from his father's letters and diaries; Sir Alan Bowness for extracts from Barbara Hepworth's and Ben Nicholson's letters to Read; Nina Gabo Williams for extracts from her father's letters to Read; William McCarthy Cooper for extracts from Douglas Cooper's letters to Read.

The Social Sciences and Humanities Research Council of Canada and the Arts Research Board of McMaster University provided me with financial assistance. The Killam Program of the Canada Council awarded me a Research Fellowship which gave me the time to write this book.

Leila Ryan pointed out to me that a biography of Read was needed, and I hope that her considerable enthusiasm for the man and his writings is reflected here. In his customary way, George Woodcock has been a staunch ally and friend. My research assistant, Anne Massey, has been indefatigable in discovering Herbert Read material. John Covolo read the typescript of this book with his customary zeal. Candida Brazil, my editor at Weidenfeld, has been exemplary, as has her copy-editor, Peter James. While in London, I have profited from discussions with my good friends Caroline Kirby, Rosanne Musgrave and, especially, Heidi Woodhead. My wife, Christine Dalton, and my children, Alex and Vanessa, have given me – at their expense – the time and the space in which to write this book.

Before he died, Herbert Read sold the vast majority of his papers to the McPherson Library at the University of Victoria in British Columbia. I have been greatly assisted in making use of this considerable archive by Dietrich Bertz, who has an unrivalled knowledge of this material. I am deeply appreciative of Dietrich's many kindnesses.

Preface

Herbert Read is one of the most celebrated English men of letters of this century. During his thirty-year reign as taste-maker and cultural impresario, Read was involved in a wide variety of activities. He wrote essays and books in which he attempted to come to grips with contemporary trends in painting and sculpture; he was a virulent castigator of English philistinism, his championing of the surrealists in 1936 being one of his best-known ventures into the arena of public controversy; he was one of the founders in 1947 of the Institute of Contemporary Arts; he was a staunch defender of his close friends Naum Gabo, Barbara Hepworth, Henry Moore and Ben Nicholson; he was a poet of considerable accomplishment whose own inner landscape is best glimpsed in his verse; his autobiographies are moving accounts of his search for personal and intellectual identity; his own novel, *The Green Child*, is a vivid exotic fable about the search for the self; his writings on the English romantic poets brought those then neglected writers to the attention of many new readers; as a publisher, he was imaginative and resourceful, promoting, for example, Denton Welch's *Maiden Voyage* and *In Youth Is Pleasure* and the novels of Samuel Beckett; he was a friend of Jung and one of the first literary critics to use psychoanalytical methods; he espoused his anarchist convictions in pamphlets such as *Freedom: Is It a Crime?*; he was a member of the anti-nuclear Committee of 100.

In a *Punch* drawing from 1964, one gallery-goer asks another: 'Do you think Sir Herbert Read takes something to keep him so avant-garde?' As the cartoon demonstrates, Read in 1964 was still the best-known promoter of modernism in the English-speaking world. He was famous, but fame had been dearly bought. His reputation as the defender of 'advanced' art was, as far as he was concerned, a dubious distinction. For him, such notoriety implied failure. Failure because, as the cartoon intimates, 'avant-garde' was still, as far as most Englishmen were concerned, a strange, uncomfortable notion, a concept which raised xenophobic shackles. Failure because Read's reputation rested on his writings on art – not on his poetry, his novel or his literary criticism. For him, art criticism had been an accidental occupation, into which he had haplessly wandered and then been trapped. Failure because Reed had acquired the reputation of approving everything that was contemporary. In reality Read despised, for example, the Euston Road School and towards the end of his life he became increasingly distrustful of many of the new isms. Failure because modernism could be regarded as an eccentric blind alley, down which no sensible English person would want to stray.

Read saw himself as an Englishman who had resolutely espoused English culture. True, he had wanted his fellow countrymen to be aware of significant developments on the Continent and in the United States, but he had done this so that British art could hold its own with the art of any other nationality. Although Read defended some of the formalist notions of Pater, Fry and Bell, he was really a disciple of John Ruskin, the man who had attempted to place painting and sculpture on the same level of accomplishment as literature. Like Ruskin, Read was severely criticized for his attempt to reform an iconoclastic nation, united in its antipathy to the sensuousness of the visual. Again, like Ruskin, Read was a latter-day romantic, who valued works of art and literature which engendered the strong, direct feelings of their makers: 'In the end, art should so dominate our lives that we might say: there are no longer works of art, but art only. For art is then the way of life.'

Modernism for Read was a formalist aesthetic which recognized the primacy of the artist's romantic vision. Read's own taste in art tended towards classical expression (geometric, abstract art) rather than figurative, brightly coloured or emotive works of art. He saw abstract art as the prime modernist way to accomplish the modern artist's full potential as creator. Read is therefore often seen, incorrectly, as someone who denigrated the traditions of English literature and painting. Yet his autobiographies, novel and poetry are strongest when they evoke the pastoral landscape of Yorkshire. And his defence of Wordsworth, Coleridge and Shelley displays a fascination with their search for the immanent and transcendent. Read, a classicist by temperament, was entranced by and defended romanticism.

For Read, modernism could help twentieth-century England find a new, revolutionary 'way of life'. In defining modernism as a movement which rejected forms of expression which no longer conveyed any real meaning, he remained sympathetic to a plurality of new movements (imagism, vorticism, cubism, expressionism, surrealism, constructivism, abstraction, abstract expressionism, action painting) which gave the writer and artist the opportunity to re-explore the world and its past. A painter, such as Paul Nash, interested in the tradition of landscape painting could find that commitment revitalized by contact with surrealism. An artist of different proclivities, Henry Moore, could use an amalgam of surrealism and abstraction to explore the timeless theme of mother and child and, in the process, give birth to works of art essentially English.

Ultimately, Read was interested in fusing that which was distinctly English and often parochial to that which was European and cosmopolitan. He saw the provincial and the cosmopolitan as twin strands in his own character and he attempted to intertwine them. Read was an ideal spokesman for being both English and modern because he was aware of those often contradictory impulses within himself.

Today, Read's name is still cited virtually every week in major newspapers and magazines as a thoughtless promoter of the new or as a deeply intuitive defender of the contemporary. Because he was careful not to rock the boat of modernism in any of his books, articles or lectures, he does appear at times, as one critic recently put it, 'inert'. Or indiscriminate: the implication being that the same person cannot admire, say, Jackson Pollock and Mondrian, W. H. Auden and W. B. Yeats. These views of Read are distorted.

Although Read was generous in his embrace of many different kinds of modernism, he was zealous in insisting that such works demonstrate a commitment on the part of the artist to uncover the unknown, to explore visual possibilities which are hidden or dormant. At the end of his life, Read discerned the emergence of a new sensibility which was more playful and parodic and, at the same time, less respectful of the autonomy of the artist. In pop, op and minimal art, he was dismayed to see the genesis of post-modernism.

In Read's personal life there were also many conflicts. He was in the best and worst senses a self-made man: he had strong inner drives which motivated him, but he could be ruthless in fulfilling those aspirations. Another incongruity can be seen in the extraordinary lengths to which Read, the spokesman for the unconventional in art and literature, went to present himself to the world as the epitome of an

English gentleman in dress and manner. In the forties, Read was a credible defender of anarchism and pacifism because he had been the recipient during the First World War of both the Military Cross and the Distinguished Service Order. Although Read desperately wanted to be valued as a poet, his reputation, he increasingly recognized, rested on his role as defender of modern art. He was an agnostic who was fascinated by religious belief. By temperament, Read was a gambler, a man who took many risks. In his own view, he played for high stakes and lost some important bets.

During a long career, Read published over sixty books and more than a thousand articles and reviews, but throughout his life, he was restrained in speech; he was also at times excessively diplomatic. Beneath these surface traits, he was a man of very strong, often volatile, feelings. His 'voice' in letters to close friends was unhampered and often unrestrained: he spoke directly and sometimes harshly. This study, by its use of unpublished letters, shows this very real side of Read: he emerges as a passionate man who attempted to prod his fellow countrymen into an awareness of the modern world. His feelings about the art and literature of his time are shown fully, and, since he was concerned with both modes of expression, the interactions of those often disparate worlds are also chronicled here.

Much of the force of Read's beliefs emerges only when his inner conflicts are linked to his public concerns. Behind the seemingly complacent façade of modernism can be discerned, his irritation with and resentment against T. S. Eliot; his sometimes bitter quarrels with Barbara Hepworth; his hostility towards Wyndham Lewis, Graham Sutherland, William Coldstream, Francis Bacon, W. H. Auden and John Betjeman; his disputes with Douglas Cooper, Stephen Spender and Edward Dahlberg. There is also his selfless sponsorship of young writers such as Henry Treece, Sidney Keyes, Alex Comfort and Denton Welch. In addition, Read's deeply troubled first marriage is delineated fully.

In this biography, I have described all aspects of Read's career as one of the foremost English intellectuals of this century, examining both his accomplishments and his failures. As his conflicts come into focus, his courageous defence of the modern becomes both more understandable and more human. Read spent much of his life in an often selfless quest for the new. In a deeply patriotic way, he attempted to prepare his fellow countrymen for the contemporary world. But, like men, all modernisms come into being in order to die, and, at the end of his life, Read saw the creed he had fought for being torn asunder. Although Pound, Moore, Hepworth and Nicholson survived him, Read was the last English spokesman for a set of beliefs about art and literature which emerged early in this century, flourished in the twenties and thirties, and was superseded by the unimaginatively named post-modernism.

1   The Leaf and the Stream

1893–1903

In a time beyond memory, the Vale of Pickering had been a vast lake. As the waters receded, they left in their path a fertile plain. In this landscape, where the land remains sculpted by the long-vanished water, the sea had eaten through the hills to leave behind an earthly paradise. The once menacing sea is an almost forgotten presence.

Herbert Read's earliest recollections were of a lush, idyllic world whose existence was vaguely threatened by an alien force. All 'life is an echo of our first sensations', he claimed, and as a child he was acutely aware of 'forces outside'. For him it was a world where closeness to nature went hand in hand with a vivid awareness of its austere and forbidding countenance. At night, a child could be aware of the velvet stillness of the fields but, suddenly, the low of a cow could be transformed into the 'abysmal cry of some hellish beast, bringing woe to the world'.

To outsiders, the villages on the fringe of the moorlands were places of exile. A benighted parson assigned to a parish there exclaimed that such locales were 'not found out when they sent Bonaparte to St Helena; or else they never would have taken the trouble to send him all the way there!'[1] For him, such places had no redeeming virtues – they seemed to have sprung rudely from the soil.

Muscoates Grange, the farm on which Read was born on 4 December 1893, was at the western end of the Vale, where the land was flat and surrounded by misty hills. The family could see the moors to the north, the wolds to the south, 'meeting dimly in the east where they were most distant'.

Almost because of its remote other-worldliness, the Vale teemed with stories of fairies, hobs, wisemen and witches. It was a place touched by an eerie supernaturalism, reflected in local legends such as 'The Hagmare of Orrer', 'The Giant's Lapstone' and 'The Fairy Cow of Wardle Rigg'. The eighteenth-century witch, Betty Strother, had

1

practised white magic nearby, and her equipment included a looking glass, a crystal ball, cubes and a garter. To those who called on her for assistance, Betty sold talismans (sigills) into which were cut hearts, skulls, ships and other icons which brought luck to their possessors. Throughout the nineteenth century, tales of 'shape shifting, of witches turning themselves into toads and in particular into hares prevailed'.[2] At the time of Read's birth, the aura of truth still clung to those narratives.

Daily life in the Vale at the end of the last century was devoted to coaxing a livelihood from a usually willing soil. Ring games, Christmas parties, bee smotherings and occasional visits to the outside world of Whitby and Scarborough were the gentle pleasures of this existence. So cut off was the world of the Grange that when Read's father went to York or Northallerton the children had only a vague wonder of the exotic places he visited: the 'toys he brought back with him might have come, like sailors' curios, from Arabia or Cathay'.

At the conclusion of the nineteenth century, however, the steam engine and the threshing machine threatened the time-honoured methods in the breeding of cows, sheep, pigs and bees and in the cultivation of gooseberries, plums and apples. And, beyond the Vale itself, there was the railway. The mechanical gradually was making its presence known; the quiet life at the edge of the moors would soon be in flux. It was in this remote land about to be jarred by the industrial that Herbert Read came into being. Throughout his life, he was to have a strong sense of the harsh but beneficent place where he had been born; at the same time, he knew that the Vale had been ravaged by the onslaught of the machine. During his childhood such threats had been only rumours, but they had vaguely disturbed 'his childish consciousness'.[3] Read graphically recalled that invasion of alien forces, as it impinged itself on him as a young boy:

> But one day he goes to the high-road,
> sees carts and carriages pass
> and men go marketing.
>
> A traction engine crashes into his vision
> with flame and smoke
> and makes his eager soul retreat.

'I know that my Saxon family has a continuous history of 500 years in an isolated valley in England. It was probably there for 1500 years,' Read claimed.[4] Since at least 1725, the Read family had been linked with the Duncombe Park Estate in the then North Riding of Yorkshire. The rentals for that year show that Ann Read lived at Pockley, a village two miles north-east of Helmsley. Her husband Henry had died in 1721, leaving her with six children, one pair of oxen, a mare, a nag, a hog, thirty sheep – an estate valued at almost forty pounds. Ann's children prospered, and in 1851 Edward, Ann's great-great-grandson and Herbert Read's grandfather, lived in the same place with his widowed mother. He was farming his late father's 108 acres, and he also had 187 acres at Beadlam Ridge. In addition to his Yorkshire ancestry, Read was proud of his Jacobite connections: David Edwards, a fugitive from Scotland, had a daughter who married a man with the surname of Tate; her granddaughter Jane Tate was Read's paternal great-grandmother.

The census-taker for Pockley in 1851 was John Read, Edward's elder brother. He was more successful than his sibling, and in 1856 he moved to Muscoates Grange, five miles to the south. Thirty years earlier, W. Eastmead had dispiritedly written of that spot: 'There is nothing particularly interesting in this village, the country being flat, the roads rather neglected, and the houses scattered. In consequence of the low situation of the country near it, a great part of the land is often under water, by the overflowing of the rivulets or becks which intersect country from the moorlands.' The same writer added, ominously, that after a heavy rain 'the scene is sometimes dreadful; from the higher ground, the prospect in the valley is like a sea, and many accidents have happened from the mighty torrents which roll down the channels.'[5]

But the 195 acres of Muscoates were kind to John, his yield of the land justifying the £210 in rent he paid. When he died in 1871, the tenancy of the land was taken over by his brother Edward, who moved there with his wife Mariana and his two young sons Herbert Edward and Ernest William. Herbert Edward, the elder son, continued the tradition of tilling the land. Ernest went up to Cambridge – a measure of the family's gradually increasing status. He eventually became head-master of a college founded by the Duke of Sutherland at Golspie in the north of Scotland. Another gauge of worldly achievement was the farmhouse itself, probably built in the mid-nineteenth century: its spacious rooms and expensive exterior ornamentation made it a gracious residence, betokening the elevated rank of its tenant-farmers.

In 1889, Herbert Edward, having reached the age of majority on 12 April, became nominal tenant of the 195 acres, although his father retained legal control of the property. Edward probably remained at Muscoates until 1892, when his elder son married Eliza Strickland, their neighbour's daughter.

Like the Reads, the Stricklands were prosperous farmers of the

3

North Riding. In the 1770s, William Strickland, who had spent most of his life at his own farm at Appleton-le-Moors, moved to Ouldray in the parish of Rievaulx. When he died in 1775 or 1776, he left an estate worth over £500. However, in removing himself to Ouldray, William exchanged the status of landowner for that of tenant. (He probably did this because the farm at Appleton was too small for his large family, or he may have been a victim of the Enclosure Acts.) His new farm was part of the Duncombe Park Estate, where the Reads already farmed.

The Ouldray tenancy eventually passed to William Strickland, who married Sarah Wood, the daughter of Christopher, a butcher of Pockley. William and Sarah moved to Lance Butts farm near Marton and then to Southfield farm in the parish of Kirbymoorside. The couple had nine children, of whom Eliza was the youngest.

Eliza, who was nine months older, married Herbert Edward Read on 5 October 1892. It is possible that husband and wife had been childhood playmates. In his autobiography, Herbert, their eldest son, remembered the 'sensitive face . . . soft brown eyes, and . . . close curly black hair' of a father who did not have the 'features of a normal farmer'; he also recalled a man who could passionately curse a labourer who, by taking a pregnant mare out to plough, had caused her to miscarry; his father was also a person tinged with a scholarly 'intuitive sense of reality'. Read said little of his mother, although he fondly recounted her quickness to comfort him as he awoke with a piercing shriek from a nightmare, 'perhaps to take me back with her to sleep away the sudden terror'. In his dreams, the little boy would be resting peacefully on a bank of clouds. Then the sky would darken, and the darkness would take visible shape in objects which menacingly approached in order to destroy his congenial retreat.

The Reads may have tilled the earth, but they displayed the refinement of gentlemen farmers. Distinctions between aristocrats and farmers were obliterated by sport, particularly hunting. Since hunts largely took place on farmers' land, their co-operation was essential, the two classes mixing at the hunts and the hunt balls. Herbert Edward and Eliza rode to hounds, and at such times their tenuous position as tenants was overlooked. The young child also recalled his father taking part in a tennis tournament at Helmsley Castle: 'I still see the white figures of the players set against the vivid green of the lawn.' Herbert, who in those days was called Bertie, fondly remembered his family's prestige, but his clearest recollections were of the Vale and his life in that blue and green world of sky, earth, orchard and pasture. To Herbert, it seemed that Muscoates was cut off from the rest of the world, but there were farmhouses on each side of them which were only a half-mile distant. The impression that the child had was of a remote existence in which he and his family were at one with an arcadian world.

Herbert's world centred on the farmhouse, a large two-and-a-half-storeyed 'square stone box with a roof of vivid red tiles'. He recalled the comforting warmth and pungent aromas of the kitchen, with its oak dresser, large, open fireplace, gleaming deal table and flagged stone floor. In addition to himself and his parents, there were his two brothers William (b. 1895) and Charles (b. 1897) and his sister Mariana (b. 1900). There were usually five to seven farm labourers, two servant girls and, for most of the time, a governess. The house was filled with a constant bustle, which became almost overpowering at midday when all these persons converged in the kitchen. Every day had its activity: Monday for washing, Tuesday ironing, Wednesday and Saturday baking, Thursday 'turning out' upstairs and churning, Friday 'turning out' the downstairs. There were visits from Jabez and his wondrous threshing machine, and from the blacksmith. Excursions were made to the mill at Howkeld, to Bransdale and to Helmsley; 'goodies' were bought in a sweet shop in the hamlet of Ness.

The front garden of Muscoates was like an overly formal drawing-room, a place where a child could hope to steal a forbidden apricot or climb mischievously in the monkey-puzzle tree. Left to himself, the small boy would often wander out into the green, orchard, foldgarth or stackyard. These were his four 'dominions' as well as his 'shrines', sometimes lit with 'sacred fires'. The green, for instance, was the home of the waterfowl and the pump, under which could be discovered incandescent lime-coloured lizards; it was also where pigs and fowl were slain, cattle born and the tails of horses seared. Although he witnessed prosaic brutality, this boy had a natural craving for horror. The child, he claimed, 'survives just because he is without sentiment, for only in this way can his green heart harden sufficiently to withstand the wounds that wait for it'.

Herbert Read the boy was not always 'without sentiment'. His young heart was taken aback when, in the midst of a slaughter of rats, he came upon a nest of newly born ones. Then, he was 'suddenly sad'. One day, he killed a robin, a crime which was made more awful when a cousin promised to keep it a secret. However, he could slaughter rabbits with comparative impunity, and he was successfully blooded at his first kill: 'The severed head of the fox was wiped across my face till it was completely smeared in blood, and I was told what a fine huntsman I should make. I do not remember the blood, nor the joking huntsmen;

only the plumed breath of the horses, the jingle of their harness, the beads of dew and the white gossamer on the tangled hedge beside us.' Despite such pluckiness, this boy often felt cut off from the world of the Vale. He could be broken-hearted and tearful when pet lambs and ducks were stolen away to market. One day, he crushed his little finger in a machine for making oil cake, fainted, and bore the scar for life.

Although his younger brothers performed the task easily, Herbert could never manage to milk the cows. William and Charles teased him mercilessly about this and various other deficiencies, making him even more self-conscious about them. The little boys fought bitterly to win the affection of their mother. In particular, Herbert remembered suffering from 'injured seniority' when he was expected to share 'mother-love' with his yahooish siblings. Only much later, in 1955, was he able to distance himself from William: 'I was terribly jealous of him between the age of ten and twenty, but then our ways separated and his world and mine have never touched again.'[6]

Herbert, William recalled, was diffident, afraid to step fully into the family circle, as if he did not belong there. And as if he could not – or would not – share its modest joys and sorrows. Although he wanted to be like his father, Herbert's reticence probably grew out of a very early awareness that his sensibility was different from that of Herbert Edward and other members of his family. With some justification, he saw himself as one with innate gifts set adrift among those who did not share his inclinations.

Throughout his life, Read remained extraordinarily reticent in conversation and in demonstrations of affection. Such shyness, he claimed, was a natural part of his Yorkshire or Northern inheritance. 'But reserve does not mean an absence of feeling – only a determination not to show it,' he reflected.[7] Another time he claimed that he came from a culture which regarded 'affections . . . as too sacred for publication'. This meant that feelings could not be explored except 'in the disguise of art'. This was 'not a difference of feeling, but of manners'.[8] He was a contemplative person whose instinct was to release thoughts on paper, not in conversation: 'my vocal chords *are* weak, and my thoughts are timid, except when I write'.[9] He was, Read asserted, far 'too English by nature to wear my heart on my sleeve, and this must be my excuse for my seeming lack of warmth'.[10] These are partial truths.

For understandable reasons, Read acted in a retiring manner from early childhood. In addition, he sometimes chose to be withdrawn and detached. In this way, he shielded himself from disappointment or hurt – this may well have been a bitter inheritance from his father's early

6

death. If he *seemed* to be without sentiment, he appeared less vulnerable. That piece of childhood theatrics became a part of his personality. Read's many silences – as a child and as an adult – often made the intimate side of his character a cypher to family and friends. Read led a large part of his life 'taking for granted (that is to say, not expressing or acknowledging) the reality of the affections'. As he admitted, such behaviour 'often leads to misunderstanding'.[11]

Read's own early remembrances were of a child who gave a precise, geometric, almost religious, order to his four dominions: 'Each province was perfectly distinct, divided off by high walls or hedges; and each had its individual powers or mysteries.' In this passage, the world of nature, evoked with mathematical exactitude, gives way to supernatural wonder. And this is the essence of *The Innocent Eye*, a book in which each part of the simple world of the farm participates in a sophisticated Platonic order. The charm of his autobiography lies in Read's ability to recall acutely scenes of childhood and to sketch those recollections in an abstract, sculptural way. Paying close attention to how the various objects on the farm stand in space while, at the same time, homing in on their essences, Read frequently eschews realistic description. At the time he wrote of his childhood, Read was a defender of the work of Henry Moore, Barbara Hepworth and Ben Nicholson. *The Innocent Eye* mirrors in prose the experiments in stone and on canvas of his friends. He produced a sophisticated, modernistic narrative about his early life.

For that small boy, the landscape – the earth moulded into rhythmical contours, a large over-reaching sky, the tender desolation of purple tints from the moors – touched his inmost depths. However, the separation of the boy from his landscape was, as we have seen, part of Herbert Read's nature. From the beginning, he felt apart from the world into which he had been born. As such *The Innocent Eye* is an accurate summation of keenly felt experience in which a precocious Adam orders a paradise from which, at any moment, he might be expelled. Like all true Edens, Herbert's was outside time – everything flowed into an ever widening circle.

In addition to the sanctity of nature, young Herbert was attracted to the abbey at Rievaulx and the local church. The lonely setting of the church brought a strange kind of solace: 'The inhuman stillness of the situation aided our friendliness; our Church was still where the monks who first built it twelve centuries ago had wanted it to be, in a wild valley, near a running beck, grey like a wild hawk nesting in a shelter of dark trees'. The child also discerned in the purple moors a place 'where

7

God seems to have left the earth clear of feature to reveal the beauty of its naked form'.

A sense of a providential order was rapidly supplemented by the boy's discovery of the pleasures of reading. The book which first held him, he confessed, was a lively piece of pulp fiction, *Little Meg's Children*: 'I see now that its grim pathos, too simple to be wholly sentimental, may have worked into the texture of my unfolding imagination.' There was not, Read asserted, any reflection or reasoning in this novel, but its strange repertoire of 'dingy streets and attics . . . of lack of bread and clothes, of evil and misery' held him. The perils, sentimentally and cloyingly elicited, of the fictional characters affected him deeply. But, he thought, children are protected from the real and imagined terrors in their own lives by 'a cocoon of insensibility, until such time as they have the power to counter intelligence with deeper intuitions'. The death of Little Meg's mother and the sad plight of the orphaned children particularly touched him, as in the passage where Little Meg, fighting her own despair, comforts her brother, Robin:

> When Little Meg told him Mother was dead, and lifted him up to kneel on the bedside, and kiss her icy lips for the last time, his childish heart was filled with an awe which almost made him shrink from the sight of that familiar face, scarcely whiter or more sunken now than it had been for many a day past.

Herbert's own early sense of desolation was recaptured in the poem, 'The Boy in the Barn', which begins:

> A little boy wandering alone in the night
> Went into a barn all wrecked and decayed,
> And the bats and the moths and the fluttering things
> Flew in his face and made him afraid.
> So he fell on the floor and buried his head,
> And his lantern fell down at his feet.

In the attic at Muscoates, there were maids' bedrooms, a section used for storing apples, and free space in which the only books in the house were kept. 'Once upon a time when I was a little, little boy . . . I lived in an old and lonely farmhouse. Up some narrow and creaking stairs there was a big dark garret. I would creep up those stairs with a thumping heart and enter that garret with fearful eyes, ready at any moment to spring back with a cry of fear.' As in a fairy tale, the room was filled with mysterious, unimaginable wonders. The little boy would enter boldly only if he were with his mother or a servant. Gradually, though, the place became a calm refuge. Here – accompanied by the musty sweetness of the fruit – young Herbert pored over foxed copies of sermons, devotional works and the *Illustrated London News*.

He soon 'craved for novelty' – his 'lust' for books could no longer be satisfied in the attic. Herbert made friends with the postman who daily brought the *Yorkshire Post*. This fellow was sympathetic to the plight of a youngster ardently desirous of expanding his horizons, but his own taste ran only to the lurid, pink-coloured *Police Gazette*, whose contents had nothing to do with fantasy and which, accordingly, left no impression on the child. Herbert became intrigued with music as performed by an itinerant horse trainer nicknamed, appropriately, 'Fiddler Dick', who could, when he played, elicit a sound 'conjured out of the air'. The boy found a broken fiddle in the attic and pleaded with Dick to teach him, but he could never produce a sound resembling his instructor's. The impulse to create had temporarily been thwarted.

At about the same time that his interest in books and music began, Herbert started school. On 26 April 1901, John Essex, the master of Nunnington Village Boys' School, made this entry in his log book: 'Admitted two boys from Muscoates, thus bringing my total to 54. It is high time I had assistance. These boys H Read and W Read have never been to school before and just know their letters.'[12] Although the seven-and-a-half-year-old Herbert and five-year-old William had been taught to read by the governesses who helped their mother, Mr Essex considered their skills below par.

In 1902 Essex confided to his log book: 'the lower standards are very backward and consist of very dull boys.'[13] Doubtless, Herbert Read, a child recently habituated to the powers of his own blossoming imagination, was included in that group. That precocious, secret existence was shaken by Mariana's death on 16 May 1902, two months before her second birthday. In *The Innocent Eye*, Read associated her with a music box which his father had purchased at Northallerton. It was a delightful toy but it played 'For there's nae luck about the house'. Mariana was 'fair as sunlight' and 'smiled to the tinkle of the musical box'. When she became ill, Herbert was suddenly sent away and, a few days later, he was told she had become an angel. Later, he visited her grave site at Kirkdale and grimly witnessed the 'unmeaning mound that covered her body'.

Herbert's life in the valley came to an end abruptly with his father's sudden death on 3 February 1903. Herbert Edward was returning from a hunt with friends; in a manner remarkably similar to that in Eastmead's bleak account, a storm broke. At a swollen beck, at the southern boundary of Muscoates, the horse panicked, throwing and

9

injuring its rider. Strangely, Read does not mention this but says only that his father was taken ill with a fever, no doubt an aftermath of the accident. The house became tense and silent.

> The air of anguish in every one, my mother's tearful eyes – these were obvious even to us children. One day leeches were brought, and stood in a glass jar on the shelf in the dairy. They were black, blind and sinister. But then we were taken away. I went to Howkeld, and one night I suffered intolerable earache, so that I cried aloud, and was poulticed with onions. The pain had gone in the morning, but by my aunt's tears I knew that my father was dead.

The next day Herbert was driven back to the farm, where the blinds were drawn. He was taken to see the corpse. 'The cold wintry light came evenly through the open slats of the venetian blind. My father lay on the bed, sleeping, as he always did, with his arms on the coverlet, straight down each side of his body. His beautiful face was very white, except for the red marks on his temples, where the leeches had clung.' Herbert was told to kiss that face, which was 'deadly cold, like the face of Little Meg's mother'. The worlds of art and domestic reality had chillingly come together.

Years later – in 1949 – Read recalled that the beauty and charm of Eliza had made him and his brothers quite naturally 'desperately (but unconsciously) in love with her (we were horribly jealous of each other)'.[14] Nevertheless, Herbert had from infancy derived much more solace and comfort from his father than his mother, and this made his loss the more poignant. Of course, he may have idealized his father because he died at a crucial time in his development. His father could live only in imagination and in memory. Herbert Edward's quiet manliness remained his son's standard: 'He brought some visionary quality to his life and labour. He was a man of austere habits and general uprightness.' Despite the fact that Read had from boyhood cultivated interests and inclinations markedly different from his father's, he wanted to be like him – his father's early passing probably fostered that resolve. The loss endured by this sensitive nine-year-old was accented the night his father died by the menacing clap of horse- hooves on the highroad. Soon, he knew, he would be leaving the Vale.

Herbert's memories of the next few days were muddled. There was the grave near Mariana's, the earth falling with a hollow clatter upon the lowered coffin, the dark fir trees rising in the background. Since they were tenants, the family had to remove themselves quickly. The young boy had to relinquish his dominions.

Things lost are painfully dear in memory, and despite his

realization of the hardships to be met in a pastoral setting, Herbert Read would seek for the remainder of his life to return to the site of his birth. He dreamed of continuing the kind of life from which his father had been so suddenly and horribly sundered.

Young Read had a remarkable power of self-renewal, even though he carried within himself early, sorrowful memories. His expulsion from his Eden tormented him. He may have been a tiny leaf cast adrift in a whirling stream, but his green heart eventually hardened to withstand the wounds of death and separation.

11

2   Paradise Lost

Herbert Read, now a bewildered and fatherless boy, was soon rudely plucked from his world of innocent wonder. The contents of Muscoates Grange were quickly sold, Eliza and the boys moving a few miles east to Thornton-le-Dale. There she was housekeeper to her nephew, John Cussons, who was working his own mill. A few months later, Eliza went to live with her father-in-law Edward in Kirbymoorside. At that point, Herbert and William were sent away. They were taken by Eliza and an uncle on a 'devious' train ride, stopping only to change at cavernous stations. When they arrived at their mysterious destination, they were put in a cab which rattled along the cobbled streets climbing up steep hills, past dark satanic mills, and emerging eventually on a high bare moor, at the other side of which rose the largest building they had ever seen. They were now denizens of the grim, dark industrial city of Halifax. The picturesque hills and dales of the Vale had given way to the sordid reality of the factories, employing mainly women and children.

At the ages of ten and eleven, Read claimed, the characters of boys coarsen, when they enter a no-man's land between childhood and adulthood. In his autobiography, he curtained off that part of his life as of little interest. In truth, these were years of hurt which he did not wish to relive by forcing himself to write about them. Never before had he 'lived under a cloud of unhappiness' as now fell upon him. Much later, he claimed that the 'art of the child declines after the age of eleven because it is attacked from every direction. . . . the price we pay for this distortion of the adolescent mind is mounting up: a civilization of hideous objects and misshapen human beings, of sick minds and unhappy households'.[1] In these angry words the reader can hear the man recalling his own entry into adolescence, a move made more sad by his recollection of just how much had been taken away from him when he left the tranquil Vale of Pickering.

The Crossley and Porter Orphan Home and School – the structure

12

which had loomed up before him – was of French Renaissance design, blackened by the smoke which drifted across the moor from the surrounding factories. Placed in a conspicuous position upon Skincoat Moor (now called Savile Park), the edifice dominated its environment. John, Joseph and Francis Crossley, carpet manufacturers of Halifax, who employed more than five thousand people in the mid-nineteenth century, had founded the school in 1864. The immense building – solid, stolid and ornate – had first been conceived as the setting for a superior school or Congregational training college before the Crossleys decided upon an orphanage 'open without restriction of sect or locality' to fatherless children. The school was inaugurated with the arrival of six little boys one Sunday afternoon in the summer; after an interview with the Principal, the mothers departed. Girls were allowed to enter the following year.

Places at Crossley were allocated to orphans from Yorkshire, to children who had lost both parents, to offspring of Anglican and Nonconformist parents, and especially to orphans of families whose 'temporal condition has been reduced'. In reality, the school had a strong middle-class character, which was in keeping with the Crossley brothers' original aim; in Halifax, the place was called 'the College'.[2] Children were admitted between the ages of two and ten, boys being allowed to remain only until the age of fifteen.

In 1887, the institution became the Crossley and Porter Orphan Home and School, when the yarn merchant Thomas Porter of Manchester donated fifty thousand pounds to ease the school's financial troubles. A legend has it that Porter, prior to bestowing his gift, visited the school and inspected the exterior, but never ventured into the building.

The education of the two hundred boys embraced a wider variety of subjects than that of the hundred girls who spent their afternoons knitting. The boys, dressed in drab uniforms of grey trousers and waistcoats, blue Eton jackets and porkpie caps with straight peaks of shiny, black leather, studied history, scripture and algebra; in addition, there were lectures in French, Latin, physiology and physiography. William Cambridge Barber, headmaster from 1872 to 1910, regarded drill and discipline as the cornerstones in gaining high grades in the Cambridge locals. He taught 'by machinery' and, as one old boy recalled, made the boys go to bed by 'numbers':

> When 'one' was shouted, we all knelt at our bedsides, and in this devout attitude we remained until 'two' rang out, when we immediately arose and placed our little wire baskets on our beds. At 'three' we folded our

13

coats neatly into the baskets and as number followed number we slowly disrobed, until 'eleven' found us facing a basketful of neatly folded articles, waiting patiently for 'twelve' to permit us to clamber hastily into bed and warm our chill bodies.[3]

Barber dealt with any misdemeanour with a curt Biblical quotation; he also gave malefactors huge chunks of scripture to memorize. As a result, the boys in particular always did well in the examinations in religious knowledge.

Herbert disdained Barber's exercises and the accompanying Congregational pieties. The warm, comforting kitchen of Muscoates had been replaced by 'varnished pine, hygienic distemper and stencilled friezes'. He vividly recalled Barber's regime: 'no hot water for washing at any time of the year; meat and vegetables once a day and otherwise only milk and bread, mostly dry bread. . . . no private rooms, not even a reading room. . . . There were no luxuries; pocket money was forbidden.' The students rose at 6.30 and had a three-quarter-hour prep before breakfast. Another two-hour prep was mandatory in the evening. It was a school where only mathematics was imparted with any hint of imagination. English, French and all other subjects were taught by endless rote.

Herbert Read felt that his physical needs were fulfilled at a minimal level; his spiritual cravings were completely overlooked.

> I was by disposition of a quiet nature, but no wild animal from the pampas imprisoned in a cage could have felt so hopelessly thwarted. From fields and hedges and the wide open spaces of the moors; from the natural companionship of animals and all the mutations of farm life, I had passed into a confined world of stone walls, smoky skies, and two hundred unknown and apparently unsympathetic strangers.

Read maintained that older children often suffer like animals, 'dumbly and vaguely', their only release being tears. But the code of the school denied such an outlet.

Another outlet closed to Read was sport, in which he was only average. As such, it became hateful to him. Books were the only escape open to this isolated boy. He could not buy any, and the school library, although it was stocked with adventure novels, was not one to feed an imagination rapidly struggling into being. Nevertheless, he pored over Scott, Ballantyne, Mayne Reid and Rider Haggard, later confessing, 'never have I known such absorption and excitement as gripped me when I first read *King Solomon's Mines* and *Montezuma's Daughter*'. A boy who wanted to read outside class-hours had to do so against the 'shrill pandemonium' of the playroom. Despite the constant sense of constraint he endured, Read, significantly, saw Barber as the person who first made him aware of literary form. However, he added this caveat to his words of praise: 'But I insist that the impulse to write, the love of words for their own sake, and for the sake of what they could express, was precedent.' Read still remembered 'Fiddler Dick' and asked his mother if she could spare the extra money for piano lessons. Eliza agreed to this, but his new teacher was a 'fierce Dutchman, bristling with long hair and a silk bow-tie, flashing with rings'. Herbert dropped the lessons after a year.

Read's intellect was fighting for existence, but Crossley was not the ideal place for a precocious lad. Read felt trapped. In retrospect, he was glad when at fifteen the school cast him 'willy-nilly, out into the world'. Despite his disclaimers, Read's school career was not as prosaic as he implied: he won a prize (Grimm's *Fairy Tales*) for general progress, second-class honours in the Cambridge Junior Certificate, and, on leaving school in December 1908, a Second-Class Certificate of Honour. His penchant for writing had been sharpened by his contributions to an underground school newspaper.

New boys at Crossley and Porter were usually placed with older pupils who acted as 'fathers'. F. Leach, who was assigned to Read, found him quiet, undemonstrative and a bit cold. Years later, when Leach reintroduced himself to Read at a Tate Gallery function, he received the strong 'impression that he was not too happy about being reminded of his "days as an orphan" '.[4]

At the time that he left Crossley, Read's mother moved to Leeds, where he too spent the next five years. Eliza, who had been in Kirbymoorside since 1903, had helped to manage a laundry there. From 1903 to 1908, Herbert and Eliza had seen each other intermittently. Eliza went to Leeds in the summer of 1908 because she obtained through her friend Alderman Fred Kinder, the local Liberal leader, a post with the City of Leeds Training College, first as manageress of the laundry attached to the Westwood Grange Hostel and, then, in early 1909, as matron of the St Ann's Hill Hostel, at a salary of £45. A strong enticement was the presence in Leeds of her sister Ellis.

Although Read later referred to the family home on the outskirts of Leeds, he and Eliza moved four times in quick succession. Initially he joined his mother at Westwood Grange but, when she became matron, mother and son took rooms at St Ann's. Accommodation there was limited and by 1910, when William and Charles had left Crossley, Eliza rented a house for her three sons at 24 Delph Lane, where they were

15

looked after by Miss Ashworth, a family friend. In 1912, when the hostel was closed, mother and sons moved to 7 Buckingham Mount. These two red-bricked terraced houses were in streets of 'good class' according to *Robinson's Leeds Directory* of 1907–8. There were certain standards beneath which Eliza would not sink.

In his autobiographical writings, Read obliquely hinted at dissension between himself and his mother, referring in an offhand manner to an adolescent's inability to override the wishes of his elders. In truth, Herbert and Eliza quarrelled bitterly when they were forced together in 1908. Herbert was a surly teenager convinced of innate intellectual superiority. Eliza, William and Charles thought Herbert insufferable. He was now a brilliant young man who anguished over the deep gaps separating himself and his family, who in turn remained unsympathetic to his frequent demands. They thought him pretentious and overbearing whereas he felt that he was more painfully aware than they of what had been lost by his father's premature death.

If Herbert had a heightened sense of having been dispossessed, so did Eliza. Her life had been torn apart by the deaths of her only daughter and, soon after, her husband. She had to take a series of lowly paid jobs in order to keep her remaining children together. Having endured disruption, she was over-anxious about the futures of her three sons. In the process, her manner became rigid and over-controlling. In a precarious attempt to prevent her children from suffering further injury, she risked alienating them.

Acutely sensitive young people are often destined to be at odds within families where intellectual achievement is not valued. Herbert and his mother constantly picked on each other. Eventually, Eliza would burst into tears, Charles and William comforting her when the intransigent Herbert stormed from the room. Quarrels – usually centred on Herbert's refusal to accept that his family was destitute and that he must trim the sails of his ambitions – left the two younger brothers edgy and bitterly resentful of their awkward sibling. William felt that his mother and elder brother were twin personalities inextricably linked in conflicting quests for dominance within the family. Indeed, William increasingly realized that his brother's austere and reserved character was a replica of his mother's.

Although their similarities drove them apart, Herbert and his mother loved each other deeply. When Eliza died at the age of forty-seven on 9 December 1914, five days after Herbert's twenty-first birthday and a month before he enlisted, her son found it difficult to distinguish between dire reality and comforting delusion: 'So strong was the psychic shock that when I found myself in a strange country and amidst new surroundings, I began to be haunted by such vivid dreams that for months I existed in a state of uncertainty. Was she really dead? Or had her death occurred only in one of my obsessive nightmares? I did not dare to give expression to this real state of uncertainty, but as the months passed, there came no confirmation of her existence.' This phantasmagoric 'uncertainty' between waking and dreaming betrays just how crucial Eliza was to her son. At one level, this passage displays how much he missed her – it was psychically impossible for him to admit that she was dead. He obviously experienced a great deal of guilt, such guilt leading to 'obsessive nightmares'. Above all, his existence was deeply tied to his mother. Could he be alive if she were dead?

In 1908, Read was 'persuaded' by his mother and her 'advisers' (probably her sister, her brother-in-law Ernest Read and Alderman Kinder) to apply for a clerkship at the Leeds, Skyrac and Morley Savings Bank. On 22 January 1909, he was given the job at a salary of £20 per year. He set aside a shilling a week for 'culture': he had stealthily determined to become Prime Minister. Read was delighted that he had a three-year contract because at the conclusion of his stint he would be nineteen years old, the usual age for university entrance.

The bank's head office was in the centre of Leeds, with three branches in the outlying working-class districts. Junior clerks such as Read were disseminated on monthly rotations to the branches. Each morning, Read went to the head office, where the branch manager gave him a cash-bag. That person then accompanied him to the assigned spot, where, under supervision, he entered transactions in ledgers and pass-books. The branches closed at three and, as soon as he could carry the ledger and cash-bag back to the city centre, he was free.

This dreary job unleashed an ambition on Read's part to become a doctor. He admired his physician cousin, Archibald Gardner, his father's closest friend, but Gardner's inability to save Herbert Edward's life had left him a broken man. He, perhaps at Eliza's insistence, eventually dissuaded Herbert from medicine. Eliza wanted Herbert to make the most of the 'good opening' at the bank. As his interest in politics awakened, Herbert determined to become a lawyer, a decision with which his 'mother and her advisers were well pleased'. At once, Eliza devised a scheme for him to be articled to a solicitor. However, Herbert wanted to be a barrister. He conceived of the former calling as one devoted to 'drab realism' whereas the latter had 'romantic' possibilities. Barristers, Eliza insisted, were more expensive to educate. Her son weakened, allowing negotiations with a solicitor to begin. At

17

that point, he sat for a matriculation exam, which, when he passed it, became a Rubicon filling him with self-confidence.

Now the battles between mother and son heated up. Herbert wanted to go to university and held out – despite persistent maternal harping on the danger of exchanging the uncertainties of vague ambition for the certitude of the law. A compromise was finally reached: university was to be the prelude to a legal career. Secretly, Read had determined to devote himself to literature. He persuaded one of his uncles – on the strength of a legacy of £300 left to him by his grandfather but payable only on his twenty-fifth birthday – to advance the necessary funds. Herbert touched his uncle's heart and mortgaged his future for the bright, but nebulous promise of education. The young man saw himself as a 'silver knight on a white steed . . . riding to quixotic combats, attaining a blinding and indefinable glory'.

Gradually, this dreamy, slightly vain young man had become entranced by the secret world of poetry as he wandered 'through areas [of Leeds] in which factories were only relieved by slums, slums by factories – a wilderness of stone and brick with soot falling like black snow. Drab and stunted wage-slaves drifted through the stink and clatter; tramcars moaned and screeched along their glistening rails, spluttering blue electric sparks.'

In 1911, the population of Leeds was almost 450,000, its previous concentration of textile factories having given way to industries such as iron smelting, brass founding and tailoring. The continued rapid growth of the city meant that the notorious back-to-back slum houses were still in abundance. Standing in the midst of crowded, sooty streets were the massive public buildings such as St Peter, St John's, New Briggate and the town hall. Austere monumentality and monumental poverty were yoked violently together.

This ghastly environment gradually penetrated Read's 'true-blue' Toryism, which had been fed on the novels of Disraeli. When he had first arrived at Leeds, he had joined the local branch of the Conservative Party, distributed its leaflets and 'worshipped my King with a blind emotional devotion'. Since the city had contrasted harshly with the country, Read's first impulse had been to retreat back to inherited political prejudices against the 'wage-slaves'. But the world of poetry moved him in a vastly different direction, that turn being taken under the guidance of a 'father-substitute', William Prior Read.

While waiting for a post in the Indian Civil Service, William, Herbert's younger brother, had taken a temporary job with the man who shared his name but to whom he was not related. 'He was a man of small proportions, gentle manners, and in physiognomy bore a close resemblance to . . . William Blake. He had two passions – the reading of poetry and the cultivation of flowers.' William Prior was from a Quaker family from the Isle of Axholme. Like the brothers, he had been orphaned at an early age. He had been placed in the care of two rich, cultivated maiden aunts, who educated him with the intention of making him a keeper at the British Museum. But he rebelled against such a narrow scheme, and, eventually, after various misadventures, settled into tailoring, a calling which he loathed. Herbert felt an immediate bond with the older man: they were orphans who rebelled against the aspirations of female relations.

William Prior's home in Stanley Drive overflowed with volumes of Ibsen, Turgenev, Chekhov, Yeats, Browning side by side with those of Fiona Macleod, William Cullen Bryant and Francis Thompson. The older man's taste may have been undiscriminating, but this hardly mattered to a young man who could at long last feast on a varied literary diet.

Character, Read claimed, 'is only attained by limitation', and this is certainly true of his years in Halifax and Leeds. He had been tested by the stigma of being an orphan, by the boring work to which he had given himself over, and by the endless disputes over 'prospects' with his mother. In William Prior, he came upon a person whose real, inner life centred on literature. Also, just as he was about to be consumed by the meanness of his surroundings, the older man's 'kindness balanced the sorrow' of his early life. He saved Herbert 'from a bitter heart, and so early damnation'.

Herbert had discerned an innate love of learning in his father. It was Herbert Edward who had brought the music box back from Northallerton, his son recalling his 'intuitive sense of reality and right values which are not acquired by the mere process of reading'. Herbert obviously saw himself as the person in the family who had inherited this same delicate sensibility, but he also realized that such proclivities had to be nurtured. And this was the crucial link between Herbert and William Prior. The older man shared with the younger an inborn devotion to learning – more crucially, he kept that spark alive in him. Suddenly, the 'incantations' of Blake fell upon Herbert 'like an apocalypse'.

Indulged by the tailor's frequent gifts of books and inspired by his passion for poetry, Herbert began to write verse, and, naturally, he showed him his first efforts. The fact that William Prior was not a particularly astute critic was irrelevant: 'he encouraged me with his

19

praise and was for a long time the only audience I had'. The 'precedent' impulse to write had been unleashed: 'It descended on me like a frenzy, and a day was not perfect unless it gave birth to a poem.'

Herbert's recollections of his friendship with William Prior were serenely benign: he dedicated his first book of poems to him. William, Herbert's brother, had a different memory. He had also responded to the warm fellowship of his employer, whom, of course, he had known first. He recalled that Herbert, in his search for approval and admiration, had pushed him rudely aside, the older man eventually responding with greater affection to Herbert than to him. This sibling rivalry in pursuit of a father wounded William, who was already enduring the agonies of the constant bickering between his tearful mother and dour elder brother. The sheer opportunism of Herbert appalled him.

Read was attempting to forge a friendship with a person who reminded him of the patient, sensitive father he had lost at the age of nine and whom he now saw reincarnated. Herbert wanted to be like these two men. The reality was that his nature was often more like his mother's: passionate, frequently turbulent, and sometimes capable of cold disdain. Like his mother, Read was ambitious, although he disagreed with Eliza on what constituted worldly success. He did realize early on that ambition must be tempered with charm, and at seventeen the stern, uncompromising teenager gradually gave way to a man of gentle austerity who could act, when necessary, 'without sentiment'.

3   Awakenings

At the age of fifteen, Herbert became devoutly religious, swept up in a wave of 'devotional ecstasy' centred on the services of the Church of England. Liturgy, litanies and creed did not intrigue him, however. He would be carried outside himself when he fixed his gaze on a face, a lamp or candle flame. His whole being 'would hang on this bright point, whilst around [him] swirled the music of the organ, the voice of the preacher, the soaring Gothic arches'. This had been Read's way of bringing his consciousness into touch with a supernatural being. But, gradually, this fever abated, to be superseded by an uneasy scepticism.

As the prospect of confirmation approached, Read's new un-orthodoxy flustered him. The ceremony had been postponed until William left school in 1911 because Eliza wanted the boys to undergo the ceremony together at St Michael's, Headingley. Doubts paralysed Read, who did not dare reveal his qualms to his mother or brother. He simply could not memorize the Creed, whose sentences became a 'meaningless succession of syllables'. Acutely conscious of not wishing to mislead William or upset his mother, he stumbled through the 'painful farce' of a ceremony. He even went to communion for several months. Finally, he could endure it no longer. He gave up his prayers and, then, attendance at church. Eliza was puzzled and hurt. She used her own considerable powers of persuasion against her obdurate son and, when these failed, she summoned relatives and friends to assist her. But her eldest son's 'unbelief was now too positive'. Despite her pleas, he could not – or would not – relent.

Read's break was particularly painful because his father had been a strict Christian: 'Only a blizzard would have prevented him from driving the five miles to church every Sunday.' Prayers and readings from the Bible had formed an integral part of life at Muscoates. Thus Herbert had the additional guilt of rebelling against his adored father

21

when his belief in Christianity faded. Years later, Read claimed that he had not abandoned God.

> I did not deliberately forsake God.
> Rather I clung to Him
> > like a child to its mother's skirts.
> But the garment was whisked away
> > I fell to the ground.

A dawning conviction that religious institutions were instruments of social oppression further deepened his disdain for the Church of England. Such feelings are vented in 'Christ's Mass', obviously indebted to Blake's *Songs of Innocence and Experience*:

> The church is warm
> Where the good folk swarm
> To hear the little boys with their faces so bright,
> Clothed in their surplices wimpled and white,
> Raise their sweet carols and joyfully sing: –
> 'Peace and good will to all men bring'.

> But out in the sleet,
> In the dismal street,
> Women and children, wretched and dank,
> Hunch in a ragged and woeful rank;
> Rickety, rickety, doubled with croup,
> They wait for penn'orth of hot pea-soup.

Read's unbelief was agnostic rather than atheistic. Genuine religious belief he respected, but he was suspicious of those who clung desperately to the conception of an after-life.

By the time he entered Leeds University in 1912, Read's faith was centred on words, in the mysterious ways in which they could be arranged to capture the truths hovering at the edge of consciousness. A bit earlier, the 'frenzy' of being a poet had overwhelmed him. Now he wanted to refine those skills, only through the mastery of which could he hope to become a professional writer.

The University of Leeds had come into existence in a haphazard way. The Leeds School of Medicine was founded in 1831; the real nucleus of the future University arrived only forty-three years later with the Yorkshire College of Science, an institution which set out to fill an urgent need for courses in engineering, agriculture, mining and metallurgy, areas of expertise essential for those who intended to become farmers, manufacturers, scientists and teachers. In 1887, the

College reluctantly amalgamated with Victoria University, an offshoot of the University of Manchester. Following the dissolution of Victoria University in 1904 came independence and the title, University of Leeds.

The newly chartered institution belonged to the second generation of nineteenth-century English universities. Its immediate predecessors – University College, London and Owens College, Manchester – were intended for the 'middling rich' and those with 'small, comfortable trading fortunes'. In contrast, Oxford and Cambridge were aristocratic preserves. From the time of its Yorkshire College inheritance, Leeds University was committed to natural and applied science, with humanistic studies taking a lowly second place. Lyon Playfair, one of the founders of the College, had squarely faced this issue: 'Our universities have not yet learned that the stronghold of literature should be built in the upper classes of society while the stronghold of science should be in a nation's middle class.'[1]

Such a belief in two cultures did not sit well with young Herbert Read, when he registered at the University in 1912. During his first year he read French, English, History and Geology for his intermediate BA with the intention of taking an honours degree in History. The following year, having switched to the Intermediate L.L.B., he was reading Logic and Social Economy. When he matriculated, Read had determined to pursue a course not 'strictly *utilitarian*'; in his second year he shifted to his 'proper studies'. He resolved the conflicts between disparate pursuits by deciding to take two degrees.

This pragmatic young man furnished and decorated a room in his attic, where he studied and wrote. Here he had undefined 'rare extasies' to the contemplation of which he would return with a 'wistful longing'; at such times, he grandiosely proclaimed, 'I would even love myself for what I have been.' He was certainly aware of stirrings which he desperately wanted to bring into being.

By and large, Read found himself an anomalous figure at an institution which largely disavowed the pursuit of literature (425 of 663 full-time students taking degree courses in 1914 were enrolled in programmes in science, medicine and technology). His purpose in life was fixed but in an extremely indeterminate way; his fellow students were bent on becoming schoolmasters, clergymen, scientists and technicians. Read found such goals crude and calculating.

They were interested in one thing only – in getting the best possible degree by the shortest possible method. They were anxious to memorize

23

and eager to anticipate the testing questions. Their career was plotted and they were careful not to stray from the thin line which marked an easy path through the world of knowledge. Perhaps they had been caught young, in a machine which hitherto I had accidentally escaped.

The sheer variety of subjects which Read undertook in his second and subsequent year (Latin, Logic, Roman Law, Jurisprudence, Common Law, Constitutional Law and History, Political Economy, Social Economy, European History) led to dizzying mental congestion. He faithfully attended lectures, then studied into the night. During the few daylight hours when he was not at lectures, he was drawn to a seat in the library adjacent to a high bookcase containing 'like a mountain veined with shining gold'[2] the works of Dostoevsky, Ibsen and Nietzsche. He would open a textbook but, almost immediately, his eyes, imagination and hands would be drawn, in an orgy of acquisition, to one of the books in the case. Thus was disciplined education swamped, Read retaining a contempt for the gradual manner of education advocated by Cardinal Newman.

Storm Jameson, who entered Leeds University three years before Read, saw her institution as existing in another world from the Oxford evoked in Compton Mackenzie's *Sinister Street*. 'The difference did not lie in the disenchanting grime, the ring of steel furnaces and mills belching smoke by day and flames by night, the ceaseless beat of industry in our ears, the total lack of everything implied in talk of dreaming spires and punts idling between fields yellow with buttercups. It lay deeper – in a thin thread of spirit joining us tenuously to the mediaeval universities.'[3] Jameson also craved 'an elegance I had discovered I lacked'.[4] This sense of inferiority also haunted Read, who, although he had no conscious desire to have attended prep or public schools or Oxford or Cambridge, felt cut off from the inherited traditions such places automatically bestow.

In particular, Read sharply bemoaned the lack of an Oxbridge tutorial system at Leeds, but when he sent F. W. Moorman, Professor of English, two poetic dramas, heavily indebted to Yeats and written in North Riding dialect, he received unstinting praise. The teacher, who a few weeks earlier had lauded Read's essay on witchcraft and Elizabethan drama, had been pleasantly startled to discover that one of the many students scribbling notes in front of him had dared to attempt such difficult verse. Moorman took Read up, encouraged him and asked to see more of his writing.

Through another paternal figure at Leeds, Read discovered the power of 'advanced' art. In 1911, two years before Read enrolled, Michael Sadler became Vice-Chancellor of the University. Previously, he had been Director of Special Enquiries at the Board of Education for ten years, followed by eight years as Professor of the History of Education at the University of Manchester. From the outset, Sadler distrusted his new institution's insistence that earning a living was the primary goal of education. During his twelve years at Leeds, he resolutely refused to have his freshness of outlook dulled by bureaucracy, being convinced that pragmatic concerns had overwhelmed the University from its very beginning. 'Leeds, hampered by poverty, had put up with unworthy buildings, with almost slum layouts for some of its extensions, with pinched salaries, with a starved library, with a makeshift Refectory and Common Room, with a third-rate athletic field. Nevertheless, by sheer weight of character, of brain-power and public-spirit the University won through. But to the end of its life it will bear the marks of the struggle, like a thrown tree on a West Riding moor.'[5]

Sadler was an astute collector of art, and, according to Roger Fry, he civilized Leeds. 'The entire spirit had changed from a rather sullen suspicion of ideas to a genuine enthusiastic and spiritual life. He showed what *can* be done, but rarely is, by education.'[6] Six watercolours by Mari Bauer were Sadler's first acquisitions in 1909. In rapid succession during the next three years, he purchased, among many others, two Fantin Latours, three drawings by Puvis de Chavannes, four Gauguins, a dozen small Constables as well as works by Steer, Augustus John and William Nicholson. Sadler was not a particularly wealthy man, but he was married to a woman with far more money than he. Mrs Sadler did not mind spending twenty-five pounds on a watercolour, but she balked at the acquisitive fever which began to dominate her husband's every waking moment. Sadler's bank manager also rebelled, and purchases sometimes had to be cancelled and pictures sold off. For Sadler, as for many collectors, prudence became an intermittently practised virtue.

In the early summer of 1911, at the Allied Artists Exhibition at Albert Hall, Sadler's son, also Michael, purchased half a dozen small square woodcuts – 'strange . . . semi-representational, and with an element of hieratic rigidity'[7] – by the Russian artist, Wassily Kandinsky, who lived in the small town of Murnau, thirty-five miles south of Munich. The following summer, when father and son were planning a visit to Bavaria, the younger man wrote to the painter, asking if they could visit. Kandinsky responded warmly to this overture, and that August the Sadlers stayed with him and his mistress, Gabrielle Münter. Sadler senior was immediately taken with the forty-six-year-

25

old exile with his 'dark olive skin, a thin black beard, a gentle voice & sweet smile & a Mongolian look'. He found Kandinsky's paintings 'primitive-looking', being touched by the artist's inclination to talk of 'mystical books . . . the lives of the saints . . . and strange experiences of healing by faith'.[8]

Although he did not yet possess a keen interest in abstract or semi-abstract art, Sadler bought the first paintings and drawings by Kandinsky to enter England. Also, he persuaded his son to translate the artist's treatise *Über das Geistige in der Kunst* (1912) into English (*Concerning the Spiritual in Art*, 1914).

In his pre-First World War paintings, Kandinsky evoked an intensely coloured and vividly pagan world, derived from the landscape of his retreat in the Bavarian Alps. For him, the surfaces of nature were only a means – though a significant one – to uncover hidden, primal forces. Kandinsky's treatise, in a complementary manner, called upon artists to express their inner lives in abstract terms; artists, he claimed, like musicians, did not have to rely excessively on the material world. At this time, Kandinsky himself was moving tentatively towards complete abstraction.

Herbert Read's introduction to abstract art came at the time he visited Sadler's grim mansion, Buckingham House, at 41 Headingley Lane. His entrée through the back door came when he secretly took tea with Miss Wallace, Sadler's housekeeper and a close friend of Eliza. The critic who would later advocate a metaphysical art, which 'denies the reality or sufficiency of normal perception' because the inward eye allows a glimpse of an even 'more marvellous world',[9] probably experienced his first epiphany in the presence of the bright, gyrating forms of Kandinsky.

In 1912, a further opportunity for Read to see strikingly contemporary paintings, drawings and sculptures was provided by Frank Rutter's appointment as Curator of the Leeds Art Gallery. Rutter, in his mid-thirties when he arrived in Yorkshire, had founded the Allied Artists Association in 1908. A principal reviewer for the *Sunday Times* and editor of *Art News*, he had written the outspoken *Revolutionary Art* (1910). In 1912 he was instrumental in having Wyndham Lewis' nine-feet-square *Kermesse*, which he called 'a whirling design of slightly Cubist forms expressed in terms of cool but strong colour contrasts',[10] placed on exhibition. This advanced, opinionated, volatile man was eventually enrolled among the 'blessed' in the vorticist litany of those who were true friends of art. In Leeds, he became one of the blasted.

Rutter took the job at Leeds in response to the pleas of family and friends to abandon his precarious freelance existence in favour of steady employment. Not surprisingly, Rutter, who had lived most of his life in London and Paris, never felt himself to be anything but a stranger in Leeds. He had thought the city a 'go-ahead place' because the gallery had bought Orpen's *The Red Scarf* and the University had appointed Michael Sadler Vice-Chancellor. Quite soon after taking up his post, he became enraged at the repressive control exerted by the City Council. As well, the 'gross' taste of the same city fathers oppressed him. One day, he conducted three members of an Art Gallery Committee round a spring exhibition. A heavy silence prevailed as they strolled through galleries hung with paintings by Orpen, Sargent, Steer and William Nicholson. Then, they reached the room set aside for local artists. 'Here the trio at last came to a standstill before a portrait worthy of a place on the lid of any chocolate box. Immersed in aesthetic thought before this painting of an attractive young woman, they stood awhile in silence: and then one councillor nudged another, remarking, "Eh! A wudna mind takin' yon t' Blackpool for a week-end." '[11]

The Curator's taste led him to battle for the acquisition of a Pissarro. This painting was considered too modern by Rutter's overseers, who gave his obstinacy in this instance as the reason for his dismissal in 1917. Actually, Rutter was fired because he became mixed up in a successful plot to free a hunger-striking suffragette named Lillian Lenton, who had been released from Armley prison into his care. Mischievously, he arranged for her to be smuggled out of his heavily guarded home.

If Sadler's and Rutter's adventures in modernism intrigued young Herbert Read, A. R. Orage, who had left Yorkshire for London in 1905, cast the deepest shadow in the formation of his sensibility. Born in 1873, Orage lost his father early and was brought up in poverty, in the village of Fenstanton in Huntingdonshire, by his mother, who earned a little money by taking in washing. When he was a young teenager, she asked the local squire to give her son work as a labourer. Young Orage's intellectual capacity became evident to his patron, who helped him become a pupil–teacher. Eventually, he made his way to a training college, qualified as a teacher and became an employee of the Leeds School Board at Chapel Allerton in September 1893. In that same year, the Independent Labour Party was formed, the young schoolmaster quickly becoming one of its most enthusiastic supporters.

Deep-set eyes below heavy eyebrows, a prominent nose, a birthmark which broke across his face like an irregular sunburn, and a red necktie were what friends remembered about Orage's appearance. They also

27

recollected his virile magnetism, which often led to touchy situations with women.

> His gospel, always preached with his tongue in his cheek, that every man and woman should do precisely what he or she desires, acted like heady wine on the gasping and enthusiastic ladies who used to sit in rows worshipping him. They wanted to do all kinds of terrible things, and as Orage . . . had sanctioned their most secret desires, they were resolved to begin at once their careers of license. They used to 'stay behind' when the lectures were over, and question Orage with their lips and invite him with their eyes, and it used to be most amusing and a little pathetic to listen to the gay and half-veiled insults with which Orage at once thwarted and bewildered his silly devotees.[12]

Orage's sexiness became legendary in Leeds and, later, London. However, his marriage was unhappy and childless. After he had drifted to London, he took up with Beatrice Hastings, who so mesmerized him that he took part in the assault by the suffragettes on the House of Lords in the spring of 1907. He was arrested, the only man among seventy-five women.

Orage's friend Gerald Cumberland was dubious about his espousal of 'divine nonsense', a snide reference to the young schoolmaster's obsession with mysticism. First, there was Plato, then Madame Blavatzky. 'His interpretations of the "Secret Doctrine" and "Isis Unveiled" fluttered the dovecotes of Theosophy', another associate, Holbrook Jackson, recalled.[13] Then, Orage became absorbed by the *Upanishads*, the *Bhagavad-Gita* and the Society for Psychical Research. He was constantly searching for a guru who could unlock the secrets of all mythology. Perhaps it was natural that, like Havelock Ellis, Yeats and Shaw before him, he eventually discovered Nietzsche, who had died in 1900.

The German philosopher's denigration of a social order leading nowhere, his advocacy of the Superman and his hostility towards liberalism, decadence and asceticism were warmly received by many English intellectuals, who craved remedies for a sick culture and society. The employment of Nietzschean principles, they argued, could restore heroism to an increasingly unheroic age. Behind the apparent materialism of such a stance, Orage insisted, was a thoroughly mystical view of the world. For him, Blake's substitution of a mystical–revolutionary vision of the universe in place of a corrupt political and religious order which over-valued rationality anticipated many of the German's ideas. 'Blake is Nietzsche in English,' he proclaimed.[14]

Orage was also attracted by Nietzsche's antagonism to Apollo (reason) and his championing of Dionysos (energy).

> Apollo is always on the side of the formed, the definite, the restrained, the rational; but Dionysos is the power that destroys forms, that leads the definite into the infinite, the unrestrained, the tumultuous and passionate. . . . Dionysos without Apollo would be unmanifest, pure energy. Apollo without Dionysos would be dead, inert. Each is necessary to the other but in active opposition.[15]

The eternal battle between these two forces would always rage within Herbert Read, but as a university student he turned, like Orage, from the Christianity of Blake to the secularity of Nietzsche, who became his mentor. The young man inclined towards haughtiness profoundly identified with the philosopher whose disdain for the ordinary was one of the chief reasons for his popularity with intellectuals. For Read, this was a new terrain: 'It was as though I had tapped a central exchange of intellectual tendencies; from Nietzsche communications ran in every direction and for at least five years he, and none of my professors or friends, was my real teacher.'

Although the German philosopher eschewed traditional religious values, his notion of the Superman foresees that some individuals will rise above ordinary humanity; as such, his philosophy has a supernatural component. Nietzsche's aesthetic also makes allowance for an art and literature not bound by traditional notions of structure and form; in inviting a quest for the 'unrestrained' it welcomes the experimental, the search for the new. A contempt for the ordinary and a disdain for democracy go hand in hand with a belief in the Superman and the search for unhampered forms. The paradox is that such an aesthetic is politically repressive but artistically daring. Although his interest in the 'forms of things unknown' was unleashed by the German philosopher, Read would later see the political implications of Nietzsche's writings as sophomoric.

Surprisingly, revolutionary, frequently Nietzschean, notions of art were almost as widely debated in Leeds in 1911 as they were in London, where the doctrines associated with vorticism, imagism, post-impressionism, and 'significant form' were being propounded by intellectuals – and ridiculed in the popular press.

Vorticism began in about 1911 as an attempt to anglicize futurism, the Italian movement which produced emotionally expressive pictures which depict the sensations of movement and change. The vorticists also aspired towards the non-representational, emotive aspects of cubism. In their borrowings from foreign movements, Wyndham Lewis, David Bomberg and T. E. Hulme were opposed to the essentially French influences which had dominated Roger Fry's Bloomsbury. Fry and Clive Bell believed that an 'aesthetic thrill' was experienced in appreciating the formal properties in a work's 'significant form'; they dismissed subject matter, anecdotal content and moralizing. Although they too were formalists, the vorticists felt that Fry and his followers were timid, unwilling to grapple with movement and abstraction. According to them, Bloomsbury was too tied to the post-impressionists, Cézanne in particular. In their rejection of Fry, Bell and – quite soon – futurism, the vorticists conceived of themselves as a whirling, dynamic, violent force which could lead to an artistic renaissance in England. Their revolutionary desires were in accord with Nietzsche's – and Orage's – espousal of Dionysos.

In contrast to vorticism, imagism was a much tamer affair. It aspired to direct treatment of a subject, to immediate rejection of any word which was not absolutely essential, and to the condition of music. Just as vorticism wanted to find a new pictorial language, imagism – by its very name committed to the visual – wanted to discover a new verbal language. Ezra Pound, its principal apostle, yearned for a 'granite' poetry: 'We will have fewer painted adjectives impeding the shock and stroke of it. At least for myself, I want it so, austere, direct, free from emotional slither.' T. E. Hulme in 1909 had described such verse as visually concrete: 'It is a compromise for a language of intuition which would hand over sensations bodily. It always endeavours to arrest you, and to make you continuously see a physical thing. . . . Images in verse are not mere decoration, but the very essence of an intuitive language.'[16]

The forum for debate in Yorkshire was the Leeds Arts Club or 'Platonic Lodge', founded in 1903 by Orage, Holbrook Jackson and A. J. Penty. During their years in Leeds, Sadler and Rutter were active members of this assemblage, whose published statement of intent was bland: 'Our object is the study of the ideas expressed in art and philosophy, religion and politics, and to consider these ideas in their actual bearing upon social life.'[17] In reality, the Club was apostate and esoteric. Edward Carpenter espoused a radical sexual philosophy, Mary Gawthorpe defended militant suffragettism, Shaw asked, in 1905, 'Should Leeds Be Burned?', and Wyndham Lewis on 16 May 1914 pontificated on 'Cubism and Futurism'. Jackson fondly recalled how the Club was born out of a 'contempt of pedantic philosophy and dead art', upon an insistence of the 'necessity of applying ideas to life'.[18] He was also proud of the notoriety the Club achieved, despite the fact that it never had more than a hundred members. The audiences were usually small, 'except when there was a lion hunt, and particularly on the famous occasion when the lion was G.B.S.'[19] Ultimately, in Jackson's view, Leeds was amused but otherwise unmoved.

At first, the Club's premises were on Park Lane but eventually it transferred to Blenheim Terrace, where Read attended meetings. Rutter, who became president of the Club, defended Fry's and Bell's notion of significant form. Rutter also encouraged an approach to drawing which attempted to represent musical sound. In addition, he promulgated the view that it was valid, in contradistinction to their meaning, to represent the emotional resonances of words.

Tom Heron, three years older than Read, was a member of the Club at the same time. Heron, who was born in Bradford, later went into the textile industry, eventually starting Cresta Silks in 1929. He remembered Read as shy and timid, neatly and correctly dressed, listening intently to all that was said. When a painting was being examined, he would scrutinize it sharply; 'when anyone was speaking, he would lower his head and look at him . . . as though his face was just as important as the words. Occasionally, he would wait his time and put in a very carefully articulated question or comment. And if he wasn't satisfied with the answer . . . then he'd return to the charge.' Heron and Read openly quarrelled about Tom's status as a conscientious objector. Read even accused him of being a 'Christian anarchist', one who obeyed the laws of the land only when he approved of them. In turn, Heron glimpsed in Read a smug 'contentment with the scheme of things and his own niche in it'. When Read later joined the army, Heron told him that the tidiness of it suited him.[20]

At twenty, Herbert Read was exposed to – and participated in – heated discussions at the Leeds Arts Club about the future of painting, poetry and the perilous connections between them. The notion of sister – or, rather, warring – arts was with him from the outset. For the next seven or eight years, his own sketches were done in a vorticist manner. His poetry became resolutely imagistic.

Despite some remnants of Toryism in his political beliefs, Read welcomed the new ideas about art with which Sadler, Rutter and Orage had invigorated Leeds. In marked contrast, the eccentric, passionate Jacob Kramer, the first artist whom Read knew well, abhorred the doctrines being preached at the Club. Only a year older than Read, Kramer, born in the Ukraine of an artistic family who had settled in the Jewish colony in Leeds by 1900, was firmly set in his ways by 1911. He rejected both post-impressionism and cubism as deviant movements, harbingers of decadence. In 1912, Sadler assisted him in obtaining a scholarship at the Slade. By 1915, he had spent some time in Paris under Sadler's patronage and was a member of the London Group. Although he exhibited with the vorticists, his naive figurative style was fundamentally at odds with the aims of that group. He believed vehemently in a realist mode of representation in which a transcendent symbolism was readily visible.

Self-consciously, Kramer, habitually dressed in a greasy mackintosh and battered slouch hat, made himself into a latter-day Blake. Roger Fry considered him a 'bloody fraud'.[21] He was also renowned for being violent, as when he started a fight with Augustus John in the midst of Roy Campbell's bohemian wedding celebration at the Old Harlequin night-café in Beak Street in 1922. Campbell, who had retired upstairs with his bride, descended in his pyjamas in order to restore order: 'A strangled protest and assent at once came from Kramer; and stiffly and slowly, his shoulders drawn up, his head thrust out, he put his biceps away.'[22]

Once, when Kramer was offered the use of Jacob Epstein's London flat, he thought that his then wealthy friend would not miss some of his Persian carpets. He sold a few, pocketed the money and waited for the outraged complaint which was never uttered. A bit later, when Kramer was travelling, Epstein was allowed to stay in his Leeds flat, whereupon he sold six of Kramer's paintings.[23] Kramer's resolute nerviness was upstaged the evening he was drawing a cadaver at a local medical school. When one of the limbs moved, the artist quickly fled the premises.

From the outset of their odd friendship, Read and Kramer disagreed about modernism. In a bout of youthful enthusiasm, Read threw himself 'into a vortex'. As he later recalled, 'Jacob had his own firm position on the edge . . . and was not to be seduced by any manifestoes that ran contrary to his nature.' Kramer attacked futurism and assured Read that there was no such thing as post-impressionism. Although Kramer could see the attractions of cubism, he reluctantly rejected it. 'Cubism in my estimation succeeds in conveying the idea of a dynamic force, and one is immediately struck with the impermanency of the whole thing, because the impression that it leaves upon the mind is momentary, and because of this spontaneity cannot find a place. It is not subject to the process of development.' In place of any form of art which drifted towards non-figuration, Kramer sprang to the defence of realistic symbolism: 'When the natural and the spiritual element impinges itself upon my consciousness, a terrific struggle . . . ensues, and it is by the greatest effort that I am ultimately able to transmute the base substance of detailed naturalness into the essence of spirituality, the latter always predominates, owing to its essential vigour and direct appeal.'[24]

If Kramer was moving in what some considered a regressive direction, he was not uttering cautionary words in isolation. He was echoing sentiments shared by Harold Gilman, Spencer Gore and particularly Charles Ginner, who in 1914 defended 'neo-realist' ideas in the *New Age*. Indeed, Kramer was probably following Ginner, who argued that, although 'mere beautiful pattern' or 'subtle and delicate arrangement of words' were the foundation of good paintings and poems, such works must represent 'some intelligible idea or outlook on life'. Ginner wanted realism, sound colour values, structure and elements of abstraction to be fused. He despised narrow allegiance to "Art based on formula'.[25] For him, this was the death of art.

Although Read shared some of Kramer's reservations about cubism, he disliked his emphasis on the 'spiritual', which Kramer saw as an independent force *outside* the artist. Read flatly disagreed:

> When you say that the more conscious you become of the element of spirituality which is inherent in everything, to that extent you are filled with a sense of abiding happiness. I think you deceive yourself to this extent: that the element of spirituality is not in the things, but in the image of the things in your mind.[26]

Does the artist's symbolic world originate only from within himself or should he attempt to link exterior realities to his inner life? The friendly quarrels between Read and Kramer in 1912–18 reflected battle lines being drawn at the very same time in London between post-impressionism and vorticism, futurism and vorticism, vorticism and neo-realism, post-impressionism and cubism. All of these disputes centred on the question of what was the most effective method of representation, the various answers ranging from minute photographic realism to complete abstraction. For the next few years, Read was a fierce partisan of vorticism.

In his early essays in the *Gryphon*, the student magazine at the University, Read characterizes the artist as someone who rises above the common herd, as in his lavish praise of Francis Thompson's 'genius-endowing Poverty', which he hailed as 'veritably god-like and life-giving, so that, personified, we give it a place in our Olympus'. This precocious and slightly pompous man of letters discerns elements of the

Superman in Strindberg but then realizes that common human failings bring his hero crashingly down to earth.

> A curious face – a face that betrays the man. There is only one word to describe it – it is *pug*. Still, there is beauty in it; especially in those eyes which reflect, even in a photograph, an inward strife and pain. . . . The bristling moustaches round the mouth seem almost like issuing flames. . . . And flames did in truth issue from that mouth – flames that might have burned a deal of rubbish, but were destined to flicker and to die.

These are a young person's haughty words. Nevertheless, Read uses sharp, vivid language, which exhibits a critical mind ready to grapple with important issues, such as the rights of women. Strindberg 'attacked woman as a sex; he revealed her innermost soul by means of all the realistic art his genius was capable of. And this play [*Miss Julie*] is the supreme expression of his misogynist views. . . . The best proof of the strength of the play is the hatred women bestow on it.' Ultimately the Swede was praised for his ability to transcend the limits of realism and to deal with some 'of the greatest psychological conflicts that the soul of man is capable of'. Read concluded by reprimanding Strindberg for dying with a 'Christian platitude on his lips'.[27] Scorn would not come easily to Read as an older man, but, understandably, his youthful rebellious spirit bubbles to the surface in this 1914 essay.

Read was absorbed in 1913–14 more with verse than with criticism. In attempting to define a more distinct literary personality, he was increasingly pulled in the direction of imagism. Earlier, he had been dominated by the archaic neo-romanticism of Ralph Hodgson, whose verse 'seemed to come from a world of gipsies and highwaymen, they were sometimes sentimental, and they had a simple, insistent rhythm which haunted the mind.' A concern for 'pretty jingle and infectious rhythm' gave way, under Pound's influence, to 'fused ideas . . . endowed with energy'. One of his first series of poems opens with citations from Ezra Pound: 'Emotion creates the Image'; 'The Image is more than an idea.' His poems from 1915 show the influence of the American exile, as in 'Fancies':

> Wrapped in a purple night of thought,
> I saw gold stars a-roaming.

The strong sexuality entering Read's verse can be seen in 'Despair' (1915):

> She gazes with her dim, grey eyes
> into the gathering mists,
> And scarlet moths,
> flock to her lips
> to suck the honey there.

Another poem from the same year is even more redolently sensuous:

> The lady in the leopard's skin –
> She'd roses in her waving hair,
> And roses in her peaked breast;
> But other roses bloomed for me
> Within her dark and dancing eyes.

The likely muse of such verse was Read's future wife, Evelyn, whom he met in about August 1914, just before or after the outbreak of the war, when he had plunged into a debate on morality at the University Union. He taunted the group with his unconventionality and was startled when an unknown lady supported him.

A month younger than Herbert, Evelyn – Read usually called her 'Robin' – was the daughter of Arthur Roff of Bradford, a drysalter who made medicines which he sold in marketplaces throughout Yorkshire; her mother Beatrice was from Halifax. Evelyn entered Leeds University in 1912 with a King's scholarship, eventually taking an ordinary B.Sc. degree in 1915 in Botany with Zoology and Education as subsidiary subjects.

During Herbert's and Evelyn's first year in university, Eliza was diagnosed as having inoperable cancer. The impending loss of his mother may have hastened his courtship of Evelyn, whose precise intelligence resembled Eliza's. If his mother was resistant to the very idea of university education, Evelyn had a correspondingly sceptical, rigid outlook. In his liaison with her, Read was drawn to someone who shared his mother's straitlaced coldness. He became even further separated from the warm sensitivity he associated with his father. The wound inflicted by that death was pushed more deeply inside him.

From the outset, Herbert played, a bit too self-consciously, the devil's advocate to Evelyn's overly rational angel. Sex was an immediate barrier in their courtship, when Evelyn refused Herbert's pleadings to sleep with him. Although her would-be lover craved unconventionality, Evelyn did not believe in sex without marriage. In *Death of a Hero*, Read's friend Richard Aldington claimed that during the three or four years preceding 1914 'young men and women were just as much interested in sexual matters as they are now, or were at any other time. They were in revolt against the family or domestic den ethic.'[28] Herbert

35

wanted to rebel. Clearly, Evelyn did not. Despite such basic differences, Evelyn's claims upon her future husband's devotion can be glimpsed in 'Entrance':

> Outside
> I hear her steps . . .
> Her questing eyes will roam
> The blue dusk of my room.

Then her eyes are 'lit / With the brightness of stars'.

Intellectually, Read was a very advanced young man at the outset of the war – eager for experimentation. Emotionally, he was still withdrawn. Strong conflicts divided him, this being reflected in his devotion to a woman who raised serious objections to the new ideas he was championing. He was obviously unsure of the modernisms he proclaimed, Evelyn's doubts encompassing nagging fears of his own. Only when he became surer of his way would their paths divide.

4 The Contrary Experience

'Democracy always seems to me to be lacking in ideals. If only we could graft on to it the idea of a Super-*race*.' Such were Read's political beliefs in January 1915. He was trying to fuse Nietzsche's austere disdain for any sort of compassion for the masses with his own growing concern for the factory workers of Leeds. By 1911, he had renounced his Tory beliefs, but he had nothing with which to replace them. He studied Marx, Bakunin, Kropotkin and Carpenter; at the same time, he distrusted the two extremes of socialism, collectivism (control of the means of production by consumers) and syndicalism (control of the means of production by organized bodies of workers): 'Both are fundamentally wrong: society must be regarded as an entity – a co-ordination of consumer and producer.' Three years later, he realized that he was vaguely socialist. The war would strengthen and clarify this inclination.

To Read's equivocal socialism was attached a nebulous pacifism. He saw the Great War as a conflict between rival imperial forces, which could be halted only by working-class action. The failure of such aspirations was his first object lesson in political disillusionment. Nevertheless, like so many young men of his generation, a Kiplingesque notion of patriotism beckoned him. His still undefined notion of himself as a writer would be crystallized, he thought, in the throes of conflict. Action – not contemplation – offered an unsullied means to purify the uneasy fires burning within him.

Read's involvement with the military began about 1910, when he still contemplated becoming a doctor. In the vain hope of acquiring practical experience, he joined the local territorial unit of the Royal Army Medical Corps. Two years later, at university, with an impetuousness he later disdained, he transferred to the Officers' Training Corps. In 1912, war was still a remote possibility, the Corps providing Read with his sole physical diversion. He 'enjoyed the game very much'. While, as he said, he was 'happily at play, [he] was caught by the war'.

37

When England entered the war on 4 August 1914, Read knew it was impossible to be both a happy warrior and a concerned socialist. A week later – on the 11th – he applied for a commission in the Territorial Force. Meanwhile, Eliza's deteriorating health held him back from pressing this claim. Death 'robbed' him of his mother on 9 December. Thoroughly devastated, he asked Michael Sadler to support his application of 21 December for a temporary commission in the Regular Army. Fifteen days later, on 6 January, he was made a second lieutenant in the Green Howards and posted to Wareham in Dorset, to which he had to travel by way of London.

Despite his sorrow at Eliza's death and his imminent entry into a new way of life, Read, who had never been out of Yorkshire, immediately upon arrival at King's Cross hired a taxi to take him to Waterloo by way of Cork Street, near Elkin Mathews' bookshop in Vigo Street, just off Piccadilly Circus. The 1890s, when he and John Allen published *The Yellow Book*, had been the zenith of Mathews' career, although many distinguished Anglo-Irish writers remained on his list.

Earlier, in 1909, Mathews had taken the young American Ezra Pound in hand, helping him find his first footings in literary London. Although the large bundle of poems which Read had with him that day were not imagistic, Pound's publisher gave the intrepid young man a warm welcome and told him that he would contemplate publication if the young soldier paid a reader's fee. The anonymous judgement – delivered a few weeks later – was dismissive: the poems were slight and imitative. Only a selection made by himself, the reader claimed, would pass muster. Undeterred, Read insisted on making his own choice and paying the publication costs. Six months later, only twenty-two copies having sold (an additional seventy-two were distributed to libraries and friends), the author, repenting of his presumptuousness, had the remainder of the edition of 250 pulped.

The title of the volume – *Songs of Chaos* (dedicated to William Prior Read) – and its epigraph from Nietzsche ('One must have chaos within one to give birth to a dancing star') came well after the composition of the poems. In January 1915, Read was just beginning to feel the full force of Pound's influence and thus approached his publisher; in June, he embarrassedly realized how badly these poems missed the mark of imagistic tautness and compression: 'The intensity with which I wrote some of these poems is still a vivid memory – it was not an intensity of emotion leading to expression, but an emotion generated by the act of creation.' Now, Read understood how much he had been using the voice of others, as in this Yeats-inspired pastiche:

> When Niodr arose from the burning deep
> And bade the waves no longer weep: –
> Niodr arose with a golden harp
> And touched the strings that never warp,
> Bidding the angry waves be still,
> And the Vanir gather to obey his will.

Read's overture to his favourite poet's publisher hints of hubris; his decision to pulp displays resolute honesty.

His introduction to London had been surprisingly congenial, but Read immediately had to continue on his way to Wareham, where he found the barracks stifling. Unfortunately, he had stumbled into a very select coterie, most of his fellow officers being from public schools, a high proportion of them from Eton. Read's sense of inferiority began to consume him. Slater, a master at Eton, seeing his new comrade with a copy of *Erewhon Revisited*, good-naturedly exclaimed, 'That I should find someone reading Sam Butler in the British Army!' Read was not so lucky when he accidentally left a copy of Orage's *New Age* behind in the officers' club. A junior subaltern discovered it and thumbed it for a minute or two. Slowly, the colour deepened in his florid face. He turned suddenly to address the room and, holding the paper up as though it were unclean, he shouted in a loud voice: 'Who brought this bloody rag into the mess?' The hostile question did not bring Read to his feet. He sank deeper into his chair, as his opponent pitched the magazine into a waste-paper basket. For the future, Read confined his mess reading to the *Tatler*, perusing the *New Age* in his tent or cubicle.

If Read's fellow officers were a snobbish, intolerant lot, he was almost as piqued with those under his command. He found his position as one of a group of 'little, homage-receiving gods' to be quixotic. His increasing sense of the claims of democracy had gradually made him eager to know the working class first hand; soon, he realized, he had swallowed the idealized newspaper fiction about such men. In a letter of 28 January, he complained: 'They are a rough lot – mostly miners from Durham and Middlesbro'', who were always 'grumbling about their food and pay'. He was sorely vexed that they were not there for 'spiritual motives'.

Like many other officers, Read was in an intolerable position. Officers and men were allotted separate quarters, messes, uniforms, weapons – they also shared widely different visions of life, differences reflected in accents, diction and syntax. Read despised the anti-democratic stance of his fellow officers, and yet, confronted with discontented subordinates, his own inclination to distrust the common man surfaced.

39

Discord gave way to harmony only when Read – together with his men and fellow officers – confronted 'primitive filth, lice, boredom and death' in the Ypres Salient in November 1915. When he arrived at a small French town en route to his base in Flanders, he was struck by how 'woefully English' the place was. As for many others, any trace of domesticity vanished for him within a week of his arrival at the Front.

> I have now seen 'the real thing'. A trench in winter, wet and cold, the stench of decay, and even ghastly death. And what is my keenest impression? Only the inexplicable unreality of it all. Danger I did not realise, nor did I experience fear. I slept when I could, and my sleep was the sweetest I've known since infancy. And even when I saw the first man killed, I did not know whether to laugh or cry.

This emotional numbness was interrupted by nightmares about Eliza's death. The 'terrible fragility' of existence thus made itself known to him in both his waking and his dreaming lives.

Read was not afraid to die, although a year before such an apprehension had frightened him. Rather, he arrived at a calm which surpassed the religious resignation of many of his compatriots. The stench of rotten flesh was everywhere, hardly suppressed by the chloride of lime sprinkled on especially gruesome remains. And yet, with clear honesty, Read confessed: 'Now I know death to be merely an ending – untimely, perhaps, and, for those who know my hopes, an occasion for regret. . . . The only sorrow I feel is for the high projects of my ambitious spirit.'

Such reflections were made amid Read's multitudinous duties as an officer: he inspected, encouraged, visited and comforted the men under him; he would deal with enquiries brought by runners, and he censored letters. These were day activities. After evening stand-to, the real work began. He would supervise repairs to the wires, construction of saps and the storage of bombs and the other munitions. Also, he led patrols and raiding parties. Or he guided his men back to the relief trench: 'Every stray shot that cracked and hissed past seemed to shred our nerves. We went on, stumbling into crump-holes and tripping over tangled wires, panting in the agony of exhaustion.' As morning approached, he would have to be certain that no man was visible above ground. And these final tasks were done amid the frequently flooded, always smelly and congested trenches. Like Wilfred Owen he had 'not been at the front', he had 'been in front of it'.[1]

Like many other soldiers, such a hell made Read aware of landscape in a heightened way, in which a once green pastoral world stood in sharp deviation to the ravaged land which it had become: 'The sky was a wide and still harmony, in contrast to the conflict within it. . . . The sun shone on the bright silver planes of the Fokkers, whilst shells burst all round them, leaving white fumes like blossoms scattered on the sky.' At the same time that he was touched by the destruction of land, Read became less aware of the differences between himself and his comrades – his men and fellow officers. In 'My Men', where he declared his affection for those he commanded, there is – as in many war poems – a homoerotic tinge:

> A man of mine
>   lies on the wire;
> And he will rot
> And first his lips
>   the worms will eat.
> It is not thus I would have him kissed,
>   but with the warm passionate lips
> of his comrade here.

In January 1916, Read was devastated when a shell 'blotted out with its reverberating riot a lad who had been to me the embodiment of flagrant vitality'. And this incident may have led to the grim 'Truth for a Change':

> Such a lad as Harry was
> Isn't met with every day.
> He walked the land like a god,
> Exulting in energy,
> Care-free,
> His eyes a blue smile
> Beneath his yellow curling locks;
> And you'd wonder where a common labourer got
> Those deep Rossetti lips
> And finely carven nose . . .
> I saw him stretch his arms
> Languid as a dozing panther,
> His face full to the clean sky –
> When a blasted sniper lay him low:
> He fell limp on the muddy boards
> And left us all blaspheming.

Read's ambition to become a writer flowered amid the débris of war, as can be seen in this powerful, imagistic 'impression' of Ypres:

> Sunset licks thy ruins with red flames. The flames rise and fall against the dusking sky: against the dusking sky flames fall and die. Heaped in the black night are the grey ashes of desolation. But even now the moon

41

blooms like a cankered rose, and with soft, passionate light kisses the wan
harmonies of ruin.

Read wrote three similar 'Fables from Flanders' which he sent off to the
Gryphon.

One evening that March the orderly brought the daily 'Comic
Cuts', the news bulletin published by Headquarters and which the
Captain read aloud in a kind of vaudeville back-chat. The final
paragraph contained a curt note announcing the death of Henry James
on 28 February 1916. The ghosts of Maggie Verner, the Princess
Casamassina and Daisy Miller rose up before Read, who was silenced to
tears.

Later that month, Read was accidentally wounded and briefly
hospitalized in France before being invalided back to England. He
remembered waking on a Sunday morning, the ward bathed in
sunlight. He became aware of a minister holding a service, at which
some attractive nurses 'like angels in a vision' sang. Briefly, Christianity
seemed beautiful, but when the padre administered communion to a
dying soldier, Read was revolted. Two days later, the crossing to Dover
was like a nightmare. 'The lapping of the water mingled with the moans
of the suffering,' while Read and some others played cards. Later, he
drank some whisky and subsequently managed to set fire to his
bandages while lighting a cigarette.

A grey, foggy light greeted the ship as it reached port. The prospect
of spending May in Yorkshire at first made Read exuberant, but soon, in
the midst of homecoming celebrations, a depressing sense of reality
took over as he became aware of the 'dead ecstasies and passions of dead
men'. Would he ever be able to banish such spirits? But then he
remembered that at the Front the 'beautiful wan ghosts' had been the
final reality: 'And so I became possessed of a wild energy, crying
"Unreal, unreal! All is unreal, and only Death is ultimate." '

The immediate impact of Read's first stay at the Front was a
stirring defence of Georges Sorel's *Réflexions sur la violence* (1914),
when T. E. Hulme's translation appeared in 1916. Trained as a civil
servant, Sorel (1847–1922) discovered Marxism in 1893 and, four years
later, became an ardent defender of Alfred Dreyfus. By 1902, Sorel
denounced both the Socialist and Radical Parties because they accepted
democracy and constitutionalism as preparatory stages for a new social
order; in place of tame measures, he favoured revolutionary
syndicalism, an anarchist movement which stressed the spontaneity of
class struggle. In *Réflexions*, he specifically promoted violence as a valid
way of destroying existing political systems. Sorel also insisted that in

order for the working classes to be inculcated with revolutionary fervour the concept of general strikes had to be promoted, such an idea helping to generate a collective will to insurrection.

At the outset of the war, Read had struggled with the idea of democracy; in 1916, he advocated proletarian violence in the wake of the class conflict which, he was certain, would be unleashed following the end of the war. Read also claimed that, inevitably, war had led to a bellicose spirit in *all* Englishmen, over whom had passed, like a wave, 'a grand revival of the sentiment of glory – a new realisation of heroic values'. However, Read's place now remained firmly with his enlisted men. He realized that the end of the war would lead to an intensification in class feelings; this rigid demarcation in a world of vanity and bitterness would prepare the ground for the fulfilment of Marx's hypotheses: 'and the fatalistic revolution will be in sight'. He felt strongly that the increasing strength of capitalism would set the stage for a more 'virile' proletarian class to overthrow it.

Read considered guild socialism, which advocated industrial self-government through national worker-controlled guilds, the appropriate instrument of upheaval. This movement, which had originated with A. J. Penty, one of the founders of the Leeds Arts Club, sought to revive the spirit of medieval craft guilds and argued that workers should strive to control industry rather than government. At a meeting of the Leeds Arts Club in 1913 or 1914, Read had denigrated Penty's ideas as 'completely dead. . . . Aren't you on the wrong street?' By 1916 he had changed his mind: such notions could be the means of revolution, especially as Penty was outspoken in his attack on machinery and in his pleading for revolution, not evolution. In contrast, Read found the Fabians 'intellectual fogies' who resisted action. Later, Read would return to his earlier view that the guild movement was anachronistic.

Now Read proclaimed himself an anti-romantic. He had no ideals, he declared, that had not been smashed. Like Sorel, he had come to believe in the depravity of man. 'Romanticism is – in literature – the confusion of the human with the divine. . . . Once you regard the divine as something subjective, something within one as a matter of course, then you get all the absurd sentimentality and romanticism that vitiates all literature since the Renaissance.' In response to these outdated beliefs, he was a pessimist who saw 'life at its real worth'. A bit self-consciously he proclaimed, 'Life is dynamic: death is static.'

From June 1916, Read was with the 11th Yorkshire Regiment at Rugely Camp, Staffordshire, 'a dreadful place' where he was supposed to be on light duty. In fact, the work was plentiful and monotonous. 'I

43

think I shall flee to the Front for a little peace at the earliest opportunity,'
he sarcastically said. His only immediate consolation was the
camaraderie, much more ardent than any he had experienced at school
or university.

The war dissipated Read's reserve. His anti-romantic poems and essays
are, almost paradoxically, alive with pure, often angry, feeling. In
contrast, his letters to Evelyn are overly intellectual, completely lacking
in spontaneity and, for the most part, affection. The emotions released
by war are absent in his missives to her, all of which were destroyed. In
1962, when he added *War Diary* to his autobiographical writings, Read
published his letters to her as 'scrolls from a tomb [which] bear witness
to the preoccupations of a lost generation'. The resulting diary is made
up of extracts from seventy-six letters written between 28 January 1915
and 14 November 1918. Read instructed his typist (his daughter
Sophie) to remove all salutations, closings and endearments, and later
he blue-pencilled many passages in the typescript before it was sent to
the printer. Then, he burned the letters. (None of Evelyn's letters to
him have survived.) Earlier, he or Evelyn destroyed the letters in which
he frankly discussed the sexual aspects of their courtship.[2] The *War
Diary* was therefore not a complete record. Yet it provides an accurate
reflection of the distrust and discord upon which this unlikely marriage
was eventually launched.

From the outset, Evelyn and Herbert shared a distaste for many of
the assumptions, particularly religious, which shaped George v's
England. Perhaps too resolutely, they proclaimed their individualities.
For them, the prospect of mutual dependency was excessively threatening. On 27 August 1916, Herbert told Evelyn: 'I quite agree with you
that only they who stand alone, stand firm. I think you rather mistake
my meaning in venturing to put faith in an individual. I don't mean to
pin my faith in life upon any person.' This was a hurtful truth, as was his
view on marriage which, he said, 'should be a purely individual contract
capable of dissolution at the will of the parties to it'. He could also be
condescendingly old-fashioned on the nature of women, who, he
claimed, 'do not look for depth in persons or in things. They are satisfied
with the sparkle. This would seem to be a biological failing.' Petulantly,
he told her in July 1916: 'You don't seem to know whether you are an
optimist or a pessimist. . . . Can you reconcile these two attitudes? Or
must I believe with the crowd that feminine logic consists largely of
caprice?'

On her part, Evelyn remained unconverted to her lover's point of view. At times, disgusted with his complacency, she attacked his 'ill-cut glossiness' and called him 'artificial – self-conscious – cynical – unsympathetic – inconsistent'. She also said he lacked 'zest for life'. In turn, he dubbed her a 'Puritan Rat' who tried to curb his exuberance.

At times, Read's façade of resolute self-sufficiency deserted him, his uncertainties coming out into the open, as in these reflections of 13 October 1917:

> You are wildly, tragically wrong. You ask me to be sane, which is to be sincere – to speak my mind with all the truth I am capable of. I would rather have left it to a more opportune occasion – that's what I meant. Nowadays I feel that all my enthusiasms, all the ideals which I have the spirit to strive for, are as uncertain as my life. I did not wish to appeal to you in this uncertain attitude . . . but your letter compels me.
>
> Know then, that for the last two years I have been rather an elaborate hypocrite. Here is my story. When I first knew you 4 [sic] years ago I made of you a rather romantic idea and devotee.

Herbert had been trying to redefine what Evelyn meant to him. He had obviously been tempted to break from her, but, as he told her a month later: 'Our friendship and all that it might be remains to be explored. I feel that I have in my hands something very precious – something that holds a world of wonder and joy, if only I can keep it there.' Still, as Read's fellow Yorkshireman J. B. Priestley recalled, the war provided an ambience where 'a wholly masculine way of life uncomplicated by Woman'[3] was hailed with relief. Read's own ambivalent feelings towards women – a mixture of admiration, devotion, distrust, sexual attraction – are encapsulated in these two letters, among the most 'censored' of those in the typescript of the *War Diary*.

More than anything else, the *War Diary* traces Read's rapid – often rabid – intellectual development. At one point, he tells Evelyn, 'You must not grumble if books overwhelm my letters.' This is not an understatement. During 1916–18, he reports on his reactions to, among others, Wells' *The New Machiavelli*, Plato's *Republic*, *Don Quixote*, the novels and stories of Henry James, *Biographia Literaria*, *Under Western Eyes*, Hazlitt's *Essays*, *The Return of the Native*, *Jude the Obscure*, W. T. Watts-Dunton's *Aylwin*, D. H. Lawrence's poetry, Ford Madox Ford's *The Good Soldier*, W. H. Hudson's *Green Mansions*, *Purple Land* and *Crystal Age*, Arthur Waley's translation, *170 Chinese Poems*, *Lord Jim* and Wyndham Lewis's *Tarr*. He also discusses Henri Bergson, Benedetto Croce, Arnold Bennett, Richard Steele, Thucydides, Rider Haggard, Tennyson, Gabriele d'Annunzio, Samuel Butler, Kipling,

Goldsmith, Lamb, Swift, Chesterton, Jules Romains, William Morris, Karl Marx, Robert Louis Stevenson, Gilbert Murray, William Archer, Edwin Muir, George Meredith, Matthew Arnold, John Masefield, Guy de Maupassant, Dante Gabriel Rossetti, Nathaniel Hawthorne and the Brontë sisters. Later, during the offensive at St Quentin, Read carried the Everyman edition of Thoreau's *Walden* with him; like the American writer, Read was a reclusive rebel.

At Rugely, Read designed a fashionable studio: '15 × 12. Floored with antique matting – Greek couch (some people call it a camp-bed) – my walls decorated with a series of Japanese prints, three charcoal sketches of Watteau's, two of Whistler's, three or four of my own productions (note the conceited company I keep), a shelf of books, an oak table, a writing table and a few photographs of friends.' From this comfortable, secluded vantage point, which included the services of a Scots cook, Herbert Read, clad in his dressing-gown, could pronounce on the essence of the twentieth century. This bookish soldier would have agreed with Siegfried Sassoon, 'I didn't want to die – not before I'd finished *The Return of the Native* anyhow.'[4] Read had also begun his first, later abandoned, novel.

Read's poetry and prose had been transformed by Ezra Pound, the war and the philosophy of violence. His own attempts at drawing were vorticist. 'I see no reason', he asserted, 'why decorative art should not be as abstract as music.' For him, design could take hints from nature, but it should not imitate it slavishly. It was possible to have an aesthetic representation of an idea. Read's own design on the front of a little collection of poems he sent Evelyn was, he told her, 'a pattern representing the emotional contest of my soul. *Perhaps* you will be able to divine suggestive form in it.' The accompanying poems were attempts to express an emotion felt by the poet 'with the object of inducing that emotion in the sympathetic reader'. He ended with a credo:

> The nobler the emotion induced the greater
>   the work of art.
> The noblest emotion is the joy in abstract
>   beauty.
> And, of course, beauty is truth.

This proclamation, an uneasy combination of Keats and Pound, contains the seeds of Read's later work as a poet and critic. He was attracted towards the precise use of words for achieving beauty, truth and joy; at the same time, he knew that he was attracted towards the spiritual, quasi-religious values to which abstract art can aspire. Also, he increasingly realized, his own skills were verbal rather than visual.

Evelyn disdained abstract art because it was 'above the people'. This 'damning heresy' infuriated Herbert; art, he instructed her, should always be experimental. In addition, she was inclined to think that the common man had the capability of appreciating 'high' art. Her lover was adamant: 'NEVER. The average man does not know what art is. He revels in the incidental and the sentimental and all things vile and nude. Pears Annual is his level.'

Read stoically and good-naturedly accepted the scornful amusement with which his fellow officers greeted his 'select, futurist' efforts, continuing to draw in a vorticist style throughout the war. In April 1917 he wanted to sketch a fine-looking 'huge negro in an azure-blue uniform' but the fellow seemed to have better things to do than pose. In any event, Read did not have the courage to ask him. Two months later, half a dozen of his 'weird drawings' which were exhibited at the AAA show at the Grafton Galleries sold.

Although stranded under canvas in Staffordshire, Paris and London were the centres of Read's world. He told his uncle Ernest that instead of completing his degree at Leeds, he intended to settle in one of those cities. Read was also in touch with Frank Rutter, with whom he founded the journal *Art and Letters*, a rival to the inappropriately named, as far as Read was now concerned, *New Age*, which had become 'too fond of assuming the rôle of despot among the moderns and of course, despotism in matters of the spirit, like art and literature, is disastrous.'

When Evelyn read such aggressive remarks, she might well have reflected that Herbert, whose tyrannical tendencies she was rebelling against, did not know himself very well. *Art and Letters*, he instructed her, was opposed to realists, romanticists and even 'Abstracts (poor me!) who do not relate their art to life at all'. Read informed Evelyn that Rutter, disgusted with the City Council, had left Leeds and was now working at the Admiralty.

Together, Read and Rutter intended to espouse Morris rather than Marx, quality over quantity. Although Read was co-editor as well as co-founder of the magazine, army regulations prohibited him from publicly claiming direct responsibility for its day-to-day operations. A critique of Joyce's *Portrait of the Artist as a Young Man* was Read's initial contribution to the journal. It was also his 'first shot' as a reviewer. Despite clarity, radiance, economy, exactness and purity, he found the book 'pathetic': Joyce 'is apt to make sensual perception the reality of life, and to neglect the intenser spirituality of our being. With his eyes to heaven, he must yet consider the stench in his nostrils.'[5] This book touched too near the bone. Read would have found a parallel to his own struggles against mother, religion and patriotism in Joyce's careful evocation of the awakening of his artistic consciousness. Read – himself a twenty-four-year-old Dedalus – was probably threatened by the thirty-five-year-old Irishman's stark, comical and satirical portrait of his younger self. Read was sufficiently unsure of himself in 1916–17 to embrace wholeheartedly 'silence, exile and cunning'.

At times, Read's intellectual pursuits had to take second place to his army duties, as when he accepted a draft out to Étaples ('Eatables' or 'Eat Apples' the infantry called it) in June–July 1916 and spent a day in Boulogne. When, in August 1916, the 11th Yorkshire Regiment was disbanded, Read, who became an acting lieutenant on 1 September, was posted to the 2nd Training Reserve and in January, after a bout of bronchitis the previous month, was transferred to the 7th Yorkshire Regiment at Brocton Camp, also in Staffordshire. From there, he returned in April to France, eventually becoming a member of the 10th Yorkshire.

At Brocton, Read and eleven other officers lived in a wooden hut situated upon a high waste land. This group quickly became 'Our Society', among whom were Gunga, the Elephant, Uncle, Karl Marx, Sir Henry Irving, Piccanninny and Hen, who had 'very henny legs' and 'a hennier walk'. When Read defended socialism at the expense of imperialism at a camp debate, he received only six votes from the officers present. He was characterized by the leader of the opposing motion as 'a nice keen little boy' who would eventually develop into a real democratic imperialist. 'May my brain rot first,' he told Evelyn.

Read 'WAS *NOT* SICK!!!' on the boat to France. On 7 April, he reached his base where brown tents extended for miles across sand dunes, which the moonlight bathed with a 'mighty romantic' glow. But Read felt decidedly unromantic when he learned that his luggage could not follow him until the next day. His reaction to his second extended stay at the Front was, as he admitted, melodramatic: 'I don't want to die for my king and country. If I do die, it's for the salvation of my own soul, cleansing it of all its little egotisms by one last supreme egotistic act.' Cold and weary England was not worth dying for; socialism was.

Added to metaphysical discomfort was the usual filth of the trenches. On 8 May Read was finally able to have a wash: 'But still I haven't had my clothes off for 9 days and see no immediate prospect of getting them off. And never a BATH since 20 days ago.' Spring he experienced in 'an abortive sort of way'. He and his comrades somehow remained dirty but cheerful, dressed variously in gladrags, steel helmets, 'Tommy's clothes' and gas respirators. His captain played the flute, 'like any pagan from Arcady'.

Read's renewed sense of friendship with his companions modified his previously intense, sullen patriotism. At times, he rightfully feared that he was becoming a 'dreadful moralist', but his capacity for radiantly selfless courage had been released, almost ready to be tapped. *Art and Letters* 'bloomed' in June, but Read was only moderately pleased. He did not consider his treatment of Joyce adequate, but he thought his poem 'Curfew' in the same issue inspired:

> Like a faun my head uplifted
> in delicate mists:

> And breaking on my soul
> tremulous waves that beat and cling
> to yellow leaves and dark green hills:

> Bells in the autumn evening.

Just before being told that he would be going off on a 'death and glory job', Read had taken up Bertrand Russell's *Principles of Social Reconstruction*, in which the distinction is made between creative and possessive impulses. Read concurred with Russell that out of 'the former proceeds all good: out of the latter all evil'. The test was finally upon him. Now he would discover on which side he should be placed. Would he cling to life in a cowardly way or would he take a leap into the unknown?

In July 1917, the Fifth Army was attempting to move north-east against the German First Army. As part of that operation, Read – who had been gazetted lieutenant on 1 July – and another officer were asked to train volunteers for a raid on the enemy's trenches, where they were to kill as many as feasible and bring back at least one prisoner. Forty-seven out of a possible sixty offered their services, and the party, infected with 'low villainous cunning', set off on their perilous assignment on a dark, dirty night. Everything went well until, about 150 yards from the German trenches, they suddenly realized that the enemy was approaching them. Read and his colleague had not planned for this eventuality. The other officer quickly retreated to organize the men into a defensive position, leaving Read.

I could now see what was happening. The Huns were coming out to wire

. . . and were sending out a strong covering party to protect the wirers from surprise. This party halted and took up a line in shell-holes about twenty yards from us. Then some of them began to come forward to reconnoitre. We lay still, looking as much like clods of earth as we possibly could. Two Boche were getting very near me. I thought we had better surprise them before they saw us. So up I get and run to them, pointing my revolver and shouting 'Hände hoch' (hands up), followed by my trusty sergeant and others. Perhaps the Boche didn't understand my newly acquired German. At any rate they fired on me – and missed. I replied with my revolver and my sergeant with his gun. One was hit and shrieked out. Then I was on the other fellow who was now properly scared and fell flat in a shell-hole. 'Je suis officier!' he cried in French. By this time there was a general fight going on, fire being opened on all sides.

This mêlée finally led to the object of the raid being accomplished: an officer, who had won the Iron Cross at Verdun, was taken. The next day, Read took him down to Brigade, and during the hour walk they enthused in broken French about Beethoven and Chopin. When they discovered they were fervent disciples of Nietzsche, they became sworn friends. At least, that was what Read told Evelyn.

In the late 1920s, when he rewrote this incident for *Ambush*, a collection of prose pieces about the war, Read claimed that during his conversation with the German officer he 'stammered in broken enthusiasm about [Nietzsche's] books, but got no response'. When he left the man at Headquarters, Read 'gazed at him eagerly, tenderly, for [he] had conceived some sort of vicarious affection' for the man he had done his best to kill a few hours before. 'I waved my hand as he left, but he only answered with a vague smile.' The later account is obviously fictionalized, Read's youthful, raw feelings being transformed by artful memory. The reconciliation which ends the earlier version is wistfully unrealized in the subsequent account, the glowing optimism of youth having been destroyed by the dreary rigour of adult experience.

The story of the German army officer in *Ambush* is prefaced by an account of cowardly Lieutenant P, who had been in France for four months when he was chosen to lead a raid with Read. As the time for the foray draws near, he owns up to an overwhelming fear: 'He began to confess to me; to bemoan his fate; to picture the odds against us.' Read, who finds him repugnant, urges his fellow lieutenant to approach the Colonel, but he 'just hung his head and looked stupid'. Finally, Read reports P to the Colonel, who removes him from the mission. A few months later, P is killed in a bombardment in a night of 'confused darkness and sudden riot'.

The story of P is an intriguing preface to the story of the raid, providing as it does a foil to Read's bravery. Probably it is not a true story. Rather, it is a symbolic account of divisions within Read himself. His actions – for which he received the Military Cross – displayed incredible bravery, but he was in touch with the other side of valour: the fear of losing one's life, the cutting anxiety that his promise as a writer might be unrealized. And he may have not been fully aware of those conflicts until he sat down, ten years later, to cast his experiences into semi-fictional accounts.

Later that month, the army, like a 'benevolent old gentleman', arranged a 'joy-ride' to Amiens, passing through the valley of the Somme and past Albert. In September, just before leaving for a month in England, there was constant scrubbing and polishing which gave the broken-down village where they lodged a 'Bond St atmosphere'.

On this leave – and doubtless on others – Herbert must have met up with Evelyn, who since January 1916 had been a third-form science mistress at a girls' school in Bristol. Despite the austere reserve of his letters, the lush, pastoral prose poem 'Cloud Form' from *Ambush* exhibits his intense sexual feelings for her. At the close of the school day, a nameless teacher walks rapidly towards her lodgings when her attention is attracted to the still, warm sunlight in a sloping meadow. Although tired and a bit sad, she is restless, lies down, takes a moment to retrieve a letter, rereads it and slips it back into her bodice. She looks up to see a motionless white cloud.

> The faint fragrance of the meadow, the crepitations of a few insects, a bird in the wood behind – scarcely invaded her senses in this stillness and space. Soon everything was gone, except the cloud. This lambent whiteness seemed to fall till it hovered in the immediate space above her. And then slowly it began to penetrate her. The warmth and the glory and the whiteness possessed all the channels of her flesh and animated them with an unknown life. The ecstasy seized her limbs and in a tremor she awoke.

Then the woman hears a scurrying sound, but she is alone. The frank – but extremely impersonal, almost morbid – sexuality of this passage displays the strong attraction Herbert, absent at the Front, felt towards Evelyn, but she is an unaware recipient of his Zeus-like embraces. In fact, they terrify her. The conflicts about sex between Herbert and Evelyn – in the lost courtship letters – are here transformed into an Ovidian myth. In 'Nocturne' from *Eclogues*, Read's second volume of verse (dedicated to Evelyn), the speaker's erotic longing is much more direct – and human:

> I will make this girl a bed of ferns
> Beneath the trees,
> And she shall come to me naked and shy
>   in the starlight,
> And when I kneel to kiss her body
> Faunish I will be aware of its human scent. . . .
> We will be silent in the world;
> And if she think good
> We will go down to the green pool
> To lie with our bellies in the cool grass
> And drink together.

Read analysed himself further in 'Kneeshaw Goes to War', which appeared in the fourth issue of *Art and Letters*. At the outset of the poem, Ernest Kneeshaw is supremely unaware of others.

> He might at least have perceived
> A sexual atmosphere;
> But even when his body burned and urged
> Like the buds and roots around him,
> Abash'd by the will-less promptings of his flesh,
> He continued to contemplate his feet.

The war does not immediately change this ironically named man: 'still his mind reflected things / Like a cold steel mirror – emotionless'. At Boulogne, his thoughts 'flooded unfamiliar paths. . . . Whilst he yet dwelt in the romantic fringes'. Then, exposed to the desolation of war, he feels himself a 'cog in some great evil engine'. Subsequently, during the second wave of fighting in a merciless battle, he claws the earth with a pick, cleaving the skull of a corpse. He shrieks, becomes impotent with fear, and then is hurled by a 'hot blast' into 'the beautiful peace of a coma'. Much later, minus a leg, he wanders the hills back in England, where, at last, he welcomes the pleasures of the flesh. But Ernest is guilt-ridden, believing himself a Judas who, at one crucial moment, betrayed his body to fear.

The power of fear is a theme that obsessed Read. At the outset of the war, Read, like Kneeshaw, had been haunted with the anxiety that he would not act in a courageous way. More significantly, Kneeshaw was probably a pun on Nietzsche, Read's intellectual hero, and the name may be an ironic comment on his own over-earnest development, his predilection for reason over passion. As such, the poem shows Read's capacity for self-irony and demonstrates an attempt to exorcize that demon side of him which lacked zest for life. The war brought Read to a real awareness of himself as a person who could – in the case of his men – care deeply for others. The tragedy was that this knowledge, coming amid carnage, was purchased at such a high price.

Read returned to France in October 1917 and was immediately thrown into a milieu of vague, anxious rumour about future offensives. On 10 January, still in the midst of protracted apprehension and little activity, he told Evelyn that the 'game was not worth the candle' and noted, approvingly, the rapid growth of pacifist opinion among his men. He predicted – incorrectly – that the censor would snip out this comment. Life in the trenches remained relatively calm in March, the fighting between his cat and a wandering setter being a momentous event. Then, suddenly, uneasy calm gave way to 'raging hell'.

On 21 March, the Germans began a drive at dawn through heavy fog, striking the right flank of the British sector – the Third and Fifth Armies – along a sixty-mile front. The Fifth, spread thin on a forty-two-mile front lately taken over from the French, collapsed, exposing the Third Army's right and forcing its withdrawal. Read's battalion was rushed up the line, and for six long days and nights they were besieged by the enemy. When Read's colonel, C. V. Edwards, was wounded on the second day of the onslaught, Read took command. Regularly, he and his men would be surrounded, fight their way through, only to be circled again. The new leader's canniness and grace under pressure eventually got the battalion to safety.

Read's cunning masked a nervously beating heart, as when a bullet hissed close to him: 'I thought: then this is the moment of death. But I had no emotions. I remembered having read how in battle men are hit, and never feel the hurt till later, and I wondered if I had yet been hit.' Later, the war and his childhood came eerily together when he and his men had to plunge into a stream: 'The men had to toss their rifles across, many of which landed short and were lost. The sight of these frightened men plunging into the water effected one of those curious stirrings of memory that call up some vivid scene of childhood: I saw distinctly the water-rats plunging at dusk into the mill-dam at Thornton-le-Dale, where I had lived as a boy of ten.' The circumstances were not dissimilar to his father's fall at the swollen beck.

Despite nagging doubts on his part, Read's calm assurance in command had been a remarkable success, leading to the Distinguished Service Order. However, Read's nerves were badly frayed. When his good friend, Captain Colin Davison, 'radiant as ever', came to see him, he was too 'sick' to share the news of those horrifying events with him. In the following days, he later told him, 'my heart seemed closed to you'.[6]

Two months later, Read became an adjutant but was sent back in June to England, where he was ordered to the 3rd Battalion at West Hartlepool, in preparation for transfer to the Royal Flying Corps (he became an acting captain on 27 October). Read briefly considered staying in the army, just as his political inclinations were developing in a manner increasingly antithetical to military discipline.

By October 1917, Penty's insistence on transforming England's industries into units of local guilds seemed unduly insular to Read. He now believed that only a cosmopolitanism which abolished national distinctions could stop future wars. He realized that Penty could counter with the argument that small organizations prevented national units and, thus, national economic aspirations leading to war. 'Of course,' he rejoined, 'that is familiar to us as philosophic anarchism and is very attractive as such *but* – is it practical?' An even more profound change had overtaken him by April 1918 when he proposed 'beautiful anarchy': 'I hate mobs – they fight and kill, build filthy cities and make horrid dins. And I begin to think that their salvation and re-creation is none of my concern, but the concern of each individual.' Read had obviously become suspicious of the power of any political system to legislate for the good of mankind. Anarchy had now become an attractive alternative to corrupt, fumbling governments.

That July, when a medical board rejected his transfer to the Flying Corps, Read was not unduly disturbed. The cruellest blow of the war came on 5 October, a month before the Armistice, when his brother Charles was killed at Beaurevoir. Herbert mourned him in 'Auguries of Life and Death':

Some well-meaning fool
called him an unconscious Sidney
proudly dying in the surge of battle.
Many said
he paid the supreme sacrifice. . . .

Let us be frank for once:
Such foisted platitudes
cannot console sick hearts.
Rather this alone is clear:
He was a delightful youth
irradiating joy, peculiarly loved
by hundreds of his fellows.
The impulse of his living
left a wake of laughter
and happiness in the hearts of sad men.

Read had entered the service an aloof young man, known as 'Baby Read's brother', so marked was the contrast between his austerity and Charles' eager friendliness. Many uncertainties remained when the Armistice arrived, but Read had learned that his fear of death had been linked to tremendous reservoirs of courage. His notion of the Superman had been punctured by the claims of democracy, socialism and anarchy; isolation had given way to brotherhood. To his surprise, his inherent gentleness had led to military glory. Ironically, the contrary experience of war, harrowing as it had been, had helped to heal some of the divisions within him. In a sense, his life was renewed because death had so nearly taken it. And, of course, this ambitious man now had the freedom to launch himself upon the world of art and letters.

5 Killing the Nineteenth Century: Classical Modernism

Read's first real exposure to London literary life had come while he was on leave in the autumn of 1917. Just before that, he had been impressed with a slim volume of verse, *Prufrock and Other Observations*, and suggested to Rutter, whose task it was to secure contributors, that they ask the author to write for *Art and Letters*. Rutter invited T. S. Eliot, then a confidential clerk at Lloyd's, to dine with them at the Monico in Piccadilly Circus. The restaurant had a faded, rococo elegance suited to the twenty-nine-year-old Eliot's austere correctness. He expressed cautious interest in *Art and Letters*, but it was decidedly a wait-and-see curiosity. Moreover, he was 'abashed by the apparition' of a dashing military hero from the trenches. Read, who had come straight from the Palace where he had received the Military Cross, intimidated him. Eliot felt compelled to explain that he had applied for a commission in the Naval Reserve but had waited in vain for a call-up. Read, whose pacifist tendencies were on the upsurge, was indifferent to Eliot's patriotism. The reserved young American and the taciturn Yorkshireman reached a tentative understanding that day which eventually led to the publication in *Art and Letters* of essays by Eliot on Marivaux, Marlowe, Webster and Euripides. The poems 'Burbank with a Baedeker' and 'Sweeney Erect' also first appeared there.

When they met in 1917, Eliot was still a relative newcomer to London. He had studied at Harvard, the Sorbonne and Merton College, Oxford. In July 1915 he had married an Englishwoman, Vivien Haigh-Wood, and their first attempt to settle in London was in the Bury Street flat of Eliot's former tutor, Bertrand Russell, who rented a tiny closet room to them. Eliot's parents were displeased by his marriage and his desire to remain in England. His posts at the High Wycombe Grammar School and, later, the Highgate Junior School did little to alleviate degrading, constant penury. He resigned from Highgate in December 1916, briefly lived off his considerable wits, and joined the Colonial and Foreign Department at Lloyds at 17 Cornhill in March 1917. Earlier –

56

in the summer of 1916 – Tom and Vivien had moved to a small flat at 18 Crawford Mansions, a dingy area south of Baker Street.

Eliot had established a semi-secure niche for himself only six months before he met Read. Although he was a mere five years older than his English friend, he immediately played the elder statesman to the younger subaltern. Read's intellectual development had taken place largely in isolation; Eliot had been directly exposed to some of the finest minds (George Santayana, Irving Babbitt, Harold Joachim, Henri Bergson) of the time. Eliot had the advantage of five years of intense, dedicated reading; also, he had the same handicap in a relentless commitment to the craft of poetry. A more subtle building block to superiority was, strangely, Eliot's Americanness. Englishmen, who might have had an understandable inclination to condescend to the Harvard Brahmin and to treat him as a rash foreigner, were quickly dissuaded by Eliot's perfect conformity to the stereotype of the reserved, self-deprecating Englishman. As Read said, 'If anything gave him away it was an Englishness that was a shade too correct to be natural'.

Eliot never practised camouflage. He was simply himself. As such, he was received, sometimes critically, by Bloomsbury and the Sitwells. Ottoline Morrell, who invited him to Garsington Manor in 1915, thought him frozen: 'I found him dull, dull, dull. He never moves his lips, but speaks in an even, mandarin voice. . . . I think he has lost all spontaneity and can only break through his conventionality by stimulants or violent emotion.'[1] Eliot, according to Stephen Spender, 'always exercised some privilege of post-dating his age'. By inclination, he was a person of quiet, understated authority. From the outset, Eliot was more than a mentor or friend to Read. He became a stern father whom he could emulate, rebel against and, at times, loathe.

When Read arrived back in London on 24 October 1918, Frank Rutter obtained a room for him in pleasantly disreputable Half Moon Street. Despite the busy Mayfair streets and the proximity to Piccadilly, he responded with great enthusiasm to the beautiful quiet, 'silent as a mountain top', of the city. In contrast to exploding fusillades, the noises of the frenetic metropolis soothed him. He became a new man, his eyes brightly gleaming as he zealously embraced the planning and plotting necessary to a literary career.

Since the early 1900s, London had been a battleground of conflicting literary and artistic allegiances. This was the fray into which Read now threw himself. He had spent precious years on the sidelines –

now he wanted a starring role. But, he was soon to find out, so did many other young men. As we have seen, Read had long been intimately aware of imagism and its antagonistic riposte to neo-Georgian pastoralism. His best poetry had assimilated the lessons taught by Ezra Pound. Read's drawings had carried him towards the strident, action-filled semi-abstractions of vorticism. He prized precision, energy and hardness. As he edged into London in 1918, vorticism was almost over and imagism was being seriously challenged.

One of the first books Read picked up at the end of the war was Wyndham Lewis' *Tarr* – an attempt to capture vorticism in prose – which had been published in June. 'The style is vivid,' he said, 'but that is about all.' Still, he realized that it was an important book, being impressed by its lively evocation of 'nasty people'. There was a more important reason for reading this novel: 'Wyndham Lewis is the ringleader of "les jeunes" and has a personality *and* a BRAIN.' When he finally met him, Read was overwhelmed. His own reaction to *Tarr* should have prepared him on 26 October for the brusque, energetic, handsome, Canadian-born talker whom Edward Marsh called a magnificent 'buffalo in wolf's clothing'. Lewis cultivated blackness in his high-crowned hat, his buttoned-up, uniform-like coat, his Inverness cloak, his beard and long dank hair. His alabaster face and protruding eyes provided the only contrast in his appearance. Lewis, who laid claim to the 'tarnished polish' of the English public schools and the gilded cafés of half a dozen European capitals, was well aware that he attempted a precarious existence poised between bohemianism and starchy respectability: 'Outwardly, I have been told, I looked like a *moujik*: but if so it was a *moujik* who bought his clothes in Savile Row or Brook Street and his most eccentric shirts in the Burlington Arcade.'[2]

Earlier that day, while looking for Lewis, Read met Ezra Pound at his 'den' at Holland Park Chambers in Kensington. 'As you would *not* expect,' Read told Evelyn, 'he speaks in a quiet soft voice and though affected in appearance is delightfully normal in manner.' Pound, resplendently handsome in his tallness, yellow-gold hair, small red spade of beard and penetrating green eyes, was yet another foreigner in search of an English reputation.

Both Lewis and Pound were rampantly aggressive. 'What's the use of England being an island,' Lewis once asked Augustus John, 'if you're not a *volcanic* island?' In short order, he attacked the 'bedroom idealism' of Walter Sickert, proclaimed 'Phallic aesthetics', lambasted Roger Fry's Omega Workshops as a 'curtain and pincushion factory', mocked the futurist Marinetti's facile admiration of technology: 'you Wops insist too much on the Machine. You're always on about these driving-belts, you are always exploding about internal combustion.' Sometimes hidden were Lewis' many talents.

In the *Wild Body* stories and in paintings such as *Kermesse*, Lewis was trying to join abstraction to terrifying new forms, particularly machines. David Bomberg, a fellow vorticist, saw in Lewis 'a Slade man honouring the same pledge to which I was staking my life – namely, a Partizan'.[3] Lewis and Pound were linked by similar, fraternal bonds. In addition, they regarded themselves as outsiders trying, with the help of the likes of native-born assistants like Bomberg, Roberts and Wadsworth, to impose modern art upon a reluctant nation. In 1919, Read purchased his first original work of art – one of Wadsworth's extremely geometric graphics: his sympathies had remained resolutely vorticist.

Pound's energies tended to be channelled into a series of assaults on publishers and magazines. He was endeavouring, sometimes too desperately, to find a suitable 'rag-bag' in which to stuff the 'modern world'. From the moment he arrived in London, he wanted to find out how 'Yeats did it'. Pound's obstacles tended to be self-imposed: he was too eclectic in the range of material – troubadour lyrics, Ernest Fenollosa, Arnaut David, the Elizabethan dramatists – from which he attempted to construct a contemporary style. When he first settled in London, he had been an enthusiast for writers as diverse as Browning, Rossetti, Dowson, Symons, Margaret Sackville and Rosamund Watson. Only gradually did he move towards absolute rhythm and visual accuracy. His preoccupations with other writers often removed Pound from his own sensitive responses to his milieu. All in all, as he told James Joyce in December 1918, he was better 'digging up corpses of let us say Li Po, or more lately Sextus Propertius' than in perserving 'this bitched mess of modernity'.

Read was intrigued by Pound and Lewis. He did not share the Sitwells' penchant for making fun of Pound. On the other hand, he found it difficult to take him seriously: 'Apart from his exotic appearance, he rattled off his elliptic sentences . . . twitched incessantly and prowled round the room like a caged panther.' Quite soon, Pound's voice had a 'harsh nasal twang'. Read's cautionary disdain was reciprocated by Pound, who in 1920 said: 'H. Read I never have swallowed, not as a *writer*'; a year later, he called him 'too bloody dull' for his *Little Review*.[4]

Initially, there was a measured friendliness between Read and Lewis. Read told Evelyn: 'he is not half so ferocious as you might imagine.' They 'palled' together that October. 'I think he rather likes me because I am not of the "damned pseudo-artistic riff-raff",' he complacently informed Evelyn. At Lewis' Great Tichfield flat, Read met Iris Barry, who had just become pregnant: 'He had a nice girl there "to pour out tea" – I did not catch her name, but she is a young poetess who has not yet published. Quite a nice girl.' Read's conventionality can be seen in this aside, which is of course meant to assure Evelyn that one could be both resolutely modern *and* assiduously moral. He also told Evelyn that she bore an uncanny likeness to 'Mrs. Ezra', Dorothy Shakespear: 'I was absolutely startled by her resemblance (in feature) to you. And she is perfectly charming as well. So I could not help but be captivated.'

Lewis was pleased to provide *Art and Letters* with a story 'The War Baby', a drawing and a cover design; he was flattered when Read asked him to 'decorate' *Naked Warriors*, his new book of verse. The project fell through when the publisher, Cyril Beaumont, would not pay Lewis a minimal fee of £10, as he complained to Read in December 1918: 'Were it for you, I would gladly do them for nothing. The fact that I had drawings in the book would insure a certain number of sales amongst people who for the moment, you might not reach.'[5] His involvement was confined to a design for the book's cover. But Lewis was pleased that 'The War Baby' was to appear in *Art and Letters* without 'having his balls cut off; or rather Kunt treated for appearance before a bestial public'.[6] Read liked the lustiness of 'War Baby' and hoped that the 'printers would have the decency to print it unaltered'.[7]

Despite his inclination towards a rigorous aesthetic, Read remained intimidated by Eliot, Pound and Lewis. Lucien Pissarro, the French-born neo-impressionist who had lived in England since 1890 and who specialized in cottage gardens, copses and orchards, became for Read 'a vivid foil' to Lewis: 'In another ten years people will talk of a Pissarro landscape as they now talk of a "Turner sunset" or a Whistler nocturne. There is something amazing in the life-long patience and modesty of this man. It inspires with some sort of awe.' Read was confused. He truthfully observed: 'It is confoundingly difficult to see a clear path in my future.' This observation captures perfectly the contradictions within Read as he tried to discover his way among the prevailing claims in art and literature. He wanted to be a member of the vanguard, but, as he came into direct contact with it, he was inclined to draw back. Despite the strident letters to Evelyn, he was, like her, inclined to be unduly orthodox. Carefree bohemianism, as practised by Lewis and Pound, frightened him.

In contrast, the patrician bearing of the Sitwell brothers was much more tolerable. Osbert and Sacheverell wanted to buy into *Art and Letters*, and Frank Rutter quickly arranged a meeting at the Café Royal on 26 Ocober, the same day Read met Lewis. Plainly relieved by the brothers' ordinariness in comparison with the ringleader of 'les jeunes', he was immediately won over: 'They are sons of Sir George Sitwell – aristocratic, wealthy, officers in the Guards, Oxford University and what not. But *also* furious socialists, good poets (Sachie very good) and very young (about my own age). They are crammed full of enthusiasm for the future and it is with them that I can imagine myself being associated a good deal in the future.' However, the Sitwells represented the 'beastly self-complacency' of the upper classes that Lewis despised, and two days later Read's own insularity had been shaken: 'The Sitwells are rather too comfortable and perhaps there is a lot of pose in their revolt.' However, he felt he ought to stick with the brothers English: 'But they are my generation whereas Lewis's is the generation before and it is with the Sitwells that I must throw in my lot to a large extent.' In turn, Osbert was very observant. To him, Read was 'like a Roundhead; he is extravagant only in the lengths to which austerity carries him'. The streak of puritanism which Osbert discerned he attributed to Read's early struggles. Only when the 'premature seriousness' was banished by a smile, he pointed out, did the gravity in his face suddenly and pleasantly vanish.[8] As a droll comment on Herbert's solemness, Osbert presented him with a stuffed owl in a glass case.

Lewis was eleven years older than Read, and Osbert Sitwell only a year. But the barrier that Read felt was one of attitude, not age. Lewis thought the Sitwells practised a 'special brand of rich-man's gilded bolshevism'. The brothers were certainly eager to fill the vacuum left by the decline of imagism and vorticism with their own alternative Bloomsbury. Intellectually, they could not compete with the likes of an Eliot or Lewis, but they had style and satire. Read certainly did not feel intimidated, despite the wide social gap separating him from these aristocrats. He was quite willing to collaborate with Osbert in planning 'manifestos and generally making ourselves heard in the land'.

During this packed week in October 1918, 'the most *truly* wonderful in my life', Read was also taken up by the painter Charles Ginner, who had been actively involved with the Camden Town and London Groups. Earlier, during the war, Read had met Ginner and Harold Gilman through Rutter. He had found Ginner a 'funny stick' who, comprising a pair of glasses, straggly moustache, small voice, and rumpled clothes, never knew whether he had had dinner or not. Gilman was 'similar but neater'.

Read became a 'new man' in this heady London atmosphere of conflicting views as to how poetry and painting should be practised. He squeezed in time to see the Ballets Russes. He considered taking over the Allied Artists Association to which he wanted to add a publishing and book-selling business 'starting cautiously and in a small way, but gradually working up a great independent Authors' Press'. Read's letters are also crammed with references to other new faces: Nina Hamnett, Harriet Weaver, Dora Marsden, P. G. Konody, Richard Aldington. In the midst of all this breathless activity, Read's supposed reason for being in London – the DSO investiture – became a 'boring affair'.

Although delightfully over-stimulated by this whirlwind week, Read retained his capacity for shrewd judgement, as when he sorted out his impressions in a letter to Evelyn of 30 October: 'Of all this crowd I begin to distinguish the poseurs and the real talents. Lewis and Eliot are by far the most *important* figures. They have *strength*: I see that well. Pound is a curious mixture. He makes his undoubted talent less effective by his personal expression of it. He does not allow his brains frank egress.' Read was also in grave danger of not discovering the candid truth about himself. What 'frank egress' would he take? What kind of a modern would he become – a Pissarro, a Sitwell, a Pound, an Eliot?

Having been exposed for the first time to literature and art among the 'veritable lions' that October week, Read felt, not surprisingly, deflated when he arrived at his posting at Westbere in Canterbury. As he wandered around that city, Read realized that an inexplicable blindness to reality had led him to consider staying in the army. Previously, he imagined an officer's off-hours would allow him scope to develop his literary talent. Still, Read had to earn a living. His work as an officer had made him – and others – aware of his considerable skills as an administrator. Only briefly, politics beckoned as an alternative to the army. On 10 November he cancelled his application to the War Office for a regular commission and left the army in January 1919. When he arrived in London the following month, he remained unsure of his future.

While at Leeds University, Read had been taught by Arthur Greenwood, then a thirty-three-year-old lecturer in Economics and a founding member of the Yorkshire (North) District of the Workers'

Educational Association. During the Leeds municipal strike of 1913, Greenwood's open support of the strikers had irritated the University authorities, and, shortly before the outbreak of the war, Greenwood went to London as General Secretary of the Council for the Study of International Relations. He was a protégé of the Webbs and, by 1916, had written extensively not only on international relations but also on child labour and juvenile unemployment. Three years later, Greenwood had become a member of Lloyd George's secretariat and from 1917 to 1919 was a principal at the Ministry of Reconstruction (he had stood unsuccessfully as MP for Southport in 1918). Read, who shared his former teacher's idealistic concern with social welfare, confided in him. Greenwood urged the anxious young man not to return to university and suggested that his talents indicated a career in politics or the civil service. Specifically, he recommended that Read should take up an administrative post in the Labour Party hierarchy – such a job could be used as a stepping-stone to Parliament; or, he offered, he could recommend him to the Ministry of Labour. Read's talents, he felt, would, after a brief probationary period, lead to a permanent post in the First Division.

Read opted for the Ministry, which he joined later that month. He was appointed to the Trade Board and took part in the negotiations for the setting up of the Whitley Councils (joint boards of employers and unions) in several industries. When it was decided to set up a similar mechanism in the civil service, an officer was needed by the Treasury to oversee its implementation. Read's obvious administrative ability having attracted favourable notices, he moved to the Treasury in August 1919. Earlier, in February, at the outset of his time in the civil service, Wyndham Lewis had generously remarked: 'I am so glad to hear that you are getting demobilized & going to take up your quarters in London. Also the Ministry of Labour sounds a lively post at present.'

Lewis's blithe expectations were not realized. At first, Read fervently hoped that his ability to co-ordinate details, write minutes and prepare summaries was simply part of his literary aptitude. But the sheer drudgery soon made him aware that he was in danger of killing any such talent. In the army, he had been 'gagged, bound hand and foot' to government propaganda; similar inhibitions prevailed once again. Also any sense of leisure had evaporated: 'I rarely left the Treasury before half-past six or seven, and by the time I had reached home, for a late dinner, I was tired and exhausted. The more I contemplated the course ahead of me, the less I liked it. My colleagues around me were for the most part absorbed in their departmental work:

it was their main interest, to which they willingly devoted all their energies.'

Read's considerable left-over energy went into the building of a literary career. He had partially withdrawn from *Art and Letters* after Osbert Sitwell had become a one-third partner in November 1918 (the magazine ceased publication in 1920). Now, he tried to focus his after-work hours on fiction. Also, he became known as someone who could be seen at important events, as Arnold Bennett's casual remembrance of a June 1919 evening at Osbert's house at 2 Carlyle Square shows: 'A good dinner. Fish before soup. Present W. H. Davies, Lytton Strachey, Woolf, Nichols, S. Sassoon, Aldous Huxley, Atkin (a very young caricaturist), W. J. Turner and Herbert Read (a very young poet).'

When the Sitwell brothers, in an attempt to place themselves even more squarely in the forefront of contemporary art, exhibited Modigliani, Derain, Vlaminck, Soutine, Matisse, Utrillo, Dufy, Zadkine and Archipenko at Heal's Mansard Gallery in the Tottenham Court Road, Read acted as a shopman with them, 'selling catalogues, answering enquiries, and often quieting, or trying to quiet, protests' about the outrageous paintings and sculptures.[9]

During his first days in London, Read lived at 24/29 Nottingham Terrace, York Gate, in close proximity to Madame Tussaud's. When he married a bit later, he moved to 35 Beaumont Road, Purley. He called his 'little house in the suburbs' 'Muscoates', after his childhood home. From the outset, Herbert was reticent about Evelyn. He casually mentioned his engagement to Osbert while they were walking across Trafalgar Square. 'He stopped and stood with a look of great distress on his face, as though I had told him I was about to commit suicide.' Osbert assured him that he was making a grave mistake, marriage being a form of economic servitude and spiritual death. Osbert was obviously speaking of his own fear of marriage, but he might have been troubled because Herbert was yet another young man upon whom Edith Sitwell had a crush. Previously, Herbert had made omelettes for her. She certainly responded in stony silence to his announcement. He realized that he had been expelled from 'the happy life of [her] youth'; before, she had thought him 'shy and charming': 'We used to have large tea-parties on Saturdays, and Herbert Read and two others, sometimes four others, of our very intimate friends used to stop on afterwards, and help cook the supper.'[10]

Read's response to Osbert and Edith was sharp: 'There was no reason why I should have told her; or Osbert. My future wife was quite unknown to them and not literary.' A reflection – prompted by Osbert's strictures – suggests marriage was for him a grim but natural necessity: 'But celibacy also is a spiritual death. We deceive ourselves if we think we can plan our lives against the grain of our physical dispositions.' As early as 1919 Read felt trapped, but that year he and Evelyn were married on 7 August at the Register Office at North Bierley. Arthur Roff, Evelyn's father, William Prior Read and Herbert's brother William were the witnesses.

Read felt imprisoned by his marriage and his job. As far as he was concerned, the civil service tapped his vitality, leaving him little room to develop his capacity as a writer. His discontents are readily apparent in his 'Apology for E.S.'. Eugene Strickland and Read first met in April 1919. They shared an office in Whitehall, overlooking Horseguards Parade. Once they were thrown together, their differences became all too apparent: 'I was not destined to stay in the Civil Service – my real ambitions lay elsewhere, in the world of literature. But Eugene Strickland was a born administrator.' Strickland criticized Read's lack of drive. The two men drifted apart. After their paths had diverged, Strickland sent Read a curious memoir in which he revealed that he had once felt destined to be a poet. However, at school, he learned to speak in two languages:

> – the inner language that expressed my feelings and the outer language that I addressed to other people to satisfy their expectations. I answered the questions that tested my knowledge of the world, and discovered, as all children do, that in order to please my parents and teachers, I had to acquire a knowledge of external facts – of numbers, measurements, grammar and history. The language of my feelings I might still use for intimate occasions, to convey to those I loved my affections and desires; but it so happened that my family life came to a sudden end in my tenth year . . . My sensitive antennae recoiled into my innermost being, and for eight years I remained a dumb and frightened animal.

At Oxford, the repressed language of emotion was expressed in poetry, which could be shared with a few select friends. He also learned that poetry is 'not the direct expression of feeling, but is rather the art of inventing forms to contain our feelings'. Then Eugene came to the unhappy realization that it was difficult to survive as a poet. His aspirations pulled him in contrary directions.

> The thought of my own father's brief and obscure life was perhaps always present to my consciousness. . . . But I had worldly ambitions – not so much for the sake of wealth or social rank, but of power and active participation in public affairs. Already my thoughts were turning to those

65

professions, such as law and politics, which were open to the arts of eloquence. I saw myself addressing vast audiences, swaying their emotions, inducing their loyalty. Then came the war, and you know the rest. My poetic reveries were put away with my civilian clothes; five years later the clothes were moth-eaten and the reveries had vanished.

For many years afterwards, Read, seeing Strickland rise higher and higher in the administrative bureaucracy, compared his humbler achievements to those of his former friend.

Of course, 'Eugene Strickland' is a fictional alter-ego of Read himself, and this 'apology' is in large part an attempt to isolate a part of himself which he found repugnant (in 1920, Read submitted an essay under this pseudonym to the *Athenaeum*). In creating such a character, Read could analyse estranged aspects of himself and, in so doing, reject them. Like Lieutenant P and Kneeshaw, Strickland represents a self who could, given a chance, have come into being. One of Read's Yorkshire ancestors was Emmanuel Strickland. More significantly, Eliza Strickland was Herbert's mother's maiden name, and the career of 'E.S.' is similar to the one she had envisioned for him.

What this curious disguised autobiography reveals was the temptation Read underwent to abandon his ideals and to succumb to the pressure of worldly success. In 1919, he had become shackled to a system which he despised but at which, paradoxically, he showed an ingrained aptitude. Also, Read's discomfiture at not having attended Oxford or Cambridge can be seen here in a fine piece of reverse snobbery: Eugene Strickland, the Oxford man, sells out, but the person from the University of Leeds does not. Read's strong sense that his father's premature death overshadowed his subsequent existence is movingly elicited when 'Eugene' states that from the time of his father's death he was 'thrown into an alien world where there was no use for a language of feeling'. However, in the early twenties, Read, very much like 'E.S.', tried to abandon 'feeling', which he increasingly saw as a kind of vice.

Glum determination and long nights are difficult to endure, especially if their end is hard to discern. Friends such as Eliot, Lewis and Flint reassured the would-be writer. In March 1920, Read told Lewis: 'I am fairly settled in my somewhat bourgeois existence: hoping for eventual emancipation via "free" talent – false hope perhaps.'[11] Evelyn wanted her husband to persevere, but she had an inherent suspicion of his new friends. Her shrewd, strong mind was distrustful of bohemenianism in any guise. Much-needed, exuberant assistance came from rascally, plump Ford Madox Hueffer (later Ford), whom Read had met at Redcar in 1918, when he had 'mopped up' a staff job over the older man's head, just before the fateful October week in London.

Although, at first glance, Read incorrectly guessed that Ford was little more than a stylist, he was immediately taken with the idea of having a friend who had known Henry James '*intimately*'. Ford also told the younger man about H. G. Wells, Pound and Rebecca West ('great fun she, he says, but promising'). The forty-five-year-old Ford, who had collaborated with Conrad on three books, served in the Welsh Regiment from 1915 to 1919 and had been badly gassed. A sometimes incautious liar, he told Read that he was married to Violet Hunt the novelist (in 1931, Ford's wife Elsie successfully sued *Throne* magazine for describing Hunt as Mrs Ford Madox Hueffer); in fact, by 1919, Ford had a new mistress, Stella Bowen.

Despite the fact that he was from a generation antecedent to 'les jeunes', Ford felt an instant camaraderie with them. He once described himself accurately as a 'sort of half-way house between nonpublishable youth and real money – a sort of green baize swing door that everyone kicks both on entering and leaving'. In 1913, Pound asserted that he would rather talk about poetry with Ford than with any man in London. For Ford, poetry had to be as well written as prose: 'Its language must be a fine language, departing in no way from speech save by a heightened intensity (i.e. simplicity). There must be no book words, no periphrases, no inversions.' In September 1919 he urged Read to visit him: 'I rather want to put you in touch with some new periodical & publishing ventures that may help you if you are still inclined for a (part) literary career – & the sooner you get in the better, because, though these look like being lasting concerns One Never Knows.'[12]

Another backer was Richard Aldington, with whom Read became 'very pally' in October 1918 when he blandly described him as a 'jolly open-faced English type – 26 years old – and quite boyish. Altogether a friend to be.' Although it is severe, Virginia Woolf's assessment of 1924 is more accurate: 'a bluff, powerful, rather greasy eyed, nice downright man, who will make his way in the world, which I dont much like people to do.'[13] Woolf's back had been put up by Aldington's extraordinary aggressiveness, to which some friends eventually reacted by rejecting him. By the end of 1918, Aldington's marriage of 1913 to H.D. (Hilda Doolittle) was largely over, although he remained convinced that she – and not Pound – was the greatest of the imagist poets.

For Read in 1918, Aldington, only a year older than himself, was a legendary figure who had written for the *Egoist*, *Poetry and Drama*, the *Little Review* and the various imagist anthologies. Read and Aldington lunched that first day, then strolled up Charing Cross Road, browsing in the bookshops. A glimpse of Aldington's virulence can be espied in a remark to Read of January 1919, when he urges his new friend to come to terms with the fact that poets have the potential, although a severely limited one, to revolutionize society: although 'our ability to put the wind up the governing classes is minute compared with that of the least Trade Union', it is 'about time we returned to the brigandage of our illustrious predecessor, F. Villon'.[14]

When *Naked Warriors* appeared later that year, Aldington was spiritedly approving. However, barbed compliments were an Aldington speciality, as when he called Read's attention to 'a slight tang of Lewis in your prose episode'. He added: 'forgive me for this, which will annoy you'.[15] Nevertheless, Aldington was correct about 'Killed in Action', where Read tries too hard to find a verbal equivalent to Lewis's war canvases. The following passage, with its metaphors of rape, incest and necrophilia conjoined to a stark black and red colour scheme, is typical of the entire piece: 'Now riven and violated; a wide glabrous desolation; a black diseased scab, erupted and pustulous. The black shell-holes were like earthly lips puckered to kiss – lips of Mother Earth, incestuously desirous – parched, sucking lips eager for his wet red blood.' Outrage was Read's aim here. And in the Preface:

> We, who in manhood's dawn have been compelled to care not a damn for life or death, now care less still for the convention of glory and the intellectual apologies for what can never be to us other than a riot of ghastliness and horror, of inhumanity and negation. May we, therefore, for the sake of life itself, be resolved to live with a cleaner and more direct realisation of natural values. May we be unafraid of our frank emotions, and may we maintain a callous indifference to the prettifying of life. Then, as the reflex of such stern activity, may we strive to create a beauty where hitherto it has had no absolute existence. From the sickness of life revealed let us turn with glad hearts to the serenity of some disinterested beauty.

The poems in *Naked Warriors* – and in *Eclogues* which was also published in 1919 – veer between the tranquil horror of 'April' –

> To the fresh wet fields
> and the white
> froth of flowers
>
> Came the wild errant
> swallows with a scream

– and the heavy-handed irony of 'The Crucifix' –

> His body is smashed
> through the belly and chest
> the head hangs lopsided
> from one nail'd hand.
>
> Emblem of agony
> we have smashed you!

'E.S.W.' in the *Gryphon* was deeply angered by Read's attempt to immortalize the sordid: 'If Mr. Read's muse has developed, it may be doubted whether it has improved. *Naked Warriors* leaves one with a nasty taste in the mouth. . . . The ugliness of war, of life in general, is only too painfully self-evident, and though the scavenger and the sanitary inspector are very necessary, we need men not only to point out to us the hidden filth and dirt and uncleanness, but to help us get rid of them, and to show us the beauty that there is in things common and unclean.' As far as Read was concerned, life after the war was a sordid mess.

Although Read's verse had remained decidedly imagistic, he had become uncomfortably aware, as had Pound, that the movement was going to seed: 'their sea-violets and wild hyacinths tend to become as decorative as the beryls and jades of Oscar Wilde'. In order to survive, he claimed in 'Definitions towards a Modern Theory of Poetry' in the third number of *Art and Letters*, the poetry must pursue 'significant form which is achieved by unity, vitality, exactness, concentration and decoration'.

Read's appropriation in 1918 of 'significant form' from Clive Bell's *Art* (1914) shows how deftly he could intermingle literary and art criticism. He could also praise the 'peculiarity' of David Bomberg's show at the Adelphi: 'And the way he will explore all the possibilities of an idea in a series of drawings seems to indicate that his mind is of that objective, scientific sort that alone is capable of wonders. Mr. Bomberg is possibly a great artist.'[16] Read also took the opportunity to castigate the public's tendency to tag artists with labels. He had an affection for such philistines similar to the one he entertained 'for the largest hippopotamus in the Zoo'.[17]

When *Art and Letters* ceased publication in the spring of 1920, Read, who had earlier expressed disgust at the increasingly staid *New Age*, in search of a suitable market for his work submitted a war story to that journal in February 1920. Orage was curtly dismissive:

> You are quite at liberty to call me anything you please but I cannot

pretend that the measure of your emotional experience is necessarily the measure of mine. . . . The Lord forgive me, but I find [the war story] dull in every sense but the . . . personal one of considerable interest in your psychology. It is not my place of course to offer you advice; but if I did, it would be to urge you to forget the war . . . and to bring into consciousness what your unconsciousness throws up. . . . What did your soul learn in the Great War?[18]

Orage was hostile to war literature. His disparaging comments must be seen in that light, but he also realized that Read was obsessed with the war, as if he could not move forward from those harrowing experiences. In effect, he told Read not to blame the war for personal unhappiness. Although he objected to the use of the word 'soul', Eliot praised *Naked Warriors*, assuring Read that he had been deft in the presentation of Kneeshaw.

Ford Madox Ford continued his paternal interest, but he was decidedly put off by Evelyn's claim that he and Stella were too bohemian: 'tell Mrs Read that Stella and I are not aesthetes. At the present moment she is cutting ham sandwiches to take on the river for the day!!!!'[19] Ford and Evelyn disagreed about the civil service. Ford advised Read to stick with it. To a large extent, Evelyn's attitudes were contradictory. She did not like his London friends. And yet she realized that her husband's happiness was centred on concerns – antithetical to the civil service – which involved him with persons she distrusted. She was caught in an impossible position: she thought her husband's friends would come between her and Herbert, but she wanted to nourish the pursuits which gave him obvious pleasure. Finally, Evelyn, lamenting the friends, urged him to resign.

Another way out with which Read flirted was to abandon his government job, return to Yorkshire and eke out an existence as a writer there. Ford scoffed at him for considering such a move, telling him that such a retreat offered only penury and starvation. He reminded his protégé that a reproduction of the Venus de Milo had, until recent memory, been concealed behind aspidistras at the Leeds Art Gallery. To go back to Yorkshire, he warned, would freeze any hope he had of becoming a real writer: 'Don't let yourself undergo that hardening process; it is a very stupid one; and try to forget that you come from the Sheeres at all. . . . Whitechapel is really a better lieu de naissance.'[20] Ford's cavalier notion that the civil service was an elegant profession for a gentleman did not sit well with Read, who was there to earn a living. Finally, he decided to remain where he was, having come to the realization that he would never have sufficient free time to become a novelist.

That painful reflection meant he would have to ignore this piece of advice from Ford: 'You may not like novel writing but it would be a good thing to stick to it as to avoid turning your soul into a squirrel in a revolving cage.'[21] For Ford, the novel was the only literary genre to which a serious man should apply himself. Only there was the possibility of finding a 'New Form'. And, he prodded Read, such a quest was the only worthy occupation of a writer. Read, who shared his friend's commitment to modernity, nevertheless pushed his own future in the direction of poetry and the essay. A disciplined worker, he set aside time each night to write. By so doing, he kept his interests alive for, as he said, 'the creative impulse dies if not given a quick chance to materialize'. In January 1921, Read became private secretary to the Controller of Establishments, but the promotion brought him little joy. Again, he thought of throwing his job up and returning to Yorkshire.

Despite Orage's earlier rejection of the 'dull' piece of war fiction, Read began in 1921 to frequent his tiny office in Rolls Passage. The editor, who frequently called his paper 'No Wage', had a tiny cubicle with cartoons pinned to the walls. There was also the 'manager': the dark, disapproving Alice Marks. Read sometimes attended the 'editorial conferences' held in the warm basement of the ABC restaurant in Chancery Lane. Orage also officiated over discussions at the Kardomah Café in Fleet Street and held lunches at the Sceptre, off Regent Street. Katherine Mansfield told him: 'you taught me to write, you taught me to think, you showed me what there was to be done and what not to do'.[22] Read could have said the same of this quirky man. Many years later in 1958, he told Henry Miller: 'I worshipped Orage when I first came to London and began writing under his tutelage. But everything of his evaporated, and now he is only a memory.'[23]

Orage was sufficiently impressed by Read's expanding skills to ask him to take over his literary column, 'Readers and Writers', which was signed R. H. C. Read wrote twenty-five of these between 14 July and 29 December 1921. Ford was outraged: 'Curse you! Just as in H.M. Army you mopped up that staff job over my head, so you have mopped up the New Age Lit. Page. . . . Thus do the ungodly grow fat on the too early works of the righteous.'[24] As Read later admitted, he now began to neglect Ford, whose novels, with the exception of the Tietjens series, he did not admire; he was sure that Ford now considered him 'a lost soul'.[25] Meanwhile, Orage leaned heavily on Read, upon whom he bestowed an astute mixture of occasional praise and frequent blame: 'Beware of too often choosing subjects unfamiliar to your readers. Enlighten them about things they *think* they already know.'[26] As 1921

71

wore on, Read complained to Orage of nervous exhaustion, of having taken on far too many responsibilities.

One reason for Read's debilitating tiredness was that he found it difficult to say no to an intriguing proposal, as when Orage casually mentioned in May that he was thinking of approaching F. S. Flint to edit the manuscripts of T. E. Hulme, who had been killed at the Front in 1917. At the time of his death, Hulme's papers were with Ethel Kibblewhite, his mistress, who asked Orage to edit the huge mass of untidy material. Read immediately proposed himself as editor. Hulme, who even more than Lewis had evolved the critical theories at the heart of vorticism, had espoused an anti-democratic, anti-romantic aesthetic. By presenting his papers to the world, Read would be propagandizing a rigorous, virile modernism.

If self-doubt ever intruded itself into the consciousness of Thomas Ernest Hulme, he concealed it. Hulme, who was born in 1883 at Gratton Hall, Endon, North Staffordshire, began to make his mark as a ruffian when he was sent down from St John's College, Cambridge, in 1904. According to J. C. Squire, his departure led to the 'longest mock funeral ever seen in the town'. Hulme rode on a hearse 'astride the coffin with his friends in deep mourning grieving beside him'. After an eight-month stay in Canada in 1906, Hulme returned briefly to England in 1907 and then went to Brussels. In the next five years, he developed his anti-democratic, classical theory of art.

Hulme was not an original thinker, but he had the remarkable ability, like Read, to synthesize the work of others. When his one-time mentor, Henri Bergson, was accused of being partial to egalitarianism, he rejoined: 'Bergson no more stands for Democracy than he stands for paper-bag cookery.'[27] In 1912, Hulme left Cambridge for Berlin, where he came under the spell of Wilhelm Worringer, whose *Abstraction and Empathy* (1908) came to dominate him.

Worringer made a crucial distinction between 'geometric' and 'vital', between classicism and romanticism. Specifically, he argued that geometric art was a manifestation of essential truths, quasi-religious in nature, which displayed man's clinging to a perfection beyond himself. 'Vital' art, usually representational, in which the consciousness of the artist is central, was considered humanist, and thus decadent. Geometric art was God-centred; vital art was overly concerned with puny human feelings. The notion of Original Sin was central to geometric art; vital art did not recognize the fall of man. Hulme had been well on the way to such beliefs before he went to Germany, but that trip inflamed him with a stronger sense of purpose in spreading the gospel of abstraction. Pound, who always retained a strong romantic inclination, dismissed Hulme as talking 'a lot of crap about Bergson' but F. S. Flint said Hulme was the 'ringleader' in insisting on 'absolutely accurate presentation and no verbiage'.

Hulme was as intent on shocking his friends in his personal – as well as his professional – life. As David Garnett recalled, he courted scandal. 'Hulme would suddenly pull out his watch while a group of his acquaintances sat talking with him at a table in the Café Royal. "I've a pressing engagement in five minutes' time", he would say and stride out of the building. Twenty minutes later he would return, wipe his brow, and complain that the steel staircase of the emergency exit at Piccadilly Circus Tube Station was the most uncomfortable place in which he had ever copulated.'[28] Hulme's exhibitionism – particularly his espousal of mechanical sex – was part of a carefully conducted campaign on behalf of his brand of modernism. Wyndham Lewis aptly called him a 'very talkative jolly giant, arrogantly argumentative, but a great laugher'.[29]

At the Leeds Arts Club, Read had been exposed to many of Hulme's doctrines, which have many points in common with Nietzsche. In promoting Hulme, he was spreading ideas to which he had long been an ardent convert. Despite intellectual comradeship, Read felt Hulme's character repulsive:

> He was an aggressive, bullying, truculent fellow, intensely disliked by most people. He played with ideas in a casual, careless sort of way, but undoubtedly had a nose for the right sort of ideas, rather than an intellectual sense. He roused people, inspired them with curiosity & the right kind of curiosity – but nothing more. . . . there was little solid thought there. . . . no consistency, no 'moral fibre'. . . . I think he would have 'organised' us all a good deal = to that extent his loss is deplorable.[30]

Although his puritanical side may have disdained Hulme, the dead soldier's role as impresario of modernism remained crucial to Read. Since his own destiny was to continue the fallen soldier's work, he welcomed the opportunity to edit the aptly named *Speculations*, which was published in 1924.

Orage continued his watch on Read, but the older man's enthusiasm for P. D. Ouspensky, the mystical anti-Bolshevist Russian mathematician, philosopher and journalist, put him off: 'after a trial-run of a dozen lectures I turned away'. However, his work at the 'No Wage' brought him the kind of attention he sought. In December 1921, Orage was at a party at the home of Sydney Schiff, the collector, novelist and translator of Proust, who warmly praised Read: 'Lewis was present & became interested & your name was canvassed as that of a new star!'[31] Earlier that year, Read had warned Lewis that his range in his magazine *Tyro* was too limited – he was not sufficiently emulating the satirical precision of either Rowlandson or Hogarth.[32] The seeds of enmity had been sown.

Read's existence was split between seemingly endless days at the office and long nights in his study. His life changed dramatically in 1922 when a letter which needed the signature of the Controller of Establishments landed on his desk. The Treasury, it announced, had approved two additional assistant-keeperships at the Victoria and Albert Museum. 'In a flash' he saw his escape. Read took the letter to his boss and blurted out his request. Read's supervisor was understandably surprised that his subordinate wanted to exchange a much coveted post worth £400 for one of £250. Read, who often casually neglected long-range financial goals, was embarrassed but firm – and won his superior's reluctant approval. Shortly afterwards, Read went for an interview, was hired and was posted to the Department of Ceramics, a subject about which he then knew nothing.

Read went from a tedious job to one which was '*too* interesting'. Now, he had the pleasure of not being able to make a clear distinction between work done in office hours and work done at home. His new responsibilities demanded that he sharpen his eyes. Previously, he had been concerned with images in poems. For him, art and literature gradually fused together, as they had for Ruskin and Pater.

Again, Yorkshire was very much in Read's mind. In April 1922, he told his friend the poet Wilfred Rowland Childe: 'We must definitely turn our backs on London & all its erudite sophistications. . . . My idea is to neglect & ignore the London cliques & critics entirely. . . . I am sure that London is utterly dead. . . . I am weary of it all.' Read's toying with the idea of a Yorkshire literary movement shows not only how discouraged he could become but also how deeply implanted within him was his nostalgia for his first ten years at Muscoates Grange.

At about the same time, in a peevish aside, Read vented his contempt for Joyce's *Ulysses*: 'a book written for & addressed to one man only – the author of it. It is the reductio ad absurdum of all the modern movements in art-literature.'[33] Read may have been responding with disdain to the romantic side of Joyce, who explores his hero's emotional responses to wife, lost son and Dublin.

Read managed to keep up an alliance with Wyndham Lewis, who was hoping to publish excerpts from Hulme in *Tyro*. Despite surface friendliness, Read had now become suspicious of Lewis, who in a jealous rage had once threatened to kill Hulme, having tracked him down to a house in Frith Street and seized him by the throat. Hulme dragged Lewis down the stairs into Soho Square, where he hung him upside down on the railings. Increasingly, it was Lewis' 'cageyness' which irritated Read – every meeting was conducted as if they were conspirators. 'More often than not we met in an A.B.C. – with our backs to the wall.'[34] When Read, along with E. M. Forster, was invited in October 1922 to dine with the Woolfs at their Richmond home, he told, with Virginia's approval, 'amazing stories' of the 'Wyndham Lewis pigsty'.[35]

By March 1922, Read had finished work on a new volume of verse, *Mutations of the Phoenix*. He submitted this collection to Harold Munro's Poetry Bookshop, although it was the Woolfs who published it in 1923. Munro, rightly worried that imagism was not readily visible in this new group of poems, asked Richard Aldington to vet them. Aldington realized immediately that this verse intended to 'throw over' its predecessors, himself included:

> our poetry was the poetry of the emotions and of beauty, of instinct and sudden impulse. . . . Read (and others of his 'school') try to create poetry from thought and the operations of the intelligence; psychology and character interest them; beauty is a phenomenon not a passion; they analyse love, they don't overflow with it. . . . We committed many follies, but they are wise; we were as silly as doves, but they as subtle as serpents.[36]

Aldington's perceptive criticism reflects the difference between the imagist movement and Eliot's metaphysical style in poems such as *Prufrock*. He is also distinguishing between *Naked Warriors* and *Mutations*. Read's lush, disciplined use of vivid metaphors has unfortunately given way, under Eliot's influence, to cerebral ruminations, as in the opening of 'The Falcon and the Dove':

> This high-caught hooded Reason broods upon my wrist,
> Fetter'd by a so tenuous leash of steel.
> We are bound for the myrtle marshes, many leagues away,
> And have a fair expectation of quarry

or in the concluding stanza from 'Equation':

> Earth is machine and works to plan,
> Winnowing space and time;
> The ethic mind is engine too,
> Accelerating in the void.

In his critique, Aldington suggested that Read's only serious rival was

Tom Eliot, who is 'an older hand, has a mind which is wonderfully athletic and well-trained'; he also noted that *Mutations* was not as good as the book Eliot had in manuscript.[37] That unpublished poem was *The Waste Land*.

Aldington hit upon precisely the dilemma which now confronted Read as poet and critic. He was a deeply intellectual person, who had strong literary and critical skills. Those talents were dwarfed by Eliot's, and it was Eliot, not Read, who would produce a considerable body of poetry and criticism articulating the classicism of Hulme. Eliot and Read were drawn together partly because of their devotion to the ideals of that slain soldier, but in the next few years the influence of Eliot would become intolerable to Read. He would be constantly over-shadowed, and he would have to revolt against the notion of a work of art as phenomenon. Ford Madox Ford, who told him in April 1921 to get out of his cocoon, had the correct measure of the precocious Yorkshireman: 'I don't believe you are the chilly intellectual . . . that you think yourself: you are a temporarily unthawed emotionalist. And a day will come.'[38] Eventually, the day arrived when Read decided to put up a counter-faith to Eliot. Then, he would preach passion.

6   Reviving the Nineteenth Century: Romantic Modernism

'My intellectual debt to Eliot has been enormous, but he has been rather like a gloomy priest presiding over my affections and spontaneity.'[1] In this poignant aside in a letter of April 1943, Read apologized to the poet and publisher Richard Church for his pervasive lack of generosity. Read suspected that the reason for such behaviour on his part stretched back to his friendship with Eliot. As the twenties wore on, Read realized more and more that Eliot's influence upon him was pernicious and destructive. At first, he did not know how to mount a rebellion. However, as early as 1921, Read, even though he was pleased to 'bleat with the goats' of the anti-romantic tradition, confessed to Aldington that his 'contempt for spontaneous poetry was to some extent strategical'.[2] Gradually, Read's strategy would lead him to become a proponent of the 'profuse strains' of a modernism strongly indebted to Wordsworth and Shelley.

Read's early flirtations with romanticism, a movement that both he and Eliot *publicly* abhorred in the twenties, were based on the assumption that all poetry must have a large component of emotion in it, feelings which, in turn, must be engendered in the reader. Hulme was stridently classical, but his attempt to recruit Coleridge and Bergson to his side by expropriating their belief in the intuitive and fluid shows inherent contradictions. Similarly, Eliot might have wanted to eradicate his personality from *Prufrock* or *The Waste Land*, but these poems are in large part successful because they engender a profound sense of emptiness, ennui and dislocation in the reader – and these were the emotions Eliot *felt* when he wrote those poems. In practice, classical and romantic tend to be doctrinaire labels, as in this pronouncement of 1924 by Eliot: 'A new classical age will be reached when the dogma, or *ideology* of the critics is so modified by contact with creative writing, and when the creative writers are so permeated by the new dogma, that a state of equilibrium is reached.'[3] Throughout the war, Read had eagerly sought such a 'new dogma' and during the early days of *Criterion*, he was its enthusiastic promoter.

Following the demise of *Art and Letters* in the summer of 1920, Eliot was anxious to set up a new and better magazine, perhaps modelled on the American *Dial*. In late 1921, Eliot asked Richard Cobden-Sanderson, a self-employed publisher who, with his wife Sally, gave lavish parties at his Hammersmith home, to finance such a venture. In turn, Cobden-Sanderson approached Lady Rothermere, the wife of the owner of the *Daily Mail*, the *Sunday Dispatch* and the *Evening News*. She was intrigued by the idea of herself as the patroness of a review devoted to literature and painting. According to Aldington, who told the story in his habitually tactless way, it was Sydney Schiff who 'introduced Eliot to Lady Rothermere's gang, but as I wasn't in on that particular racket I can say nothing definite'.[4] Subsequently, Eliot attended séances at her home at which Ouspensky, the mystic friend of Orage, presided. Disclaiming virtually all control over editorial policy, Lady Rothermere put Cobden-Sanderson in charge of the magazine's finances, layout, corrections and mailings.

Eliot wanted his magazine to look austere, and he also decided early on that it was to be a quarterly. The only thing he was not sure of was a name; it was Vivien who suggested the arrogantly self-aggrandizing *Criterion*, the name of the restaurant where she and a former lover, Charles Buckle, had frequently dined. Lady Rothermere's idea was for a magazine which would be 'chic and brilliant . . . which might have a fashionable vogue among a wealthy few'. This was what Eliot told Read in October 1924. What Eliot wanted was for *Criterion* 'to be a work of renewal, stirring up the hopes and enlivening the imagination of educated people who might recognize some worth in tradition'.[5] These antithetical aims hint at the discord which eventually overwhelmed the relationship between patron and editor. From the outset, Eliot attempted rigorous control of the magazine, although he was embarrassed by any suggestion that he was power-hungry. Despite what he *told* Read, Eliot wanted to dominate – he was a born despot. Later – in June 1925 – Aldington would accuse him of not having offered help to others: 'Eliot has funked his responsibilities to us since 1921. . . . in the first flush of enthusiasm for the Waste Land, he could have had us all organised. But he couldn't make up his mind!!!!! Piddle.'[6]

Eliot had placed himself in an impossible position: he was damned if he sought power, and he was reviled if he rejected it. Aldington, even though he served as assistant editor until the beginning of 1924, was fractious, and Wyndham Lewis, whose brilliantly coloured semi-abstract prose and painting Eliot admired, refused to partake in the venture. The team – among others, Eliot, Read, Aldington, J. B. Trend, Alec Randall, F. S. Flint, Richard Church, Bonamy Dobrée, Frank Morley and Harold Munro – first lunched weekly at the Cock in Fleet Street. Then to suit Read and his colleagues from the Museum (A. W. Wheen, K. de B. Codrington, W. A. Thorpe and Geoffrey Tandy), lunches were moved to the Grove in Beauchamp Place, South Kensington. However, the actual *Criterion* meetings took place once a month in the evening in a small private room at the Ristorante Commercio in Soho. These dinners were later moved to the Soho Hotel.

As he assured Read, Eliot wanted to write to the limit of his convictions, and genuinely thought that he did not wish to impose them on others. The American exile, hostile to psychological criticism, frequently conducted himself as if he did not have an unconscious. However, he did sound an ominous warning: it was essential to find persons who had an impersonal loyalty to a faith not antagonistic to his own. Although Eliot tolerated freedom, he was suspicious of it. Early in the 1920s, a bond of classicism tenuously held the critical sensibilities of Read and Eliot together.

More vital than ideology was the sense of shared purpose which dominated the *Criterion* group. All of these men had jobs which occupied their days; their real work – and purpose in life – was a steady engagement with literature. The 'faith' which they professed was centred on a credo which insisted that the life of writing touched the deepest parts of human sensibility, that such concerns were at the heart of civilization. Literature *was* life. Unlike their Bloomsbury colleagues, they were not additionally absorbed in gossip or friendship or personality. Feelings were considered trivial, and there is a resulting metallic edge to their letters, a glum starchiness which Eliot, surprisingly, punctured in rare moments of whimsy. Literature aside, Read and Eliot habitually talked of taxes, death duties and, especially, cheese.

At home, Read was a diffident husband, not overly concerned with his wife's emotions. When he reached Purley by six or seven, he would be exhausted after a busy day at the Museum. Nevertheless, he would quickly vanish after dinner to his study, where he usually had several projects in hand. Evelyn, alone during the day, would crave his attention, and when she did not receive it, began to feel more and more isolated. Her loneliness was partially relieved by the birth of John on 7 June 1923. John's earliest and most persistent memories were of his

79

father's cool detachment and his mother's sometimes overweening devotion. In 1937, Read, realizing how emotionally numb he had been in the twenties, told the Swiss critic Häusermann that he could have profited from psychoanalysis. However, he had held back. 'It is also admittedly due to a certain caution – to a feeling that I must not wade too deep into these waters or I shall drown. Ideally I should have submitted myself to analysis about 1925.'[7]

In addition to acting as Eliot's coadjutor at the *Criterion* and to participating fully in the administrative life of the Victoria and Albert, Read published between 1923 and 1929 over twenty articles and reviews dealing with glass and ceramics in journals such as the *Burlington*, *Country Life* and the *Connoisseur*. His closest associate at the Museum was Bernard Rackham, the younger brother of Arthur, with whom he wrote *English Pottery* (1924), the first modern classification of all branches within that field. At the very same time that he was desperately attempting to become a poet and essayist, Read's work at the Museum sharpened his visual sense, making him intensely aware of another type of aesthetic experience – one which is routinely closed off to those solely devoted to literature.

Earlier, during his time in Leeds, he had become interested in the pictorial arts; subsequently, he had experimented with vorticist designs. In the mid-twenties, he became more and more aware, in contrast to Eliot, of his lively response to the visual. After *Criterion* lunches, as Frank Morley, the big-boned, sometimes gruff American who also worked at Faber, recalled, Read would take two or three people back to the Museum to look at a vase or a piece of jewellery. 'Eliot was always very slow to respond. . . . Herbert, on the other hand, was very much at ease with a physical object.' In 1942, Read told Denton Welch that he had 'never known a man with less plastic sense' than Eliot.[8] Read had now found an arena where he could not be bested by his American friend.

Read's literary criticism was also developing in a manner contradictory to Eliot. In a *Criterion* essay of 1923, 'The Nature of Metaphysical Poetry', he echoed ideas found in Eliot's *The Sacred Wood* (1920): 'Metaphysical poetry is determined logically: its emotion is a joy that comes with the triumph of the reason, and it is not a simple instinctive ecstasy.' These remarks stand in diametric opposition to 'Psycho-analysis and the Critic', published two years later in *Criterion*. This was an essay to which Eliot was decidedly 'antagonistic'. Here, Read discussed the origins of literature, 'the processes of mental activity'. He welcomed psychology as a tool which can help to show how a work of art derives from the personality of its maker. For Eliot, such speculations were prurient and voyeuristic.

Read's own adolescent rebellion against Eliza may have been in his mind when he wrote this approving comment on Adler's theory of personality, which claims that every neurosis is an attempt to free oneself from a sense of inferiority in order to gain a sense of superiority: 'the most general period for the formation of the superiority-complex coincides with the most general period for the outburst of the poetic impulse. I mean the time of the awakening of the adolescent sexual instincts, the time of the withdrawal of parental protection, the period of instinctive disorders and social control. I think there can be no doubt that the artist is born of this conflict.'

The Oedipus conflict, according to Read, was a worthy tool in explicating *Hamlet*: 'the artist is initially by tendency a neurotic, but in becoming an artist he as it were escapes the ultimate fate of his tendency and through art finds his way back to reality'. The essay also displays an early flirtation with Jung's theories of archetype, unconscious symbols, introversion and extroversion: 'The poet, in fact, is one who is capable of creating phantasies of more than individual use – phantasies . . . of universal appeal. . . . Jung's theory springs from that general principle of contrasted attitudes . . . introversion and extroversion, a fundamental division of the self which may be traced in every activity . . . the opposition between subject and object, between thought and feeling, between idea and thing.'[9] Such reflections are abhorrent to Eliot, who attacked Read: 'What does [Herbert Read] mean by unconscious symbols? If we are unconscious that a symbol is a symbol, then is it a symbol at all? And the moment we become conscious that it is a symbol, is it any longer a symbol?'[10] Defiantly, Read would have answered yes to both rhetorical questions.

Aldington, angry because he could not get a poem published in the magazine of which he was assistant editor, fuelled Read's increasing irritation with Eliot. The imagist, who was well connected, had served in a similar capacity at the *Egoist* and, more crucially, was a good friend of Bruce Richmond, the editor of the *Times Literary Supplement*. Perhaps he had been appointed because Lady Rothermere or Cobden-Sanderson had wanted a watchdog. In any event, Aldington saw his work at *Criterion* as thankless, as when he discovered in proof a snide reference by Pound to the Pope. He exploded: 'The law of libel in England is severe; Roman Catholics are sensitive; and anyway I don't think it urbane to call the Pope a s.o.b.' Aldington himself was unguarded about Eliot in letters to Read: 'I don't profess to know what

Eliot's influence on me has been; I suspect that, like Pound's of old, it is rather negative than positive, warning me off, rather than hurrying me on.'[11] Aldington also maintained that Eliot was purposely blocking Read's career by not introducing him to Richmond: 'One thing in Pound's favour – he was never afraid to shove forward a new man. T.S.E. hasn't the energy (or the disinterestedness?) to do it.'[12]

In 1925, Evelyn had a miscarriage, about which she told her son John years after the event. Soon afterwards, she became ill with a thyroid condition. Her husband was more concerned with Eliot, Aldington and a literary career. Also, unfinished business from the war haunted him, as the publication by the Woolfs in 1925 of *In Retreat* demonstrates.

Read's increasingly fraught friendship with Eliot was further strained when, having joined Faber & Gwyer, he suggested to Read that he switch from the Woolfs to his new firm. Virginia thought Eliot treated the Hogarth Press scurvily: 'Today [30 September 1925] we are on Tom's track, riddling & reviling him. He won't let Read off that book, has been after him 3 or 4 months.'[13] However, Eliot attempted to place full responsibility for where *Reason and Romanticism* was published squarely on Read's shoulders. He did not wish to get embroiled in a fight with the Woolfs. Having engineered the fracas, Eliot told Read he was free to make up his own mind.[14] Despite growing reservations, Read, still steadfastly clinging to Eliot, warned Aldington: if 'we link Eliot's brains to a big commercial undertaking, we must have done the trick. We march on to a triumph. But in bickerings, false pride, & mutual mistrust we shall all be lost.'[15]

Aldington, certain that Eliot had poached on his preserves (a biographical series), had been bitterly wounded once again. That matter was amicably resolved, but Aldington was afraid to confront him with his deep dislike of Pound, Lewis and Joyce. He vented his spleen to Read, who informed him in January 1926: 'I quite agree about Lewis & Pound. Joyce is a more difficult case, but still pathological.'[16] Read also told Aldington that he had been badly disappointed by Routledge's promotion of his Hulme book: 'Bad display, bad boost, lack of persistence & strategy.'[17]

Plans for the Reads to visit the Aldingtons at Malthouse Cottage at Padworth in Berkshire had to be postponed when it was discovered that the 'Reads' 'nice, clean, athletic dog' might fight with their hosts' cat. Evelyn's sister, who was with the Reads on an extended visit, would not babysit the beast, as Read complained to Aldington on 3 March: 'the upshot is that my sister-in-law does not very much relish the idea of being left here on her own. . . . We will palm off the bloodhound somehow, and bring nothing but peace and plenty.'[18]

In February, Aldington had reviewed *Reason and Romanticism* and sent a proof of his piece to the nervous author, who offered his unabashed thanks: 'I'm honestly a little bit flabbergasted at having brought it off. I won't say it was unconsciously done – that the thing just wrote itself – that wouldn't be quite true. But the effect it seems, is out of proportion to my effort. I have still to show whether it was a fluke, or whether it is in me.'[19] Read's insecurities surface in this unguarded note of gratitude, where he also spoke of 'fear' as something the mind '*could* rise above'. With some difficulty, he had been able to conquer such feelings during the war; now he was fighting to establish a career as a critic, and he was desperately afraid of failure.

The title of Read's first book of criticism reveals its author's divided loyalties: *Reason and Romanticism*. Reason is given an uneasy pride of place, but the growing claims of 'feelings' are vindicated. 'Literature is, after all, mainly an expression of emotional states. . . . emotion is the original substance of all aesthetic forms, for even intellectual forms cannot have value as art until they have been emotionally apprehended.' Eliot may possibly have agreed with this statement, but he would never have emphasized 'emotion' to the degree found here. Much more strongly than his friend, Read wanted to hold the twin strands of intellect and passion together. Yet Read still clung to Eliot's classicism in *English Stained Glass*, also published in 1926, where he asserts that the restoration of reason 'as the supreme instrument of human knowledge' was the greatest achievement of the thirteenth century.

That same year, Read published another book, *Collected Poems*, weighed heavily towards the verse in *Songs of Chaos*, *Eclogues* and *Naked Warriors*. In these poems Read still presented himself as an imagist deeply troubled by the war. The feelings which that experience had unlocked were just beginning, with considerable trepidation, to find their way into his criticism.

Read's former publisher, Virginia Woolf, was cited by Read in a *Times* leader of March 1926 as a model of good prose. She duly entered this information in her diary and caustically added: 'such a charming man'. Under the auspices of the Victoria and Albert, Read travelled to Spain by way of Gibraltar in the spring of 1926 (24 April–27 May). His enthusiasm for the landscape of hot yellows and brilliant greens led to a wry retort from Aldington: 'I am glad to know that you are back and that you enjoyed Spain in spite of its romantic appearance.'[20] Almost as if in anticipation of the bitter civil unrest that was to overwhelm that country, Read described Spain as a 'place where the serpent bites its own tail'.[21] In June 1926, he was gratified that his versifying was well known enough to be parodied by *Punch* in 'More Jackdaw in Georgia. The Poets at the Round Pond':

> Sing, a saucer of light,
> You Pond;
> Rest in your folds of green baize.
>
> I will sing too,
> Assuming rusticity
> in an attitude of peace
> On a bird-soiled chair. . . .
> This is the apex,
> This is the triumph,
> This is the glory.[22]

Still, Read's ambitions were largely unfocused. He did not want to write a monthly column for *Country Life*. Aldington, who had engineered such a possibility, told him that he should find out if he pleased or repelled that magazine's readers. In any event, Aldington reminded him, poets were better off in twentieth-century London than under Louis XIV: 'The South Kensington or reviewing is a better job than bum-sucking a duke.'[23]

By August 1926, Read was uneasily immersed in the unsteady plans for the future of *Criterion*. In the spring of 1925, Lady Rothermere had summoned Eliot to Switzerland, at which meeting she informed him that the journal was 'not, to her mind, chic enough; in fact, it was not chic at all'.[24] Despite this, she was willing to continue her backing, provided Eliot found other patrons. Bruce Richmond's advice was eagerly sought – he became 'the Secret Agent in the whole thing'.[25] Finally, Eliot's new employer, Faber & Gwyer, agreed to share the equity of the *New Criterion* with Lady Rothermere; after a few issues, Faber made the journal into a subsidiary company.

The first issue of the 'new' magazine appeared in January 1926. Partial freedom from Lady Rothermere meant that Eliot no longer even had to try to appear fashionable, and the revamped *Criterion* introduced a policy of greater austerity. Politics, theology and non-literary matters came to dominate in a way that had been previously impossible. Eliot's editorial stance increasingly became that of a general defending reason from an onslaught of insidious foes: 'But we must find our own faith, and having found it, fight for it against all others.'[26] He also claimed that there was a new discernible turning in art 'toward a higher and clearer conception of Reason, and a more severe and serene control of the emotions by Reason'.[27] 'Reasonable' writers included Sorel, Hulme, Babbitt and Jacques Maritain, whereas those who represented passion, 'that part of the present', which according to Eliot was 'already dead', included H. G. Wells, Bertrand Russell and Bernard Shaw. Eliot's disdain for Shaw is perfectly enshrined in the cutting remark: 'in his long series of plays Mr. Shaw reveals himself as the artist whose development was checked at puberty'.[28]

Slowly, but in an increasingly sure way, Read found that he could not share Eliot's views. An Eliot supporter, John Gould Fletcher, thought Read had become a spy at the *Criterion* meetings. He disdainfully recalled: since 'he considered beauty of equal, if not superior, value to mankind, as either goodness or truth, I was convinced that he was, in fact, a disguised Romantic'.[29] Read had nowhere else to go. Although he felt that Eliot was wrong about literature, art and politics, there was no alternative group to which he could turn. He also considered Eliot's intellect superior to his own. Above all, Read was a loyal person.

Meanwhile, Eliot was moving steadily towards the Church of England (he was converted in 1927) and his 1928 declaration of himself as 'classicist in literature, royalist in politics, and anglo-catholic in religion'. In his usually constricted way, Eliot did not tell Read of his conversion, Read's first intimation of the move coming after he had spent the night at Tom and Vivien's small house in Chester Terrace: 'I woke early and presently became conscious that the door of my room, which was on the ground floor, was slowly and silently being opened. I lay still and saw first a hand and then an arm reach round the door and lift from a hook the bowler hat that was hanging there. It was a little before seven o'clock and Mr Eliot was on his way to an early communion service.'

Eliot's demeanour in 1926–7 pushed Read in the direction of 'anarchist, romanticist and agnostic'. He had also come more and more to the realization that true heroism does not consist of a single, unswerving dedication to any cause. He increasingly saw such behaviour as a kind of cardboard humanity. In 1928, he praised T. E. Lawrence as a person 'full of doubts and dissemblings, uncertain of his aim, his pride eaten into by humility and remorse, his conduct actuated by intellectual and idealistic motives. It is no disparagement to say that out of such stuff no hero is made.'[30] This moving verbal portrait is more about himself than Lawrence, about Read's strong sense of 'no heroism' within himself. He was a man of profound uncertainties who remained untouched by the transcendent confidence which now infused Tom Eliot. When Wyndham Lewis wrote to complain about an unpleasant review he had received in *Criterion*, Read was compassionate: 'I was served the same way myself a short time ago. It is not playing the game, I agree, but I don't think Eliot is quite conscious of what he is doing. Perhaps he has not got the "party spirit", in which case he should not lead a party.'[31]

Read papered over his disagreements with Eliot when he praised him – years afterwards – for commissioning *Reason and Romanticism* for his first Faber list: 'though the Reason of it owes something to Eliot, the Romanticism was my own. It was already my declared purpose to seek some reconciliation or "synthesis" of these opposed faiths. If Eliot had any desire to check me at that time, it was all done with a very gentle rein.' Later, Read would also insist, with great acuity, that Eliot was 'a romanticist paying lip service to the concept of classicism'. At times, Read's own classicism reasserted itself, as when he praised Wyndham Lewis in the *Nation and Athenaeum* as 'a great and scandalously ignored painter . . . a brilliant protagonist, by far the ablest pamphleteer of his generation, by far the most active force among us'.[32]

Read's largely repressed quarrel with Eliot left him tired and dispirited, as Aldington was quick to pick up in November 1926: 'You sound a little weary – overwork, my boy.'[33] In January 1927, Eliot was urging Read to get his edition of *Sentimental Journey* ready as soon as possible: if he wanted to attract the favourable attention of the *TLS* editor, he had to publish something which Richmond's public could understand.[34] Another piece of war prose – 'The Raid' – was published in *Criterion* this year, but the central event was the move from Purley to Broom House at Seer Green near Beaconsfield in Buckinghamshire on 15 June. That winter, Read was 'upset by all the harassments of building a new house & getting rid of an old one'.[35] On 12 May, the Purley house had not yet sold, causing additional strain.[36]

Broom House, which Read had a hand in designing, displays the residual conflicts within its owner: the exterior was semi-Tudor but the interior was resolutely contemporary. Although he was aware of modern 'abstract harmony' in architecture, Read never wished to live in a 'crystal cabinet'. Sixteen years later, he recalled:

> . . . I built this house
> By an oak tree on an acre of wild land
> Its walls white against the beechwood
> Its roof of Norfolk reed and sedge.

> The mossy turf I levelled for a lawn
> But for the most part left the acre wild
> Knowing I could never live
> From its stony soil. . . .

> A secular and insecure retreat –
> The alien world is never far away.
> Over the ridge, beyond the elms
> The railway runs; a passing train
> Sends a faint tremor through the ground
> Enough to sever a rotted picture-cord
> Or rattle the teaspoon against my cup.

Evelyn, more isolated than she had been at Purley, wanted her family from Yorkshire to move in with them. Read firmly resisted this suggestion.

Just as he and Evelyn were drawing more and more apart, Read was an uneasy witness to the breakup of Tom and Vivien's disastrous marriage. He recalled Eliot's wife as a 'frail creature who had not been married long before she began to suffer from serious internal ailments' which 'exasperated an already nervous temperament and she slowly but surely developed the hysterical psychosis to which she. . . finally succumbed. Posterity will probably judge Vivien harshly, but I remember her in moments when she was sweet and vivacious; later her hysteria became embarrassing.' In reminiscing about Vivien Eliot in 1966, Read might well have been recalling Evelyn's similar – but much milder – demeanour early in their marriage. Significantly, Read portrays Vivien's mental illness as if it operated in a vacuum independent of Tom: she had 'an already nervous temperament' and 'developed' a mental illness to which she 'succumbed'. Read indirectly absolves Eliot of any blame, portraying him as a hapless witness to psychosis. He completely fails to take into account that Eliot's icy passivity may have contributed to his wife's distress, just as he never seemed to realize that his own remarkable detachment from his own wife might have exacerbated her increasingly frail state.

Towards the end of 1927, Eliot put Read's name forward for the Clark Lectureship at Trinity College, Cambridge. Surely, Eliot asked, the Museum would let him off once a week for eight weeks?[37] Although this was a tempting prospect, Read was then more concerned with the two books which were published in 1928: *English Prose Style* and *Phases of English Poetry*. The former is a handbook on rhetoric, which Graham Greene has said should be 'compulsory reading for any would-be writer'.[38] The other treatise is relentlessly categorical in its treatment of the poetry of nature, the poetry of love, pure poetry. Nevertheless, Read's grapplings with romanticism are plainly evident here, as when he praises Wordsworth's drift in the 'direction of sincerity of expression'; yet Read is careful to claim that there was in 'Wordsworth always this intense struggle to find objective expression for his intensely subjective feelings'. Moreover, Wordsworth is shown to have 'rejected too much' of the previous tradition, the book ending in substantial agreement with Eliot's stance that the poet's most personal feelings must, if they are to touch the reader, be presented in an impersonal manner. Read was in a fervently Eliotesque mood in an essay of 1927 when he deplored the possibility of a work of art being an expression of personality: 'my only answer is Bah!'.[39]

Books such as *English Prose Style* supplemented Read's meagre Museum salary, but they also distracted him from his real ambitions, as Aldington reminded him in 1926: 'It is perhaps a little unlucky in one way that you can make so much out of your technical books. It naturally makes you discontented with the much smaller money for belles lettres.'[40] Roger Fry despised the prose book, 'partly because he don't a quarter understand Sterne and also he's one of this neo-Thomist lot with a whole bag of metaphysical nostrums on his back'.[41] At about the same time, Virginia Woolf assured Vita Sackville-West that she was a 'true British Grenadier', who stood up 'resolute in the full flood' of scoundrels such as Eliot and Read.[42] Praise for Read came from the twenty-nine-year-old American poet and critic, Allen Tate, when Frank Morley took him in October 1928 to a *Criterion* lunch where he met Eliot and Read for the first time: 'Herbert Read is the best mind in England. . . . Eliot, of course, was due to be the most interesting, but he is a Sphinx.'[43]

The year 1928 brought another trip to the Continent on Museum business, this time to the South of France. Read's third book directly resulting from his work at the Victoria and Albert was published the following year: *Staffordshire Pottery Figures*. This type of ware, made of salt-glazed stoneware, was displaced by porcelain. According to Read, this event had not taken place until aesthetic sensibility had been destroyed by mass production in the nineteenth century. Read's distinction between pottery and porcelain is the crucial underpinning of this volume:

> The porcelain figure was destined to grace the mantelpieces of the aristocracy and rich bourgeoisie; the pottery figure was never meant to be

more than a cheerful ornament in a farm-house or a labourer's cottage. The potter who made the figure was himself a peasant with a simple mind and a simple sense of humour. But because of this simple sense he often strays unconsciously into a realm of purer forms. He blunders into beauty.

Read is defending works of art which come spontaneously from impulses in the labourer's heart. He might well have been comparing the farm house in which he was born to the labourer's dwelling, knowing that his origins were similar to the peasant's he describes so sympathetically. In a work apparently divorced from his literary criticism, he comes to recognize that the purity of language and feeling that he had praised in Wordsworth was part of his own heritage. Read's soon to be reawakened interest in politics is hinted at here in the implied contrast between complacent capitalist and intuition-filled worker.

Despite the extra money his books brought him, Read was under constant financial constraint, as he told T. E. Lawrence, who condescendingly retorted: 'Your economic shift is hard luck. . . . Perhaps if you are really a poet, leisure will return to you some day, as it did to Hardy. After all, it's quite a good life time if a man writes *two* good poems in it.'[44] Bonamy Dobrée, who was teaching in Egypt, chastised him for preferring Wordsworth to Milton: 'You can have no notion, no glimmering of an idea, not the most shadowy conception of the gulf, the irremediable burning gulf, that lies between me and a man (can he be a man?) who can for a moment entertain the thought, much less write, that Wordsworth is a better poet than Milton.'[45]

Jokiness aside, Dobrée had become concerned with the degree to which *Criterion* had now become a 'Religio-Political organ'. Apprehensively, he told Read: 'It seems to me to have lost its freedom. . . . we are asked to condemn the Revolution because it was not Anglo-Catholic! I am beginning to feel a little uncomfortable in that galley.'[46] On 29 April, Dobrée congratulated Read on his third book of that year, *The Sense of Glory*, and shrewdly observed that his friend's obsession with glory was a substitute for religion.

Glory for Read was a sense of communal – and individual – triumph over barbarism. The subjects of these essays (Froissart, Malory, Swift, Vauvenargues, Sterne, Bagehot and Hawthorne) displayed varied, honest attempts to obtain or regain that virtue, of which the ultra-rationalist Descartes is the great enemy. Twentieth-century man had lost 'the habit of faith. We neither love deeply enough, nor feel deeply enough, nor think deeply enough.' Significantly, glory could be 'only fully realized in solitariness'.

Without doubt, Evelyn felt that her husband lived too much within himself. She penned this cryptic comment in 1929, the year they went to Austria on holiday: 'Beginning of Anxiety symptoms. Too strained & strenuous a time. . . . Too much silence.' Aldington continued to sound his warning that Read was devoting far too much time to literary criticism: 'What you have done in criticism is great and valuable, but you have much to say about life as well as about thought and literature, and the satisfaction of creative work is very, very great.'[47]

Aldington's advice, meant kindly, would later torment Read; in 1929, it was one of a series of anxieties gnawing at him. He told Glenn Hughes, who asked him to write a chap-book on Eliot, that he could not do it. 'In a sense I am too closely associated with him for me to want to objectify him. . . . In any case, I don't think close personal friends ever write very well of one another.'[48] A month later, Eliot asked him what he felt, in a general way, about professorships. Herbert Grierson wanted to put Read's name forward for a professorship of fine art at the University of Edinburgh. Read, who constantly felt 'sweated' at the Museum, agreed to let his name stand.

When Read was writing the Clark Lectures in the autumn and early winter of 1929 (the lectures were delivered in 1930), he was engulfed in an overwhelming sense of personal and professional uncertainty. His marriage was on the rocks. He was afraid that he had devoted far too much energy to criticism at the expense of poetry. He was not sure where his increasing interest in the visual arts was taking him. He strongly dissented from the critical stances taken by his friend Tom Eliot, who had garnered far more approbation for his poetry and criticism than had come his way.

Read's writings on literature often reflect inner turmoils, and this is particularly true of *Wordsworth*, which the reviewer in the *Times Literary Supplement* accurately claimed was 'fuller of theories of life and philosophy than it is of Wordsworth'.[49] Read's description of Wordsworth's Yorkshire ancestry leads to a long passage which is far more autobiographical than biographical.

> Yorkshiremen are imaginative like all northerners, but a matter-of-factness, a strong sense of objectivity, a faculty for vivid visualisation, keep them from being profoundly mystical. The same qualities make them wary in their actions, and canny in their reckonings. But their most extraordinary characteristic . . . is their capacity for masking their emotions. It is not a question of suppression, nor of atrophy; the normal feelings of the human being are present in more than their normal force, but banked up against this impenetrable reserve. No doubt, as a

protective device, this iron mask has had historical advantages. And in the domestic sphere it ensures a business-like dispatch of those affairs, such as births, deaths and marriages, which tend to choke up the existence of a more expansive people.

It was 'impenetrable reserve' that Evelyn had to deal with in her husband's demeanour; she could not see the 'normal feelings' of a husband and a father, and Read's 'business-like' attitude towards domesticity troubled and hurt her. In turn, Read perceived his early infatuation with Evelyn as a horrible mistake which had trapped him in a loveless marriage. In *Wordsworth*, Read was examining the barriers between himself and Evelyn. Perhaps they were too much alike or perhaps reticence was too strong a feature of both their personalities. Read was trying to touch the deepest parts of his self, but by 1930 that secret, romantic self had been irrevocably cut off from Evelyn. In the same book Read was also attempting to rid himself of the spectre of Eliot. He wanted to make his own mark as a critic by directly opposing his friend's teachings. At long last, he knew himself to be a romantic.

Read claimed that there were two Wordsworths: Man and Mask, Reality and Myth. He wanted to reject his Mask and his Myth, but he did not know how to do this. Poetry remained for him much 'more intimate & real'[50] than the writing of essays but, increasingly, he gave himself over to criticism. He could no longer be a disciple of Eliot, and he wanted to leave his wife. And yet, he realized full well, a tremendous struggle lay ahead. As he said: 'an endowment of sensibility is one thing, the capacity to transfer sensibility into thought is another'. And, he knew, to transform it into action is even more difficult.

7   Time Regained

> It cannot be read for pleasure; it is terrible, almost unendurable, in its realism and pathos. . . . It merely tells the story of a generation of men who, though they may have escaped its shells, were destroyed by the war. For these men, the war lasted too long to be an adventure; it withered something in them that had never come to full growth. . . . No idealism is left to this generation. . . . death destroyed even this, and we were left with only the bare desire to live, although life itself was past our comprehension.[1]

These are Read's harrowing reflections on Erich Maria Remarque's *All Quiet on the Western Front*, a book of nightmarish evocation of the war from the German perspective. In this passage, Read is eulogizing not the dead but those who, like himself, survived in order to return to a living death. Although the war had brought Read camaraderie, it left him with a strong sense that all life is war, that conflict and, finally, defeat are inevitable.

The German novelist told his story in a more sensational manner than his predecessors, paving the way for Graves' *Goodbye to All That* and Aldington's *Death of a Hero*, both published in 1929. Read championed the publication of Remarque's 'severe, masculine, brutal' book, later writing of it the most felt of his many book reviews; rarely, in any public statement, did he allow rage to come to the surface. In the wake of Remarque's phenomenal success, Aldington 'sailed to fame', Read said. Ultimately, he felt, his friend's triumph brought desolation to their relationship.

Read's review of war literature in *Criterion* was responsible for a quirky letter of commendation from the acerbic Cambridge don F. R. Leavis, who concluded: 'I am not supposing that my approval is worth anything to you. In any case, you don't know me & will, of course, do nothing more than put this in the waste-paper-basket.'[2]

The spate of war literature in 1929 prompted Read to recast some of his own memories into *Ambush* (1930). In the same year, he

92

published a pamphlet, *Julien Benda and the New Humanism*, in which he espoused the ultra-conservative French critic's attack on 'sentimental humanitarianism which is the love of human beings in the concrete, an affair of the heart, an emotional exaltation'. Benda claimed that intellectuals no longer defended idealistic or disinterested values; they had been corrupted by the masses. Read, strongly attracted to Benda's notion of the intellectual as one who must stand apart from the affairs of ordinary men, put himself in the position of defending a person of fascist tendencies. Despite the Wordsworth book, Read remained tormented by the conflict between reason and passion. Here, he briefly returned to the side of Eliot.

Relations between Herbert and Evelyn disintegrated further in 1930. She was even more lonely. Also, now suffering increasingly from her thyroid disorder – her delicate frame becoming puffy as the illness took over – she insisted, without success, that her family move to Broom House. On 21 March, Read blandly told Jacob Kramer that Evelyn had been 'rather ill, & is not yet better'.[3] That summer the unhappy couple went to Vence for a short holiday. On the bus from Cagnes to Vence, they met a 'dispirited and sombre' Englishwoman who asked their advice about finding a place to stay. The Reads took her along to their hotel, where she engaged a room. The next day, when she saw that Herbert had a camera, the lady asked him to take a snapshot. He agreed, and she then told him that she wanted a photograph of D. H. Lawrence's grave and tombstone, where Lawrence's symbol, the pheonix, was patterned in coloured pebbles. The novelist had died on 2 March and the woman was Louise (Louie) Burrows, the Ilkeston schoolteacher who was one of the prototypes for Ursula in *The Rainbow* and the subject of the phallic love poem, 'Snap-Dragon'. Although their coy friendship had been over by the early 1910s, Louie remained obsessed with Lawrence and told Read that the novelist had treated her badly.[4] Read's own hostility to Lawrence was reinforced by this encounter. Both men were deeply tinged with puritanism; both tried, in differing ways, to touch the pagan parts of themselves. In Lawrence, Read glimpsed some of his own, repressed conflicts, and he did not like what he saw.

By 1930 the pull of the visual over the literary was in full swing. Read had decided early on not to review contemporary poetry: a fellow poet could not, he maintained, adopt a sincere critical attitude to the work of a contemporary: subconsciously he would be inhibited by comparisons with his own verse.[5] In a more lighthearted moment, he claimed that,

93

like a tight-rope walker, he had to keep his eye on his own line: 'If I look to the right or the left I am in danger of losing my balance.' Poets, like horses, he also observed, should wear blinkers, 'lest they should become agitated by those who trot alongside'.[6]

On 25 September 1929, Read's essay, 'The Meaning of Art', appeared in the *Listener*. Ensuing articles were so popular that one of the magazine's editors, R. S. Lambert, wrote three months later asking for a weekly piece of about 800 words on 'any subject connected with art you may think fit for the fee of £5.5.0'.[7] Eventually, there were fifty-four articles, rearranged and modified to become *The Meaning of Art* in 1931.

In his first extended foray into the visual arts, Read asserted, following Worringer and Hulme, that there were two types of art – geometrical and organic. Read did not feel that organic art, which aspired to recreate persons, landscapes, objects as they appear to the eye, needed a defence. However, he had no fundamental objections to representational art. Instead, he concentrated his efforts on 'abstract' art and its presence even within 'realist' art:

> We must not be afraid of this word 'abstract'. All art is primarily abstract. For what is aesthetic experience, deprived of its incidental trappings and associations, but a response of the body and mind of man to invented or isolated harmonies. Art is an escape from chaos. It is movement ordained in numbers; it is mass confined in measure; it is the indetermination of matter seeking the economy of life.

Such claims reach back to his defence of Hulme, but Read's newly established romantic principles lead him to emphasize the 'feeling' behind abstract art. 'The work of art is in some sense a liberation of the personality; normally our feelings are inhibited and repressed. . . . Art is the economy of feeling; it is emotion cultivating good form . . . . A work of art is not present in thought, but in feeling.' Read also asserts that all these departures from exact imitation are 'purposive'. The artist has a will to create form – he wants to make a symbol for something 'super-real'.

The link between abstraction and symbolization is a vital one for Read in that abstraction allows the artist the opportunity to explore new directions in the creation of symbols; the painter or sculptor need not be confined only to the realist tradition. This is the central point of Read's championing of abstraction: it can unlock doors previously thought closed. He is also at pains – like Worringer before him – to point out that abstraction is not a new phenomenon, its presence being readily visible in Byzantine and Chinese art.

Read is clearly bothered by the unwillingness of the English to pursue new approaches to art which had found favour on the Continent. Cézanne, Gauguin, Van Gogh, Picasso, Chagall and Klee are praised for their contributions to modern art. Then, Read suddenly turns to England: 'The other artist I would like to mention is an English sculptor. . . . We may say without exaggeration that the art of sculpture has been dead in England for four centuries; equally without exaggeration I think we may say that it is reborn in the work of Henry Moore.'

Read was looking in 1931 for an avant-garde English artist who embodied a modernist aesthetic. He found such a person in the sculptor. Read had met Moore, who was five years younger, in about 1929, when they were introduced by Sir Eric Maclagan, the Director of the Victoria and Albert Museum and an early Moore collector, in his office. Moore, a miner's son from Castleford in the West Riding of Yorkshire, was, like Read, an exceedingly reserved person.

After a stint in the armed forces, Moore studied at the Leeds School of Art and the Royal College of Art. His first one-man show at Dorothy Warren's gallery in late 1928 was favourably mentioned by *The Times* as one in which 'materials' took precedence over 'nature'.[8] Moore's first major public commission had come the same year: a relief symbolizing the West Wind for the London Underground at 55 Broadway.

In July 1929 Moore had married Irina Radetzky, from an upper-class Russian family; she had immigrated to England by way of Paris in about 1922. The newlyweds moved to a studio-cum-villa in a portion of a Victorian house at 11A Parkhill Road in Belsize Park, near Hampstead and within easy walking distance of raffish Kentish Town to the south. Barbara Hepworth and her husband, John Skeaping, had migrated in 1928 to 7 The Mall, an alley of studios off Parkhill Road, and it was she who found 11A for her fellow sculptor and his bride. In 1929, Moore was well known to fellow members of the avant-garde. An ambitious man who hankered after wider acclaim, he mingled the representational with strong elements of the abstract and primitive. These borrowings gave his work an obvious symbolic edge. He was not content merely to show a mother and child; he wanted to depict the idea of Mother and Child.

Just before Moore's second one-man show, held at the Leicester Galleries in April 1931, Read asked if he might visit him in Hampstead to see his work. Henry and Irina gave Read supper, and showed him sculptures and drawings. Read remained silent; the Moores thought he was appalled. The next morning a letter arrived from Read expressing his fervent admiration for what he had seen and telling the Moores he would be writing an article for the *Listener* (22 April 1931). Moore later remembered: 'I was surprised, absolutely staggered when the article came out at the amount of appreciation and understanding he'd got out of that experience.'[9] Although *The Times*, *Observer* and *Manchester Guardian* praised the Moore exhibition, Read's endorsement was uttered in a general climate of disdain, as in the *Morning Post*: 'The cult of ugliness triumphs at the hands of Mr Moore.'[10]

Then, as later, Read was greatly moved by Moore's work, but there were other influences at work. Both Yorkshiremen shared a strong sense of being outsiders in the art establishment. Also, Read was looking for an Englishman who embodied the truly contemporary. Having found such a rare person, he proclaimed him: 'Henry Moore, in virtue of his sureness and consistency, is at the head of the modern movement in England.' This brave, unfettered artist 'has no regard at all for the appearance of the object (if there is one) which inspires his work of art'. Moore is shown to be essentially concerned with the '*translation of meaning* from one material into another'.

Read's identification with Moore was exceedingly close – almost as if Moore were the artist he would have become had his talents lain in that direction. The defence of Moore in 1931 – and in later years – has a strong autobiographical edge. Like Read, Moore's feelings were buried beneath a seemingly calm surface. He excavated pent-up emotions in his carvings and sculptures – he was loath to express them in words. Moore's virility is apparent in all photographs of him as a young man, but, like Read, his sexuality was often fully unleashed only in his work. Moore and Read, men of great feeling, paid a high price for their precocity, with which they were never completely comfortable. Their close friendship was one of shared responses which hardly ever found a voice in conversation or letters. Although Read sometimes seemed to ignore English art, he was anxious to promote in his alter ego *modern* English art, feeling that more traditional artists had their allies.

When W. G. Constable became Director and first Professor at the Courtauld in December 1930, Read wrote a warm letter of congratulation. However, he did not mention that he was in the midst of deciding whether or not to abandon the Victoria and Albert in favour of the Watson Gordon Chair at Edinburgh. Herbert Grierson, who had been Regius Professor of English there since 1915, had earlier made overtures through Eliot, who thought an academic job might resolve some of his friend's financial and professional problems: a professorship would offer more security and, perhaps, writing time. Eliot did have some misgivings. In his experience it was rather exasperating to have professorships dangled in front of one, and he could not see why anyone would accept such a job unless he was desperate.[11] Read needed the money, but he thought his ability to write might be further stifled. Aldington had unwaveringly strong misgivings when Read turned to him for advice:

My feeling is that when the English bourgeoisie (particularly Cambridge) get hold of an artist they try to make a professor out of him. It seems to me, they've buggered poor old Tom Eliot up. . . . It's a damn shame, because he has genius. For Christ's sake don't let them do that to you, Herbert. A poet is a man who produces poems, and I feel there is masses of stuff in you awaiting expression just as soon as you get the key to release it. Of course, it is absolutely open to you to say you'd rather be a first-rate critic than a second-rate novelist. And I feel that even the simulacrum of creation represented by the writing of a second-rate novel makes one so much happier than the sordid sterility of criticism.[12]

Aldington put his finger on an anxiety troubling Read. Was he a writer or a critic? Were these inalienably distinct callings? If he wanted to be a poet and novelist, Read realized that it was probably best to avoid the academy. On the other hand, a critic could easily be at home in a university environment, especially the Gordon chair, which was the only full-time professorship in art history in the British Isles. Read would be the second incumbent: the first, the archaeologist Baldwin Brown, had held the chair since 1880. It was an agonizing decision. In addition, Read's literary interests worried Grierson's colleagues; Read was dumbfounded when one of the faculty members who interviewed him expressed the opinion that he ought to have spent all his life 'preparing to fill a chair of Fine Arts!'[13] There was a further complication: Eric Maclagan wanted Read to succeed him as Director of the Victoria and Albert. Should he seize the opportunity in front of him or practise patience?

In the midst of this quandary, D. S. MacColl informed Read that he loathed his article on Wilson Steer and the English Tradition in the *Listener*. MacColl, a close friend of the impressionist Steer, and later his biographer, told Read the piece was badly flawed, doctrinaire and insulting. In particular, he thought it wrong to label Gainsborough a bourgeois, to say that English painters lacked courage and vision, to claim that English art was deficient in architectural structure, and to elevate Matisse at the expense of Steer. He scolded Read: 'though it is convenient to talk about the "architectural" and "plastic" sides of painting, after all the *pictorial* is the indispensable centre, & the deciding element is *colour*'.[14] Read pleaded guilty to a few of MacColl's charges, but he held to his admiration of Matisse over Steer. Although Read had a good eye, his interests were largely theoretical. MacColl was justifiably criticizing Read for being too concerned with ideas behind works of art rather than their physical presences.

At the Victoria and Albert, Read felt crushed. At Christmas 1929, for example, he had felt obliged to get work done. Two days later, Eliot told him that he was sorry that the Museum job 'sweated' him so much: if he and Vivien had known that Herbert had had to put in hours at his office during the holidays, they would have invited him over for a lunch of cold turkey.[15]

In his mind, Read juxtaposed the ornate classical austerity of Edinburgh against the frenzy of London life. In the eighteenth century, Edinburgh had been a true centre of the Enlightenment, and scholars–teachers at the University such as Saintsbury and Grierson had tried to rekindle the intellectual life of the city. For precisely these reasons, Grierson had recruited Read, who thought the Presbyterian inheritance of the city was buried in a misty past.

By the spring of 1931, Read had decided in favour of Edinburgh, where he had been promised one term off (out of the usual three) each year for writing. More money and more time were seductive entice-ments, and on 26 May 1931 the announcement of Read's appointment appeared in *The Times*. As he confessed to Middleton Murry, the decision left him 'fussed', 'overwhelmed' and 'unprepared'; neverthe-less, he dreamed of 'infinitely more liberty'.[16]

From the outset, Edinburgh failed most expectations. The cost of moving up was greater than anticipated, and the Reads' overdraft became larger. Since Broom House had been let, they decided not to buy but to lease from the University 'a large, ugly, but comfortable mansion' at 9 Tipperlinn Road, where the services of a butler were provided. In contrast to London, the social life of the city, Read found, was old-fashioned and exacting. Despite such drawbacks, Read told Richard Church: 'There are too many Rip Van Winkles, but there is an interesting younger generation. I don't seem to miss *London* at all.'[17] One of his first projects was to design a huge modernist desk (approximately ten feet long) for his new study. On 28 October, Read refused an invitation from David Bomberg to lecture: 'if I had still been in the south I should have been glad to help. I have only just begun the work here, but I like it very well, and Edinburgh is a delightful city to live in.'[18]

98

Read's inaugural lecture two weeks earlier on 15 October began with a tribute to Baldwin Brown and a brief lamentation concerning the sorry state of art history in the curriculum of English universities. In contrast, this discipline had fared well in Germany and the United States. Then Read acknowledged the necessary evil of vocational training. But, to counteract such evils, a new emphasis had to be placed on sensibility. This led him to the centrality of art. 'In the end, art should so dominate our lives that we might say: there are no longer works of art, but art only. For art is then the way of life.' Since he wanted to imbue his students with the proper spirit to combat the ascendance of technocracy, Read proposed to teach a course on the history *and* theory of fine art.

> Art, just because it demands an intuitional apprehension, cannot be dismissed as history. It is a present activity, and I should regard my duties as but half done if, in teaching the enjoyment of the art of the past, I did not also lead my students to enjoy the art of the present day. Art to-day is a testimony to our culture, a witness to its positive qualities and to its limitations, just as the arts of the past are to the cultures of the past. We cannot fully participate in modern consciousness unless we can learn to appreciate the significant art of our own day.

Read wanted to inspire his students with an 'intuitive sympathy' and 'pureness of heart' so that they would not approach contemporary art with closed minds. In this talk, Read's mentor was Ruskin, who claimed that 'mental sight becomes sharper with every full beat of the heart' and whose programme in aesthetics was intended to allow the participants 'to forget [themselves] and enter, like possessing spirits, into the bodies of things about' them. In order to accomplish these goals, Read would ask his students to cleanse their minds of any preconceptions they had formed about art; then, he would show them examples of primitive, classical, medieval and subsequent cultures, until the present was reached. On the way, he would demonstrate how an understanding of art enriched one's understanding of history; he would talk about how artists exploit their materials. In such an environment – 'not an atmosphere of analysis and research, but . . . an atmosphere of creative initiative' – he would hope to awaken the habit of enjoyment in his charges.

He would feel 'self-justified' if he could 'inspire enthusiasm rather than impart knowledge', Read confided to William Rothenstein.[19] He certainly became a cult figure in the city: 'During the past two years,' one observer noted in 1933, 'bright Edinburgh people revived conversationally moribund tea parties by posing the question: "What do you think of Herbert Read? I mean, what do you really think?" After that you couldn't get people out of the house.'[20]

Read's surviving lecture notes – one talk on sculpture ranges from ancient Greece to Gill, Brancusi, Zadkine, Moore and Hepworth – clearly demonstrate that he followed the recipe he outlined in October 1931. Much later, various bits of gossip suggested that Read had been treated in a hostile way by the faculty and students in the Department of Art History. Read himself is the likely source of such rumours. At least once, his slides were supposedly placed in the projector upside down; his championing of El Greco was disdained. Geoffrey Grigson tells such an anecdote:

> 'Do you tell us, Read, that this Picasso of yours doesn't know what his picture will be when he starts it?'
> 'Yes,' came Read's answer to this right-minded academic colleague. . . .
> 'Oh, well . . .' and that was the end of the matter (and very soon came the end of Herbert's professorship).[21]

Read's predecessor, Baldwin Brown, did not have great sympathy with most of Read's objectives. However, he is thanked in the acknowledgements to *The Meaning of Art* and due accord was paid him in the inaugural lecture. Relations between the two men were strained, not openly antagonistic. Upon arrival, Read had found the rooms of his department filled with plaster casts of classical architecture and asked for their removal. They remained firmly in place, and he was delighted when some rambunctious Tory students, supporters of Churchill's reappointment as Rector of the University, charging through the department on their way to place a pennant on the Dome, hurled many of the casts to the floor, reducing them to a dusty pile of bric-à-brac. After Brown died on 12 July 1932, Bonamy Dobrée asked Read: 'Now that he is dead, will you be getting rid of the casts cheap? If so, what about some for our garden?'[22]

Unfortunately for him, Read's First Ordinary class of one hundred met at half-past three in the afternoon, just as the pubs closed. Once or twice, inebriated students became rowdy, flinging bread rolls across the room. Opinions differ as to Read's effectiveness as a teacher. Nigel McIsaac, a student at the Art College who sneaked into the lectures, found him efficient and organized. Read habitually arrived one minute late, gave a brief outline of his topic, developed his points coherently, finished three or four minutes early, concluded briefly, bowed to the class and exited. A. C. Davis, who was taking the course as an elective, thought Read diffident. David Daiches' reactions support Davis: 'He seemed unsure of himself, his ideas did not appear to be well organized nor was his presentation effective.' As Daiches remembered, Read did not seem particularly interested in his students' efforts: 'Our first class assignment was to write an essay on "The Significance of Primitive Art" (on which he had been lecturing) and I eagerly awaited his comments on my own essay on the subject. Imagine my disappointment when I got the essay back with the sole comment – pencilled at the end: "Yes, but please write on one side of the paper only." '[23]

Neither largely suppressed antagonisms on the part of colleagues nor Read's ineffectiveness as a teacher should have been insurmountable barriers. As sole professor and, therefore, head of a small department, he had absolute control of its teaching. Also, he was backed by Grierson, a strong ally. To a limited degree, Read came to see Edinburgh in 1931–3 as stuffy, uncongenially provincial. Nevertheless, public dissatisfaction really arose because of personal scandal.

Among the recherché pleasures of 1930s Edinburgh was the salon of André Raffalovich and Canon John Gray, sometime friends of Aubrey Beardsley, Walter Pater, Lionel Johnson and Oscar Wilde. By 1889, when he was twenty-three but looked fifteen, Gray, who had been forced to leave school at thirteen to become a metal turner, had met Wilde. Gray, largely self-taught in languages, music and painting, was then a clerk in the Library of the Foreign Office. Wilde courted Gray, giving his celebrated hero his surname; Gray returned the compliment by signing his letters to him, 'Dorian'. The two were lovers – briefly. Wilde even defrayed the printing expenses of Gray's first book, *Silverpoints*, in 1892. Raffalovich, a wealthy Jew whose family had emigrated from Russia to Paris, was two years older than Gray and famed for his extraordinary ugliness and rapacious homosexuality. Wilde's relations with Raffalovich were strained early, probably because of almost identical streaks of cynicism. Raffalovich entertained in ostentatious splendour of which Wilde proclaimed: 'André came to London to start a salon, and has only succeeded in starting a saloon.'[24]

The Russian, who had previously authored squibs against Gray and Wilde for their excessively florid prose styles, fell in love with Gray when he met him in November 1892. Their relationship was partially forged by a shared antagonism to Wilde. After their former friend's trial, Raffalovich published in 1895 an abusive pamphlet, *L'Affaire Oscar Wilde*.

Sexual passion was eventually transmuted into religious devotion.

101

Gray entered the Scots College at Rome in 1898, his fees probably being met by Raffalovich, who frequently visited him there. Gray was ordained a Catholic priest in December 1901 and four years later became rector of the newly created parish of St Peter's, Morningside, Edinburgh. In that year, Raffalovich, who in 1898 had joined the Third Order of St Dominic, a confraternity for laymen, moved to 9 Whitehouse Terrace in Morningside. He financed in large part the building of St Peter's, which was completed in 1907.

Raffalovich's home was filled with his own carefully arranged floral designs and with paintings by the late impressionists, giving the place a pleasantly claustrophobic feel. His library, in contradistinction to Gray's at the presbytery, was worldly – one shelf was filled with books on homosexuality. For twenty-five years, invitations to Raffalovich's Sunday luncheons and Tuesday dinner parties were much prized. Read, a celebrity from London, was someone to be cultivated. At a lunch at this garishly splendid house in the autumn of 1931, Read was placed next to Margaret Ludwig, a recent convert to Catholicism. Ludo, as friends called Miss Ludwig (her family nickname was 'Golly'), was vivacious and headstrong – and outspoken. A friend recalled her as 'small, dark eyed and with a very deep voice. Speaking rather slowly, she would make capricious remarks with an air of intense solemnity.'[25] Margaret spoke and dressed with assurance, but she was deeply unsure of herself. Her poise was a thinly applied veneer.

Ludo's childhood home was 78 Beaconsfield Place in Aberdeen, but it was her family's German ancestry which pervaded the household and her childhood memories. Both her parents were half-German, her father having a keen sense of being an outsider in Scots society. Charles Ludwig, who worked as a shipping agent, had been brought up a Catholic, but he had permanently blotted his copybook when he brought a Protestant bible into a Catholic Church. Later, Charles was a primordially repressed Victorian parent. When one of his sons was dying of leukaemia, he and his wife Helena did not wish the other children to know. At the time, Ludo was six and, in the midst of a squabble, she cuffed this younger brother in the head. When her father heard of this, he summoned her into his presence and denounced her wicked behaviour. The little girl was chilled by this humiliating experience. She felt tremendous guilt, but, on the other hand, she had performed her supposedly nefarious deed in the midst of a quite ordinary brother–sister fight. She was traumatized by the injustice of her father's imprecations, coming to the conclusion that men were not to be lightly trusted.

The uncertainties of life in Beaconsfield Place were greatly relieved by the pleasures of music. Helena played the piano, and all eight of the nine children who survived to adulthood found a warm consolation in the family orchestra, string quartet or any of the other recitals which were the centre of their evenings. At such times, the emotional poverty of the family was offset by the passions conjured up by Beethoven or Brahms. Such moments were precious to all the children, and Ludo eventually followed the lead of one of her older sisters in deciding to become a musician, although she was convinced that her own approach to music was dilettantish. When she was seventeen or eighteen, she went to Glasgow to pursue further studies in the violin and viola, stayed there for three years, then journeyed to Cologne, where she lived for a further three years. Her professor there was the Catholic composer Walter Braunfels, and her first stirrings towards Catholicism were aroused by his Masses. The Braunfels were related by marriage to the aesthetician Adolf von Hildebrand, whose *Problem of Form in Painting and Sculpture* was published in 1907. In that household, so receptive to music and painting, Ludo felt happy and secure. Irene (Munza) Braunfels, Walter's daughter, became her friend and confidante.

Later, when playing the viola in an orchestral recital at Cologne cathedral, Ludo was struck by the radiant confidence of the guardians who protected the sanctity of that place. This was in direct contrast to the discordant murmurings of the crowds in Berlin and Cologne. Catholicism appealed to her because of its calm assurance in the wake of the violent upheavals which were beginning to overtake struggling, post-war Germany.

When Ludo returned to Scotland to take a degree in music at Edinburgh, she flirted with Catholicism, but it took three more years before she decided to enter the Church from which her father had stormily expelled himself. The 'distressing necessity' to rebel had been part of Margaret's decision to abandon the Episcopal Church in favour of Catholicism. As she said, it is 'the great honesty of finding out a thing for yourself that complicates matters'.[26] A friend, Theo Hunter, introduced her to a parish priest, Father Rice, who, although he drank a bit of whisky and smoked cigarettes, was a fervent and articulate proselytizer of his religion. She was received into the Church in his smoke-filled cubicle of a room, where a calm assurance took her over. Finally, it seemed, she had found the peace which had, up to that time, eluded her.

At Aberdeen, Ludo had been a close friend of Janet Grierson, Herbert Grierson's daughter. Now that they were both in Edinburgh,

103

they were often together and played piano–violin duets. Ludo joined a string quartet, and eventually she acquired a studio in a backlane behind Princess and George Streets. She even became more outspoken, as when Donald Tovey, who did not really like music for voice, cocksurely asked his class, 'None of you, of course, will know Isolde's last words?' One of Ludo's sisters had years earlier driven her to distraction with that aria and, quickly, she put up her hand and sang the final lines from the 'Liebstod'. The professor was flummoxed. Music was the centre of Ludo's life – previous boyfriends had come from that sphere of interest – and now she had found religious certainty and, after receiving her Bachelor of Music degree on 27 March 1930, a post in the music department at the University and its Reid Orchestra. Janet Grierson had even engineered an invitation to Whitehouse Terrace.

In a brief moment, Ludo's world was turned upside down when she sat next to Herbert Read at the Gray–Raffalovich table, over which Gray's now obese presence loomed. Ludo and Herbert exchanged a long glance, falling in love immediately. She was twenty-five in 1931, thirteen years younger than he. Her only thought was: 'I am going to have that man.' She only learned that Read was married when, the next day, she saw him out walking with his 'shabbily dressed' wife. This was in contrast to the green silk flapper dress and patterned stockings which she wore at that time. Herbert was just as struck with Ludo as she with him. His marriage had been sour for years, and Ludo's glamour diverged sharply from Evelyn's wary demeanour, her face and body now bloated from the thyroid deficiency. When he called at Ludo's studio for the first time, Herbert presented her with an arrangement of white lilac and garlic.

Herbert and Evelyn were disastrously similar in demeanour. This had bred contempt. Outwardly, Ludo's outspokenness contrasted sharply with Herbert's withdrawn manner, but her loquacity masked pervasive insecurities. Although Read was frequently unsure of how to conduct himself in public encounters, he had a strong sense of inner worth. In every way, this was an attraction of opposites, a union where differences led to harmonious confusion. Read pursued Ludo and, increasingly, she found it impossible to resist his quiet charm. Although she was torn between her allegiance to her newly adopted religion and her love for a married man, Ludo eventually put her trust in the human rather than the superhuman. Like her father years earlier, she rebelled against the strictures of Catholicism. But a pervasive sense of guilt filled her every waking moment.

★

Although their relationship remained chaste while they were in Edinburgh, Evelyn's suspicion that Herbert and Ludo were having an affair gave way to a feeling of certainty when Herbert suddenly insisted that a grand piano be moved into their Tipperlinn Road home so that Miss Ludwig could have a place to practise, her studio not being large enough for the piano. John Read, eight at the time and a witness to his mother's futile anger, felt displaced. An obvious, tangible feeling of uncertainty entered his existence. For the boy, that piano became a not very subtle symbol of intrusion. His already tenuously connected family was falling apart. When Ludo visited Tipperlinn Road, John frequently stuck his tongue out at her. She responded in kind.

Read's obvious disappointment with Edinburgh was lightened considerably by his liaison with Ludo. Also, he discussed with Gray and Raffalovich the possibility of creating a modern art centre, modelled on the Bauhaus, in Edinburgh. After the war, Read and Frank Rutter had planned an artists' co-operative. Read's new scheme was much more ambitious. In an unpublished essay, 'Proposals for a Scottish Philanthropist', he envisioned a central institution which would co-ordinate and unify the various cultural strands in the city. Housed in a functional building, the institute would have lecture rooms, music rooms, an exhibition gallery, a film workshop and a laboratory for experimental projects. 'In Germany,' Read claimed, such an institution 'would be created by public enterprise, but here I doubt if our civic traditions would rise to such an occasion. But what a magnificent opportunity for a philanthropist! It is within the power of one man to implement the artistic renaissance of a nation. Surely such a man exists.' He obviously did not, but Gray and Read might have hoped that the wealthy Raffalovich would be stirred by the challenge. A cryptic comment in a letter from Read to Gray of 28 April 1932 probably refers to this doomed venture: 'I hope I have not raised your hopes too high – You will perhaps think it . . . is remarkable for what it avoids rather than for what it achieves. But I find a pleasant toughness in it.'[27]

Although his plans for a centre for contemporary art came to nought, Read's affair with Ludo led him in the summer of 1932 to write *The Innocent Eye*, his poignant account of his Yorkshire childhood. That work is obviously imbued with the spirit of Wordsworth's *Prelude*. And, the influence of Hepworth and Moore can be detected in the stark, relief-like manner in which essentials are captured. Nevertheless, here for the first time Read found his own speaking voice as a latter-day romantic. His creativity, previously locked up by literary and art criticism, was unleashed. In meditating upon and writing about his past, he was explaining himself to Ludo, putting into words what his halting conversation failed to capture. In so doing, he finally touched his innermost core, that part of himself which wanted to be a writer not a critic, that portion of the self which had suffered cruelly as a child. Significantly, Ludo's copy of *The Innocent Eye* is inscribed: 'from BIG READ'. This autobiography concludes with the loss of Muscoates and, by implication, the end of childhood. Read could write that poignant account only when he was about to leave his wife and start a new life with Ludo. The trauma of a new parting – this one initiated by himself – allowed him to write of that early, unresolved wound.

In *The Innocent Eye*, Read recalled an incident, which later became a portent of his love for Margaret Ludwig. In the early twenties on a moonlit evening in Bavaria, he had arrived at his destination, a castle which had been converted into a hotel. The porter told him that all the guests were in the music room and directed him to a small balcony which he could enter without disturbing the audience.

> The room was in darkness, except for an electric lamp at the far end of the room, above the dais where the music was being played. It was a violin sonata, and I was immediately held, not so much by the music as by the image which came into my mind as I gazed at the woman playing the violin. Her slender body was like a stem on which nodded, to the rhythm of the music, a strange exotic flower. The corolla of this flower was a human face, very white beneath an arch of raven black hair, and it seemed to brood over the coiled tawny petals of the instrument, preserving an essential stillness in the midst of the force that agitated them.

A beautiful, calm moment in the past had merged magically with the present.

Evelyn stood by in largely muted rage at her husband's behaviour. In July 1932, she and Herbert went down to Leeds, where he was awarded a D.Litt. (honoris causa) by the University. The couple stayed with Read's brother William and his wife Flora. Soon after they arrived, Herbert told Evelyn that she needed more appropriate clothing for the ceremony, suggesting that Flora go shopping with her. Evelyn protested, she would go alone. When she arrived back from her expedition, she was garishly dressed, the final touch being bright red gloves. Her husband was furious, becoming even more cross when she refused to borrow a pair of Flora's gloves. Evelyn was dressing symbolically, wishing to remind her husband of scarlet women.

One of the Leeds graduands that 4 July was Rayner Heppenstall, later a producer at the BBC, who met Read at a party that evening.

106

Denton Welch, when he met Heppenstall in 1948, was struck by his exotic demeanour: 'He seemed slow, almost drugged; he had the sort of composure that puts one at a disadvantage, if one is afraid of gaps in the conversation. One rushes in with trite things, with anything to break the dreadful, imposed, uneasy Buddha calm.'[28] He also noticed that his eyelids 'seemed often to be sliding down, like rather sluggish drops of porridge'.[29] That summer, Heppenstall remembered Read as 'Tall, erect, with dark hair waving thickly over his right temple . . . at forty he was an attractive figure.'[30] The young man was amazed when, on being introduced, Read instantly recalled the few poems Heppenstall had managed to place in *New Verse* and *Adelphi*.

Read's increased introspection in the wake of his involvement with Ludo led to 'The Personality of the Poet', the central essay in *Form in Modern Poetry* (1932). He was trying, as he told a friend in March 1932, 'to reconcile his own view of personality in literature with T. S. Eliot's "tradition" '.[31] However, this piece becomes a covert attack on Eliot, not a synthesis of classical–romantic ideas. Read was particularly concerned with the famous dictum in *The Sacred Wood*: 'Poetry is not a turning loose of emotion, but an escape from emotion; it is not the expression of personality, but an escape from personality.' Read, indebted to Freud's concept of the ego, defines personality as the coherent organization of mental processes; as such, personality contains conscious and unconscious elements. In contrast, character is more an exterior phenomenon which by repressing them prevents elements of the personality from being displayed and acted upon. Personality is private, romantic and lyrical; character is public, classical and rhetorical. Character tends to be fixed early; however, true change can be achieved only through modification of the personality.

Obviously, Read thought he was on the threshold of such a change. This essay also shows the conflicts within Read, himself a would-be poet, his affair with Margaret and the writing of *The Innocent Eye* bringing him to the painful realization that he had placed far too much emphasis on character. Up to 1932, Read thought his own existence had been too outer directed, he had been in danger of destroying his lyrical side. The decision to leave London had been partially dictated by the wish to have more time to write, but it soon became apparent that he had merely exchanged one set of chains for another. His personality, like the older Wordsworth's, was in danger of extinction.

Tom Burns of Sheed and Ward, who published *Form in Modern*

Poetry, made many objections to 'The Personality of the Poet', pointing out flaws in logic and consistency. Read held firm, although the 'Grand Inquisitor' made him write a long preface explaining his 'heresies'.[32] By contrast, when Frank Morley of Faber asked Arthur Wheen to read *The Innocent Eye*, his former colleague immediately understood, as he told Read, that 'your *whole* intention was . . . not to write an account of your childhood, but to show that the artist's vision is childhood's vision – that both the child and the artist see things innocently as for the first time, as they were in the beginning. That you were a child and are an artist. That it was because of this double intention that you wrote in what I called a "painterly" style.'[33]

Despite Wheen's kindly assurances, Read remained divided about his worth as a critic and a creative writer. He was certain that Eliot would despise *Form in Modern Poetry*, and he feared his disdain: 'although I disagree fundamentally with many of his dogmas, I respect his judgment beyond anybody's'. He was relieved when Eliot wrote to him on 15 September to tell him that, on the whole, he found *The Innocent Eye* convincing. Still, Read knew that his literary and visual sensibilities were, to a large degree, in conflict. When William Rothenstein called his attention to the fact that *The Innocent Eye* was 'romantic' whereas much of the modern art he admired appeared 'classical', Read admitted that a gaping wide contradiction *seemed* to exist: 'But I am much more eclectic than you assume, and can admire good representative work in painting as well as, say, the work of Max Ernst. . . . But it is difficult to make such divergences of feeling & taste fit into a logic of life & art, but I think I shall go on trying.'[34] In truth, Read was coming more and more to realize that abstract art had a strong emotive basis; on such grounds, he would become its resolute defender.

Read's growing sense of a new creative self can be seen in 'The End of a War', published at the end of 1932 in *Criterion*. Significantly, it is 'a', not 'the', implying that 'The End' is the record of an individual's response to various kinds of war, not simply the 1914–18 conflict. The poem recreates an incident which took place on 10 November 1918, the day before the Armistice was signed. Read, then back in England, had heard of an English battalion which, in pursuit of remnants of the retreating German army, encountered a severely wounded enemy officer on the outskirts of a French village. He told Lieutenant S that the village had been evacuated two hours earlier. The English troops entered the village and were ambushed: a hundred men and five officers were slaughtered. The remaining English eventually routed the

Germans, mercilessly bayonetting them. Lieutenant S's corporal then returned to the dying German officer, who seemed to be expecting him; his face did not flinch as the Englishman's bayonet ripped him apart. Later that night, the corporal found the naked body of a young girl in a gardener's cottage. 'Both legs were severed, and one severed arm was found in another room. The body itself was covered with bayonet wounds.' Lieutenant S is called upon to investigate, but he can find no evidence as to why this ghastly deed was perpetrated.

The poem is divided into three sections: 'Meditation of a Dying German Officer' and 'Meditation of the Waking English Officer' are the outer portions of the triptych, flanking 'Dialogue Between the Body and the Soul of the Murdered Girl'. The German is a pragmatist who has found a purpose to life in service to the fatherland:

> I fought with gladness. When others cursed the day
> this stress was loosed . . .
> then I exulted: but with not more
> than a nostril's distension, an eager eye
> and fast untiring step.

The officer is able to give blind loyalty to the war because, unlike his friend Heinrich, he has no belief in God. Rather, he has faith in self, friends, confederates and the state.

> This good achieved, then to God we turn
> for a crown on our perfection: God we create
> in the end of action, not in dreams.

In the final analysis, the German officer has the courage of his atheistic convictions: 'God dies in this dying light. The mists receive / my spent spirit: there is no one to hear / my last wish.' For his part, the English officer has questioned the meaning of war:

> When first this fury caught us, then
> I vowed devotion to the rights of men
> would fight for peace once it came again
> from this unwilled war pass gallantly
> to wars of will and justice.
> That was before I had faced death
> day in day out, before hope had sunk
> to a little pool of bitterness.
> Now I see, either the world is mechanic force
> and this the last tragic act, portending
> endless hate and blind reversion
> back to the tents and healthy lusts

109

> of animal men: or we act
> God's purpose in an obscure way.

Ultimately, the English officer is complacent: he tells his German counterpart: 'You die, in all your power and pride: / I live, in my meekness justified.' The English officer's thoughts mingle into 'light celestial / infinite and still / eternal / bright'.

The mechanical bravery of the German officer may have been Read's ironic reflection on his own behaviour during the war, when – without any religious conviction – he was prepared to die for his country. The English officer's saccharine self-confidence would have been repugnant to him. No easy answers are found in the middle section where the Body continually questions the complacent assertions of the Soul, which insists that the girl died for God and country:

> I filled
> your vacant ventricles with dreams
> with immortal hopes and aspirations that exalt
> the flesh to passion, to love and hate.

The Body rejoins that another emotion became a significant factor in the girl's existence: 'My wild flesh was caught / in the cog and gear of hate.' The Soul asserts that the 'cry that left your dying lips / was heard by God'. The Body contradicts this: 'I died for France.' These disagreements lead to a final clash of convictions:

> BODY
> Such men give themselves not to their God
> but to their fate
> die thinking the face of God not love but hate.
>
> SOUL
> Those who die for a cause die comforted and coy;
> believing their cause God's cause they die with joy.

The joy of the Soul is 'coy' – much too self-righteous in its cosy beliefs. The Body comes to the conclusion that a God who condones the existence of war is more to be despised than embraced.

The conflict between Body and Soul was a central concern of Read's. He had no patience with metaphysical speculations about the life of the soul after death, believing in the world as it existed before his eyes, whether in a poem or a painting or another person. Although he was quite willing to explore the symbolic meaning of a work of art or a relationship, Read's explorations began with the physical, with something or someone who can be seen or touched. The poem is an 'end' to his obsession with the war, to any flirtation with religious belief and to a marriage which had become one of soul, not body. In 1935, Henry Miller in response to this poem astutely told Read: 'You revive in every line the image of the sacred body, the feeling of body, *for* body, the feeling of a cosmos and of our relatedness to it. You are absolutely right and unshakeable when you rest in the body as a poet.'[35]

An increasing sense of the wrong job and the wrong wife led Read to fantasize about returning to London to launch a publishing firm. Frank Morley reminded him that such ambitions required a great deal of capital: 'Fabers, so far as big money, a broken reed. We have small capital, & need a quick turnover to keep alive.' His advice: 'hold on a moment, old timer: stick it, laddie. . . . I believe in miracles, but they gotta be rigged.'[36]

Read was in London in February 1932 to attend the Seven and Five exhibition at the Leicester Galleries; later that year he wrote a short introduction to the exhibition of carvings by Barbara Hepworth which opened at Arthur Tooth's gallery in November. 'Stone and wood [in her work] yield their essences to give form a concrete significance.' Then he went on to make further claims for Hepworth's work:

> That some of Miss Hepworth's creative conceptions should recede into a symbolic world of abstractions is not a feature that should deter the disinterested spectator: art is a servant . . . in any sphere of the human spirit – and not least in this marginal world between consciousness and unconsciousness from which emerge strange images of universal appeal. . . . modern artists like Barbara Hepworth step boldly in a new venture which may succeed in redeeming art from its present triviality and insignificance.

Read's strong words would be repeated again and again on Hepworth's behalf and Moore's. That autumn, Read felt that his own poetry was gaining recognition when Geoffrey Grigson asked him to contribute to *New Verse*.

Back in Edinburgh, Read's second academic year began quietly. Evelyn and Ludo were friendly enough to attend Herbert's lectures together. The two women were an odd couple: one pale and dowdy, the other vibrant and alluring. Evelyn was a diligent taker of notes; Ludo just listened. The Reads often entertained students, faculty and members of the Edinburgh intelligentsia. One visitor, Hugh MacDiarmid, wrote on 2 January 1933 to thank them for a pleasant New Year's lunch. Despite being an ardent nationalist, MacDiarmid found Scotland a 'howling void' and told Read: 'You can imagine from this how glad I am to find you in Edinburgh and have occasional meetings with you.' However, he sadly reflected, he and Read were too much alike: 'we are too shy to talk frankly and freely on real issues and tend rather to confine ourselves to small talk'.[37]

David Daiches remembered seeing Read regularly at the Edinburgh Film Guild, which showed avant-garde films (mostly foreign): 'I recall his sitting in front of me, wearing a beret, with his little boy beside him.'[38] Read's attitude toward film – then and later – was ambivalent: 'I do admit that there are great films, and that we get from them a sensation of some sort which stimulates, thrills, terrifies. But in my own experience at any rate this sensation is ephemeral – I find that very few fixed impressions remain, and I think the psychological reason is that the stimuli follow one another so quickly that they cancel each other out, and what remains is an indistinct composite image.'[39]

Read remained profoundly discontented, the New Year making him poignantly aware that time was passing him by. He told Aldington of an overwhelming sense of ennui and entrapment. Although he turned over his options ceaselessly, decisions evaded him. As usual, Aldington provided unequivocal advice:

> First, you must decide (in whatever way you do decide things) whether the life of your creative instinct and its expression in literature is really more to you than anything else. Second, if you decide in the affirmative, your next step is to go straight as an arrow for the way of living which you believe most likely to attain that end. . . . As to Safety First, does it always work out so, especially in the present chaos?[40]

Aldington did have a cautious side, however. He told his friend to use his approaching leave to get down to the writing he *really* wanted to do. At the same time as he voiced his frustrations to Aldington, Read expressed similar feelings to Richard Church in an unguarded way on 25 January 1933:

> the bourgeois & academic life seems to press so closely round me here & I am already longing to escape – escape from what superficially is an ideal job. But inwardly I know & have always known that there will be no satisfaction until all my energies are devoted to my writing. Why should we waste six months every year on people who cannot appreciate you, who drain away all your energy & in the end remain blocks of granite? . . . One must have such a strong faith in oneself to go straight for the goal.[41]

Morley, to whom Read had again vented his frustrations, warned: 'not every seeming way out is a true Exit'.[42]

Obviously, Read spoke candidly to his three confidants about his

112

professional anxieties. He was reluctant to confess that these difficulties were augmented by his marriage, which was rapidly dissolving. His love of Ludo had inspired him to write a piece of autobiography and an important poem. He knew the directions in which he wanted to move. Yet he was consumed by guilt.

The showdown between Evelyn and Herbert took place while they were on holiday on the Isle of Islay in the late spring of 1933. John was sent out to a nursery at the resort, when his parents had reached the breaking point. Previously, John had been forewarned of a rupture by the incident with the piano – no one actually bothered to explain to him what was going on until about 1935, when he was twelve. In the family photograph album, Evelyn sardonically wrote 'Cheated' under a photo of Herbert. The discomfiture in his face, she is implying, demonstrates that he has not obtained what he wanted in marriage. In a notebook of John's, she cryptically stated: 'Everything in house here upset & unusual & unsettled.' Her most explosive statement she wrote on the back of an early profile photograph of herself. It reads in part:

> *The Slave Driver!*
> The Criminal!
> When I gave you these I hardly knew how to pay
>   for them.
> Yet you hardly *thought* of that when you
>   badgered for them!
> And you *pity* Margaret![43]

Who, Evelyn asked, was the *real* 'Slave Driver' and 'Criminal'? Who had cheated whom?

In June 1933, Herbert and Ludo escaped Scotland for Cologne,[44] where the Braunfels welcomed them, these friends giving a much needed sanction to the couple's flight. In an acidic draft of the letter he eventually sent to Sir Thomas Holland, the Principal of the University, Read claimed that although a 'private life' and 'a public position' could be maintained at a place such as Cambridge, he realized that 'such a position would not be tenable for a moment in Edinburgh, & therefore to save the University a public scandal' he tendered his resignation. Read's contempt for the conventions he was flouting can be discerned in the words he deleted: 'I have left my wife & in due course I expect to be divorced ~~for what~~ on an undefended charge of ~~what the law is pleased to call~~ adultery.'[45] Read was sorely missed by some of his students. According to one, he had used his knowledge as a 'personal force': 'Mr

Read may be happier now that he is not Professor Read (he always looked startled when he was given his title) – but will we?'[46]

On 13 July, Aldington congratulated Read on his decision to leave Edinburgh and Evelyn: 'Your card reached me just too late to get a reply to the poste restante. I was unwilling to write you at Edinburgh (visions of intercepted letters). . . . This is great news, and I send my warmest congratulations and hopes for the future. I haven't any doubt about you, with your talents, your courage, your energy and your self-control. This will be an enormous release, and you'll go like a race-horse now.'[47]

Mischievously, Raffalovich told Ludo that she had met a fate worse than death: 'Now, you'll have to live in Bloomsbury!' Although Charles Ludwig wrote Read a polite note[48] accepting the elopement, in a vituperative letter, written in German, he told his daughter that he had been publicly shamed by her doings: he had overheard some men at his club discussing the errant Professor and his mistress from Aberdeen. Herbert playfully told Ludo: 'If it wasn't for you, I would have gone to London for Moore.' Ludo, who had comfortably established herself in the musical circles of Edinburgh, did not appreciate the joke. Not surprisingly, her insecurities reasserted themselves, as agonizing guilt replaced religious certainty.

Her life, Evelyn increasingly realized, had come to an end, even though she outlived Herbert Read by four years. Although Read later suggested that his marriage broke up in 'very similar circumstances' to Eliot's, this is not really true. Unlike Vivien, Evelyn's behaviour became markedly bizarre only after her husband left her. Evelyn and John moved to a flat in Edinburgh in 1934. Gradually, 'acute paranoia', as one of her doctors called it, took over. Certain fixed ideas would obsess her, pushing out other, more ordinary concerns. Friends urged her to return to teaching, but she pleaded looking after John as an excuse. (Her sole income was the £400 a year alimony paid by Read.) Evelyn became violently anti-sex, later accusing a professor at Edinburgh of having propositioned her, and forbidding John to go to any film which might have 'chorus girls' in it. She locked herself up in her bedroom and would not eat. For a while, her brother-in-law William was startled to discover she saved empty cornflake boxes, filling a spare room with them. The rest of the flat was filled with packing-cases, furniture, books and newspapers piled up to the ceiling. As a young child, John had seen his mother as excessively straitlaced but much involved in his emotional development. He always perceived his father as detached and awkward. In a sense, John lost both parents in 1933.

114

John Read lived with his mother until he joined the army in about 1941, when he was eighteen. He obviously exerted a stabilizing influence on her and, when he left home, her mental health deteriorated even further. Evelyn's father, also an eccentric, went to live with her when John departed; he died in about 1943, and Evelyn was two years afterwards institutionalized. One day John was abruptly summoned by his commanding officer, who brutally proclaimed: 'Read, your mother has finally gone completely bonkers!'

Evelyn had a sorry existance moving from Craig House, Edinburgh to The Retreat, York to a place in Norwich, where the keeper was a man with a hook arm in a wheelchair. Later, she was in Shropshire at Church Stretton and, finally, Stafford. She remained aware of her various surroundings, but she was oblivious of her oddness. Although she endured shock therapy a number of times, she never forgot anything in her dismal past. She claimed to be a rationalist and expressed a violent hatred against the Catholic Church and those who professed it. In direct response to Ludo's Catholicism, she became a member of the Spanish Civil Defence Committee. At the end of her life, she was a tiny, withered woman, intensely withdrawn. Her eyes would focus on a visitor's face, then they would flicker abruptly, and, as suddenly, her attention would be diverted to the floor, the ceiling or another face. She abruptly clutched at things, then, as quickly, she would release her grasp. Her tremendous intelligence remained intact, but she was a person uncomfortably mired in her enmity towards those who she thought had wronged her.

In the summer of 1933, Herbert and Ludo arrived back in England. His departure from Edinburgh and the University had been accomplished with more flair than he had anticipated or desired. He had not told Evelyn that he was leaving. When he had not shown up after a few days, she reported him missing to the police. Years later, Herbert Grierson told David Daiches: 'If Read had consulted me, I would have told him how to keep his Chair *and* the girl.'[49]

When André Raffalovich heard of little John's unhappiness, he wrote to Eric Maclagan's wife asking her to persuade her husband to intervene. The Director of the Victoria and Albert did that on 13 August. Having considered the situation, he flatly told his former subordinate:

> you have no right to do it whatever justification you and the girl you love may feel for it. . . . [Margaret Ludwig] can never be happy if she puts up this unbreakable barrier between herself and her religion. I can't speak about your wife; as you know, I only met her a few times, and I have no

115

right to assume that she does not acquiesce in what you propose to do. But Raffalovich at any rate has no doubt about your boy's feelings, and I do not see how under any system of ethics you have the right to hurt him to that extent even if it is for the sake of fulfilling your own highest destiny and bringing happiness to someone whom you feel means even more to you.[50]

Earlier, on 27 July, Read's brother William fully supported his decision: 'I don't think your letter was such a shock as you thought it would be. I handed it to Flora who said "I don't find it difficult to understand and I am very glad that he has found someone to give him the necessary incentive to make the break." ' William, fearful of what would happen to John, promised to keep an eye on him.[51] Years later, Read grimly – and with considerable self-complacency – spoke of 'paying alimony for thirty years, a grievous burden, and one more cause of my routine labours. Life is full of these man-traps. You may have remarked how many of the great writers avoided matrimony, and that those who did not always suffered more than the rest of mankind.'[52] In 1961, when Muriel Spark sent him a copy of *The Prime of Miss Jean Brodie*, which is set in Edinburgh, Read assured her that she had captured the atmosphere of time and place perfectly. He was filled with nostalgia: 'For I suppose it was my prime too, and equally disastrous & joyful things happened to me then.'[53]

In a poem from this time, 'Night Ride', two lovers are huddled together as the bus they are on hurtles through the night; they wake 'cold / to face the fate / of those who love / despite the world'. In 'Time Regained', the poet suggests that 'a hurt's that done' may be forgotten by the mind. It is possible, this poem intimates, to circumvent guilt and yet pay a price for earthly happiness. This was a momentary sad reflection. Read hoped to burn the past. Now, he believed, he had the freedom to become the writer he felt lay dormant within him. Days of glory, he hoped, awaited him.

8   Art Now: International Modernism

In the summer of 1933, Herbert and Ludo arrived in London penniless. Ludo thought of rejoining the Reid Orchestra, but when she went back to Edinburgh she was rebuffed. Aldington tried to help Read land a job as literary adviser at Heinemann. Henry Moore lent the destitute couple 11A Parkhill Road, on the frontier that divides the two worlds of Hampstead and Camden Town, while he and Irina were vacationing in Kent. However, Ludo did not move in with Herbert immediately – she briefly stayed with a friend's mother. Moore jokingly referred to Read's 'summer of sin'. Another friend, Valentine Dobrée, was prim, being shocked that Ludo, a recent convert to Catholicism, would get up early to go to Mass and upon her return snuggle back in bed with Herbert. Eliot, who had left his wife the year before, did not approve of Read's taking up with another woman.

Support for Read came that summer, reluctantly, from an unexpected quarter: Roger Fry. He told Kenneth Clark that he was willing to support Read's candidacy for the editorship of the *Burlington Magazine*. Although he distrusted Read's art criticism, he nevertheless recognized his curiosity and range of interests, 'which is more to the point than great learning along narrow lines'.[1] The year before, Read had attacked the fundamental notions inherent in Fry's theory of art, although he had done this politely. He praised the subtle painter's eye Fry brought to his criticism, but he suggested that he was too concerned with 'plastic values' and the 'what' of a picture: in his opinion, Fry was prone to reducing the essential values of art to an apprehension of formal values, and he disapproved of the way in which Fry in *The Artist and Psychoanalysis* had 'made mincemeat of those innocent psychologists who judge a work of art by the symbolic value of its concrete imagery'.[2] According to Read, Fry denigrated the symbolical in favour of an aesthetic in which form and content become one. Fry was a Francophile; Read recognized the importance of French art but he was

117

really a partisan of Northern art. Obviously, Read felt that Fry was a bit anti-intellectual and reductive. On the other hand, Fry distrusted a philosophy of art which was concerned with meaning at the expense of artistic competence.

Although he was desperate to put together a number of jobs which could keep him afloat, Read hesitated about the *Burlington*. It did not pay very much (£500 a year), and Read had hoped that more lucrative opportunities would come his way. Fry told him that he could *treat* the *Burlington* as part-time work, but that it must be called a full-time job as that would be the grounds for 'firing' the unsatisfactory Robert Rattray Tatlock, the editor since 1920, who also worked for the *Daily Telegraph*.[3] Finally, on 4 August Read agreed to succeed Tatlock and offered an apology to Fry for taking so long to reach a decision. He also warned him again that he would have to combine the *Burlington* with other work. The first issue of the magazine under Read's direction was December 1933, the new editor's essay on English art being the first item. Read had also told Fry that he would like it understood that the scope of the magazine had to include a 'modicum' of modern art. Agreed or not, Read did not move the *Burlington* that 'modicum'. However, he did eagerly publish the work of young scholars who had yet to establish themselves: Ellis Waterhouse, John Pope-Hennessy, Denis Mahon, Erwin Panofsky, Friedrich Antal.

During that first summer on Parkhill Road, a small job paid £20: the text for the first book on Moore, published in 1934 by Anton Zwemmer, the Charing Cross Road bookseller. On 19 July, Read took Paul Nash's advice and asked the BBC if he could broadcast on art. Ludo practised her viola in a room filled with wood carvings by Moore, and she recalled 'one specially of a little figure that I always longed to own; but of course we had no money in those days'.[4] This boxwood figure they nicknamed 'butter-girl'. Later, when Ludo joined a string quartet which was playing Bartok she asked David Higham, the literary agent, for his candid opinion: 'I had to tell Ludo that to me it sounded like cats on the roof.'[5]

The Moores' return to London meant that Ludo and Herbert had to move again but, luckily, only to 3 Mall Studios off Parkhill Road. Barbara Hepworth and Ben Nicholson, who were living together at No. 7, found their new home for them. Cecil Stephenson, a painter from Bishop Auckland in Durham who had trained at the Leeds School of Art, the Royal College of Art and the Slade, had lived since 1919 – his model railway ran out into his garden at the back. In 1932, obviously under the influence of his new friends, he began to paint in an abstract manner.

The seven stable-like studios, with a detached one at the end, were built by Thomas Batterbury in 1872 for lease to working artists. Red-tile roofs, chimney pots, open timber construction, red-brick walls and three skylights were features common to the units. The little path to the studios was slightly smelly – as Ludo said, 'smelly greenery, London greenery' – and the doors to the studios were tiny. Then, suddenly, there was a large room in front, with a huge window, a large garden outside and a 'monastery garden' beyond.

Ludo and Herbert took full advantage of the spaciousness of No. 3, in time filling it with tubular furniture by Mies van der Rohe, the desk made by Read when at Edinburgh, a set of curtains designed by Ben Nicholson, a white skin sofa, sculptures by Hepworth, paintings by Nicholson and Alfred Wallis. Ludo did not like their Aalto furniture: 'We had a round table, with a round cover, covered with linoleum and rather nasty little chairs, plywood stools; you always tripped over them.'[6] The floor was covered with white linoleum; the woodwork was pale blue, and the walls were white. Ben came in to see the results of this interior decorating. 'Wait a minute,' he said and returned a few minutes later with a round cork table mat which he had painted scarlet – it was still wet in his hands. He seized a ladder and nailed the disc halfway between the top of a painting by himself and the ceiling. The room, Read recalled years later, 'was transformed by this accent of colour, perfectly placed'. Off this room were three small rooms: a kitchen, bathroom and bedroom, which became Munza Braunfels' when she came to live with Herbert and Ludo – she acted as cook and chauffeur. Up the stairs was a covered platform, the main sleeping area. Quite often, the flat was filled with music from the gramophone, such as Douglas Bing's rendition of 'Miss Otis Regrets'.

The Heath, including Parliament Hill, gives to Hampstead an arcadian splendour, almost as if this portion of north London has been sliced away from the tribulations of urban life. In 1814, John James Park called it 'a select, amicable, respectable and opulent neighbourhood'. Byron, Keats and Constable settled there in the nineteenth century. The chance of enjoying a pleasant mix of city and country life attracted, at the beginning of this century, writers as varied as H. G. Wells, John Masefield, J. B. Priestley, John Galsworthy and D. H. Lawrence.

Prosperous, fashionable artists in the late nineteenth century had gravitated towards Fitzjohn's Avenue, west of Hampstead. Hampstead proper was pleasantly dilapidated when Mark Gertler moved there in 1915. Henry Lamb had a studio on the top floor of the Vale Hotel; later,

119

in 1924, Stanley Spencer took over this place, where he painted *Resurrection*. Four years later, Skeaping and Hepworth in the wake of their second successful joint exhibition moved there because of the large amount of room they could rent at a reasonable price. Hepworth alerted Moore to Parkhill Road. In 1933, Hampstead was on the verge of becoming the modernist fortress in London. Within the next five years, Naum Gabo, Bernard Meninsky, E. L. T. Mesens, Moholy-Nagy, Piet Mondrian, Paul Nash, Adrian Stokes, Marcel Breuer, Walter Gropius, Berthold Lubetkin, Desmond Bernal and Sigmund and Anna Freud settled there – or in near proximity.

On Boxing Day 1933, Jim Fairfax-Jones opened the Everyman as a cinema, specializing in avant-garde European films, the offerings in 1934 including Eisenstein's *Thunder Over Mexico*, Lang's *M* and Riefenstahl's *The Blue Light*. Read, an avid but dispassionate film-goer, relished this place. The Everyman's Foyer Gallery, run by Tess Fairfax-Jones, showed Paul Klee for the first time in England; David Bomberg, Anthony Gross, Fred Uhlman, Barbara Hepworth, Ben Nicholson, among many others, had shows there in the thirties.

A buoyant optimism filled the writers and artists who in the thirties chose the cheap accommodation and rural beauty of Hampstead, almost as if the world could be remade in a brighter way than hitherto. The abstract, geometrical work of Hepworth and Nicholson of this period exemplifies this confidence, as in Nicholson's declaration of 1934: 'What we are searching for is the understanding and realisation of infinity – an idea which is complete, with no beginning and no end and therefore giving to all things for all time.'[7] Nicholson's theosophical, transcendental vision, highly indebted to, among others, Kandinsky and Mondrian, conceived of the artist as the harbinger of a new social order. Finally, it seemed, it was possible to escape the horrors of the war.

Barbara Hepworth arrived in Hampstead in 1928. Ten years younger than Read, she was from Wakefield in Yorkshire. She had trained at the Leeds School of Art and the Royal College of Art. From 1924 to 1926 she held a West Riding scholarship in Italy. At Florence in 1925, she married a fellow student, the sculptor John Skeaping, whose work was and remained decidedly naturalistic. Barbara, brown-haired with a high sloping forehead, delicate eyebrows, straight nose, firm mouth, was much more sexually reticent than Skeaping, an aggressively handsome man who soon found his wife 'very un-sexy'.[8] In 1929, attracted to Eileen Frielander, he arranged to spend a weekend with her, which he boasted, was 'an eye-opener, or more correctly a "fly" opener'.[9] In a slightly more placid way, Barbara in 1931 took up with Ben Nicholson, who left his wife Winifred, a painter of delicate, radiant still-lifes. Ben, the son of the painters William and Mabel Pryde Nicholson, was attracted to non-realistic approaches to art from his student days. A man of studied, determined passion, he was the antithesis of his exuberantly grandiose father. Barbara responded enthusiastically to her new companion's interest in non-representational art, her work turning almost at once in a markedly abstract manner.

Nicholson and Hepworth were immediately touched by Read's strong support. Barbara was taken with his quietness: 'Whenever he was in the presence of a new work, of any kind, he was totally silent and he probably wouldn't speak for half an hour. But the silence itself was a great inspiration because one began to look at the work through his eyes.' She also felt that he responded to the 'sensuality of what lay underneath the skin' and allowed the 'creature' within the sculpture to speak to him. Nicholson could be prickly, but his friendship with Read kept on an even keel. Read's relationship with Hepworth was much more intricate.

Ben and Barbara shared an almost merciless dedication to work coupled with an often ruthless ambition. Nicholson's desire for fame was accepted matter-of-factly by his peers. He had been born into the art world. Of his lineage there was no question. Like Read and Moore, Hepworth was an outsider, and outsiders, she felt, had to prove themselves. In a manner similar to Read's, she sometimes sacrificed intimacy on the altar of career. Her friend Margaret Gardiner recalled that Barbara:

> totally redefined the meaning of the word 'work' for me. Work was at the centre of everything for her; it was what sustained her through all the stresses and strains of her life. . . . By 'work' she meant, of course, carving, not chores. . . . Some of Barbara's acquaintances found it hard to understand her attitude to work – they thought her stand-offish and were offended if, when they dropped in casually, she would say 'Sorry, I'm working' and would firmly shut the door.[10]

Hepworth craved recognition, even more so than her fellow pupil at Leeds, Henry Moore. With a great deal of justification, she felt that her femaleness thwarted her being taken seriously. Also, she was in conflict: did a woman have the right to covet recognition and acclaim? Was it possible to be both a good mother and a successful sculptor? Hepworth

121

answered yes to both questions, but she paid a heavy psychic price. Her striving took the form of a life-long competition with Moore.

One way of deciding this thorny issue was to look to Herbert Read, who had given her unstinting praise in 1932. His opinion as a fellow Yorkshireman and leading advocate of modernism meant a great deal to her. In such situations Read was a masterful politician, avoiding any occasion when he might be called upon to answer loaded questions. Hepworth suspected that Read's deepest sympathies lay with Moore. Such unresolved questions gave a lively frisson to their relationship. In addition, Read's mixed feelings about women were unleashed.

Barbara Hepworth's art appealed to the intuitive, feminine side of Read's nature. Yet, as with Eliza and Evelyn, he still saw women as controlling and punitive. Although he remained a strong supporter of her work, Barbara felt, rightly, that she never received the unstinting approval given to Moore, with whom Read maintained a less volatile – fraternal – relationship. She resented this and would confront Read with his inconsistencies. Then he would fight back. These sparks led to bickering which, in turn, forced Herbert and Barbara to grapple with what they truly felt about art.

Skeaping's feelings about Read had not the slightest tinge of ambiguity – he hated him: 'his style of writing struck me as a specious use of pseudo-intellectual jargon. . . . I felt instinctively that this man was dictating to us what to do.'[11] He mentioned his disdain to Edith Sitwell, who immediately concurred: 'That crashing bore. . . . Sachy and I went to dinner with him some weeks ago, passing a long and tiresome evening. Finally I said to Herbert, "We really must be going now, our last bus goes at 12.30 and we daren't miss it," whereupon Herbert looked at his watch and said, "But Edith, it's only 9.15." '[12] For Skeaping, Read was simply not enough of a vagabond, and Read never had any sympathy for bohemian untidiness: his hair, suit, shirt were always immaculate but blended into an appearance which was, one friend recalled, 'touchingly natural and attractive and informal. His bow ties in particular took a fine path between dandyism, undress and a certain old-fashioned respectability.'[13] Read's unconventionality could be glimpsed in his omnipresent berets, which were replaced by more conventional porkpie hats in the late forties.

Another difficult friend was the irascible Geoffrey Grigson, who founded *New Verse* in 1933, the year he turned twenty-eight. A strong proponent of Auden, whose proletarian, political verse did not appeal to Read, Grigson was at bottom an enthusiast for the poets and artists of the Romantic landscape: Palmer, Clare, Wordsworth, Hardy – this was a tenuous bond between him and Read. Grigson, who was a disciple of the even more difficult Wyndham Lewis, also valued 'individuality' in art and poetry, feeling that abstract art promoted collectivity and socialism, which would ultimately water down and impoverish English life. In January 1935, he attacked Nicholson's work: 'Admirable in technical qualities, in taste, in severe self-expurgation, but too much "art itself", floating and disinfected.' Grigson admired Moore's less controversial work and liked to stroll from his home in Keats Grove to Parkhill Road and the Mall Studios for frequently acrimonious chats.

Grigson's view of Read was derived from Wyndham Lewis, who now claimed that Read never looked a picture in the face, although he knew the kind of picture to look in the face.[14] Lewis also told Grigson that in November 1933, shortly after the publication of his volume of verse, *One-Way Song*, he met Read by chance by the ticket machines at Piccadilly Circus Underground. Fumbling in his attempt to start a conversation, Read blurted out: 'I didn't know you wrote verse, Lewis.' The artist maliciously rejoined: 'I never knew it was so damned easy, Read.'[15]

Like Grigson and Lewis, Read too could be haughtily dismissive, as when E. M. Forster invited him and William Plomer to lunch to meet Somerset Maugham, who presumably might be able to give these struggling young writers some help. The occasion was an unqualified disaster, Read pugnaciously lecturing Maugham about 'contemptible people who write for money, like you'.[16]

Such jarring moments were rare in 1933. As far as Read was concerned, a radiant glow had settled over the Mall Studios – and his life. In the delicate 'Other' he distilled the intensity of his passion for Ludo:

> Other faces
>   are like lamps unlit:
> Yours is a net
>   in which a thousand stars are caught;
> the sky around
>   is darker for their deft withdrawal. . . .
> Other lives
>   drift to the Sirens' rock:
> Your music
>   issues in the wind's wake
> muted and immortal.

Ludo, who felt the constant tug of her Catholicism, was shocked at the number of unmarried people who lived together, including herself and Herbert. On such grounds, she did not like Adrian Stokes, although she realized that others 'found him beautiful. He had enormous wide eyes, which went nearly to the back of his head.'[17] Stokes, a painter–critic who had begun an analysis with Melanie Klein in 1930, had in *Sunrise in the West* and *The Quattro Cento* applied psychoanalytical methodology to Renaissance art. Almost ten years younger than Read, Stokes, educated at Rugby and Magdalen, went to Bombay shortly after Oxford. There, he became fascinated with Indian culture and mysticism, which formed the basis of his first book, *The Thread of Ariadne*.

To Margaret Gardiner, Stokes was like a magnificent bird: 'tall, with a crest of unkempt fair hair, blue eyes, sweeping eyebrows like wings and a beak of a nose'.[18] A relentless explorer of the truth about himself and the nature of art, Stokes was an active promoter of Hepworth and Nicholson. In November 1933, indebted to the Kleinian emphasis on the baby's intense love–hate response to the mother, he wrote: 'So poignant are these shapes of stone by Barbara Hepworth, that in spite of the degree in which a more representational aim and treatment have been avoided, no one could mistake the underlying subject of the group. In this case at least the abstractions employed a vast certainty. It is not a matter of a mother and child group represented in stone. Miss Hepworth's stone *is* a mother, her huge pebble its child.'[19] Despite different emphases, the friendship between Read and Stokes was founded on their enthusiasm for abstraction. That friendship had a shaky start. Stokes was at first stand-offish, remembering all too well that Read in *English Prose Style* had used an excerpt from *Sunrise in the West* to illustrate metaphors concealing meaning.

Ludo's sense of remorse led to conflicting feelings about sexuality, not terribly dissimilar from Evelyn's. Read claimed not to experience pangs of guilt, although he attacked the Catholic Church in his hostile review of Christopher Dawson's *The Modern Dilemma*: 'When a new St Francis has arisen to reform the Faith, when the church has sold all it has and given to the poor, when it has condemned . . . usury upon which the capitalist order is based – then it will have force enough to bring into its ranks those who . . . are determined to preserve an integrity above the false values of all creeds that subordinate the spirit of man to the tyranny of material ends.'[20] For the remainder of his life, Read, who was not anti-Christian, remained virulently anti-Catholic, being particularly antagonistic to that faith's totalitarian control of its members. In April 1938, he told a friend: the Catholic Church has 'no

Herbert Edward Read, Herbert's father, in his early thirties

Muscoates Grange

Eliza Read with her three sons (left to right: Herbert, Charles and William)

Crossley and Porter School, Halifax

ABOVE: Evelyn Roff, *c.* 1916–18

LEFT: Herbert Read in military uniform, *c.* 1917–18

ABOVE: T. E. Hulme, 1914

LEFT: A. R. Orage

AEROPLANE LANDING.

Read drawings, *c.* 1917

THE ROAD TO POLYGONVELD.

AN OLD SOLDIER.

Wyndham Lewis with his portrait of T. S. Eliot, 1938

Broom House

Evelyn Read with John

BELOW: Jacob Kramer's portrait of
Herbert Read, *c.* 1930

RIGHT: The formal Read, with
Arthur Wheen, *c.* 1925

The casual Read, *c.* 1930

Evelyn Read, *c.* 1933

Margaret Ludwig, *c.* 1932

guts, no vitality; only a dead weight of worldly possessions and a contempt for human suffering'.[21]

Obviously, Read became hostile to Catholicism because he was an uneasy witness to the anguish Ludo endured as she pondered the wide gap between her daily existence and the dogma of her adopted religion. After Ludo's sister Frances – known as 'Fuzzy' – converted to Catholicism, she asked her confessor if she could stay with Ludo, now, presumably, a fallen woman. The priest told her that she could visit her sister but that she could not sleep under the same roof. At night, Fuzzy retired to the outhouse. Much later, when Ludo wanted to travel to the Vatican to see the Pope, Herbert said that such a trip was unnecessary and that under no conditions would he pay for it.

Despite protestations on Herbert's part – and the resulting strain on their relationship – Ludo remained a devoted Catholic, although she was not allowed to receive communion since the Church considered her to be in a state of mortal sin. Friends, such as fellow convert Graham Greene, felt that Ludo was too rigid in her adherence to Catholic doctrine. Since her heart was pure, she had nothing to fear, they told her. Her son, Piers Paul Read, has aptly described his mother's feelings about religion:

> her respect for my father's intelligence was reverential – she had German blood in her veins – but never for a moment was she inclined to adopt his agnosticism. Her faith was stronger than his reason, and almost as if to propitiate the God whom she had offended by her adulterous liaison, she brought us all up in the religion which denied her its sacraments and condemned her to Hell-fire.[22]

Ludo's determined adherence to Catholicism became an instrument of revenge against the man who had usurped her from that creed. Now, a domineering rigidity began to mask her many insecurities.

Read's own strong religious inclinations were transmuted into a concern with the transcendental reality which hovers at the edge of some works of art. The search for such a metaphysic is constant in his art and literary criticism, giving it a neo-Platonic flavour. An agnostic, Read sought a higher reality, a central concern of English abstract art in the thirties.

In 1933, life was an agreeable mixture of work, visits, conversation, disagreements and shared purposes for Herbert, Ludo, Ben, Barbara and the Moores. Shopping expeditions from their commonplace part of Hampstead were to shabby Kentish Town, where there was a Catholic church. As Ludo recalled, 'And there was a movie there, just opposite the passage. You said a prayer, nipped out of the church and into the movies.'[23]

Herbert and Ludo's studio became a place of parties, Geoffrey Grigson recalled: 'It was where nationalities and generations mixed (with a notable absence, though, of Auden and his closer friends). Braque might be there, or Jean Hélion, from Paris, or Eliot gayer than his reputation, actually singing "Frankie and Johnnie".'[24] A favourite party game was to unroll some wallpaper, turn the blank side up, and attach it to a long table with drawing pins. This was then made into a sea chart with headlands, straits, reefs, islands, whales. Everyone present was then handed a piece of coloured chalk. In turn, each player with eyes shut 'started a sailing line from harbour at one end, and advanced towards the other end, trying to avoid being wrecked on one or other of the obstacles. Each player, before his turn, was allowed a long look at this gay coloured entertainingly drawn sea-course.'[25] Nicholson and Moore always won.

Read's place within what he blandly called 'a nest of gentle artists' was further secured by the publication of *Art Now* in 1933. A *Punch* cartoon of January 1934 shows the 'moderns' storming the Royal Academy, the enclave of the 'ancients'. The images in this drawing are derived from the plates to Read's new book. Douglas Cooper, Freddy Mayor's partner in one of the most progressive art dealerships in London and an avid collector of cubist art, helped Read to select the illustrations. The physical appearance of *Art Now* was mildly revolutionary: it was one of the first books to be printed wholly in sans-serif type. Reginald Wilenski in the *Listener* claimed that Read had 'an altogether broader vision than Fry. . . . Read believes in the psychological approach to the study of art and is willing to accept all that modern psychologists can supply as data.'[26] Bryan Guinness, in a sympathetic review, felt that there could be some justice in the complaint that *Art Now* contained futile philosophical speculation of little value to artists themselves.[27]

The text, based on lectures given at three institutions (University College, North Wales, Bangor; the Courtauld; Armstrong College, Newcastle-upon-Tyne – the annual Charlton lecture) is a more striking, propagandistic defence of modernism than that found in *The Meaning of Art*. An autobiographical touch enters the text when Read asserts that the discoverer of a new, symbolic vision of the world was not Cézanne or Van Gogh but Paul Gauguin, who threw up 'his post in a bank and even deserted his wife and family to devote himself to painting'.

126

GETTING READY AT BURLINGTON HOUSE
An attempted gate-crash by the Moderns is frustrated

In this *Punch* cartoon of January 1934, many of the pictures reproduced in *Art Now* are repulsed at the portals of the Royal Academy.

127

Nevertheless, Cézanne's justly celebrated claim – 'I have not tried to reproduce Nature: I have represented it' – is approvingly quoted, and, as in his book on Wordsworth, Read speaks enthusiastically of the centrality of feeling: not 'mere fellow-feeling, of feeling *with*, but rather a form of imaginative identification of the self with the object, a feeling *into*'. Modern artists, Read insists, attempt to create works which involve an active participation on the part of the viewer.

Contemporary art, Read maintains, derives its authority from the *Philebus*, where Plato approvingly speaks of the beauty of lines and curves, which 'are not beautiful relatively, like other things, but always and naturally and absolutely'. Modern artists have returned to this concept of art because of the omnipresence of machines, 'objects, expressing in their lines and volumes a certain functional perfection to which we cannot deny the name of beauty'. But there is a profounder reason for abstraction. Modern man has become dangerously aware of the advent of chaos, especially in the guise of war. Quoting Worringer's *Form in Gothic*, Read points out that some artists have always responded to such forces by attempting to establish 'a world of absolute and permanent values placed above the shifting world of appearances and free from all the arbitrariness of life. They had therefore remodelled what was living and arbitrary . . . into invariable symbols of an intuitive and abstract kind.'

In *Art Now* Read also gives his blessing to a type of art – automatism, of which surrealism was the principal school – which disavows the real world. Here the artist wants to recreate that portion of life which is 'submerged, vague, indeterminate':

> A human being drifts through time like an iceberg, only partly floating above the level of the consciousness. It is the aim of the Surréaliste, whether as painter or as poet, to try and realise some of the dimensions and characteristics of his submerged being, and to do this he resorts to the significant imagery of dreams and dream-like states of mind.

Read closes his book by bestowing his approbation on these two, often radically different approaches. In each, the signature of true modern artists can be seen, artists who are trying to harness 'mental conceptions' to the materials in which they must work. 'The act of putting pencil to paper, brush to canvas, becomes an instant [in which] the personality, and indeed, the spirituality of the artist is revealed.' Read's defence of both camps is quintessentially romantic, each method attempting to reach truths often hidden from reason.

As he told Wyndham Lewis, Read preferred abstraction – its

definiteness and precision appealing to the pristine, puritanical part of his makeup. On that score, abstract art for him was extremely intellectual, in which the artist regards the real world as a point of departure. On the other hand, he did emphasize its strong emotional component, its relentless quest for a truth beyond the self. The business of defending a plurality of modernisms was, he also told his old friend–enemy, 'a serious, even a religious' endeavour.[28] In a self-critical vein, he confessed that he was 'guilty of sympathetic flutters for any poor devil who is trying to be sincere'.[29]

The approach of war hangs ominously over the book. In the Preface Read mentions the rise of the Nazis. He pleads for art to be separated from politics, for peaceful toleration and for a public which, having become more and more disgusted by the drabness of modern life, seeks the inner world of the imagination, the key to which is held by the artist. Read's own politics within his Hampstead community are revealed in the plates: four Moores, two Nicholsons, one Hepworth.

Not surprisingly, Evelyn was not the most receptive critic to her estranged husband's ideas on modernity. Much earlier, she had distrusted his friendships with artists and writers. In 1933, she had no doubts about this. When Read presented her with a copy of *Art Now*, inscribed 'For Robin', she entered a number of rejoinders in the margins. Read claims: 'In short, the good artist is very rarely interested in anything but his art'; Evelyn retorts: 'True, which makes them extremely difficult to live with. They do not keep sufficiently in touch with everyday realities.' Read says: 'The inner world of the imagination becomes more and more significant, as if to compensate for the brutality and the flatness of everyday life.' Evelyn: 'For me that is impossible. I do feel that one can still preserve, in spite of all this mechanical environment (which I do not accept), a sense of the eternal mysteries.' The modern artist's attempt to turn his perceptions inwards seemed to Evelyn 'complete introversion & on the highway (deliberately) to insanity'. When Read spoke of symbols 'of a general validity', she countered: 'then all will react to the pictures in the same way'. On page fifteen Read claims that 'we are without courage, without freedom, without passion and joy, if we refuse to follow where' the modern artist leads. This led Evelyn to her most poignant reflection: 'Dartington Hall tries to preserve & to perpetuate the life of superior times. So did Broom House. And we had nearly won through.'

Financial difficulties continued to plague Herbert and Ludo. Llewelyn Griffith, a friend of Read's, reminded them that Gustav Holst was still director of music at St Paul's Girls' School and might need a viola teacher. Read complained to Eliot that he had to review books in order to survive. His old friend was sympathetic, assuring him that no able man should be forced to review books after the age of thirty-five.[30] He hoped a better supplement to the *Burlington* could be found. In his increasingly straitened circumstances, Read reviewed films for the *Spectator*.

Although Read's stated preference was for abstract rather than surrealistic art, his twin defence of those often conflicting allegiances in *Art Now* made him the ideal co-ordinator of Unit One, spearheaded by Paul Nash, who had made a cryptic allusion to the possibility of such an alliance in the *Listener* of 24 September 1932: 'A marriage has been arranged – and will shortly take place.' Nash, who was to become Read's neighbour in nearby Eldon Grove in 1936, was the *'grand seigneur'*: 'if one wanted to be unkind one would say he was a little pompous', Read claimed. In 1933, Nash radiated a 'more polemical spirit' than his Hampstead confederates.

During the ensuing nine months, Moore was the fellow artist with whom Nash was in contact regarding the proposed assemblage. On 17 January 1933, he told Moore in confidence: 'I have been anxious to get four of us round a table for a preliminary talk. Yourself, Wadsworth, Wells Coates the architect & myself. I wish to limit the company to these as, between us, I feel we represent the most stable & least biased members of the rather difficult collection of people who are likely to constitute a group.' Nash suggested that they call themselves 'Contemporary Group', mentioned that Zwemmer's, Tooth's and Lefevre were sympathetic, and named the artists who were to join the new phalanx: John Armstrong, Edward Burra, John Bigge and Ben Nicholson. Nash felt unable to 'judge sufficiently' of Barbara Hepworth: 'I heard from Ben & I shall write to him more guardedly until Barbara is decided upon! . . . Ben is a good fellow but I do not regard his judgment as entirely sound – & I believe you agree on this.' Hepworth eventually obtained a place, as did Colin Lucas, the architect, and Frances Hodgkins, who soon resigned and was replaced by Tristram Hillier. In April 1933, the Mayor Gallery showed work by Wadsworth, Nicholson, Armstrong, Hillier and Moore next to pieces by Braque, Léger, Dali, Miró and Ernst. This set the stage for Nash's letter to *The Times* of 12 June 1933 announcing the formation of a group which would stand 'for the expression of a truly contemporary spirit, for that thing which is recognized as peculiarly *of today* in painting, sculpture and architecture'. He also claimed that there was 'nothing naive about Unit One'.

It is composed, mainly, of artists of established reputations who are not very concerned as to how other English artists paint or make sculpture or build. But they have this in common with the Pre-Raphaelites; in the sense that those artists were a brotherhood, they are a unit: a solid combination standing by each other and defending their beliefs.

The Mayor held a show in October 1933 linked to the publication of *Art Now*, and work by the Unit One artists was prominently on display. Read and Cooper also stressed the new brotherhood in the selection of plates. In addition to Moore, Nicholson and Hepworth, there were two Nashes and one each by Burra, Bigge, Wadsworth and Hillier (Alfred Wallis, Ivon Hitchens, Francis Bacon and Wyndham Lewis were the only other English artists whose work was reproduced). Bacon, whose work Read despised, gained his entry through Cooper, who commissioned an art deco rug and tubular chairs from the young designer. In later years, Cooper would display these objects in order to ridicule them.[31]

Nash's assertions about the buoyant spirit of Unit One were purposefully bland. He and Moore were, in varying degrees, receptive to abstraction and surrealism. Although they incorporated elements of each in their work, their strong artistic personalities controlled and guided such borrowings. The other members of the group, especially Ben Nicholson, were not as open to compromise. Simply put, Nicholson believed that there was room for only one modernism. From its outset, he wanted to squash surrealism. Throughout the 1920s he had waited for recognition, and he did not want a new representational approach to painting to become dominant. In 1923 he had, in response to an invitation from Ivon Hitchens, joined the Seven and Five Society, founded in 1919–20 as a foil to Bloomsbury by seven painters and five sculptors, who felt that there had 'been of late too much pioneering along too many lines in altogether too much of a hurry'.[32] By 1926, Nicholson was elected their first chairman and in 1934 he engineered a rule that only non-representational works would be eligible for future shows and proposed a new name: Seven and Five Abstract Group.

Nicholson was an astute but bellicose politician. In April 1944, he offered this unsolicited criticism to Read of his Penguin monograph on Paul Nash, a Slade classmate of Ben's and one of his resolute defenders:

you do these appreciations of an artist's work terribly well but a lot of it is an act of friendship rather than sound criticism. I think you give him a *scale* which he simply does not possess. . . . As a water colourist he is a master but as an oil-painter he is completely insensitive & hasn't the dimmest idea of how to handle the medium. That 'Soul visiting the

131

Mansions of the Dead' . . . surely it is an appalling piece of sissy sentimentalism?[33]

Nicholson is expressing disdain for a close friend's work to another close friend. The dislike is sincere enough, but it is done in a particularly cutting way which denigrates Read as well as Nash. Nicholson was fully aware that Read was supposedly more comfortable with abstract as opposed to surrealistically inspired work, and he is capitalizing upon that. He is also trying to manipulate the opinion of an influential critic.

In 1933, as soon as he became involved in Unit One activities, Read, who lived only four doors down from Nicholson, knew full well that he would have to balance two factions. To remedy a potentially divisive situation, he devised an 'emetic' – a questionnaire, which he hoped would trigger responses, if not direct answers, to the questions posed. Read's own concerns seep through in this document: did they consciously use symbolism? were they influenced by Freud? were they interested in machinery? did they use numerical proportions? did they wish to retain the natural appearance of objects? did they create designs which had no apparent relation to natural objects? 'Do you believe that art in England must develop on national lines or do you think that the art of the future will be completely international?'

The diverse answers he received to his questions did not disconcert him, Read improbably claimed. Society was in transition and, consequently, unfixed. Did not artists have the right to similar anomalies and inconsistencies? This allowed him to balance Nicholson's metaphysical abstraction against Edward Wadsworth's naturalistic abstraction. Read approvingly clung to Moore's claim that only the observation of nature keeps the artist from working to formula. Read added: 'But nature, in this sense, includes such relatively abstract things as pebbles and bones.' Read's brush with university life is transparently evident: 'the very potent wine of modernism will never be poured into the old bottles of the academic tradition. . . . "Academic" has become a term of abuse, and it may never be possible to redeem it.' Overall, the Unit One book displays the seeds of dissension within the group. In late 1934, a vote was held to determine which members were to survive – a unanimously favourable response being required to retain membership. Only the two middle-men, Nash and Moore, passed the test.

Moore's political sense – in contrast to Nicholson – was subdued and remarkably subtle. In 1933, he earned £300 a year as a teacher at the Chelsea School of Art, his income being supplemented erratically by the sale of sculptures, the materials for which were expensive. When Read arrived at Belsize Park in 1933, Moore received him as a friend, but he knew that Read's rapidly rising position as the defender of modernism in England could be extremely advantageous to him. He arranged for Zwemmer to pay the relatively large sum of £20 for an introduction of a few thousand words to the 1934 book, the first devoted to him. Moore also made a contribution to the printing expenses. To a large extent, Moore's eventual international acclaim can be linked to Read's partisan sponsorship, as in his concluding remarks to the Zwemmer book:

> The life of an original artist of any kind . . . is hard; only an unfailing integrity of purpose can carry him through those years of financial failure, of public neglect or derision, which are his inevitable lot. All but a few are compelled to compromise. There has been no compromise in the life of Henry Moore, and now, in the fullness of his powers, he offers us the perfected product of his genius.

This purplish passage could be autobiography as well as biography. In 1933–4 Hepworth's sculptures were decidedly non-representational, her work less organically based than Moore's – and it had greater subtlety in nuance and transitions. It should have appealed to Read with greater force than Moore's.

Meanwhile, in part inspired by his Hampstead friends, Read wrote during a six weeks' holiday in the summer of 1934 – 'an unexpected break' – his only novel, *The Green Child*. He built a wooden hut, six by four feet, in the garden behind No. 3 and wrote 'incurrente calamo'. Earlier that summer, he confided to Edith Wharton: 'I am in London again, editing the Burlington Magazine and writing dull practical books. But I am bound by a contract to produce a "work of fiction" this year, so something must happen.'[34]

Just after the war, Read had hoped to become a novelist like Wharton or Henry James. Now, he used his unanticipated freedom to write fiction, but not the classical kind of Jamesian novel he had once envisioned. Just at the time he was praising paintings and sculptures which used designs which had no apparent relation to natural objects, he moved away from the psychological reality of the fiction which he had once held sacred. Automatism and surrealism liberated his abilities as a writer of fiction: *The Green Child* has a casual disregard for the usual laws of cause and effect. He told a friend in 1936: 'It was queer how the book wrote itself; I had nothing much to invent – only the local colour. The details of the myth were waiting in my mind. And it was only afterwards that I began to see their significance.'[35]

133

Much later, Read assured Jung: 'it was . . . the spontaneous elaboration of an Old English legend. . . . I hope no one will ever accuse me of having consciously written a fantasy to illustrate Jungian themes.'[36] And yet Read must have been aware of such possibilities when he wrote the book, which tells the life story of a Yorkshireman, Oliver, who as Olivero becomes president of a republic in South America, renounces power and returns to his native county. There, he finds a stream running back to its source and, while investigating this phenomenon, witnesses and then interrupts a grisly night scene in which Kneeshaw, the miller, is forcing a woman to eat. 'It was then that he noticed a peculiarity in her flesh. . . . The skin was . . . a faint green shade . . . and through its pallor the branches of her veins and arteries spread, not blue and scarlet, but vivid green and gold.'

Suddenly, Olivero remembers the Green Child who appeared on the day he abandoned Yorkshire. He then reminds Kneeshaw that he had been his teacher, having left the village because the pupil had wilfully broken a model railway engine, which spilled out on to the floor like a disembowelled animal. 'When that spring snapped, something snapped in my mind.' The two men fight, the miller is accidentally drowned, Olivero and the Green Child flee and follow the stream's *ascending* beck until they reach its source, step on quicksand, and sink below the surface of the pool. The two adventurers descend within a bubble of air and then ascend into a pool in the caverns where the Green People live. This Hades-like world is one of precise order, devoid of passion. Olivero is initiated into this alien culture where he eventually dies, thus becoming part of the 'crystal harmony' of his new race.

The narrative is not told in chronological order: the encounter with Kneeshaw and the Green Child in Part I is written as a modern fairy tale; Part II – which occupies more than half the book – is concerned with Olivero's picaresque adventures and rise to power and is the only portion of this work which adheres to the conventions of nineteenth-century fiction; after this elaborate flashback, Part III takes up where Part I leaves off and has a superreal quality similar to the visit to the Houyhnhnms in Book IV of *Gulliver's Travels*. Read, commenting on the structure of his book to Richard Church, said it was a triptych: the different parts 'represent three aspects of existence: Recollection, Action and Contemplation. It is not quite the same as Inferno, Purgatory and Paradise, because I don't believe in hell, or even in remorse.'[37] He told another friend that the 'day-dream-world' of Part I led to action. 'But Action inevitably leads to disillusionment, retreat, contemplation.'[38]

134

Jung certainly had reason to suspect that this fable had been written under his influence. Kneeshaw can be seen as a dark shadow of the protagonist; the Green Child is an anima or soul-image, with whom Olivero undergoes a symbolic baptism. Read's claim that he did not knowingly construct the book to such a prescription must be accepted. However, he must have been aware of his hero's Voltaire-like condemnation of the Jesuits, and Catholic rite may have been his target in the sinister eucharist Kneeshaw attempts to administer. Somewhat dubious is Read's assertion that he did a modicum of research on the South American scenes in Part II. W. H. Hudson's heroine Rima in *Green Mansions* is clearly mirrored in the Green Child, and Olivero's journey over the pampas recalls the same author's *The Purple Land* and *El Omber*. And Read must have had Hudson's *The Crystal Age* in mind. The protagonists in that book live in a passionless society not unlike that of the Green People. Read had read Hudson during the war, and it could be that Hudson's influence operated on a subliminal level in 1934. The source to which Read freely admitted was 'The Green Children' from Keightley's *Fairy Mythology*.

What is apparent is that *The Green Child* is deeply auto-biographical, probably to a much greater degree than Read was aware. As a child, he had been expelled from his earthly paradise by his father's death; after a traumatic incident, Oliver chooses exile from Yorkshire. Since Read saw *The Green Child* as a continuation of *The Innocent Eye*, the encounter between Oliver and Kneeshaw – recalling the circumstances of Oliver's departure for South America and war – dramatizes the trauma of Read's leave-taking of 1914. Also, a contrast is developed between the man who seeks his fortune away from Yorkshire and the man who stays behind. Kneeshaw, vastly different from the character of the same name in 'Kneeshaw Goes to War', is brutish, but he is a man of the soil: 'He was unread and almost inarticulate, facing the problems of life with direct instincts, acting from day to day as these instincts dictated.' Also, before his encounter with Olivero, Kneeshaw had shown kindness to the Green Child, to whom he is married. In contrast, Olivero is more sophisticated and compassionate, but he lacks Kneeshaw's earthiness.

Read's desire to return to Yorkshire as against his uncertainty whether he had lost touch with his roots is dramatized in the struggle between the two men. Read's early conflicts with his family – particularly his mother – are also encapsulated here. The arrogant young man whose destiny lies outside Yorkshire is contrasted to Kneeshaw, who represents those left behind.

135

The colourful, exotic locales of the middle portion of *The Green Child* tend to obscure its martial atmosphere, and war had long been a subject of Read's poems and semi-fictional prose. Oliver becomes Olivero and, in a similar way, the war helped to transform the personality of young Herbert Read from Yorkshire countryman to worldly sophisticate. Olivero becomes a leader through mistaken identity, and Read may be commenting on his own unlikely heroism. Olivero's political power is a form of benign dictatorship. When he becomes tired of wielding control, he arranges his own assassination. Read's anarchy, his own lack of enthusiasm for any kind of established political system, is obliquely dramatized in this portion of the narrative.

The journey Olivero and the Green Child take to her anaemic homeland occupies the final portion of the book. Olivero too readily accepts the Utopian vision, especially the concept of an art linked to crystals which

> while retaining the apparent structure of each class, departed from the strict natural order in some subtle way. Aesthetic pleasure was a perception of the degree of transgression between the artificial form and its natural prototype, and the greatest æsthetic emotion was aroused by those crystals which transgressed most within the limits of probability.

As he comes to die, Olivero envisions himself becoming a piece of crystal:

> All absolute things, absolute beauty and absolute good, and the essence or the true nature of everything, these are not apprehended by the fickle senses, but achieved by the body itself when it casts off the worm that has devoured it and filled it with itches and desires, and takes on a state of crystalline purity. . . . having got rid of the fluctuations of the spirit, we shall be pure and become part of the universal harmony, and know in ourselves the law of the physical universe, which is no other than the law of truth.

These passages reflect many ideas developed in *Art Now*, but *The Green Child* ends in a cold, sardonic way, its protagonist becoming, as it were, a piece of abstract sculpture. Life has imitated art. At a conscious level, Read may have meant the ending as a defence of geometric modernism, especially that movement's often uneasy tension between 'artificial form' and 'natural prototype'. However, he was well aware that most Utopian works consciously undermine the perfect states being described.

In 1949, Read acknowledged that there was a 'certain sense in which form kills life, and my "Green Child" was written to demonstrate that fact'. More importantly, the strength of *The Green Child* resides in the elements of automatism and surrealism which give it its hypnotic power: the nightmarish encounter between Kneeshaw and Olivero, the rapid transitions between the landscape of Yorkshire and the sub-terranean residence of the Green People, the sheer amount of fantasy in the evocation of those creatures, the fairy-tale ambience of the Green Child's earthly existence. Although he would later claim that surrealism was essentially an English impulse, Read's power in his only long piece of fiction comes, paradoxically, from his ability to employ the form of modernism to which he had consigned a secondary place in his own aesthetics.

Read's claim of 1937 for the extraordinary transformation surrealism effected on Paul Nash could well be a defence of his efforts in *The Green Child*:

> We are – in poetry as well as in painting – still very much at the stage of experimenting with the dream world. It is not a tractable world; the dream is elusive, and its essential element, the symbol which gives it its strange logic, is the first to escape us. And it is possible that the dream world is a dead or deathly world. . . . The perfect poem or the perfect painting is something more than a dream; it is that synthesis of the dream and of reality which surrealism has represented as the desirable attainment, but rarely attains.

The conflicts in Read readily manifested in *The Green Child* did not escape Wyndham Lewis, who told him in January 1938: 'What you do yourself in the literary art is so perfectly dissimilar from what you so pertinaciously push in the visual art that the secret of this duality would be for me quite impenetrable had I not known you in the days when Hulme was lecturing on "Abstract Art".'[39]

Was Read Olivero who is divorced from his origins or was he Oliver, the man who leaves Yorkshire but who must return there? Was the cold subterranean existence of the Green People where he belonged or was his true allegiance to the earth of his native county? Does the book end in Paradise or Inferno? *The Green Child* is filled with unsettled conflicts, its strength deriving from its uneasy swerving motions, its haunting open-endedness. The choices in 'Apology for E.S.' were easy; they are not so here.

In any event, Read felt that he had unlocked his creativity in a sustained piece of prose fiction. Still, he was desperately afraid that he did not have a future as a creative writer – would he exist *only* as an interpreter of other people's work? *The Innocent Eye* in 1932, 'The End

137

of a War' in 1933 and now *The Green Child* seemed to belie that fear. Was his 'wandering wakeful spirit' at long last about to be fulfilled?[40]

9   Brave, New Machine World

The mid-thirties were, as Read dubbed them in a short poem, 'Inbetweentimes', placed 'above the shadows and the dust / secure in an alien night'. An uneasy, false sense of security had filled him as early as 1930, when in the German elections the Nazis gained 107 seats from the centre parties. A certainty of impending doom is vividly captured in 'A Northern Legion' where a historical incident – a Roman war party marching forward to extinction – is likened to the eventual fall of Europe.

> Endless their anxiety
> marching into a northern darkness: approaching
> a narrow defile, the waters falling fearfully
> the clotting menace of shadows and all the multiple
> instruments of death in ambush against them.

In 1933, Hitler became Chancellor of Germany and the Enabling Law giving him dictatorial powers was enacted; the boycott of Jews had begun. Despite the enormous popularity of Oswald Mosley, many prominent refugees chose England, Hampstead in particular. Walter Gropius, the former Director of the Bauhaus, arrived in 1934 and went into practice with the architect Maxwell Fry; László Moholy-Nagy, later to be Director of the New Bauhaus in Chicago, left Germany for Amsterdam in 1934, moving to England a year later. The architect Eric Mendelsohn came that year, as did the designer Marcel Breuer. The Russian Constructivist Naum Gabo settled in Fortune Green Road in 1936 and two years later a studio was found for Piet Mondrian at 60 Parkhill Road, Moore's street. Now, at Herbert and Ludo's, one could encounter the solemn dignified company of Gropius or find oneself face to face with slow-smiling Moholy-Nagy. The tranquillity of the Mall Studios was partially disturbed when Barbara Hepworth gave birth to triplets on 3 October 1934. Read and Rayner Heppenstall were playing rummy, and Ben looked in every now and then to report progress and

139

take a hand. Realizing how much her work would be disrupted, Barbara cried – despite Ben's cheerfulness – for days.

Although the frightening surge of Nazism was apparent in England by 1934, hope still prevailed, a sense that renewal was still possible if – somehow – a design for living, previously hidden, could be uncovered. From 1919, the Bauhaus had preached a doctrine of functionalism in which excesses of the past could be stripped from design and architecture. The resulting spare and sometimes severe lines were meant to suggest a life reduced to essentials, in which all men could live in harmony. The Bauhaus also stressed the centrality in modern life of the designer–craftsman who could, if given a chance, infuse industry with his vision. England's response to the gospel of the Bauhaus can be most readily seen in Sun House on Frognal Way, Kent House on Ferdinand Street in Chalk Farm, the Penguin Pool at London Zoo, and the Highgate High Point Flats. The earliest of these buildings is Lawn Road Flats, which was opened in July 1934. Wells Coates, the dapper, volatile Canadian engineer-turned architect, persuaded Jack and Molly Pritchard to finance this commitment to transient living. According to Coates, permanent tangible possessions were a burden – life now had to be devoted to travel, new experiences, 'freedom'.[1] Coates' boldly modern building, likened by a later resident, Agatha Christie, to a giant ocean liner moored against a bank of trees, had 'minimum' flats but compactness was offset by services: bed-making, shoe-cleaning, laundry collection, window-cleaning and hot meals from a central kitchen. From 1937, an 'Isobar' on the ground floor even provided snacks. Ludo did not like the rook pie which the Flats' cookery club prepared one evening, and she was distracted by the kindly Gropius' broken, baby English. He told her that immediately upon arrival in England he had been stirred by the signs 'Take Courage', thinking how 'wonderful it was that the English should be so moral as to have such huge advertisements'.[2]

In 'The Nuncio', Read gives a vivid portrait of the power of the new architecture, largely inspired by the Bauhaus:

> Our structures are of steel and glass
> their subtle struts not obvious
> we build with space in space
> and by ingenuity produce
> our aerial houses high towers
> our winding stairs –
> all is in light

above-board and ought
to win the approval of the masses.

These lines are spoken by the insidious Nuncio, and Read's own reservations about architectural Utopias can be gleaned here.

It was impossible to know in 1934 if England was poised for extinction or rebirth. Despite trepidations about the coming of a 'Hitler Terror', Read tried to provide in *Art and Industry* (published in October 1934) a blueprint for renewal, building upon *Art Now*:

> at every stage we need the abstract artist, the artist who orders materials till they combine the highest degree of practical economy with the greatest measure of spiritual freedom. . . . The artist must design in the actual materials of the factory, and in the full stream of the process of production. His power must be absolute in all matters of design, and within the limits of functional efficiency, the factory must adapt itself to the artist, not the artist to the factory.

The shifting political climate of the thirties led Read to veer between two opposing claims. Here, he asserts that artists can change society. At other times, in a more pessimistic mood, he saw the artist's destiny being shaped by society.

Art and Industry is a freely acknowledged crib of Bauhaus doctrine, denouncing design based on outdated notions of ornament. The products of English factories are meaningless, Read claims, because they do not touch the spiritual lives of the consumers. Abstract art, however, has the power to counteract this degenerate tendency. Two heroes from the past emerge in the book, Josiah Wedgwood and William Morris: 'Wedgwood was the industrialist who thought of art as something external which he could import and use; Morris was the artist who thought of industry as something inconsistent with art, and which must therefore be reformed or abolished.' English industry must revert to these earlier, sane principles, Read maintains. He also takes the opportunity to denigrate art education in England: 'But if academic education may with benefit be abolished, another form of education, education in appreciation, must be developed. The general principles of harmony and proportion, and the development of sensuous and intellectual perceptivity, must be taught on a new and extensive scale, especially at the elementary stage of education.' Nine years later, in *Education Through Art*, Read fully developed these proposals.

The impact of *Art and Industry* ultimately resides not in the text – which rehearses ideas, although in a more focused way, from *The Meaning of Art* and *Art Now* – but in its illustrations of chairs, radios,

141

sofas, cooking utensils by Chermayeff, Mies van der Rohe, Aalto; porcelain by the State Porcelain Works in Berlin and Wedgwood; fountain pens by Montblanc. These are juxtaposed to classical and early industrial designs, which were carefully selected as harbingers of the kind of modern design being promoted by Read. Abstraction is shown to be a natural tendency in the history of design.

Read, fully aware that this book should exemplify contemporary style, insisted that Herbert Bayer, a student at the Bauhaus under Kandinsky and Moholy-Nagy, be the designer. Stanley Morison, himself an inventive typographer, was furious, venting his spleen to a colleague: 'This Mr Bayer, not content with being ignorant of the function of italics, deepens his ignorance by wilfully shutting his eyes to the utility of capitals.'[3] Nash, a friend of Morison's, had been advocating – particularly in *Room and Book* two years earlier – notions of interior design virtually identical to Read's. The painter was also fussy about layout, telling Read on 17 November 1934 that he liked this aspect of the book. He then commented on the illustrations: 'It makes me rather sick to see how good most of our English earlier work *was*. . . . How excellent most of the German & Dutch stuff *is*.'[4] In his review, 'Art and Machine Now' in the *Listener*, Noël Carrington attacked Bayer's virtuosity but was sympathetic to the book itself: 'The gist of Mr Read's æsthetic creed is that machine art must be *abstract art* and that in trying to make it conform to laws of humanistic art . . . we have been merely on a false track.'[5]

In 1933, Read had favourably reviewed Stephen Spender's *Poems* in the *Adelphi*: 'Mr Spender is conscious of his social heritage of chaos and despair, and is moved to rebellion, and even to hope.'[6] By September 1934, the twenty-five-year-old Spender and Read had become friends, the younger man telling the other that he looked forward to the new edition of his poems. He also commiserated with him: 'I do hope that you won't have to go on doing the kind of work you dislike.'[7] Although Read did not share Spender's at this time zealous Marxism, their rapport introduced each man to opposing points of view: the plain diction and political concerns of Spender mingling with the symbolism and automatism of Read.

The two men also discussed sexuality. Read once told Spender that he thought a person could choose or not choose to be a homosexual. Read was well aware of such an inclination within himself. This is evident in the dream poem, 'Love and Death', from about 1935, where homoeroticism, latently expressed in the war poems, is confronted directly. Here the speaker, immured in the 'stink and lust of urban life', is sleepless. From the shadows of the street a girl emerges; the speaker takes her to his room. 'Her dress she soon discards / And falls into my arms and laughs and cries / And tells me life was sad until I came.' The speaker romances the girl against a landscape of golden sand and endless fields of evergreen. She, it turns out, is a mirage and is followed by a boy dressed in rags.

> Once again
> The figure strips and stands
> Lank and angular against the glow.
> His eyes are sunk so deep I cannot see
> Their colour, nor discover their intent.
> His cheeks are drawn about his jaw
> And every joint articulate.
> He puts his bony hand against my breast.
> I do not shrink – indeed, I feel
> His still appeal and in his mind
> Find a cool retreat.

The landscape now becomes an icy shore with swollen waves. The muffled sound of guns in the distance pushes the poem back to the war, the landscape of *Naked Warriors*. Suddenly, the dream dissolves, as fog drifts in over the empty street. In the bed are the girl and the boy 'lying enlaced'. The speaker knows they are dead.

In the clear Freudian context in which Read conceived the poem, the life instinct (love) is contrasted to the death instinct, heterosexual love being associated with renewal, homosexuality with 'arctic waste'. All men die, the conclusion of the poem shows, but there are various ways to live and die: one can choose an existence which runs contrary to the death instinct or one can lead a life which is a form of death. The speaker in the poem probably mirrors conflicts within the poet himself. The thin, undernourished boy may be a symbolic recreation of Read's continuing sense of having been pushed abruptly from childhood to adulthood without the benefit of a real adolescence.

When he read *The Green Child*, Spender told Read that it 'communicates a whole world of experience, a world with a heaven, and hell and with an order in life'.[8] Such praise was especially welcome in the wake of Frank Morley's open dislike of the novel: 'Couldn't there have been *some* belly in part 2, some drink somewhere, some honest fucking? Ain't you no pity? You kill your readers like flies.'[9] Richard Aldington told Read that Faber had acted 'shabbily'[10] in rejecting the book and advised him to approach Heinemann, who published the book the following year. At that time, Aldington finally persuaded that firm to take Read on as a 'literary adviser' at £350 a year.[11]

Meanwhile, Josiah Wedgwood wrote to Read about *Art and Industry*: 'It contains, I think, the best critical appreciation of the old Josiah Wedgwood, that I have read.'[12] Read's unstinting praise of Wedgwood the firm was based in large part on his admiration for its wares, such as the bowls and vases of the transplanted New Zealand architect turned ceramic designer, Keith Murray. His designs, strongly influenced by classical pottery, are done in a variety of angular shapes which reflect Bauhaus austerity. At Harrods or Selfridges, their muted colours contrasted sharply with the exuberant fantasies of Clarice Cliff.

In November, Read was – embarrassingly – caught in a crossfire between Edith Sitwell and her sworn enemies, F. R. Leavis, Wyndham Lewis and Geoffrey Grigson. That was the month she published *Aspects of Modern Poetry*, a book meant to set the 'brickbats flying'. Unfortunately, the brickbats bounced back on her when one reviewer noticed that she had plagiarized Leavis; then, Grigson pointed out parallels between what Read had written about Hopkins' sprung rhythm in *Form in Modern Poetry* and her treatment of Hopkins. Read later told Denton Welch: 'I can't go on saying that I don't believe a word of what Grigson wrote. You know what these things are. One can never put them right it seems – especially with the Sitwells.' He paused. 'Conceit isn't the word to describe their attitude. It's a sort of arrogance due, I think, to their loveless childhood.'[13] Read was not pleased to receive a snappish letter in December from Wyndham Lewis, with an accusation that he had authored a nasty squib against him in the *TLS*: 'I had not thought of you as a politician . . . and a Yes-man to all the gushings relative to Jesus, Keats, Lawrence and Marx.' Read, as he was pleased to inform the paranoid Lewis, had not written the offending piece.

So removed and hostile was Read in January 1935 to the academic life that he could, ungrudgingly, congratulate W. G. Constable on his appointment as Slade Professor at Cambridge. Read had also become increasingly annoyed with the cold shoulder given to *The Green Child* by Faber and Faber. He told Heppenstall: 'Frank Morley objected to the book because there was no sex in it; wanted me to introduce a bawdy scene or two to make things more human.'[14]

In general, Read had strong convictions – fuelled by Aldington – about the unfairness inherent in the author–publisher relationship. When Geoffrey Faber issued *A Publisher Speaking* in 1934, Read asked Victor Gollancz – known for his strong socialist convictions – to review the book. Gollancz declined; he felt that Faber and many

144

other of his ilk had not yet realized that the diseases inherent in publishing were 'merely one aspect of the general disease of Capitalism in its final crisis'.[15] Read took matters into his own hands in a piece for the *London Mercury*: 'The Sweated Author'. Here he catalogued the sorry state of publishing, in which books were not sufficiently advertised and the wrong authors promoted. Such firms 'bring books down to the level of all other popular articles – magazines, cosmetics, chocolates – everything attractive but ephemeral'. Then Read castigated royalty rates: 'Even the coal miner and the fisherman receive a greater proportion of their labour than does the author.' Finally, he proposed a solution: an Authors' Co-Operative Publishing Group, which would handle production and distribution (by mail) of its wares.[16] As we have seen, Frank Rutter and Read had seriously considered such a venture immediately after the war. Gollancz objected to this proposal: 'Could your scheme conceivably work in a Capitalist world? Isn't the right course rather to concentrate entirely on smashing the system – and using every Capitalist weapon to do so?'[17] In a less heated fashion, Leonard Woolf liked the plan, although the manner of distribution might 'debauch' the buyer who liked to browse in bookshops: 'The publishers and booksellers between them are destroying the sale of books other than "best-sellers" and publishing is already little more than a gamble in which the only thing aimed at is the creation by hook or crook of a "best-seller".'[18]

Leonard's February letter seemed to bring about a rapprochement between the Hogarth Press and its former author, when Virginia and Leonard were invited by Herbert and Ludo to dinner with the Moores on 19 February. However, Virginia continued to gaze at Read with a very jaundiced eye. He had once betrayed her, and he had set himself up as the successor of her close friend, Roger Fry, who had died the year before and whose life she published in 1940. In passages such as this, Read had challenged Fry's dominance: 'faced with the machine, mass production and universal education, [he] could only retreat into the private world of his own sensibility.'[19] In this passage, Read, in a not particularly deft way, is cutting out his own terrain.

That evening, Virginia was bristling because of an argument with Clive Bell. She arrived 'parched & throbbing'. The studio was comfortless, the wine skimpy and the conversation much too sensible: 'Respectable Bohemia is a little cheerless. . . . steel chairs, clear pale colours . . . brainy talk, specialists' talk.' The Omega Workshops had not produced comfortable furniture but at least their pieces had been bright and colourful, she must have thought. Here, in the confrontation

145

between Bloomsbury and Hampstead – between an older modernism and one seeking to replace it – Woolf thought Read looked 'devitalised', his face resembling that of a 'shop assistant'.[20]

Woolf, whose nervousness as a hostess was sometimes evident in a distraught handshake and smile of welcome, is using her own claim to literary aristocracy as the daughter of Sir Leslie Stephen to put Read in his yeoman place. Her dislike of Read has to be weighed carefully, nevertheless. Read was obviously wary and nervous in her presence. He was not a talkative person, never easily engaging in small talk. And yet he could be excessively cautious, too measured in deciding what was the right thing to do. Woolf homed in on that side of Read in her diary entry. Ludo had been put off at Virginia's loud, ringing words on entering their home, 'Is this a stable?' and she noticed that Leonard was exceedingly nervous: his palsy was more evident than usual as he ate his soup. Despite these drawbacks, Irina, Ludo and Virginia chatted politely about pots. Read had such an incident in mind when Michael Meyer asked him his opinion of Virginia Woolf: 'Remarkable, but the cattiest woman I have ever known.'

A month later, Virginia gleefully told her diary that Tom Eliot had criticized the lack of sensuality in Read's poetry.[21] Her mischievous side was further aroused that June, when Eliot told her of his party for Herbert, Ludo, her sister Maymay and Munza Braunfels. Eliot, an ardent practical joker, had armed himself with fireworks and chocolates that he thought were filled with sawdust. The 'greedy' guests eagerly consumed the chocolates, which turned out to be made of soap. In a fury, they 'set upon' the surprised Eliot who became so flustered that he forgot to set off the fireworks until his guests were at the doorstep, waiting for the taxi which was to take them back to Hampstead.[22]

That was Eliot's side of the story. He neglected to tell Virginia that, as soon as his guests arrived, he regaled the ladies with his adventures at a nudist house in London, where he had gone one evening, had his clothes leisurely stripped off, and proceeded to warm his bottom by the fireside. Ludo, Maymay and Munza did not know whether he was telling the truth, but they realized that he was trying to shock them. The women, dressed in flapper finery, were trying to look worldly. Eliot decided to put their sophistication to the test. The ladies were unnerved – and offended. Maymay, who had a fierce temper, was particularly aghast and, when she bit into one of the trick chocolates, she grabbed one from the box and shoved it into Eliot's mouth. Startled, he yelled at her: 'Mind my falsers!'

In a slightly more serious vein, Read fought with Eric Gill in 1935.

146

Even more insistent than Read on the emotional forces inherent in creativity, the sculptor insisted: 'The artist is not a special kind of man; every man is a special kind of artist.' Read maintained that art was a skill.

> It was at this point that Gill and I, in our discussions, used to diverge, for I insist that art is not merely skill to make, but also skill to express. 'Express what?' Gill would ask; and if I was careless enough to use a phrase like 'To express his personality,' Gill would be at me with the mallet and chisel he kept in his mind no less than in his hands, demanding if I had ever seen a personality, and how in God's name it could be expressed except in the making of something.

Read told Heppenstall: 'Gill's doctrine is rank heresy. . . . Great art was never written tongue in cheek (nor with penis erect).'[23]

Increasingly discouraged by constant scraping to keep financially alive, Read was reduced to writing 'straight one day a week, and spending the rest of the time trying to educate the public'. His success with *The Green Child* had convinced him that his abilities as a writer of fiction lay with fantasy. Henry James had reached 'near the top of Everest, and there's no room on that peak'.

In the summer of 1935, Herbert and Ludo rented Charleston, Vanessa Bell's house at Firle in Sussex. Since Ludo was playing the viola in the Glyndebourne orchestra, this was an ideal location for a summer holiday. The then balletomane, Rayner Heppenstall, 'broke and ill-housed', was invited to stay with them. Later that autumn, Heppenstall sent Read a damning review of *Art and Industry* , leading to these explosions from the offended author.

> Your review of Art and Industry is really rather pointless and stupid. . . . you give the impression that my book is the latest variety of Bloomsbury aesthetics.
> So now you've got this bug about luxury trades! Who are you to dictate what people shall spend their money on? Just another remnant of the good old puritan tradition. If they want to spend their national dividend on cosmetics and motor-cars, why shouldn't they? And hell, is there a more luxurious luxury than ballet dancing, about which you manage to be pretty serious? And god, it is just as important for a teapot to be right as it is for Karsavina to go through her paces properly. It is more important, for the teapot dances in every proletarian home, and at present only the rich can afford Covent Garden. . . . You miss the whole significance of my book, and perhaps of more than my book – of Ben Nicholson, for example. Don't be misled by the stupid word *abstract*; life, in this sense, is very abstract.[24]

A bit earlier, in June, Read had quarrelled with Stephen Spender about *Murder in the Cathedral*, which was first performed that month in the Chapter House of Canterbury Cathedral. Spender could not stomach Read's hostility, probably generated by anti-religious sentiments: 'Personally, I find it extremely beautiful. What I like so much is that Eliot is at all events mature: every year he has lived, all his suffering goes into what he writes.'[25] Read was still desperately trying to find his own centre as a writer. He lacked Eliot's serene religious assurance, his insecurity leading to mild invective.

Eliot was the person who indirectly introduced Read to Henry Miller, the American writer *par excellence* of the phallus. In June 1935, Eliot had told Miller, in a letter not meant for publication, that *Tropic of Cancer* – accused by some of being obscene – was 'a rather magnificent piece of work. . . . Several friends to whom I have shown it, including Mr Herbert Read, share my admiration. . . . Without drawing any generation comparisons, your own book is a great deal better both in depth of insight and of course in the actual writing than *Lady Chatterley's Lover*.' Naturally, Miller asked permission to put these unguarded comments into print. Eliot demurred but eventually his remarks were trimmed to: 'a very remarkable book . . . a rather magnificent piece of work'.[26] Miller, eager for more adulation, got in touch with Read, who told him about the *Burlington Magazine*, expressed some political opinions, and agreed with Miller that censorship was a totalitarian nuisance. Miller was delighted with his new friend, expressing his views with not always refreshing frankness: 'And this high-brow magazine you edit – can't I see a copy of it? High-brow! What's high-brow anyway? . . . Fucking around with the world, with the social pattern, the economic status, the mores, the prejudices, etc. – just a sheer waste of time. . . . This whole question of obscenity – I admit to being obscene. I want to be more obscene. I see nothing wrong with it.'[27]

Later in 1935, Miller chastised Read about *Essential Communism*, a pamphlet which attempts to demonstrate how the poet must be detached from all political systems, be they Marxist or fascist. Read claims that great artists are devoid of ideologies, asserting as a corollary that politicians should not attempt to impose ideology upon artists. Slyly, he observes that revolution in art and revolution in politics have never moved hand in hand, the beliefs of a Joyce or a Marx veering in vastly different directions. Ultimately, the artist is an individual, but one whose existence is vital to society. 'A proletarian economy without art is a practical futility. Culture, and not material civilization, is the continuing force in a society.'

In order to plan a valid economic life, governments cannot grant 'absolute liberty' to individuals. 'For, as long as we live in a community, in all practical affairs the greatest goal of the greatest number is also the greatest good of the individual. As intellectuals (a penniless class, it is true) we must be willing to surrender all material rights – to let the state take our property and put it into the common fund.' This kind of structure can be tolerated economically; however, intellectual liberty is then sacrificed. This becomes intolerable:

> The economic issues are in [Germany, Italy and Russia] confused by political opportunism. But one issue, and one only, emerges when all temporary and tactical considerations have been dismissed: the issue between capitalism and communism. Even fascism, if we are to believe its theoretical exponents, is socialistic, the aim being to control the means of production and distribution. . . . The essential doctrine of all reforming parties is communism; they only differ in the sincerity with which they profess the ideal, and in the means they adopt to realize it. Some find the means more attractive than the end.

Read's anarchist convictions now leap to the surface, capitalism being linked to the other 'essential communisms'. In the face of all these ideologies, Read proposes a 'leisure society – a society giving full opportunity for the education and development of the mind'. In a moving passage, perhaps recalling himself as a teenager, Read touches on the 'ordinary man': 'From the age of fourteen he is caught up in an endless treadmill; he has neither time nor opportunity to feed his undeveloped senses – he must snatch at the diuretic pablum of the newspapers and the radio, and as a consequence, tread the mill with more urgency.' The essay ends on a note of optimism. Although Read does not believe in the perfectibility of man, he asserts his confidence in the persuadability of man to achieve a society in which there will be neither poverty nor injustice. In this piece, Read holds no brief for any system of government, maintaining that they employ various artificial means to hold their subjects in thrall.

Henry Miller doubted that great artists were devoid of ideologies. He agreed that the only worthwhile revolution was spiritual. And he asked: 'Isn't Communism a sad *end*, rather than a beginning?'[28] Cautiously, Read would have answered yes, but he would have made a list that included nazism, fascism and capitalism. When pressed by Wyndham Lewis, however, Read came down on the side of Russia. 'I share all your aversion for their prophets and protagonists, their dialectical materialism is silly and shallow, but at least they are on the side of abstract intellectual ideals as opposed to the instinctive irrational prejudices of the other side; and they are opposed to the tradition of bourgeois capitalism which has never been any use to an artist (until he is dead).'[29]

On 18 June 1935, Read filed a petition for the dissolution of his marriage to Evelyn. That autumn, he and Ludo were ill constantly with a form of infectious jaundice, carried, Read told Heppenstall, by rats: 'but we can boast nothing bigger than mice. But it clogs the brain & reduces one to a drowsy incapacity.'[30] The New Year was to bring better health and marriage. The divorce was granted on 20 January 1936, and Herbert and Ludo were married at the Register Office, Hampstead on 12 February. They honeymooned, apparently with another couple, in northern Spain. Years later, Ludo, recalling that their stay had not been a success, noted that it had rained constantly.

Read's second marriage brought, he later reminisced, 'intense disagreements about most things – religion, society, friendships, and even domicile'. But it also had two important blessings: 'physical affinity and mutual respect'.[31] However, in an undated, saturnine piece of verse many years later Read wrote:

> Tired of this lonely life
> Gone to find another wife.
> HR
> Couldn't find one. Shot myself
> You'll find my body on the larder shelf.[32]

Although he claimed that his correspondence with Aldington had suddenly ceased 'for no apparent reason' on the last day of 1935, Read did have in his possession a letter of 1936 in which Aldington upbraided him for 'silent treatment'. Several times, Aldington had intervened on Read's behalf with Heinemann: 'You said nothing about it afterwards, nor did you write me. . . . So I could only conclude that you were disappointed with the results. Perhaps you had every right to be, but I felt your silence was rather hard on me, since I had worked loyally on your behalf.'[33] Aldington's letter of 31 December 1935, Read said, expressed his concerns about his welfare: 'I was in temporary difficulties and Aldington, always kind and considerate to his friends, was trying to find me work with a London publisher.'

Read's uncharacteristic mendacity about the existence of the February 1936 letter reveals an unwillingness to deal with his harsh

150

behaviour towards an old but frequently difficult friend. Years after the events of 1936, he may have thought that he had wronged Aldington and wanted to keep the matter from scrutiny. Read was always careful to maintain the façade of a relatively untroubled, generous person. In this instance, his scrupulous regard for public opinion demonstrates the insecurity lurking behind the mask.

The year 1936 was frenetic for Read. On 9 May, he was briskly frank with Heppenstall: 'I have had one hell of a week – Monday and Tuesday in Leeds, Wednesday and Thursday in Cambridge, surrealist committees and dinner parties – all bluster and no brass.'[34] Ludo's sister Maymay, who was staying with the Reads, was being courted by the son of a Honolulu 'merchant prince . . . but she, though touched, is not, I am afraid, touched in the right spot'.[35] (Eventually, Maymay relented and married Francis Cooke.) That summer, the Reads were again at Charleston. Ludo was kept very busy 'mozarting' at Glyndebourne, and her husband wrote an essay for that company's prospectus. Thirteen-year-old John Read accompanied his father and Ludo to Dieppe that summer; he enjoyed the raspberry jam with brown bread served by the Braques. At the tail end of the year, the couple were in Aberdeen staying with Ludo's family.

Further disintegration of the tenuous critical bonds holding Read and Eliot together came this year with 'In Defence of Shelley', Read's most controversial piece of literary criticism. Three years earlier, Eliot had in *The Use of Poetry and the Use of Criticism* attacked Read's distinction between personality and character: 'Mr Herbert Read . . . pursues his speculations to a point to which I would not willingly follow him'; he 'seems to charge himself with the task of casting out devils'.[36]

Eliot was unwilling to delve into the origins of poetry, preferring to talk about its uses. For Read, poetry was a form of knowledge, whose foundations had to be explored. Also, Eliot was hostile to any form of psychoanalytical interpretation. In *The Use of Poetry*, Eliot had denigrated Shelley, whom he called 'immature', 'puerile', 'repellent' and 'shabby'. Read responded by espousing Shelley's personality, the source of his ideas.

According to Read, Shelley's personality was one which had not been able to emerge completely from the domination of his mother; therefore, he had not been able to establish a rapport between himself and the external world: his personality was not 'objectified'. Rather, Shelley's consciousness remained subjective, subjugated to un- conscious 'primary identification', leading to narcissism and homo- sexuality. 'Such unconscious homosexuality gives rise to a psychosis of

151

which Shelley shows all the normal symptoms. It determines a line of moral conduct which Shelley exhibits in his life.' Having mounted an argument about Shelley's existence which is open to serious doubt, Read praises Shelley and his poetry for 'failing to achieve something which is not in the nature of the poet'. What, then, is the nature of the poet?

A true poet, Read argues, is a neurotic whose abnormality is to be preferred to normality. Such a person expresses, 'with an unsurpassed perfection, qualities . . . which are of peculiar value to humanity'. Verse, Read is suggesting, is a pre-logical, pre-verbal and pre-conceptual kind of knowledge. Those who are stuck in the subjective world are most in touch with the origins of poetry and most able to find the words to express the non-verbal origins of consciousness.

As usual, this piece of Read's literary criticism is autobiographical. In the essay on Shelley, he may well have been reflecting on his relationship with Eliza and their many conflicts. As a young man, his intellectual and artistic pursuits had come into conflict with her stern views of reality. She may have inhibited some of his earliest artistic impulses, leaving him in a subjective state against which he rebelled.

In the final analysis, this piece is far more interesting for what it reveals about Read than for its contribution to the study of Shelley. In 1935–6, Read began to discern cracks in his attempt, through his new marriage and his Hampstead existence, to take charge of his life in a profoundly different way. He remained unsettled and insecure. The essay on Shelley attempts to look at his own origins as a poet, to recognize his divided self, to put form to the chaos in which he once again found himself. He angrily told the as usual self-righteous Heppenstall that his 'pioneer' psychological apparatus in the Shelley essay did not deserve a sneer. An unstinting search for truth was for Read a form of heroism.

10   Surrealism and Spain

'I have come from London, where a new edition of the Bible has been published with an introduction by Herbert Read.'[1] This was the greeting in 1936 of Joseph Bard, the Hungarian painter, to Geoffrey Grigson upon meeting him at Île de Port Cros. Fame often breeds envy and then sarcasm. It also brought Read an increasingly precarious position in the volatile world of contemporary art, as he tried to rein in the conflicting schools of abstraction and surrealism: 'I was in the position of a circus rider with his feet placed astride two horses.'

Hepworth's and Nicholson's search for a 'pure' aesthetic made constant demands upon Read. In late 1931 Hepworth first penetrated a hole in a stone sculpture, deliberately robbing her work of any association with the human figure. In September 1935, Nicholson's white reliefs were shown at the Lefevre Gallery. These paintings remain the most coherent one-man modernist exhibition by an English artist before the Second World War. A month later, the Seven and Five Society, largely under the aegis of Nicholson, held the first all-abstract exhibition in England. Hepworth and Nicholson were among the English artists whose work was exhibited alongside that of Mondrian, Moholy-Nagy, Hélion and Calder by Nicolete Gray in her 1936 Abstract and Concrete show. Reginald Wilenski in *The Meaning of Modern Art* supported these developments: 'We react with satisfaction to works of art which make us realise subconsciously that all human, animal and vegetable forms are manifestations of one life.' D'Arcy Thompson's *Growth and Form* (1917), a popular book with the intelligentsia in the thirties, further enforced such beliefs, although his treatise rejected the eternal and universal in favour of the ephemeral and the accidental.

As before, surrealism, which in France was much more scientific, political and precise than it ever became in England, was tugging at Read's sleeve, largely through Paul Nash, although Moore was also

153

pulling in that direction in 1936. The term, whose name was taken from Apollinaire, was defended by Breton as a belief 'in the superior reality of certain forms of association neglected heretofore; in the omnipotence of the dream and in the disinterested play of thought.' In practice, the surrealists wanted to unleash the power of the un- conscious and to revolutionize social policy. From 1927 to 1935, surrealism in France was locked in a love–hate relationship with the Communist Party, as Breton proclaimed: 'for us, surrealists, the interests of thought cannot cease to go hand in hand with the interests of the working class'.

Many Marxists saw the aesthetic and political aims of surrealism as diametrically opposed concepts. If one cultivated the unconscious, was the plight of the oppressed not being neglected? Breton's response was that the liberation of the unconscious would make a person more aware of the poor and repressed. This was not acceptable to Read. By 1936, he saw communism, and therefore Marxism, as yet another stifling political system. He adhered to the aims of communism but was completely at odds with its ideological programme.[2] Like Breton, he was sympathetic to Trotsky's insistence on a separation of the artist from the state: he could live with Trotskyite doctrine but abhorred Stalinism.

Although his own strengths as a writer were in accord with surrealism, Read remained a fervent advocate of abstraction. He perceived the importance of the intuitive in both movements, although he realized that abstraction is more congenial to a rational approach to art: its surface coldness – as practised by Nicholson and Hepworth – is quintessentially classical. Moreover, the possibility of excess in surrealism frightened Read, and he responded to it in an extremely cautious way. He tried to tame it.

For Read, surrealism – which he habitually called superrealism – was essentially English: it was simply a tendency, although dormant, which had to be revived. It could be found in the prophetic books of Blake, the nonsense verse of Lear or *Alice in Wonderland*. The movement was 'coeval with the evolving consciousness of mankind'.

> It is in this sense, then, that surrealism is a reaffirmation of the romantic principle; and though poets and painters in all ages have clung to a belief in the inspirational and even the obsessional nature of their gifts, repudiating in deeds if not in words the rigid bonds of classical theory, it is only now, with the aid of modern dialectics and modern psychology, in the name of Marx and Freud, that they have found themselves in a postion to put their beliefs and practices on a scientific basis, thereby initiating a

continuous and deliberate creative activity whose only laws are the laws of its own dynamic.'

Read's *seeming* inconsistency – his swinging between classical and romantic – did not bother him, since he conceived of all human activity as a mingling of the two. He wanted to reconcile reason and feeling, dream and reality. In 1962, he sat in his study with two pictures facing him: 'one a pure abstraction by Ben Nicholson, the other a surrealist fantasy by Paul Delvaux. By chance their colours harmonise; if there is any contradiction in their forms, it must correspond to a contradiction in my own mind, for both appeal to me with equal force.' The conflict between these two forces was crystallized for Read in the mid-thirties by two new friends: Naum Gabo, the Russian émigré sculptor, and Roland Penrose, the wealthy English aesthete who had returned to England after thirteen years in France.

Gabo, forty-five when he arrived in England after three years in Paris, had been a student of Heinrich Wölflin's in Munich, went to Scandinavia during the war and returned to Russia in 1917. Three years later in Moscow, he and his brother made a nuisance of themselves when they pasted in various public places five thousand copies of their Realistic Manifesto, which set forth the basic principles of constructivism in opposition to productionism, which, under Vladimir Tatlin, advocated a socially oriented art using real materials in real space. Gabo, unequivocally anti-cubist, anti-Marxist and anti-materialist, claimed that the constructivist saw art only as a creative act: 'By a creative act it means every material or spiritual work which is destined to stimulate or perfect the substance of material or spiritual life.'[3] The manifesto of 1920 made four crucial points. First, art should be based on space and time. Second, volume is not the only spatial concept. Third, kinetic and dynamic elements must be used to express the real nature of time. Fourth, art should stop being imitative and try, instead, to discover new forms. Although lines, colours, and shapes possess an independence of the external world in constructivist doctrine, this type of art seeks to uncover and depict impulses and feelings universal to the human condition.

The Russian, whom Ben and Barbara had met in Paris, shared notions with them about the directions in which they felt art had to move. Significantly, Gabo's aesthetic – much more than that previously advocated by Hepworth and Nicholson – was coupled to a vision of the power of art to transform society. Such ideas appealed to Read, who had advocated abstract art along similar lines in *Art Now* and *Art and*

155

Industry. Previously, these ideas had had their largest following in England among architects such as Wells Coates and Colin Lucas, members of Unit One. In practice, 'constructive' gradually began to replace 'abstract' as a term. This change in name did not necessarily indicate a different look to works of art, but it did mean that there was an increased awareness of the utility of non-representational art.

Gabo had visited London in 1935 to discuss the possibility of designing for the Ballets Russes. The next year, he returned for Nicolete Gray's exhibition. For him London was vastly different from Paris, which was full of violence, gossip, intrigue and jealousy. Gabo himself was small and compact, his face frequently taking on a slightly puzzled look before breaking into a smile. He spoke English fluently, with a conviction that was not always justified. One day he disarmed Margaret Gardiner, who asked him why he was staring at her: 'Oh Margaret, it's that continence of yours.' In a little Italian restaurant where Ben was known as 'Mr Double Ice Cream', Gabo asked her: 'Darlink, what is on this menu?' She told him hashed meat. He was shocked. 'Hushed meat. Oh no, I don't eat hushed meat.' When he left one of his works behind in a taxi, the policeman to whom he reported the matter was flabbergasted when in answer to his question, 'What have you lost?' Gabo replied: 'A construction in space!' There was also a wistful sadness to Gabo, as in this reflection: 'Think what it takes to make a man, the years of love and care that can so easily be destroyed in a single moment.'[4]

Shortly after he had settled in London, Nicholson took Gabo to No. 3 Mall Studios to meet Read, who was sitting reading a book by the fire. 'He was wearing glasses, but he looked above the glasses, so in my impression I saw a very handsome man looking old.' Gabo's double perspective captures the renewed sense of vitality which Read's second marriage had brought him; he also discerned the weary anxiety that Virginia Woolf had called Read's 'shop assistant' look. Cecil Stephenson, Barbara and Ludo were also there. The conversation turned to a canvas by Wyndham Lewis, which was roundly castigated. Gabo objected, 'for God's sake, that is a very good painting, and in his time he has done something'. A fracas ensued, but then Gabo noticed that his new friend's face had gradually begun to shine, just as he winked in agreement.

Educated at Queen's College, Cambridge, the collector, painter and writer Roland Penrose had gone to live in France in 1922, when he was twenty-two. Penrose had been 'born in a cloud smelling strongly of oil paint, honest banking and piety',[5] his mother being from a family of bankers and his father an academic painter in the tradition of Alma-Tadema. Both parents were also ardent Quakers. Penrose first heard of modern art through Mansfield Forbes of Clare College, who effused about Cézanne and Gaudier-Brzeska. Penrose also became a friend of Roger Fry, whom his father considered a charlatan for having imported post-impressionist painting into England and thus betraying his Quaker heritage. Since James Doyle Penrose did not bestow his paternal approval, Fry, in his stead, gave an enthusiastic benediction to Penrose's decision to continue his studies in Paris. During his long absence from England, Penrose became a close friend of Max Ernst and Picasso, painted in a surrealist manner, married Valentine Boué, travelled to India and worked as an assistant to Robert Bresson, the film-maker. After his marriage broke up and his parents died, Penrose returned to England, eager to bring Gallic sunshine – in the form of surrealism – to his native shores.

Penrose settled in Downshire Hill in Hampstead. In comparison to Paris, London for him displayed a hermetic, snobbish reserve. His school and university friends had not been 'infected with the virus of Surrealism, and greeted him even in Bloomsbury with quiet tolerance or outright scorn'.[6] Through Paul Éluard, Penrose met David Gascoyne, who was visiting Paris to write a book on surrealism. In the rue de Touron, they vowed to bring the movement to London.

Back in Hampstead, eager allies were soon recruited, including Joseph Bard, Len Lye, John Banting. Paul Nash, who in a manner remarkably similar to Read had seized upon surrealism as a useful tool with which to deepen his understanding of English landscape, eagerly joined the confederation. The painter and film-maker Humphrey Jennings helped to edit the first surrealist bulletins. Young poets such as Hugh Sykes-Davies, Ruthven Todd and Roger Roughton were eager accomplices. Sykes-Davies paid Read a surrealist compliment when he told him that his face was like that of a praying mantis, with its 'very broad forehead, and then the face tapering away almost to a triangle . . . down to the extraordinary sensitiveness of the very mobile but rather small mouth'.[7]

Nevertheless, Read remained uncomfortable with the alliance between surrealism and communism, feeling that this friendship in England should be one of words rather than deeds. Real communists, he insisted, saw their group as a 'bunch of bourgeois decadents'. Also, he increasingly realized, he was in his surrealist activities 'acting a part'.[8]

By 1936 other forces in the art world, in addition to surrealism and abstraction, clamoured for attention. There were many artists who deliberately clung to traditions they had inherited as young men. In addition to their obvious indebtedness to his teacher, Paul Nash, the haunting beauty of Eric Ravilious' designs and paintings reflect an intimate knowledge of eighteenth- and nineteenth-century English watercolours. There were those who like Bomberg pursued their experimentations outside the feuding ideologies. Bloomsbury continued to dominate the London Group.

Kenneth Clark, Director of the National Gallery from 1934, attacked 'advanced' art in the *Listener* in 1935. Such art, he claimed, was out of touch with reality – it could only lead to a dead end. Read responded to this 'jagged splinter in the eye' by rounding on the young art historian: 'When, in the whole of history, has the finest culture of a period been, *at the time of its first creation*, anything but the affair of a small minority?'[9] Read chose a white on white of Nicholson's to defend his belief in abstraction's commitment to organic growth. Clark leaped on this. The more geometrical a work was, he asserted, the more removed it had to be from real life-enhancing vitality. A *Listener* reader wrote in to support Clark: 'Could Mr Herbert Read distinguish Mr Ben Nicholson's carved reliefs from similar ones prepared by any joiner?'[10] Later, Clark maintained that he had recognized Moore's talent as early as 1928, but he was initially more comfortable with the drawings than the sculptures, which he once likened to hot-water bottles.[11]

Another opponent was the Marxist art historian and critic Anthony Blunt who disliked the dream ambience of surrealism, its failure to depict a real proletarian world. As early as 1928 he had written in *Venture*, a Cambridge magazine, that surrealism was threatening to become serious. Blunt despised abstract art even more than he did surrealism. In October 1935, he denounced the Seven and Five show, castigating the group as a 'whole bedful of dreamers': 'Miss Hepworth snores à la Brancusi.'[12]

In 1933 a small group of friends headed by Misha Black and Cliff Rowe – in Black's candle-lit, orange-crate-furnished room at the Seven Dials – founded the Artists' International. Rowe had gone to Russia for a seven days' tour in 1931 and stayed for a year and a half. In marked contrast to England, he observed, every major Soviet institution acted as a patron to the arts. Trained as an architect, Black was galvanized by Rowe's stirring account of his response to Bolshevik culture.

This new group championed proletarian art, but it was also determined to stop the rise of fascism, as the first published statement outlining its activities made clear: 'We have taken part in strikes and

Do not judge this movement kindly. It is not just another amusing int. It is defiant—the desperate act of men too profoundly convinced of he rottenness of our civilisation to want to save a shred of its respectability.
HERBERT READ.

In this cartoon, James Boswell depicts some complacent, stuffy bourgeoisie in attendance at the Surrealist Exhibition and suggests that they are not at all touched by Read's words of invective.

elections, producing mimeographed newspapers on the spot, backed up by cartoons and posters. This will give us the direct experience we need of contact with the masses.'[13] The AI, which added A for Association to its name in 1935, allowed a plurality of styles, although, as its slogan indicated, it favoured realism: 'conservative in art and radical in politics'. The AIA's first exhibition, 'The Social Scene', took place in September–October 1934 in a former motorcycle showroom in Charlotte Street. Douglas Goldring in the *Studio* said that the work on display was crude. In the *London Mercury*, Read was also castigating, although he was sympathetic to the Association's objectives: 'One does not need to be a capitalist to describe the exhibition as a complete confusion of thought. . . . The whole fallacy of the conception

159

underlying this exhibition and the view of art it manifests is a confusion between art and propaganda.'[14]

After the publication of this attack in the *Mercury*, Read agreed to lecture the AIA about a distinction he had drawn there: 'The true revolutionary artist to-day is not any artist with a Marxist ideology; it is the good artist with a revolutionary technique.' In that talk, he managed to suppress his irritation with Marxism, praised abstraction as a 'transitional measure', and claimed that surrealism was relevant for the time being as a subversive device to disarm the bourgeois. In a lecture in the same series, Francis Klingender, the leading Marxist theorist in England, attacked abstraction as being 'no longer concerned with "external" reality in any shape or form'. Another speaker A. L. Lloyd claimed that such tendencies were channelling art into 'strange and rarefied grottoes, where exquisite little mollusc artists can shrink and expand in privacy'.[15] In Read's view, as he told Paul Nash in January 1938, the AIA 'should drop its spurious internationalism and turn itself into a trade-union for all grades and creeds of practising artists'. That February, Read quarrelled with the *Listener* – 'an almost final row' – over a Kandinsky exhibition: 'They did not think he was important enough for an article!' he told Douglas Cooper. 'I don't particularly like his work myself, but I think he is worth more space than the modern English woodcut.'[16]

Only the increasingly ominous news from Germany and Italy began to draw the various artistic persuasions together. In 1935, the AIA's 'Artists Against Fascism and War' exhibition – housed in a Georgian mansion in Soho Square – drew contributions from figures as diverse as Eric Gill, Augustus John, Laura Knight, Paul Nash, Lucien Pissarro, Barbara Hepworth and Ben Nicholson. Montagu Slater acutely sized up the situation in *Left Review*: 'Those whom art politics have put asunder, an exhibition against War and Fascism has joined together.'[17]

In the hazy gloom of impending global disaster, most of Hampstead's artists and intelligentsia collaborated in 1936 to stage a mammoth surrealist exhibition. The *individual* – his consciousness, his fantasies, his pursuit of dignity and freedom independent of all form of totalitarianism – was the common focal point of support from Marxists, members of the AIA and English romantics such as Read and Nash. The right to a spark of imagination was celebrated, this being the political issue which bound together the otherwise feuding isms.

There was a flurry of meetings. Since Penrose had lived in France, he was the natural emissary between England and the Continent. André Breton, Paul Éluard and Man Ray were to select the foreign entries; England would choose its own artists. In order to swell the ranks of the native-born, Penrose canvassed those of a non-surrealist persuasion – such as Graham Sutherland – in hopes of instant conversions. Nash, then at the outset of an affair with Eileen Agar, instructed Read and Penrose to approach her. She and Julian Trevelyan remembered becoming surrealist 'almost overnight';[18] the twenty-six-year-old Francis Bacon was rejected by Penrose. Len Lye and Humphrey Jennings co-directed *The Birth of the Robot*, a film for Shell Oil. David Gascoyne, Samuel Beckett and Man Ray – among others – translated Éluard's *Thorns of Thunder* into English. Roger Roughton wrote about surrealism in *Criterion*, a periodical which had previously avoided any mention of the movement. In June, *Contemporary Poetry and Prose* published a 'Double Surrealist Number'.

Gradually, all these multifarious preparations were focused on Read. As Penrose recalled, 'it became a most passionate affair'. Read's authority, in the words of Hugh Sykes-Davies, was 'unassertive, unemphatic, but entirely beyond question'. From the start, however, Penrose was fully aware of Read's divided loyalties: 'I think it was part of his character . . . to be full of inconsistencies and ambiguities, realizing that . . . art which is entirely consistent doesn't exist.'[19] Read's humility, Penrose felt, made it impossible for him to impose his views on others.

'Do not judge this movement kindly. It is not just another amusing stunt. It is defiant – the desperate act of men too profoundly convinced of the rottenness of our civilization to want to save a shred of respectability.' With these hostile words, Read threw down the gauntlet in his opening speech at the International Surrealist Exhibition, which opened at the New Burlington Galleries on 11 June, a sweltering day. Read proclaimed the dawn of a new age, but the painter Cecil Collins, who was an exhibitor, thought to himself: 'No, it isn't. It's the sunset.'[20]

Eleven hundred and fifty people crowded into the Galleries to hear Breton speak. Sheila Legge, the surrealist phantom, walked through the assemblage, her face covered in roses, dressed in a long satin dress, coral red belt and shoes, black silk stockings and long rubber gloves. She held a dummy leg in one hand and a pork chop in the other. Since the rooms were stiflingly hot, she soon had to discard the chop. Dylan Thomas offered boiled string in tea cups, enquiring, 'Do you want it weak or strong?' The newspapers were intrigued by the strange events of that day, paying morbid attention to Mme Breton's green fingernails.

Traffic had been stopped along the length of Bond Street as far as Piccadilly Circus.

Meret Oppenheim had her now famous *Fur Covered Cup, Saucer and Spoon* on show. According to Joseph Bard, T. S. Eliot, when Read took him on a tour of the exhibition, seemed pruriently interested in this object as a 'super-objective correlative of the female sex'.[21] There was Man Ray's *Lovers*, two giant red lips floating above the horizon. Further, often startling happenings made a visit to the exhibition until its closing on 4 July an even more bizarre experience than that provided by the 392 paintings, sculptures and Oceanic, African and American objects (in addition to the catalogued entries there were found objects – one contributed by Read – natural objects, interpreted, surrealist objects, and children's drawings). According to the *Daily Telegraph*, the composer William Walton, a member of the Sitwell entourage, hung a herring or kipper on one of Miró's paintings. As Duncan Grant was leaving the exhibition, Paul Nash asked him to put it outside. Even the exhibitors squabbled. The often reproduced photograph of Dali, Penrose, Mesens, Agar, Read and some of the others does not include Paul Nash. When Rupert Lee, the secretary of the Organizing Committee, telephoned Eileen to ask her to come down to the Burlington Galleries, Paul Nash was with her. Incensed that Lee had not contacted him, he refused to accompany her to the sitting. This was a minor matter compared to what could be seen at the New Burlington. For example, Dali wore his 'paranoiac jacket' with liqueur glasses filled with crème de menthe stuck all over it.

On 1 July, Dali, the supreme exhibitionist, spoke, wearing a diving suit decorated with plasticine hands and a radiator cap on top of the helmet, a jewelled dagger in his belt, and holding a pair of Borzois on leads. The helmet was old and extremely heavy – it had to be tightly secured because if it fell off it could break the wearer's neck. Ruthven Todd fastened the helmet. Dali then began speaking, but the heat in the poorly ventilated Galleries began to overwhelm him. Edward James, the collector, who was also assisting Dali, tried to use the billiard cue Dali held as a pointer to unloosen the helmet. Meanwhile, the two hounds had managed to tangle their leads in Dali's legs. Todd finally managed to free Dali, who finished his talk in a condition of 'combined paranoia and claustrophobia'.[22]

In contrast to Dali's event, Read's lecture on 'Art and the Unconscious', delivered while standing on a spring sofa, was a tame affair. Later, there were rumours that Read and several others stripped off their clothes at some surrealist gathering, but this story may derive from the likelier account of a late-night outing while Read was staying in the summer of 1937 at Lamb Creek, Becus Penrose's beautiful Georgian house on the River Truro in Cornwall. Roland had leased his brother's house for a month, and the rolling pastures near Lamb Creek became, as Anthony Penrose has suggested, the setting for unbridled hedonism: 'Surrealist arguments raged, interspersed with sight-seeing jaunts to Land's End, remote creeks and logan stones, the fascinating delights of Cornish pubs, and ardent lovemaking.'[23] One evening Eileen Agar, Lee Miller and some other women artists 'all danced naked around the disconcerted figure of Herbert Read, illuminated by the glare of a car's headlamps'.[24] Nash, Moore, Hepworth and Nicholson at various times sunbathed in the nude – plainly, Read was repulsed by such displays. A bit later, Eileen Agar was disconcerted when Joseph Bard incorrectly and improbably accused her of being in the midst of an affair with Read. The headstrong lover of Agar threatened to challenge the critic to a duel.

The reviews – public and private – of the extraordinary three weeks in June 1936 were ferocious. In the *New English Weekly*, H. G. Porteus attacked Read: 'It is difficult to believe that the author of "Reason and Romanticism" actually is responsible for such an effusion as the prefatory note to the catalogue.'[25] J. B. Priestley, Read's fellow Yorkshireman, accosted Geoffrey Grigson: 'As for Herbert Read – I hope he isn't a friend of yours – he is a nitwit. You could always take him in. . . . Did you go to that Surrealist opening? There was Herbert Read with all those Latin charlatans. Henry Moore's stuff was there. Henry Moore: he's lumpy. I don't know why all this modern stuff needs to be lumpy. What's there so attractive about lumpy things?'[26] These were private comments. In his public attack Priestley was even more damning: 'There are about far too many effeminate or epicene young men, lisping and undulating. . . . Frequently they have strong sexual impulses that they soon continue to misuse or pervert.' Read quoted these outrageous opinions in order to poke fun at them:

> I have nothing against Mr. Priestley, not even the fact that he was born in Yorkshire; but no doubt he feels none too comfortable on his bed of roses, and sympathy for the under-dog flows in a copious if somewhat muddled stream from his generous heart. . . . As a matter of fact, the Surrealists are no less aware than Mr. Priestley of undesirable elements in their midst; but they are not themselves to be identified with such elements. . . . On the subject of homosexuality . . . the Surrealists are not in the least prejudiced; they recognise that inversion is an abnormal condition due to a certain psychological or physiological predisposition for which the individual is in no way responsible.[27]

Other Fleet Street writers outdid themselves in savaging the show. The *Daily Telegraph* spoke contemptuously of the 'spiritual significance of artichokes', 'the subconscious message of a safety pin' and the 'dream value of the shrimp',[28] but the event was a *succès d'estime*. The intended target – the bourgeois – loved the show. The naughty, strip-tease carnival at the Burlington Galleries was eagerly devoured by the middle class who, in James Boswell's cartoon, are complacently juxtaposed with Read's words of invective. Almost overnight, billboards and magazine ads parodied Magritte and Ernst. The movement, suddenly chic, had been appropriated by its enemies.

Within the surrealist fortress itself, there were rumblings. When he reviewed *Surrealism*, a book of essays edited and introduced by Read and published by Faber, Humphrey Jennings took Read and Sykes-Davies to task for patronizing the movement. In their attempts to establish Coleridge and Wordsworth as ancestors, his two associates were 'looking for ghosts only on battlements and on battlements only for ghosts'.[29] The AIA's A. L. Lloyd was dismissive: 'If Surrealism were revolutionary, it could be of use. . . . Surrealism is a particularly subtle form of fake revolution.'[30]

That July, the failure of surrealism to shake England's complacency was overshadowed by the outbreak of the Spanish Civil War and the execution of the poet García Lorca. The following month, the death of an AIA member, Felicia Browne – the first British citizen to be killed in the conflict – shook artists of all persuasions. In October, two public sculptures by Epstein were daubed with anti-Semitic slogans, and the surrealists took part in a demonstration against Mosley. Paul Nash, Vanessa Bell and Eric Ravilious were among the contributors in December to 'Artists Help Spain', a project to raise money for a field kitchen for the International Column. However, David Bomberg clamoured unsuccessfully in February 1937 for the London Group to prohibit its members from exhibiting with reactionary groups. His further demand – 'that the London Group consolidate with the AIA and Surrealist Groups in their support of anti-Fascism in politics and art' – was also denied.[31]

Although their politics were decidedly left-wing, Nicholson, Hepworth and Gabo were disgruntled by the Surrealist Exhibition. And it was out of a sense of exclusion that *Circle* (1937), the manifesto of abstract–constructivist art, came into being. As Margaret Gardiner recalled, it 'was, in fact, born in an ABC shop where Barbara, Ben and Gabo had gone to restore themselves one day in 1936 after viewing the Surrealist Exhibition and where they decided that they absolutely had to do something to clear the air'.[32] Read's highjinks with Dali and associates had put him slightly out of favour, Ben and Barbara obviously feeling betrayed. Only in 1941 was Gabo completely candid with Read about his dislike of surrealism: 'I am more than ever convinced that whatever the printed philosophy of the Surrealist Art may be, the Surrealistic Movement as an artistic activity, has to a great degree supplied the poison which killed the youth of France and may endanger the coming generation if it continues.'[33] Although Read was asked to, and did, contribute to *Circle*, Nicholson, Gabo and Leslie Martin were the organizers and editors of that book. Ben and Barbara told Eileen Agar that Read, as far as they were concerned, was much too variable.

At exactly the same time, Henry Moore – neither a fully fledged abstractionist nor a fully fledged surrealist – confided to Agar that he was deeply worried about Read's promotion of Gabo. Moore had also been disturbed by the advent of surrealism, but he realized that 'the purely constructivist abstract people' were gaining a much stronger foothold than he felt proper. For Moore, surrealism became a healthy 'antidote' to Gabo, Hepworth and Nicholson. The sculptor never completely believed in what he called 'absolute pure abstraction'. Also, he was convinced that Read did not completely accept surrealism: 'I saw the Surrealist thing as (and this I think is why Herbert was so involved in it) the romantic side of the artist functioning.'[34] *Pace* Read, there were polemics and conflicting programmes within the 'nest of gentle artists'. The 'prevailing good temper' was not destroyed only by the war. Quite often, Read felt that 'guns were being fired at him from every side'.[35]

Read was not above trying to start a skirmish of his own when Geoffrey Grigson asked him to contribute a 'comment' to the double issue of *New Verse* (November 1937) devoted to Auden, whom Grigson idolized. Read began with a modicum of praise for the younger poet's vitality, exuberance and inventiveness, but then he gave full vent to his spleen – and jealousy – in a catalogue of errors: 'A certain retardation in growth. Schoolboy jokes and undergraduate humour. A cruel handshake. But more seriously: a definite backsliding in the technique of verse. . . . He is a little sentimental and indifferent to objective beauty.'[36]

Once again, Read was on a financial treadmill, hard work simply not bringing in enough money. In 1937, he began acting as a literary adviser to Routledge as well as Heinemann. In August, he told Tom Ragg, one of the directors at Routledge, that Heinemann had turned down a suggested series on British artists. He also mentioned that Ludo had just undergone a 'serious operation'.[37]

When Read recommended the obscure Samuel Beckett's *Murphy*, that novel, after two years of rejections by forty-two publishers, found a place on Routledge's spring 1938 list. Read was taken with Beckett's Rabelaisian buffoonery, his ability to combine 'learning and licence. It is also what I would call a perfect example of surrealist humour.'[38] Read met with some opposition among the firm's directors, but his reputation for choosing successful books eventually won the day.[39]

Between 27 January and 23 February 1937, Read had seven lectures to deliver. Constantly, he had to recycle material for a variety of occasions. In November, he engaged Pearn, Pollinger and Higham to act as his literary agents.[40] One labour of love was a piece on Paul Nash, where Read's close identification with that artist's romantic surrealism is evident: 'The striking peculiarity of Paul Nash is that, alone in his generation, he has dared to transform the English tradition. . . . he has not only discovered a new world: he has discovered a new form of life.'

Later that year – from July to December – Read accepted Graham Greene's invitation to write reviews of detective fiction for *Night and Day*, the elegant short-lived London imitation of the *New Yorker* best known for Greene's libellous remarks about Shirley Temple's precocious sexuality. A bit earlier, the timid thirty-three-year-old Greene had met Read by chance and was astonished a little while afterwards to receive an invitation to dinner, saying that there unfortunately would be only one other guest: T. S. Eliot. To Greene, this was like a letter from Coleridge apologizing for the fact that Wordsworth would be the only other person present. Read send Greene a poem written in red ink to accompany his first review:

> Shall it be Graham or be Greene?
>   There's nothing betwixt or between.
> Shall it be Graham or be Greene?
> Neither is Christian or intime,
> But one is milk, the other cream.
> So Graham let it be, not Greene.[41]

Read's whimsical side was further released in his review of murder mysteries, as in this measured praise: 'we can't all be tough all the time, and if you want a nice quiet story . . . then you can rely on Agatha Christie. It [*Dumb Witness*] is a neat little mystery with a sweet little doggie in it, and though we may be getting rather tired of Poirot and his Watson, he is less tiresome than usual.'[42] By December Read was very tired of Poirot when he turned to *Death on the Nile*: 'We know before we open it that there will still be the same old Poirot, an ageless eunuch, immune from the vicissitudes of life.'[43] Read's own increasing sense of weariness creeps into his closing reflections on *One Murdered – Two Dead*: 'There is no characterization nonsense; the people are pawns; the crime's the thing. There is also no poetic nonsense: the style is clear, colourless and effective. It is a dirty world, with no love and little laughter. It is the real world of murder and sudden death.'[44]

Under the pseudonym of 'James Murgatroyd', Read wrote a slightly surrealistic comic fable about the difficulties of living without a shoehorn. Greene objected to the name Murgatroyd, claiming it sounded a little too much like P. G. Wodehouse. Read wrote back: 'In Defence of Murgatroyd. It is a perfectly real name, and if I had been born in the West instead of the North Riding it might easily have been my own name.' Greene had suggested the pen-name, Bertram Meade. Read rebuffed that bit of interference: 'I once knew a man in the Ministry of Labour called that, and that is what it sounds like. I want something funny, and something vaguely evocative of something square and squat with protruding amphibian eyes; something weary and patient, like a frog in a drought.'[45]

Read's ever increasing stature as *the* critic of modern art is amusingly captured in a BBC anecdote of 1936. Joe Ackerley, the *Listener*'s literary editor, was gently upbraided by his superior for constantly taking Read out for long lunches:

Lambert (looking at his watch): Half-past three, Joe.

Ackerley: I've been out with Herbert Read.

Lambert: You seem to be entertaining him rather a lot.

Ackerley: He's teaching me about modern art.

Lambert: Yes – but is it necessary to lunch him five times a week at the Café Royal?

Ackerley: It's not only modern art. It's Korean art, Chinese art, Japanese art and Red Indian art.

Earlier, at Whitsun, Heppenstall had been plying Read with queries about his personal life. Herbert and Ludo had rented the Black House at Firle, and leisure gave Read time to write a frank letter to his sometime friend. He told Heppenstall that he no longer had the time to write poetry, but he claimed not to care since most versifying was 'bad company everywhere'. He hoped that at long last he might be elected to the Slade Professorship at Cambridge: 'It doesn't mean any settled independence (it is a three year appointment) and is too much work for £400 a year. But I shall take it if they do decide that divorce is no

167

objection (the real snag) because I have got into that sort of mill-race and can float along in it, and after all, it is cleaner work than reading rubbish for Heinemanns.' In what was for him a particularly unguarded moment, Read even answered, somewhat sarcastically, Heppenstall's questions about himself and Ludo. 'Do we fight? No; not desperately. Not at all in your tiger-cub fashion, though I've heard it is a sign of true love. I suppose we haven't time, don't see enough of each other, or are simply pacifists. Or the great virtue of not making a fuss.'[46]

On 23 September, Heinemann, on Read's advice, rejected a novel by Heppenstall. Read was blunt: the book did not tell a story. That night, he had to go to a party in London in honour of his new arch-enemy, Priestley: 'as part of the machine I must function'. Three months later, on 23 December, Ludo gave birth to Thomas Bonamy, her first child and her husband's second son, named in honour of Eliot and Dobrée. Eric Gill, a renowned convert to Catholicism, whose home at Pigotts near High Wycombe was close to Broom House, was the godfather.

The gathering storm, particularly in Spain, was at the forefront of Read's mind in *Art and Society* (1937) and *Poetry and Anarchism* (1938). The earlier book, based on the Sydney Jones lectures of 1935–6, concedes that the artist is a unit within a 'necessary social organization' and that without the support of society he 'cannot arrive even at the threshold of his potentialities'. As in *Essential Communism*, however, Read insists on a strict segregation between the artist and society: 'But having reached that threshold, he must be allowed to proceed alone, as an individual. For he can cross that threshold only within his own self.' The artist is supreme among his fellow men because he sees into another order of reality, his paintings and sculptures encapsulating – in symbolical form – that knowledge, born of inspiration. The elitism here, that the artist has a special faculty differentiating him from other men, was implicit in *The Meaning of Art* and *Art Now*. In this book – in the manner of Eric Gill – Read calls for a natural order of society where all activities would be aesthetic: 'Rhythm and harmony would pervade all that we do and all that we make: in this sense every man would be an artist of some kind and no art would be despised merely because it was mechanic or utilitarian.' Here, Read extends the transcendental possibilities of abstract art to an entire society. As in his essay on Shelley, Read still sees the artist as a neurotic, an outcast of society.

In the thirties, Read remained overly dependent on Freud's theories of art, but in discussing the 'deeper layers of the ego and in the

168

id' he moves in the direction of Jung's notion of the collective unconscious: 'If we consider that this region, this cauldron into which the artist is able to peer, is a region of timeless entities, then we seem to have some explanation of the source of vital energy.' Eventually, the limitations inherent in Freud's view of the artist as disturbed and damaged would be discarded in favour of the more serene views of Jung.

If Read did not accept Marxist or Stalinist views on the relationship between art and society, he was nevertheless convinced, as *Poetry and Anarchism* clearly shows, that a revolt against the existing social order had to take place: 'the abolition of poverty and the consequent establishment of a classless society is not going to be accomplished without a struggle'. There was every reason to believe, he claimed, 'that with modern mechanical power and modern methods of production, there is or could be a sufficiency of goods to satisfy all reasonable needs. It is only necessary to organize an efficient system of distribution or exchange.' Such idealism – Utopian hope precariously linked to an intimate knowledge of the social conditions of the late thirties (the Jarrow marches, the occupation of the Ritz by unemployed workers, the fall of Madrid to Franco) – was still possible in 1938. Moreover, Read envisioned the artist as a 'man who mediates between our individual consciousness and the collective unconscious, and thus ensures social reintegration'. Although the world was poised for global conflict, it still seemed possible in 1937–8 that pacifism and brotherhood might win out. Read thought that England could swim against the stream.

Read's aesthetic theories were challenged in 1937 by Adrian Stokes, the Hampstead friend whose baroque style Read had once attacked. (That year Stokes had moved to Fitzroy Street, two doors away from an art school at No. 12, which transferred its premises to 316 Euston Road in 1938.) In the gorgeously ornate prose of *Colour and Form*, Stokes distinguished between 'modelling' and 'carving' in painting. The former 'recharges a landscape with shape, with patent flourish' whereas the latter is capable of revealing 'the figures of the inner life'. For Stokes, 'modelled' canvases were more concerned with organization; 'carved' pictures attempted to get at the essence of subject matter. Indirectly, Stokes is praising the representational (carved) over the abstract (modelled); covertly, he is attacking surrealism and, especially, abstraction as practised by Barbara Hepworth.

Stokes had changed his mind. His book manifests a new, profound sympathy with the aims of his neighbours at the Euston Road School, which, founded in 1937 by William Coldstream, Victor Pasmore, Claude Rogers and Graham Bell, emphasized a delicate, sober transcription of landscapes, still lives, nudes and people. Increasing public awareness of political and social squalor (as well as the AIA's Marxist bent) influenced the School in its endeavour to capture the actual texture of life. Kenneth Clark was an early, ardent defender of the group.

On 16 March 1938, the AIA organized a debate between realism supported by Coldstream and Bell and surrealism defended by Penrose, Jennings and Julian Trevelyan. Evidently, the surrealists were more eloquent than their opponents, and rather sneakily they brought speechless advocates with them, a Picasso and a Miró. Read, a silent witness that evening, viciously attacked his new opponents in the *London Bulletin* of April 1938: 'We have tried to remember anything contributed to the debate by Graham Bell and William Coldstream. . . . but there is only the stammer and the sweat. . . . [the realists] are reduced to talking about the camera and Courbet. Actually our English Realists are not the tough guys they ought to be but the effete and bastard offspring of the Bloomsbury school of needlework.'[47] Read's hatred of the Euston Road School was strong enough for him to take the tack, unusual for him, of trying to have its artists refused places in exhibitions. If Read overreacted to the threat to his authority represented by this group, Anthony Blunt was too unstinting in his praise of Coldstream in the *Spectator* of 25 March: 'To the system of shocks, incongruities, obscurities, with which the Superrealists work, Coldstream opposes, above all, the quality of honesty. In art, as in morals, honesty is often unexciting at first sight. But the test comes not at the first, but at the fiftieth hour; and it is not obvious which will look duller then – a Picasso or a Coldstream.'

As he told Heppenstall, Read was the 'mouthpiece (or mug as we call it in Yorkshire)'[48] for the exhibition of modern German art which opened at the New Burlington Galleries that July. The year before, there had been a show of 'degenerate' art in Munich, the English exhibition being a riposte to the label affixed by the Nazis to contemporary art. Hitler was offended by the London show, making it known that if any of the 'modern' painters whose work was on display had not yet left Germany, they should quickly do so. The pictures on display included some impressionist and realist canvases, but the exhibition was particularly strong in the school of art hated by the Nazis: expressionism. In order not to initiate actions against the artists, the pictures were borrowed

170

from private collections, many from Paris. Kokoschka sent *Portrait of a Degenerate Artist* and a canvas which he claimed had been slashed into four pieces by Austrian customs – it was shown in the state in which it arrived. On 22 June, Read asked the BBC if it was interested in mounting a debate between an opponent and a defender of banned art.[49] Guy Burgess, who was then in charge of talks on art, had serious reservations about allowing the views of any totalitarian regime to be aired, even in the forum of a debate.[50]

That August, the Reads escaped to France, staying at Richard Aldington's place on the Côte des Maurs. They looked for Cézannes in Aix, but mainly they bathed. However, Read was in a 'state of spiritual doldrums, natural, I suppose, to my age'. He asked Douglas Cooper: 'How long does it last & in what direction does one emerge?' Read thought the coming conflict with fascism would hurry along – not cause – England's decline. England had lost the 'instinct' to survive: the whole country had to be reduced to ashes 'before the phoenix can rise again.'[51]

On 29 April 1937, German planes, in obvious collusion with Franco, had bombed the Spanish town of Guernica. Picasso's anger found stirring expression in the huge mural he painted for the Spanish Republican pavilion at the Paris International Exhibition. When Penrose asked him if the painting could travel to London Picasso agreed at once. Virginia Woolf, Fenner Brockway, E. M. Forster and Victor Gollancz were among the wide assortment of Patrons of the National Joint Committee for Spanish Relief, of which Read was vice-chairman. At the last minute, in September 1938, just as the mural was to be packaged for shipment, Chamberlain reached his notorious agreement with Hitler. Penrose thought that Picasso might withdraw permission, but the artist did not recant.

Guernica, with sixty-seven preparatory studies, overpowered the small room in which it was placed at the New Burlington Galleries from 2 to 29 October, where it attracted 3,000 viewers; when it moved to Whitechapel in the proletarian East End of London, 12,000 saw it in two weeks. Anthony Blunt denounced the picture: 'it is not an act of public mourning but the expression of a private brainstorm which gives no evidence that Picasso has realised the political significance of Guernica'.[52] Read counter-attacked:

> It has been said that this painting is obscure – that it cannot appeal to the soldier of the republic, to the man in the street, to the communist in his cell; but actually its elements are clear and openly symbolical. The light of day and night reveals a scene of horror and destruction: the eviscerated

horse, the writhing bodies. . . . It is the modern Calvary, the agony in the bomb-shattered ruins of human tenderness and faith. It is a religious picture, painted, not with the same kind, but with the same degree of fervour that inspired Grünewald.[53]

As Blunt later recalled, the quarrel 'was all carried out in the most friendly manner, because Read and I happened to be members of the [Reform] and we used frequently to meet there by chance, and one would say to the other, "I hope that you did not take my saying that you were stupid and wrong, etc., in my last letter, in any personal manner," and we would then go and have lunch together'.[54]

Gradually, the Hampstead years of shared camaraderie were drawing to a close. Late in 1937, Herbert and Ludo were among the first to leave, when they decided to live at Broom House, which had been rented out since 1931. In a lighthearted vein, Read told Douglas Cooper: 'We are resigning the studio to the triplets & moving out to my house near Beaconsfield, where I shall have a dachshund & grow roses & forget about communism and surrealism.'[55] Ludo was not quite as sanguine. Broom House was, for her, the home of the first Mrs Read. Nevertheless, the move to the country seemed to go well, 'Ludo taking to the country like a squirrel to a tree'.[56] Read kept chickens, although their uncontrolled behaviour led him to curse frequently the 'bloody birds'. Herbert and Ludo developed strong friendships with several families, the Dixons, Wheens and Morleys, but they were alienated from most of their neighbours. By local standards, Ludo dressed unconventionally: her clogs were outré; Herbert's berets were out of place. The ordinary garb of Hampstead was outrageously exotic in Buckinghamshire. As he grew older, Tom Read fervently yearned for his parents to fit into more socially acceptable norms. He desperately wanted his father to play golf, the sport played by middle-class husbands in Buckinghamshire.

Read now had to take a commuter train to London almost every day. In April, his morale tottered, although, he reflected, 'time passes and the structure still holds'.[57] June in Sussex refreshed him. Again, he and Ludo were doing their 'Glyndebourne round'. The Black House was neater and in every way more convenient than Charleston, though not so picturesque: 'no rabbits to shoot or tickle'.[58] In August, he was in the South of France for three weeks.

Despite the opportunity to escape London, Read could not leave behind a continual sense of impending disaster. His friend, Robert Payne, provided him with vivid bulletins of the desolation being perpetrated in Spain. Stephen Spender, who had flirted briefly with

172

communism, wrote in much the same manner, from Austria and Spain. Cautiously, Spender continually sought out news of anti-fascist activities. When he found such, he felt an 'almost sobbing satisfaction. External things over which I had no control had usurped my own deepest personal life, so that my inner world became dependent on an outer one.'[59]

When Read, 'a hardened professional reader', as he called himself, read Orwell's *Homage to Catalonia*, he wrote to the author: 'by far the best book I have seen on this Spanish war. . . . I don't see how anyone can doubt your honesty and objectivity.'[60] He was also actively involved in helping refugees from Franco's Spain. Ethel Mannin, the gushy popular novelist, had been touched in June 1938 by hearing Read's recital of one of his Spanish poems. Diffidence had caused her not to approach him. When she turned to his writings on art and anarchism, she could no longer contain herself and tried without success to phone him at the *Burlington* and Faber's. Later that day she wrote to say that she was 'moved and excited' by his discussion of the 'relation of art to revolutionary thought and feeling. It's something I have always insisted upon and felt, but have never seen expressed before, and the average "revolutionary" is deplorably doctrinaire, and indifferent to art.' Marxist doctrine on art having been summarily dealt with, Mannin asked Read to visit her the very next day. Flirtatiously, she asked him if he would rather 'come for the first time when there is no one else – though you'd not object to my lover, Reg Reynolds, perhaps? Like me, he is officially a member of the Independent Labour Party.'[61] Read claimed that he tended his garden at weekends.

The upheaval in Spain continued to obsess Read and in 1937–8 he wrote a series of poems on that bloody conflict. A grainy newspaper photo of the corpses of children slaughtered by the fascists inspired 'Bombing Casualties':

> Dolls' faces are rosier but these were children
> their eyes not glass but gleaming gristle
> dark lenses in whose quicksilvery glances
> the sunlight quivered. These blench'd lips
> were warm once and bright with blood
> but blood
> held in a moist bleb of flesh
> not spilt and spatter'd in tousled hair. . . .
>
> They are laid out in ranks
> like paper lanterns that have fallen

after a night of riot
extinct in the dry morning air.

Read's pacifist sympathies were momentarily overcome by Herschel Grynszpan, the seventeen-year-old Polish Jew who shot Ernst von Rath, Third Secretary at the German Embassy in Paris on 7 November 1938. Robert Payne, Read's friend, had seen Grynszpan 'arriving at the Ministry of Justice chained between two heavily-armoured fliks. His face was beautifully calm, and he walks like a peasant with firm unhurrying strides, not tired but utterly remote from the world.'[62] In response to Payne's letter, Read eulogized the valiant young man in a short poem, which reads in part: 'This beautiful assassin is my friend / because my heart is filled with the same fire.'

The grim nightmare of Spain and Germany provided for Read an increasingly ghastly parallel to his own inner landscape. He was constantly short of money, his alimony payment to Evelyn (£400 a year) absorbing a great deal of his income. Much of his time was now being monotonously consumed in travelling in to central London. In addition to caring for Thomas, Ludo was writing music for films and frequently had to be in the city. Munza had gone back to Germany, and the Reads arranged for a young German Jewess, Leonie Cohn, to enter England by way of Italy, where she was growing daily more apprehensive about her fate. After some delays, Leonie finally arrived in December 1938, whereupon she looked after Thomas and some household chores.

Although he led a busy, productive life, Read felt, once again, trapped. In such unrewarding circumstances, lack of money became emblematic of an overwhelming sense of despair. When the BBC Copyright section offered him five shillings to broadcast 'Bombing Casualties', he was furious. He reminded them that the fee was altogether inadequate: 'but I recognize that it merely expresses the contempt with which you, in common with the public at large, treat the art of poetry'. He told them to pay the fee to the National Peace Council.[63] Read confided his desperate financial situation to Joe Ackerley, who tried to get him some work. His memorandum drew a tepid response: 'Dull voice, a little dreary, but otherwise good' was one producer's lukewarm comment.[64]

In the autumn of 1938, at the time of the digging of air-raid trenches in London's parks, the deployment of the services of the Air Raid Precaution, and the distribution of thirty-eight million gas masks, Read ruefully told Heppenstall: 'I am in a tough financial depression,

174

the worst ever. To think that I have worked hard and soberly for twenty-five years, and that I am far poorer than when I began. . . . It is not very encouraging to virtue.'[65]

11 World Within a War

I believe it is vitally necessary for those of us who intend to oppose the coming war to start organising for illegal anti-war activities. It is perfectly obvious that any open and legal agitation will be impossible not only when war has started but when it is imminent, and that if we do not make ready *now* for the issue of pamphlets etc. we shall be quite unable to do so when the decisive moment comes . . . we might find it extremely useful to have an underground organisation. . . . Would you drop me a line and let me know whether you are interested in this idea?[1]

George Orwell, rightly convinced of the eventual clamp-down on all activities which might *seem* to deviate from government policy, asked for Read's help in January 1939 – the month Auden and Isherwood left for America. Nineteen-thirty-nine was a year of grim anticipation: the Tate stored its pictures in the disused tunnels of the Underground at Aldwych, and the National Gallery buried its possessions in mine quarries in Wales; Eros was moved from Piccadilly Circus to Cooper's Hill at Englefield Green; in September, all theatres and cinemas were closed, reopening fifteen days later when the raids had not taken place; in October 1939 Dame Myra Hess began to give lunchtime recitals in the empty National Gallery. Eventually, danger became boring. As Vera Brittain observed, 'when you are in it perpetually, how completely it destroys concentration upon ideas, books, music, philosophy, and other things far more interesting than the mere preservation of life'.[2] Mass Observation reported that the blackout had brought normal daily life to an end – people were 'staying in' and going to bed early. There was even a minor renaissance in publishing. Having nothing to do, Read lamented, was 'the only condition which will drive the average Englishman to a book'.[3]

Although deeply sympathetic to Orwell, Read was not prepared to go along with what he felt might be paranoia, although he was willing to allow his attic at Broom House to be used as a storage depot for the anarchist Freedom Press – or as a last refuge for a fight between that

176

group and the police.[4] As Orwell's letter to him of 5 March makes clear, Read did not favour the purchase of a printing press: 'I quite agree that it's in a way absurd to start preparing for an underground campaign unless you know who is going to campaign and what for, but the point is that if you don't make some preparations beforehand you will be helpless when you want to start. . . . I cannot believe that the time when one can buy a printing press with no questions asked will last forever.'[5] However, Read agreed with Penrose that 'our purpose must necessarily be to build up a group of revolutionary, anarchist intellectuals with a very definite programme behind it'.[6]

Read's own attitude, as he later announced, was one of fatalism. Although he could look forward to the eventual defeat of fascism, he was 'always sufficiently realistic to believe that a victory for "democracy" would make no real difference to the world situation'. Not being of military age, it seemed caddish to recommend younger people 'to adopt a course of action which I could not follow myself – like urging troops to go "over the top" from the safety of a dug-out'.[7]

In 'To a Conscript of 1940', the speaker meets the spirit of his twenty-two-year-old self. The older man tells the ghost from time past:

I am one of those who went before you
Five-and-twenty years ago: one of the many who never returned,
Of the many who returned and yet were dead. . . .
But one thing we learned: there is no glory in the deed
Until the soldier wears a badge of tarnish'd braid;
There are heroes who have heard the rally and have seen
The glitter of a garland round their head.

Theirs is the hollow victory. They are deceived.
But you, my brother and my ghost, if you can go
Knowing that there is no reward, no certain use
In all your sacrifice, then honour is reprieved.

To fight without hope is to fight with grace,
The self reconstructed, the false heart repaired.

Read's obsession with 1914–18 is evident in the marked contrast between youthful aspiration and mature wisdom. His disdain for any kind of war is probably the stronger because of his own record of heroism in that conflict – he knew what it was to experience cowardice but to transcend such feelings in heroic acts. During the new war, he was an air-raid warden, 'but not to support the war, merely to protect myself and my neighbours from the thunder-bolts'.[8] 'Historical justice demands', he assured Barbara Hepworth, 'that a rotten society like ours should fall.'[9] For Read, the hostilities brought inertia and inactivity:

'fewer trains, fewer buses, fewer theatres &c, thinner papers – all perhaps inevitable precautions. But in time with these restrictions, everybody moves at a slower pace – the very lifts seem to crawl up at half their usual speed.'[10]

A bit of winter's gloom was relieved in January 1939 when Paul Nash, the greatest painter of the landscape of the First World War, sent Herbert and Ludo a watercolour and pencil study for the surrealistic *Encounter on the Downs*. The Reads wrote to thank him, and Nash rejoined: 'It was so difficult to know what to send you. I had an alternative, the sketch design for my largish painting called Nocturnal Landscape but, I hesitated: "Frankly Freudian" it has been described as. That would never do. Ludo has warned me – *not before the child*.'[11]

In the midst of global and personal insecurity, Read decided to abandon the safety of the *Burlington*. This move had been under way since 1935 when a group centred on Ben Nicholson – Nicolete Gray, Leslie Martin and Read – had planned a Museum of Living Art, which would obviously have been devoted to abstraction. Late in the thirties, Read had broached the possibility of a modern museum with Helena Rubinstein, the cosmetics manufacturer, who had offered exhibition rooms.

Astonishingly, amid the pervasive dreariness brought by approaching war, Peggy Guggenheim, with her typical whim of iron, decided in March 1939 to open such a museum in London. Read, who had for years fervently clung to the idea of a permanent home for contemporary art – whether in Edinburgh or London – grasped at what turned out to be a succession of weak straws thrown out by Peggy. Their discussions centred on a permanent collection, based in London – of which Read was to be the director. At the outset, Read prepared a list of artists and works for Peggy. This shopping list, subsequently revised by Marcel Duchamp and Nellie van Doesburg, became the cornerstone of her collection, now at Venice. When Rubinstein was asked if she was willing to join forces with Peggy, she sensibly withdrew. Why did Read cling to such a possibility at the outset of war? He did this because he saw the establishment of a home for modern art as an act of reconstruction, knowing full well that the arts in England would have to be rebuilt – win or lose – after the approaching conflict with Germany had been resolved. It was a patriotic act, although the scheme was to go forward with American money.

Peggy Guggenheim was the archetypal poor little rich girl. Great wealth bought her much comfort and some ease – and an overwhelming sense of emptiness. In order to combat feelings of worthlessness she frenetically pursued – in order of importance – men and art: men who were artists or writers were her most prized possessions. Over a year before she decided to fund a museum devoted to contemporary art, Peggy, in the midst of her ultimately futile pursuit of Samuel Beckett and under the guidance of Marcel Duchamp, opened a gallery, Guggenheim Jeune, at 30 Cork Street, next to the London Gallery at No. 28, Penrose's showcase for surrealism. Peggy's first show was devoted to Jean Cocteau, whose drawings of male nudes with fig leaves surrounded by pubic hair almost caused English customs to refuse his work entry. Read, who was once propositioned by Cocteau, was a dubious supporter of the Frenchman's work. At the cocktail party to celebrate the inauguration of the gallery, Peggy wore earrings made of half-a-dozen curtain hooks. One observer remembered: 'She resembled W. C. Fields. Her brittle wrists and ankles were charming. She had very warm, slightly piggy eyes.'[12]

The shows at Guggenheim Jeune were eclectic. Marcel Duchamp vehemently – and truthfully – argued that Kandinsky had never had much exposure in England and persuaded Peggy to mount a one-man show, which opened in February 1938. This was followed by an exhibition devoted to an artist of Peggy's choice: Cedric Morris. In April 1938, there was an assemblage of contemporary sculpture, with works by Brancusi, Arp, Calder, Pevsner and Moore. During the second season – in December 1938 – Peggy featured leather portrait dolls and masks of, among others, Garbo, Dietrich and Josephine Baker by Marie Wassilieff, who also made celluloid hats which were washable and rainproof. A sarcastic newspaper reporter suggested that the Jeune was a good place to buy Christmas presents. Earlier in her second season, Peggy held exhibitions of children's drawings and collages. More than the others, these two shows display Peggy's strong interest in surrealism, a penchant shared with Penrose, who wanted to purchase a Tanguy left over from a previous show. A mild flirtation in the gallery led Peggy to visit Penrose at his Hampstead home on the pretext of looking at his surrealist paintings. Soon, they were in the midst of a brief amour, of which she ungallantly wrote in her memoirs: 'He had one eccentricity: when he slept with women he tied up their wrists with anything that was handy. Once he used my belt, but another time in his house he brought out a pair of ivory bracelets from the Sudan. They were attached with a chain and Penrose had a key to lock them. It was extremely uncomfortable to spend the night this way, but if you spent it with Penrose it was the only way.' This revelation did not bother Penrose – he was much more upset that she labelled him a bad painter.

179

In turn, he claimed that his relationship with her had never been significant: 'How could it be serious when she went to bed with everyone she met? She was very much in heat, one might say, anyone could jump into bed with her.'[13]

Despite her very best efforts, Read successfully evaded Peggy's net, although she put a good face on her lack of success: 'Mr. Read was a distinguished-looking man. . . . He had gray hair and blue eyes, and was reserved, dignified and quiet. . . . He soon became a sort of father in my life and behind his back I called him Papa. He treated me the way Disraeli treated Queen Victoria. I suppose I was rather in love with him, spiritually.'[14]

Although Guggenheim Jeune was a *succès d'estime*, it lost £600 a year. Peggy decided that she might as well become a philanthropist in name as well as deed, whereupon she asked Read to become the director of her proposed museum. Peggy insisted that Read give up the 'stuffy' *Burlington*, offering him in exchange a five-year contract at £1,000 a year. Peggy could be overwhelming, and Read did not know what to do. The lady could not – or would not – provide a reference. Although Kenneth Clark and Michael Sadler sanctioned the scheme, Read nervously asked the advice of Eliot, who evidently assured him that Peggy had the 'highest' reputation. Finally, Read offered to work six months free but borrowed his first year's salary so that he could buy a partnership at Routledge. Peggy was delighted: 'Mr Read could hardly believe his good fortune. He must have thought I had tumbled from heaven . . . all his life he had dreamed of making an ideal modern museum.'[15]

Although Read never envisioned Peggy as angelic, he was seizing the opportunity to provide England, at long last, with a venue for contemporary art. He showed Peggy his 'Proposals for a Scottish Philanthropist', insisted that the museum provide rooms which could be used as meeting places for artists and the public, suggested a yearly salon for young painters and sculptors, and proposed an opening show devoted to all the non-representational movements of the century. Peggy agreed to this but vetoed the inclusion of Cézanne and Matisse in the opening show or the collection. Peggy was to go to Paris to negotiate key pictures and sculptures for the initial exhibition. The two planned – after this show – to travel together to New York to study the workings of the Museum of Modern Art (Peggy thought MOMA's Alfred Barr was the American equivalent of Read).

Penrose and Mesens, who ran the London Gallery for him, wanted to get involved. They obviously saw the opportunity to make the proposed museum surrealistic. Peggy became very irritated: 'It seems that they had been offered free a whole floor in a building of a famous dressmaker's in Berkeley Square. If we accepted the gift and Mesens with it on a small salary, Penrose promised to lend several of his best Picassos. All this seemed unnecessary to me, as Mesens and Penrose were my avowed enemies by then.'[16] Peggy claimed that a terrible fight with the surrealists had broken out when she had an abstract show at her gallery, but her by then broken affair with Penrose may have contributed to her disdain. Peggy, who had just had an abortion, was in a nursing home outside London where she spent her time 'rereading Proust and making budgets to find enough money for Mr. Read'.[17] When Read visited her there, she refused the Penrose offer.

Clark expressed his delight that Read had finally decided to leave the *Burlington*: 'I should be filled with joy at the thought of you directing a museum of contemporary art.'[18] He also offered to lend anything of his which Read might like to borrow. Subsequently that June, he informed Read that he was selling his house in Portland Place and offered it as a possible home for the museum. Read telephoned Peggy with this news.

Immediately, Peggy abandoned the nursing home and Proust to see the proposed site. The house was very large. Peggy wanted to live on the upper floors, but then Ludo expressed a desire to have a pied-à-terre there. The ladies were soon arguing about which floors they would occupy. Despite the fact that 'Mrs. Read's resolution to live in the museum terrified' her,[19] Peggy decided to take the house. She never signed a lease because lawyers for both parties were on holiday.

In the midst of his fraught negotiations with Peggy, Read was being savaged by an irate Douglas Cooper, who had helped him select the plates for *Art Now* and assisted him in the Unit One project. During Read's tenure at the *Burlington*, his friendship with Cooper had grown steadily – particularly in 1938 – when the younger man provided him with a series of excellent reviews. Although he had made up his mind by 20 March, Read told Cooper that he was uncertain of the new terrain he would be confronting: 'I don't pretend that this is really a momentous step – England is perhaps too dead to be injected with any new life, & I shall merely exhaust myself in a vain effort. But nothing, in another sense, could be deadlier than the Burlington.'[20]

Rarely did Cooper have any doubts about himself or his opinions. He was from a wealthy family whose fortune had been made in Australia. The origins of that wealth were shrouded in mystery, most likely by Douglas. What seems certain is that Thomas Cooper went to

181

Australia in 1759, probably a decision made for him by the authorities. There he joined forces with a Mr Levi, with whom he founded the Waterloo Warehouse. The profits from that venture were used to buy real estate in Sydney. Daniel Cooper, the second son of Thomas, became the first Speaker of the New South Wales Legislative Assembly and was created a baron in 1863. Eventually, the title passed to Douglas' grandfather, who settled in England. From his estate, Douglas received his substantial fortune.

Throughout his life, Cooper bristled when any suggestion was made that he and his money had origins in the Antipodes. Educated at Repton, Cambridge, the Sorbonne and Freiburg, Cooper, by the time he turned twenty-one in 1932, had decided to devote one-third of his inheritance to collecting the four major cubist painters – Picasso, Braque, Gris and Léger – in every phase of their development from 1906–7 until 1914. His devotion to these major cubists was unbounded and obsessive. Eventually, he amassed a substantial collection of their work.[21] However, he was rabidly opposed to almost any other manifestation of modern art, particularly surrealism. Like Ben Nicholson, he tried to exclude opposing isms from exhibition. Cooper and Read shared a contempt for the Euston Road School, but ultimately they agreed on little else.[22] In response to Read's request for advice and support regarding the proposed museum, Cooper bombarded him with a set of peppery letters:

> You say there would not be enough money for *important* purchases: do you really think the postage stamp method of collecting . . . is worth doing? . . . what use is a guarantee for 5 years? Probably by then you will both have had a row, or one or the other will be bored: if she is bored the Museum presumably closes down & she is left with pictures bought by you & you are out of a job.[23]

Cooper promised Read that he would support any move which would genuinely be 'saving his soul'. 'I am sure the Burlington was a bore, but I should have thought it was a pleasant bore.' Read was irritated by Cooper's smug elitism, but the younger man disliked the 'unwilling public' who did not understand modern art. Read's more democratic ideas were rudely pushed aside:

> do you really think & believe that, for example, John Piper or Ben Nicholson, are either great or important painters? Would you be seriously prepared to maintain that they are on any grounds (apart from the prejudice you feel towards abstract (to my mind a meaningless word) painters) either better or more important painters than say Sickert or

Duncan Grant? . . . God knows I have no high opinion anyhow of English painting of *any* period since romanesque times. . . . I'm *afraid* artistic creation is not in the English race, there never has been a great English sculptor, nor a *great* English painter . . . It is only by standing firm on the things which one believes in & knows to be good – & after all one *knows* what is good & bad art – that one can hope to encourage appreciation of them. . . . I think, for example, that every mistake your museum makes is a nail in its Coffin.[24]

Although Read objected vehemently to Cooper's fanatical attacks on a museum which would accept a plurality of modernisms, he was shaken by the young collector's objections, especially as, with good reason, he feared Peggy's lack of stability. However, he informed Cooper that London needed not simply a permanent collection of modern art, but a place which would foster an atmosphere in which the modern tradition could prosper. Increasingly, he had come to the indisputable conclusion that Cooper was merely a 'snob collector'.

Read also felt that the *Burlington* was too tied to dealers. He had simply lost interest in the work there. More and more, he realized that he was a 'missionary, with an itch to rationalize and explain my instinctive preferences'. He had to gamble:

it is a risk I must take if I have any faith in my ideals. If, by the end of five years, the institution is a failure, I too shall be a failure, and everything I stand for. By worldly standards, I have always done the wrong thing. I was called a fool for leaving the Treasury for the V. & A. I was an even bigger fool to leave the V. & A. (prospect of the Directorship and a knighthood!) for Edinburgh; and to leave Edinburgh for the sake of what I conceived to be my personal happiness was the crowning folly of all. But I have never regretted any of these foolish moves; and though there have been difficulties of a financial nature, I have surmounted even these. I have never made any money and don't suppose I ever shall. . . . The sacrifices I have made have always been for something more valuable than position or money – but I am too aware of the self-indulgence involved in the process to want to make it an occasion for satisfaction or pride.[25]

Surprisingly, Ben Nicholson was strongly in favour of the proposal, even though he perceived that it would have a large surrealist component. He wrote to tell Read that he was disgusted with a reference in the *New Statesman* to Clive Bell as 'the critic who has done more for contemporary art than any other living' person: 'I think a Mus. of Mod. Art is exactly what is needed to counter all this still-born young Bloomsbury – they [the members of the Euston Road School] should be called the Dead End Kids?'[26] In April 1939, Read was also in the midst of negotiating his entry into Routledge. At the end of that month, he had

183

concluded an agreement according to which he would become on 1 July Routledge's literary adviser at £350 a year (he also received an additional £100 a year as a director's fee).[27]

George Routledge had opened his publishing firm at 36 Soho Square in 1843, the Railway Library (over 1,060 volumes) and the Universal Library being two of his most successful imprints. The company was reconstructed in 1902 when Arthur Franklin became Chairman. His son Cecil entered the business in 1906, becoming Managing Director in 1912. This was shortly after Routledge had taken over Kegan Paul, Trench, Trübner & Co., the acquisition of which was made to move the firm in the direction of publishing new titles rather than simply issuing reprints.

In 1939, Read was a well-known critic and book reviewer, and, with increasing dissatisfaction, had served as a reader for Heinemann for several years. Routledge wanted him to act as an 'ideas man'. He was to work an average of every other week, this arrangement having been made so that he would have sufficient time to devote to the proposed museum.

Then, as suddenly as she had determined to start a museum, Peggy, who had gone to Paris, changed her mind. She claimed that there was no enthusiasm in France for the project. 'To everybody's relief we finally gave up the idea.' Peggy was unclear about why Parisian enthusiasm was essential to the success of an English museum. Unsuccessfully, she tried to get a visa to travel to England in order to explain her new resolve to Read. Secretly, she was delighted when she was turned back: 'It was a good excuse to give Mr. Read, as I really did not want to go on with the thing.'[28]

Kenneth Clark was furious, claiming that Peggy had a moral obligation to provide him with an indemnity. She ignored this, settling half of the five years' salary on Read – minus the thousand pounds she had previously advanced. Peggy was unrepentant. As far as she was concerned, Read was £2,500 to the good, had been rid of a dull job and had joined Routledge as a partner. A trifle too assuredly, she declared that she had 'no qualms'. Then, she improbably claimed, read 'soon decided to write a book about his life and dedicate it to me. He wrote the book, but his wife may have objected to the dedication, as he omitted it. When all this was over he decided to call me Peggy, and thereafter we remained the best of friends. . . .'[29]

Kindly Edwin Muir tried to console Read: 'Am so sorry that Peggy Guggenheim has let you down; it may be a momentary panic. . . . She is quite a nice woman . . . but with such a deep sense of inferiority that she is difficult to deal with.'[30] Although Read discerned that Peggy had a 'good heart', he thought that all patrons tended to be vain. And, in the future, he shied away from schemes involving personal whims. He remained worried about the future of modern art in England: 'Our national indifference to the arts is not superficial: it is fundamental and will never change until the poison of commercial puritanism has been bred out of our blood.'[31] Meanwhile, at the advent of the 'Great Blackout', any such scheme had to wait until 'the lights come on again'. Meanwhile, it was best to 'crawl very carefully'.[32]

Read had joined Routledge under the assumption that it would be one of two posts, netting him an annual total of £1,450. Now, he had one job worth only £450. Although the £1,500 from Peggy helped considerably to resolve his short-term financial anxieties, he realized that his Routledge salary would have to be augmented by his pen – this was an obstacle he thought he had finally surmounted. Nevertheless, Read was enthusiastic about the possibilities offered by Routledge. The 'English Master Painters' series which had been rejected by Heinemann found a receptive home at his new firm. He made suggestions in July 1939 about improving the physical appearance of Routledge books;[33] in December he strongly recommended the establishment of the *Broadway Journal*, named after Routledge's location at Broadway House near St Paul's.[34]

That June, while things were still uncertain with Peggy, Herbert and Ludo went off in their 'little car' to Geneva, Milan, Brescia, Venice, Ravenna, Rimini, Urbino, Arezzo and Siena; their way back took them to Florence, Genoa, Nice and Paris, all in three weeks. That trip gave Read a breathing space. Although he had become a bit more defeatist than before, he was fundamentally an optimist, 'always ready to have a tilt at the windmill of despair'.[35] Providing a focus for modernism was, he told Cooper, more worthy of his 'energies than the hopeless task of preserving the integrity of a magazine for connoisseurs'.[36]

While Read was being defeated in his pursuit of some sort of financial equilibrium and while London was in imminent danger of bombing, Barbara Hepworth, Ben Nicholson and Naum Gabo were enjoying the relative tranquillity of St Ives in Cornwall. After their honeymoon in Italy, Adrian Stokes and his wife, Margaret Mellis, had settled there in May 1938. For them, Cornwall was a fusion of bright, brilliantly reflected light and craggy, windswept landscape. Adrian had told Ben and Barbara that, in the event of war, they could stay with him until they

185

were able to find a place of their own. Margaret Gardiner remembered the exodus: 'one afternoon in late August 1939, Ben, Barbara and the children all piled into the ancient car and drove to Cornwall, arriving at midnight in pouring rain. And the war came down on them there.'[37]

Soon after the Hepworth–Nicholsons had settled at the Stokes–Mellis house, Little Park Owles – a large, rambling house with large gardens and six acres of land – at Carbis Bay, they wrote to Naum and his wife Miriam urging them to join them. As she often did for her friends, Barbara found the Gabos accommodation at Faerystones, a small house a few doors down.

St Ives is positioned on the Atlantic coast in the Penwith district of west Cornwall, the most westerly fragment of land in England. Although Turner and Rowlandson had sketched and painted the region, it did not become a centre for artists until the 1880s. Writers such as Hugh Walpole, Compton Mackenzie, Havelock Ellis, Leslie Stephen and his daughters Virginia and Vanessa stayed there in the early part of the century. In 1920, Bernard Leach, the potter, settled there, and, eight years later, in August 1928, Ben Nicholson and Christopher Wood, on a visit there, chanced upon the naive paintings of Alfred Wallis, a seventy-three-year-old fisherman. The two were immediately taken with his sturdy, childlike renditions of sea and ships, responding to the intuitive feel for shapes and mood in his sombrely coloured work.

For Ben, Cornwall in 1939 was not a new terrain, and gradually his work was influenced once again by this remote landscape, his work beginning to take on tinges of realism. His energetic response to his new home can be seen in a letter to Read written shortly after he arrived there: 'It is very fierce & primitive & huge chunks of stone everywhere & the Atlantic & Carbis Bay & the English Channel in the distance – The sea is terrific . . . all v. foreign here – & such a balmy climate.'[38]

A similar movement towards naturalism can be seen in Hepworth's work. In 1939, however, she and her husband felt cut off from London. Bicycles, not the Tube or cars, were now the usual means of transport. Information on the war came in sporadically on the BBC. The Cornish were a bit distrustful of the newly arrived artists, and the motto 'Careless Talk Costs Lives' was extended to these strangers in their midst. For three years, Barbara ran a nursery school – she could sketch or sculpt only in the evening.

Since Read had remained back in London, he could keep Ben and Barbara abreast of what was happening there. And they could tell him of the anxieties which had arisen in large part because they were removed from their old milieu. In summer 1939 Ben confided in Read how desperate their financial condition was: 'As far as Barbara and I are concerned the lack of money has meant a loss of independence which is the devil & above all has meant never a quiet moment . . . & Barbara has had to work out the financial scheme of things so close to the bone that she hasn't been able to do any sculpture & has been laid up a great deal lately.'

Even in Cornwall, the war was a nightmarish reality, as Ben reflected in a letter to Read of August 1940: 'Perhaps this is the blackest moment before the dawn – certainly it's black alright – the whole thing is completely incredible & I keep on expecting to come to & find it's all a bad dream, very much overdone. . . . I think one must assume that one *may* be bumped off – & perhaps along with all the things one has ever cared & worked for. . . . I am hoping soon to have the brown uniform & forage cap & gun with which to collect parachutists – I only hope it's a Bren gun & not a rook rifle! & that they won't be too long issuing the things. I expect you'll have the same rigout.'[39]

Nicholson was displeased when Read told him in January 1940 of Kenneth Clark's continuing support of the dreaded Euston Road School. Sadly, Nicholson reflected: 'I think there is no doubt that Clark & the Euston boys will supplant the RA as the official art of this country.'[40] A bit later, in May 1940, Read disclosed to Barbara the full extent of disagreements within the surrealist group; he informed her that he had been viciously attacked by Mesens.[41] Among his many crimes, Read had consorted with constructivists, worked for bourgeois publishers, and was a friend of the 'religious poet' T. S. Eliot. Read told Mesens that he was 'going to please himself'. He had no intention of accepting a surrealist dictatorship.[42]

As well as providing much needed consolation to each other there were sometimes heated exchanges between Cornwall and London. In December 1940, Barbara was irritated with Read's use of the word 'classical' to describe Mondrian's work: such a term 'entirely fails to describe the romance, daring & intensity of his work. . . . Your definition of "classical" as "derivation, conformity & timidity" merely conjures up in my mind an academic point of view.' Hepworth also thought Read's use of 'romantic' had a tendency to become too vague. She understood that she herself was possibly falling victim to too much jargon, but, nevertheless, she thought many terms in current usage were useless or meaningless.

Earlier, in October 1939, Sophie (christened Sophia), Herbert and

Ludo's second child, was born. Read sent a postcard to Heppenstall: 'A fine baby, of the desired sex.'[43] A week later, on 17 October, he sent a letter: 'Sophie's delivery was "very tricky" . . . if the doctor had not been on time, Sophie would not have survived.'[44] According to his brother William, Herbert confided in him that he was much too old to start a second family. On the other hand, Leonie Cohn remembered him playing vigorously – and with great enjoyment – with Tom and Sophie on the yellow linoleum floor of the nursery at Broom House. However, Tom eventually learned, as John had years earlier, that his father's much used study was off-limits.

Having reached his mid-forties, Read had conflicting emotions about young children, but his deepest feelings may be seen in the tender and affectionate poem he wrote when Sophie turned two:

> Sleep, Sophie, sleep
> under our mouse-brown thatch:
> the sunflowers like sentinels keep
> their silent watch.
>
> In the pearly sky
> the hunchbacked moon is walking away –
> he has caught under his arm the reluctant day
> and you will be two when he returns.
>
> Two years and a day
> and a tongue that is beginning to talk.
> Oh, long may you babble like the crystal beck
> and leave learning to the owl
>
> Who is screeching in the withered oak
> on the other side of our road.
> The spiders are now weaving their midnight webs
> and the dew has formed to freshen your morning feet.[45]

The young girl is juxtaposed against the tranquil autumnal landscape, her oneness with the natural world gently elicited.

Read was a diligent, concerned and loving father, but he often was unable to express in conversation or gesture the fullness of his affection for his family, which is casually evoked in his description of a hot June afternoon at Broom House in June 1941: 'The children are running about naked in the garden . . . Ludo is spring-cleaning a bookshelf, and there is only an occasional aeroplane to remind us of the war.'[46] In a frisky aside, he claimed that the war should have inspired him to write sonnets 'in the grand Miltonic style'; instead, he felt like playing with the children. In April 1942, he was the 'dancing master' who operated the gramophone while Sophie and a neighbour's child frolicked. Thomas, who would never take part in such activities, dragged him into the study: 'I don't like dancing, Herbert. I want to draw dead men.'[47] In much more sombre moments, Herbert and Ludo debated the possibility of sending Tom and Sophie to safety in America but decided against it.

Fathers are sometimes closer to their daughters than to their sons, and this is true of Read: he reflected upon this in a letter of April 1940 congratulating Rayner Heppenstall on the birth of his daughter: 'I think you will be glad it is a girl: at least, after two sons I continue to be quite delighted with Sophie. It is quite a different feeling right from the start.'[48] Herbert's relationship with Sophie was one of gentle teasing, frequent laughter, shared confidences. One day she asked him why he was not a Catholic and thus attend Sunday Mass. Caught off guard, he impishly claimed that he reserved that day for washing his hair. As a young child, Sophie desperately wanted a pony and after the family moved to Yorkshire, Herbert purchased 'Brandy' from Graham Greene, Sophie's godfather. Graham promised that the almost horse-size beast was a gentle creature, but the animal was sometimes irascible. Nevertheless, Herbert and Sophie often went riding together, a habit which ceased only after such activity began to 'jiggle' his kidneys.

The war brought minor, as well as many major, worries. T. S. Eliot asked if there was enough space at Broom House to keep a suitcase. He wanted to pack up his winter clothes and stow them in the country. That way, if he was bombed, all his clothes would not be destroyed at once.[49] If Eliot were to die in the war, Ludo and Herbert were to consider the suitcase and its contents as their property: well-preserved pre-war clothes would one day be valuable.[50] When visiting Broom House, the taciturn Eliot frequently bestowed his sweet ration on Tom. Ludo continued to be frightened by Eliot, who was, as far as she was concerned, a 'spook'. During one of his visits, Eliot had a heated exchange with Read about stirrup-pumps, devices used to extinguish incendiary bombs.

Joe Ackerley was worried lest his correspondence with E. M. Forster should fall into the wrong hands. If, as Forster asked, he returned the letters to him, he was sure he would never get them back – and, one day, he hoped, they might be valuable. On the other hand, the letters, which contained information and gossip homosexual in nature, could lead some of his other friends into grave danger. The promiscuous Ackerley told Read: 'Some of my friends think that I

"*Oh, that's Herbert's muse.*"

Cartoon from the *New Yorker, c.* 1940–5: 'Oh, *that's* Herbert's muse.' This drawing, clipped from the magazine by Hepworth, Nicholson and Gabo, was sent to Ludo.

skate, at present, on ice so thin that I should take steps to avoid involving them in the event of my falling through.' Read agreed to put the papers away in a 'safe' at Broom House.[51]

London friends frequently asked if they could spend a few nights with them in order to get a rest. Nevertheless, Tom and Sophie were often frightened by the sirens which could be heard even at Broom House. And there were those asking for favours. The opportunistic Dylan Thomas, who never lost a chance to say nasty things about Read, pleaded with him in the autumn of 1939 for help in obtaining reviewing assignments. Remembering all too well how he been dragged into what he now considered a time-consuming racket, he advised the young Welshman, whose poetry he admired, that 'intellectual jobbing' was 'a self-destructive activity'.[52]

Denise Levertov, whose ballet school was evacuated to Seer Green in 1939 when she was sixteen, knew Read's poems and *The Green Child.* She was entranced when she learned that the Reads lived at the next house up the road. Her first visit to Broom House was with some fellow students to sell tickets to a recital. 'I said not a word, but used every minute to scan the wonderful paintings – one was a Miró, I recall – and the bookshelves, which . . . were the most enticing I had ever seen.'[53] Not long after, Ludo acted as accompanist when the regular pianist became ill. Denise volunteered to be the bearer of messages to Ludo, so that she could visit the enchanted house of books and art. Sometimes, Read would appear and she would gaze at him with adoration. Once, with a group of four or five others, Denise was invited to dinner at the Reads. This gave her the opportunity to go upstairs and peer at more paintings and sculptures and 'brightbacked books'. But she still lacked the courage to speak with her hero.

During the Battle of Britain, the ballet school gave a garden party to mark an exhibition of art by a child prodigy, Plato Chan, 'who with his mother and sister was a member of the strange assemblage of dancers, evacuees, refugees, Russian exiles, and misfits'[54] who made up the school. Read made a short speech, afte which Denise escaped the crowded room. Jealous of the wonderful conversations others, she imagined, were having with her idol, she retreated to the utmost edge of the garden and slipped behind a tall hedge, where she came upon Herbert and Thomas, then two. They too were hiding, and Read gave her an embarrassed smile. Denise fled, shouting 'Sorry!' Back at the exhibition, she heard people asking for Read. She maintained a gleeful silence – happy to be a guilty conspirator.

Read's most important book review of the early war years was devoted to Virginia Woolf's life of Fry. Not surprisingly, he was circumspect in dealing with his former publisher. Although the book may have had the 'limitations' inherent in being an insider's view of Fry, the life had 'inscape' wherein the biographer picked up the golden thread of the spirit and followed it through the mind's dark corridors.[55] Read saved his disdain for Fry himself, who, he again proclaimed, never came 'into any very vital sympathetic relationship to his own age'.[56]

Not unexpectedly, Read was not immune from attack, as when he suggested in a letter to the *New English Weekly* that Dante's Catholic dogma had little to do with the success of the *Commedia* as a work of art. This incensed arch-Catholic Eric Gill, who responded: 'This is, it seems to me, to mistake the accident for the substance – the bread and wine for God Himself, the temporal gift for the eternal remedy.'[57] Earlier, in December 1936, when Read was involved in a public debate with Gill and the Marxist critic Alick West, he began his rebuttal of Gill with this opener:'I feel like a lion in a den of Christians.'[58]

Further charges of ineffectualness were unleashed on Read in January 1941 by Stephen Spender, in his review of *Annals of Innocence and Experience* in the *New Statesman*. Spender begins by complaining that the continuation of *The Innocent Eye* (which forms the

191

first part of the new book) sits uneasily next to the earlier work. '*The Innocent Eye* and the prose extract from *Ambush* printed here are by Herbert Read, the sensitive recorder; most of the rest of the book is by Herbert Read, the thinker.'[59] Spender accuses Read of lacking, unlike T. S. Eliot, an artistic personality. 'I have read poems by him which record an instantaneous snapshot of a symptom of a love experience, but none which produced the impression of a sustained, strong continuous feeling of passion.' Spender is also unsympathetic to Read's frustrations as a writer, which, he feels, Read unfairly blames on external circumstances: 'There is a romantic side of Mr. Read's nature which seems to believe that, given slightly different circumstances, entirely different and much better poems and books would have emerged from his study, like rabbits from a hat.' Spender roundly rejects this argument: 'if this inspiration had been really forceful it would have carried everything before it, and would in the long run have resulted in a greater success than hack work of a literary and highbrow kind can do'. According to Spender, Read had spread himself too far in too many different directions.

Finally, Spender reaches what is for him the breaking point, Read's romanticism. In a passage which shows many of Eliot's prejudices, he attacks Read's articles of belief:

> In the last analysis, it is true that Mr. Read is a romantic, because he does not believe in evil and therefore he does not believe in the necessity of restraint. His anarchism and his aesthetic theories are based on Rousseau. It is possibly the lack of a belief in evil that accounts for the tenuousness and transparency of his poetry and opinions. Whatever the merits of the argument on either side, the writers with a sense of evil are also the writers who are most able to create character, and who have the most concrete vision of life. The writers who have no sense of evil tend towards abstractionism, bloodlessness and transparency.[60]

Spender, whose allegiance was to Auden as well as Eliot, is complaining about a kind of sensibility which is not, in his opinion, tough enough to deal with the omnipresent forces of evil. He wanted decisive practicalities, not indecisive fantasies.

Spender was right to be disappointed by the continuation of *The Innocent Eye*, which is much more ponderous than its predecessor. He also spoke the truth when he accused Read of lacking a strong 'artistic personality'. However, the often thin-skinned Read was sure that a personal animus was at work. This, he thought, was a particularly nasty piece of writing, coming as it did from a supposed friend. By 1940, Read's alliance with Spender – which had begun with a favourable notice by Read – had disintegrated considerably, Read feeling that Spender's was an unfixed character, as he assured the poet Henry Treece, who had also been attacked by Spender:

> You must know your enemies, but you must also understand them. If you know the unconscious origins of his aggressiveness, you can deal with him much more calmly & much more effectively. Aggression is always the counterpart of some feeling of frustration, and in Spender's case I don't think this is far to seek. He is a major poet manqué. He is not content to be a good minor poet (admittedly it is not even certain that he is *that*). But don't let him get under your skin: the irritation is exhausting. Wait until your 'coup' can be 'de grace'.[61]

One year later Read amplified his comments on Spender:

> Stephen has always been eaten up by envy, and he is only exceptional in that this feeling is directed quite indiscriminately against his elders as well as his contemporaries & juniors. He is even jealous of Eliot's reputation. . . . It is a bit steep of *him* to accuse me of inconsistency: my coat may be of many colours, but at least it is not a *turned* coat. But you are right to take the bull by the horns, or the cat by the whiskers. One kills this kind by kindness (my metaphors are getting a bit mixed). Give him all the space he wants. Invite him into the parlour, give him butter on his toast. But remember that he will never be a true friend: he will never cooperate. I know the type well – Wyndham Lewis was its representative in my generation. And because they are consumed by envy, because they cannot *love*, they end as failures. One must be infinitely forgiving with them.[62]

In turn, Spender felt that Read carried far too many 'chips' on his shoulders, as well as being unduly prone to blame external circumstances for his lack of success as a poet. He also thought – correctly – that Read could not accept the simple fact that Eliot's and Auden's talents as poets were simply much greater than his own.

A milder criticism of Read was published two months later by Graham Greene in the March 1941 *Horizon*. He knocks Read for 'sometimes [being] at pains to adapt the latest psychological theories before they have proved their validity' and for hailing 'so many new fashions in painting and literature'.[63] Not unexpectedly, Greene is uncomfortable with his friend's anarchism: 'sometimes we suspect that it means little more to him than an attempt to show his Marxist critics that he too is a political animal'.[64]

Greene's strictures, however, were kindly meant. He carefully juxtaposes the strengths of *The Innocent Eye*, *The Green Child*, *Wordsworth*, *The End of a War* and other poems with what he considers the second-rate work of art criticism. Unlike Spender, Greene sympathizes with Read's hatred of violence: 'a horror which preceded the war and did not follow it. The conflict always present in his work is between the fear and the glory – between the "milk-white panic" and the vision which was felt by "the solitary little alien in the streets of Leeds".'[65] Greene then seizes upon one of the most revealing passages in all of Read's writings:

> Glory is the radiance in which virtues flourish. The love of glory is the sanction of great deeds; all greatness and magnanimity proceed not from calculation but from an instinctive desire for the quality of glory. Glory is distinguished from fortune, because fortune exacts care; you must connive with your fellows and compromise yourself in a thousand ways to make sure of its fickle favours. Glory is gained directly, if one has the genius to deserve it: glory is sudden.[66]

Greene recognizes that the search for glory had replaced the search for God in Read's life. But, he realized, such a quest has a strong religious component, of surrender to a force outside the self. Despite the weary desperation which now threatened to overwhelm him, Read's unhesitant pursuit of glory, a rigorously self-imposed search which might never come to fruition, remained a central theme in his existence.

Read wrote a bantering letter to Greene to complain that, by ridiculing his art criticism, he was trying to rob him of his bread and butter. Greene responded: 'Alas, alas. I hate the idea that anyone should have regarded that article as an "attack". I deliberately rather exaggerated my disagreement with your art criticism, and your Freudian allegiances, so as I thought to throw into prominence the creative work for which I have so much admiration.'[67] As he confided to Henry Treece, Read accepted many of Greene's complaints: 'Did you see Graham Greene in Horizon? It was described as an attack to me before I had seen it, but coming from a Catholic it strikes me as a pretty handsome tribute.'[68]

A more serious literary quarrel occurred in April 1940 when, with the author's knowledge, Read accepted an invitation to give Sheed and Ward advice on a collection of short stories by Heppenstall. Although he admitted that the longest story in the collection was masterful, the stories as a whole were a 'mistake'. Heppenstall was furious. Read was obdurate: 'It seems to me that you ought to be grateful. . . . I do wish I could feel that I had done wrong, so that I could say I was sorry.' His only regret was that he had ignored his initial reluctance to make a dispassionate report on the work of a friend.[69] July 1940 brought the good news that London University had awarded Read the Leon

194

Fellowship (£400 a year) for research on the place of art in the educational system. These funds provided the time for him to begin *Education Through Art*. Ludo was also busy that summer translating one of Simenon's thrillers into English.

The new war continued to tax Read's sense of glory. He could not join his friends Bonamy Dobrée and George Orwell in signing a manifesto in the October 1941 *Horizon* calling for Official War Writers.[70] Earlier, in November 1939, he had flirted briefly with the idea of joining Kenneth Clark's War Artists' Advisory Committee. But he held no brief for the martial splendour which had inadvertently come his way more than twenty years before. He flatly disagreed with John Rothenstein, who asserted that the war had given the chance to some artists who had 'previously cultivated an esoteric vision' to find 'a common ground of contact with the public'.[71] Some harsh words about the 1914–18 conflict in *Annals* were deemed unpatriotic, unacceptable, and thus trimmed by Faber.[72]

Occasionally, Read's disdain for the war was partially overcome. When Rayner Heppenstall, now an enlisted man, attempted some 'conscientious tactics', Read told him he was acting like a fool. From the outset, he should have tried to be an orderly-room clerk: 'But I expect you have pretty well buggered your chances of anything like that now.' He also told his young friend that action would prevent him from getting 'broody'.

> The only other salvation is a change of heart. Cultivate your stoicism, your fatalism. You ought to know enough about life by now to realize that the *fact* of being personally implicated in the war doesn't make any difference to one's happiness. You have got the war inside you, wherever you go, whatever you do. The war is a fatality, a visitation. It is a flood, a plague, a blitz! Who are you to contract out of it? You wouldn't be any less conscience stricken if you were sitting under the bombs in London, or rotting spiritually in some 'safe area'.

Although Read thought England 'in the main, right', he knew that Hitler had made a more realistic analysis of the economic situation. It was a question of whether German brutality would, in the end, triumph over English stupidity and ignorance. Or – to put the matter in positive terms – could true humility successfully oppose arrogance?

> I would not like to have to fight again (I mean, actually shoot, stab, poison &c) but I recognize that that is an illegitimate fastidiousness on my part. But I want, desperately desire, our side to win. Because we can only win by social revolution, & if we, rather than Hitler, can carry through the

195

social revolution, I believe the world will be a better & a happier place to live in. Because we shall be gentle.[73]

Unlike Heppenstall, Read did not feel that he needed psychotherapy. In addition to writing and publishing, he made toys for the children: 'I only wish for more time, to take life easier, to sit back & watch it happening.'[74]

Read's first instinct was to retreat into the joys of his life at Broom House, whose existence was being threatened by the war.

> But well we know there is a world without
> Of alarm and horror and extreme distress
> Where pity is a bond of fear
> And only the still heart has grace.
> An ancient road winds through the wood
> The wood is dark: a chancel where the mind
> Sways in terror of the formal foe. . . .
>
> The branches break. The beaters
> Are moving in: lie still my loves
> Like deer: let the lynx
> Glide through the dappled underwoods.
> Lie still: he cannot hear: he may not see.

But, then again, the lynx may spy them out in order to destroy them mercilessly:

> Should the ravening death descend
> We will be calm: die like the mouse
> Terrified but tender. The claw
> Will meet no satisfaction in our sweet flesh
> And we shall have known peace
>
> In a house beneath a beechwood
> In an acre of wild land.

The poem dramatizes the omnipresent danger war has brought to the English countryside. Although Read does not seek extinction, his hatred of violence is so extreme that he will not sully his hands by returning violence with violence. Can one do anything in the wake of such threats to ordinary existence?

> The sense of glory stirs the heart
> Out of its stillness: a white light
> Is in the hills and the thin cry
> Of a hunter's horn. We shall act
> We shall build
> A crystal city in the age of peace

196

Setting out from an island of calm
A limpid source of love.

In an almost Miltonic manner, Read suggests that one must create a 'paradise within' when all that is without seems to be in disarray. The 'hunter's horn' from *The Innocent Eye* and the crystal city from *The Green Child* remind him that men, like himself, should be capable through the force of the imagination of creating a new order of world peace, even though such possibilities seemed very illusory, as on Thursday, 17 April 1941.

On the previous day, known simply as 'the Wednesday', the Germans had rained bombs on London in what they called 'the greatest raid of all time', which lasted eight hours, 450 planes dropping 100,000 tons of bombs. More than a thousand people were killed. Londoners had begun to wonder if the slogan in vogue – 'London Can Take It' – had any real meaning. The migration to the Underground, despite government edicts, was in full swing: 200,000 people were sheltering there nightly. A month earlier, Martin Poulsen's Café de Paris (ironically modelled on the ballroom of the *Titanic*) was hit by two fifty-kilo bombs killing thirty-four people, including Poulsen. Looters robbed the dead and wounded.[75]

That Thursday morning, Read had to walk from Bank to Piccadilly. No buses were running, and taxis were slowly plodding their way through the glass-filled streets. As he came towards St Paul's, Read found his way blocked. He had to take a series of detours past burning buildings, under a smoke-screened sky. Although it was usually difficult to get into Broadway House (wholesale butchers' stalls blocked the entrance), Read was taken that morning with the calm of his fellow Londoners: 'These people, after a night of relentless bombing, were not even bad-tempered: they were normal, unnaturally normal.' Was this bravery or apathy? 'I realized that I too was unnaturally calm, one of these millions to whom the phrase "going out to business" now meant "picking his way among the ruins".'[76]

In the midst of the horrible uncertainties that beset him and his country, Read was filled with a tremendous sense that England could be rebuilt, perhaps in a better manner than it had previously existed. 'The art which will then arise as a spontaneous expression of the spiritual life of such a society will bear no obvious relation to any art that exists now. It will incorporate . . . the eternal harmonies of all great art.'[77] At the moment of the very real threat of extinction of himself and everyone and everything he held dear, Read experienced a timeless moment in which his sense of glory returned to him in a new way. Despite all the struggles

197

he and his nation would endure, a new order of peace and brotherhood was possible. Many obstacles lay before him, but in a brief, crystalline instant he saw the way forward.

12   To Hell with Culture

The Blitz suddenly ceased halfway through 1941, to be replaced by the 'middle passage': three years of waiting for an end to the conflict – or a sudden resumption in air raids. Mollie Panter-Downes noted that the phrase 'after the war' suddenly came back into circulation.[1] The omnipresent Mass Observation claimed that there was a marked decline of interest in the news – people were indifferent to good news (such as the defeat of Rommel at El Alamein in November 1942) or bad news (Japan's attack on Pearl Harbour in December 1941). Of more concern was the penetratingly bitter cold to which England succumbed in the winter of 1941–2. American, French and other uniforms suddenly gave London a cosmopolitan look. The pubs in Fitzrovia were crowded and often dangerous. The black market flourished. In the main, the threat of danger seemed far removed, as George Woodcock reported in April 1943: 'This is a freak season, for weather and war alike, and here in London the domestic and the international scene has an air of inconsequential unreality in the mellow light of this extended autumn merging into a premature spring. Still, the people of London do not quite believe in the war.'[2]

In February 1941, Read notified Richard Church that Routledge was still standing, 'practically unharmed'. (A bit later, the office was hit badly in the spring 1941 blitz, Read's typewriter being among the casualties.) He went in to the office twice a week, but there was little to do. Ludo was well and expecting a baby in two months' time: 'That makes three – Thomas, Sophie & ? [Piers Paul].' John, up in Edinburgh, now eighteen, wanted to be a film producer. The only other news that Read had for Church was that Routledge had agreed to a 'hopeless proposition' but one which might 'break the ice at Broadway House': 'We have just taken on the Apocalypse Boys, if you know whom I mean – a group of young poets who had a volume published a year or two ago by the Freedom Press – Treece, Hendry, Fraser, Nicholas Moore & three or four others. We are going to publish an

199

anthology of their work – poetry, fiction & criticism. Some of it seems very good: it is, in any case, a pleasant change from Auden.'[3]

The 'Apocalypse' poets, facing the same dreary circumstances of existence which had led Auden to compose colloquial verse which examined the fading textures of English life in the thirties, wrote of the imminent collapse of European civilization in a stylistic medley which owes a great deal to surrealism, the Elizabethans, Blake, Dylan Thomas and Read's anarchist politics. Theirs is a poetry of myth, of a retreat back to the unconsciousness and the archetypes that Jung had excavated there. These young men did not want to face life as it was lived – they wanted to examine the underpinnings of existence in order to find out if life had any purpose. In *How I See Apocalypse*, Henry Treece grappled with the significance of the movement which he had helped bring into existence:

> In my definition, the writer who senses the chaos, the turbulence, the laughter and the tears, the order and the peace of the world in its entirety, is an Apocalyptic writer. His utterance will be prophetic, for he is observing things which less sensitive men may have not yet come to notice; and as his words are prophetic, they will tend to be incantatory, and so musical. At times, even, that music may take control, and lead the writer from recording his vision almost to creating another voice. So, momentarily, he will kiss the edge of God's robe.[4]

A poetry which seeks to apprehend 'the multiplicity of both Inner and Outer Worlds, anarchic, prophetic, whole and balanced',[5] could be accused of divorcing itself from reality and of wandering into a masturbatory, fanciful realm which had nothing to do with the threats of Nazism. Since the old formulas for civilization had, in Read's opinion, led to two world wars in the first half of the twentieth century, he was not optimistic about following them again down what he sensed was a new series of blind alleys. A different world order had to evolve, and apocalyptic poetry, since it questioned the bases upon which the old order existed, could possibly lead the way forward. As Read claimed, 'it is not war in the ordinary sense which we are enduring, but a world revolution in which all conventions' are being replaced 'by provisional formulas which are immediately tested under fire'.[6]

Apocalyptic poetry was strongly Celtic (Henry Treece was Welsh in origin and a great admirer of Dylan Thomas; Hendry, Fraser and MacCaig were Scots). Also it had questionable French connections through its dependence on surrealism. Quintessentially, it was romantic poetry, very much to Read's taste and not at all to the liking of Stephen Spender, who labelled such verse anti-intellectual, fallacious and verbose, as in his sarcastic comment on Treece: 'the problem of achieving ordered ideas for the sensitive young person under thirty in the world of today has now become so terrific that it may threaten to destroy his sensibility'.[7] As he confided to Treece, Read's views were completely opposed to Spender's:

> What I felt, and still feel, is that a trend in modern poetry which had hitherto been negative and destructive has suddenly become positive and creative. And poetry must now be positive, and prophetic. I was about the same age in the last war as you and Hendry are in this, and though your situation is entirely different, I look forward to your development with quite special sympathy. . . . You begin with suffering and experience, and you will not make our mistakes.[8]

Although Read's own verse shows few traces of apocalypse poetry, he was obviously taken with this new style, which his own literary and political writings had helped to foster. From 1942 to 1947, he developed two series, 'Routledge New Poets' (in wrappers with day-glo jackets) and 'Broadway House Poetry', which published, among many others, Alex Comfort, J. F. Hendry, Sidney Keyes, Emmanuel Litvinoff, Roy McFadden, Alan Rook, Derek Stanford, Julian Symons and George Woodcock. Read's first adventures in publishing this new kind of poetry were the anthologies, *The White Horseman* (1941) and *Eight Oxford Poets* (1942).

Of these young writers, Henry Treece was the one Read knew best. Treece, who was born in 1912 at Wednesbury, Staffordshire, had, after taking his degree at Birmingham, worked as an officer at a Home Office school for delinquents in Leicestershire and, subsequently, as an English master at various schools. He was at Barton-on-Humber Grammar School in Lincolnshire when he and J. F. Hendry published their first anthology, *The New Apocalypse*, with Fortune Press in 1939. As a child, Treece had been given only historical books – with lots of colour pictures – from which he developed his ardent sense of the past. Although obsessed with Celtic culture, he saw all of literature against the bright tapestry of epic adventures. Read had been with Routledge for less than a year when Treece approached him in September 1940 about the second anthology being compiled by himself and Hendry: *The White Horseman*. As he readily confessed, Read had long been one of his cultural heroes: 'If you'll forgive the metaphor, my head is rather like an attic store-room, its floors carpeted with odd snippets & clippings of your writings.'[9]

In turn, Read responded enthusiastically to Treece's verse, feeling that the young man was a Faber poet like himself, not a Routledge one.

201

Eliot, with whom Read lunched every other week, was looking, he knew, for a new poet, and Read decided in September 1940 to mount a convincing case for that person being Treece. 'My first loyalty, as a publisher, is to Routledge, but I am bound to confess that if there were a chance of Fabers doing a volume of your poems next year, it would be your best policy to go to them – and Eliot would pay a good deal of attention to my recommendation.'[10] Read decided, however, to wait until *The White Horseman* was launched before approaching Eliot. He also told Treece: 'there is also something to be said for *not* being another Faber poet'.[11] Since Read was certain of Treece's potential, he was also quite prepared to offer unabashed advice: 'I scrapped half my work at your age & sometimes have a twinge of regret. But if you want good fruit you must prune like hell.'[12]

Read, who remained deeply insecure about the fact that his reputation as a writer was not based on his verse, revealed to Treece that he feared that no one knew him as a poet. In response, Treece was able to offer him a mixture of good and bad news. The young man had always seen Read as a 'poet first: critic, though of major importance, has never been uppermost'. However, to test Read's own theory about his fame as a writer, he had asked two women from Bedford College: ' "Have you read Herbert Read's poetry?" Both "English" graduates (oh God!), they replied, "What, does he write poems *as well*?" '[13]

True to his word, Read aroused Eliot's curiosity about Treece at a lunch in mid-April 1941.[14] Two weeks later, Eliot, who liked the poems, had passed them on to Geoffrey Faber. However, Eliot used the possibly derogatory – for him – word 'exuberance' to characterize Treece's verse. He also observed that there was an excess of metaphor.[15] A month later, Eliot and Faber had decided in favour of Treece, but Read had landed himself in some very hot water at Routledge, his fellow director Tom Ragg being furious at his unprofessional conduct in marketing poems on offer to Routledge to a competing firm. Treece soothed Ragg when he gave Routledge an option on some prose writings.[16]

During these fraught negotiations, Eliot, in need of a new outfit, asked if Read could bring up some clothes on the train. However, he insisted, he did not want his dinner jacket.[17] A month later, he offered Read some friend-to-friend, publisher-to-publisher advice about the latest translation of a Maigret mystery story and the vagaries of selling detective fiction. Tentatively, he advised against allowing the word 'shit' and all others of its class into such books, his impression being that high-class detective fiction appealed to persons who had never seen such words in print.[18]

Meanwhile, Treece had become a friend of Read's. However, the young poet to whose work Read responded most deeply was the supremely unhappy Sidney Keyes, who was born in Dartford, Kent in 1922 and attended Queen's College, Oxford. Philip Larkin, who was at Oxford at the same time, remembered little about him except that he wore a fur hat in winter and had large disturbing brown eyes.[19] Keyes was in love with a woman, Milein Cosman, who was unmoved by his protestations – or repulsed by them. Despite clear signals to the contrary, he imagined that time would change the heart of the lady he adored. Sometimes his pleadings are a bittersweet mixture of Keats and surrealism: 'Not half an hour goes by without my thinking of you, and I dream of you continually. It isn't, apparently, Romantic nonsense that one dreams of those one loves very much. The context varies; one time I met you on a stair and as soon as I touched you, you changed to a stranger. Another time you were with me in a big empty house.'[20] Such protestations were received in stony, embarrassed silence. 'There is a kind of love so destructive that it cannot be borne,' he lamented, 'but I thought I was strong enough to bear it.'[21]

At nineteen, Keyes professed a learned romanticism quite similar to Read's in its intellectual preoccupations. Much more than Read – whose book on Wordsworth had been an important influence – he possessed an unwaveringly clear, strong poetical voice. Some writers, threatened by the appearance of younger ones who possess gifts to which they aspire, become hostile and, sometimes, punitive. Read's position as a publisher obviously dictated against such a stratagem, but his conduct in any case would have been the same: he was unfailingly generous. And Read was able to do this when he was entertaining serious doubts about his own future as a poet, the portion of his creative energy he valued above all others.

Keyes had come to Read's attention through T. S. Eliot, whom the young man had approached about a collection of poetry by Oxford undergraduates. Eliot was not interested, but he suggested that Keyes get in touch with Read. With great acuity, Keyes observed, 'Eliot and Read work together on all new poetry; they share it out.'[22] Since the very existence of poetry was under siege, Eliot and Read acted as fifth-column conspirators in the same cause. Recalling his part as a 'mole' in the service of poetry, Read said:

But the firms into which we had penetrated had very different characteristics and had to be subverted by different tactics. That Fabers were the publishers of my own poetry only added to the piquancy of the situation, and always provided a ready excuse for consultation. That certain poets fell naturally into Fabers' sphere was admitted – Eliot had been with Fabers for twelve years before I became associated with Routledge. . . . From the beginning of our 'conspiracy', therefore, Routledge was to be regarded as an auxiliary – as a position to fall back on when Russell Square was hard pressed, and perhaps (in Eliot's own view) as a refuge for poets who, though good, did not quite conform to the image of 'Faber Poetry' which Eliot had elaborated.[23]

Tom Ragg had, of course, uncovered just such a secret manoeuvre when he had upbraided Read regarding Treece.

Eight Oxford Poets, edited by Keyes and Michael Meyer, was war poetry only in the sense that it comprised verse written since the outbreak of hostilities in September 1939. In addition to the editors, Keith Douglas, John Heath-Stubbs and Drummond Allison were among the contributors. (Philip Larkin was furious at being omitted.) Read quickly agreed to do the book, asked for the manuscript to be assembled, and told Keyes and Meyer that he would come up to Oxford to discuss the project. True to his word, Read visited in June, eventually taking away enough material for the anthology (forty-one poems) and first volumes by Keyes and Heath-Stubbs.

Later that month, Keyes, having just passed his nineteenth birthday, enlisted in the Royal Fusiliers. For the next two years, constantly on the move from one military encampment in England to another, he found it difficult to write. In April 1943, he reflected: 'You have to be cheerful or commit suicide!'[24] Keyes died later that month in Tunisia – in battle. Shortly before, Keyes had visited Read at Routledge, the older man later realizing that death had been hovering in his office that day: 'When he came to say goodbye, he did it with an air of finality which at the time I thought he had assumed as a shield against false hope.'[25]

Throughout 1941, Read regularly wrote to Treece, whose life in the army seemed to consist of the 'radio, yelling babies and Army lorries'.[26] Read now felt free to express his disdain for certain writers, in particular his aversion to the tedious boredom induced by Henry Miller's phallic prose.[27] Like Treece, Read was certain that Mass Observation had simply become another form of totalitarian snooping.[28] When Treece considered pulling his punches in a counter-attack on Spender, Read was resolute: 'I don't see why your editorial should be less *aggressive*. More blows & harsher blows is what the situation demands. At the same time your tactics could be improved. Your mistake is to be too personal, too egotistical.'[29] Sometimes his young friend needed unstinting comfort, Read readily providing that as well: 'These phases of discouragement overtake us all. They are part of the creative process, [which] is always some sort of descent into hell.'[30] When Treece asked his publisher to intervene on his behalf regarding where he would be placed in the army, Read could offer consolation but no real help: 'My own boy, John, is being called up and wanted to get into the photographic or film section of the RAF, but I find I can't do anything for him – he has got to join up with the rest and then take his chance. I suppose this wholesale attitude towards human beings is inevitable in a total war.'[31]

Work at Routledge was hectic in the autumn of 1941. Books were selling, but paper was in short supply. Read wondered why, all of a sudden, people were reading. 'I'm afraid it is not the beginning of a renaissance, but only the economics of scarcity. So many luxuries are unobtainable, they "might as well" buy books.' Nevertheless, he hoped that something as a result would happen inside 'the collective skull'.[32]

In addition to his publishing job, Read was kept busy by his work for the BBC, a series of talks for the Indian Programme on Masterpieces of English Literature from Chaucer to Hardy. He also participated in a 'farce of a discussion' on modern art with V. S. Pritchett and Clive Bell, the latter refusing to 'take the thing seriously'.[33] He spoke against the motion 'That Art is not for the people' at an Oxford debate that November, claiming that the statement was fascist. A Somerville student witnessed a remarkable metamorphosis as he spoke: 'With severely limited gesture, a quiet voice and no fancy devices, he was transformed half-way through his speech into a passionate orator.'[34] However, Read, whose tests at the BBC had been abortive, knew that his 'voice did not come up to the full fruit standard, as the jam-pots say'.[35] He was also absorbed in the writing of *Education Through Art*: he had reached the stage where he 'couldn't stop. I've got to pursue my theory hell for leather. The chase is getting exciting. I think I am on the trail of something of quite revolutionary significance for education.'[36]

At times Read felt like an 'aging eagle',[37] but one determined that the voice of youth had to be heard. He was furious at Robert Graves and Stephen Spender when they suggested that the Second World War – in contrast to the first – had not generated any poetry of significance. In reply to them, he wrote a heated letter to the *Listener*, which was published on 30 October 1941:

> I do not think it is true that this war has failed to produce its poets. It is simply that the public has failed to notice them . . . because its favourite canaries refused to sing, the Press spread the rumour that all our singing birds had been scared away by the bombs. It was a lie, invented to disguise the fact that fashion, which makes the reputation of poets no less than of film-stars, cannot cope with the unexpected. . . . Above all, we must remember that this time the poet has been warned: he is disillusioned before the event, and to acquire a few illusions might be his happiest fate.[38]

By July Henry Moore had been making his shelter drawings for almost a year and had, without success, been looking for a new war subject. Read suggested that he tackle coal-mining, as England's 'underground army' was doing vital work to keep the country going. Moore, whose father had been a miner, was touched by the suggestion and avidly pursued it.[39]

Disgusted with the *New Statesman*'s hatred of totalitarian Germany and its concomitant inability to realize that its notions of socialist collectivism were German in origin, Read wrote a letter of complaint to the editor, published on 24 May 1941: 'Well, Sir, what are you going to do about it? Are you going to be consistent and gradually eradicate the concept of the state from your political philosophy? . . . Seventy years is not a long time in the history of a nation, and it may not yet be too late to return to a democratic faith based on the ideal of individual liberty.' In support of G. D. H. Cole, Read advocated that decision-making be relegated to small groups. The editor sardonically replied: 'In an age when technical change has vastly increased the power of the State, the problem of preserving the liberty of the individual or the small group becomes increasingly difficult and important. But it is not to be solved by talking about the abolition of the State.'[40]

In this piece of invective, Read also gave muted support to the war effort. His fellow anarchists told him that they were disillusioned even by this provisional backing. He retorted that if Hitler won the war, anarchism would be obliterated from the memory of man as 'completely as any of the medieval heresies'.[41] Privately, Read assured Douglas Cooper that the point of the letter to the *New Statesman* was that 'we shall never destroy Germany until we destroy the German state'.[42] A year later, in July 1942, he had changed his mind: 'A victory for Churchill would be a victory for a rhetorical unreality, for a social compromise, for the sheer weight of stupidity.'[43] In a world filled with 'gangsters and charlatans', only the pacifism of Gandhi appealed to him.[44] When William Plomer asked him in 1945 how he would vote in the upcoming parliamentary elections, Read shuddered: 'Vote?'[45]

His growing sense of the failure of art in fascist and capitalist societies is the major theme of Read's *To Hell with Culture*, the title of which comes from Eric Gill. Unfortunately, he asserts, art has become subjugated to nationalistic concerns which have nothing to do with art. He had made much the same point in *Essential Communism*, but his new pamphlet envisions the emergence of a new, truly democratic order at the end of the war. Then, the corrupt culture of the past could be discarded: 'To hell with such a culture! To the rubbish-heap and furnace with it all! Let us celebrate the democratic revolution with the biggest holocaust in the history of the world. When Hitler has finished bombing our cities, let the demolition squads complete the good work. Then let us go out into the wide open spaces and build anew.' In a deliberately Whitmanesque conclusion, Read foresees a new society which will brush aside the framework of capitalism. This new brotherhood will not lead to perfect works of art, but the fact that the artist will be 'appealing to a more highly developed form of society will induce a higher degree of perfection. The artist [will have] a more perfect instrument on which to play.'

In 'Art in an Electric Atmosphere' in the May 1941 issue of *Horizon* Read lacerated the hide-bound traditionalists who, as artists became more and more involved in the war machinery, hailed the 'eclipse of the highbrow': 'As in the last war, these reactionaries console themselves with the thought that communists and artists and the so-called *avant-garde* were a lot of stormy petrels announcing the storm that has now broken over us: that when the storm has passed there will be calm again, no noisy birds, a stable society and classical art.'[46] Avant-garde art, according to Read, encapsulates the spirit of its times; it is the harbinger of change. On the other hand, culture, he admits, can be worn like a suit from Sackville Street or cultivated like an Oxford accent.[47]

True art is original, creative, universal and revolutionary. Will England have false or true art after the war? That, according to Read, was the fundamental issue:

I can only reply that it will be an expression of the society we then establish. If we go back to the government of the Bank of England and the City, to preposterous monopolies exploiting the essentials of life, to a parliament of fools and an underworld of crime, then we shall go back to an art of convention, sentimentality and pride against which a few revolutionary protests will be more vain and ineffective than ever. But if we discard the notions of victory and defeat, if through common suffering

207

we are driven to humility and good will, then reason may prevail in human affairs and we shall build up from the ruins a society free from all the grotesque and irrational institutions of finance, snobbery and greed. The art which will then arise as a spontaneous expression of the spiritual life of such a society will bear no obvious relation to any art that exists now.[48]

The perennially acerbic Douglas Cooper wrote to Read on 6 June 1941 to compliment him on his recent publications. Cooper incorrectly interpreted *To Hell with Culture* as an attack on those 'dreadful Bloomsburies'. Good taste, he condescendingly lectured Read, was a 'natural, not a hot-house plant, it needs weeds, not vapour, to make it thrive'.[49] According to him, culture was dying in England because it was worshipped in a void by arrogant intellectuals. He also did not like the word 'rebuilding'; according to him, English civilization had to be recreated: 'You know who will rebuild – & what they will rebuild. The unholy alliance is ever-present: Clark, Bell, Mortimer, Sutherland, Piper, Reith, Lutyens.'[50] Cooper had become vorticist in his advocacy of bombs: 'People must see & get used to more & more destruction of their towns. When they have *this impression* visually & *sufficiently vividly* then they will accept the destruction of their ordered society. The destruction of slums free of charge is a *benefit* to humanity.'[51] Such oafish sentiments were against the grain for Read, but he agreed that the eradication of 'all that filthy property round Routledge's' filled him with joy.[52] Having launched a general series of invectives, Cooper went on specifically to attack the official war artists whose work was on display at the National Gallery:

> Please, Herbert, go to the National Gallery in an important frame of mind. Has Graham Sutherland any right to have & inflict his trivial vision on an ignorant innocent public? How dare the Director of the NG launch this vast *charlatanade*? And John Piper? How comes it that he does not commit suicide if he is not capable of feeling something more about wartime ruins than what he expresses in paint?. . . *Please look sincerely* at Henry Moore's gross travesties of art – they look ridiculous even beside Topolski: yet Henry was once an artist. Are these 'the producers of culture' who must at all costs be protected from military service? No, Herbert, in their & the country's interest you should plead for this insane waste of public funds to be stopped immediately.[53]

Such outbursts tried Read's patience, but he concurred with Cooper about the 'frivolity' of Piper and Sutherland; they were 'little men who made a prettiness out of war'. He disagreed completely about Moore, for whom drawing was not a 'proper medium'. Nevertheless, he lamented his friend's involvement with Kenneth Clark and the support given to Moore by Bloomsbury. Read insisted that, at the very least, Cooper give him credit for not having succumbed to that circle: 'Kingsley Martin, Raymond Mortimer, David Garnett, Clive & even the holy Virginia herself – they all always gave me a mental gooseflesh. It was instinctive in the old days, but now one sees how logical one's instincts were. These people were never real, and now the war has exposed them in all their unreality.'[54]

Six months later, Read himself was insulted by the astringent Cyril Connolly in *Horizon*. Despite the fact that he was a sometime contributor, Read saw that magazine as 'the last flicker of pre-war decadence, a post-Proustian inquest on a dead epoch'.[55] Trouble began when Connolly rejected a poem of Read's on the grounds that the diction was flat, although he admitted it was a good piece of work. As Read sarcastically told Treece, this reminded him of Stalin's complaint against one of Shostakovich's symphonies: 'he couldn't whistle the tunes'.[56] Then, in his 'COMMENT' in the November issue, Connolly announced that no poems appeared in that issue – despite the fact that the magazine received 100 submissions a week. Seventy per cent were simply the 'bottom level of trash'; the others showed 'Poverty of imagination, poverty of diction, poverty of experience': Connolly claimed that this thirty per cent of contributors represented a puritan imagination. Then, he wrote a sketch of an imaginary bad poet – John Weaver – who 'will have been published in *New Verse*, *New Writing*, and *New Directions*, and have produced one volume of verse, with an introduction by Herbert Read, called *The Poet's Thumb*'.[57] Not only had Read been humiliated by rejection, he also had to put up with a gratuitous insult which attacked his generosity to young writers.

Read complained about *Horizon* to Cooper but thought it should be allowed to survive. The paper shortage was severe, but the government's position on this vexed matter remained inconsistent: 'every day *tons* of paper are wasted on unnecessary advertisements, or publications like the Nudist & Prediction, not to mention the filthy newspapers themselves'.[58] He also agreed with Cooper about the much-lauded Sickert exhibition: 'With everyone round me talking about "the greatest English painter since Turner" & such like, I began to feel that my inability to see in him anything but a *third*-rate impressionist, and a bit of a charlatan at that, must be due to defective sensibility.'[59] Read also passed on news of Peggy Guggenheim's affair with Max Ernst, adding 'wasn't he always a bit of a cowboy?'[60]

Connolly, realizing that he had gone too far the previous year, published an essay by Read in April 1942 – 'Vulgarity and Impotence' – with a note on the contents page: 'COMMENT is again held over owing to pressure of space, and this month Mr. Herbert Read's article must be considered to replace it.'[61] Read accepted this bald statement as a peace offering.

In his new article, Read returned to many of the principles he had been annunciating since *Art Now*. Most of his remarks centre on a show at the London Museum, 'New Movements in Art: Contemporary Work in England: An Exhibition of Recent Painting and Sculpture', which was devoted to surrealist and abstract–constructivist work. Read commended the surrealistic works on display and extolled the abstract–constructivist, being especially lavish in his praise of Gabo's *Spiral Theme*. 'Creation is a much abused word, applied loosely to imitations and logical constructions: it is justified only for that absolute lyricism we call "pure poetry". . . . But even within this absolute world there is an hierarchy, and at the summit I would place this spatial construction of Gabo's.' In particular, Read was touched by the way the form hovered like a still but vibrating falcon 'between the visible and the invisible, the material and the immaterial', becoming in the process 'the crystallization of the purest sensibility'.[62]

Although they had been good friends for six years, Read had not previously written about Gabo's work. The Russian, who had waited patiently for some sort of signal, realized that, at last, Read had been 'overcome and . . . deeply moved'.[63] For Read, the Gabo sculpture was an attempt to wrest a form from the unconscious and to create a piece of art which manifested the fullest potential hidden within man. Such promise, he increasingly saw, was in danger of being eradicated by the war.

Paul Nash's pride was 'sorely wounded' by the *Horizon* article.[64] The artist was referring to Read's vehement attack on surrealism's separation from 'social relevance', a central theme in, for example, *To Hell with Culture*. Nash's reaction was very mild compared to that of Barbara Hepworth, who was deeply hurt by this passage on constructivism:

> I think it is perfectly fair to accuse these artists of egotism. . . . More particularly, they suffer from the illusion of the *transcendence* of the work of art. . . . The work of art is only ratified in the organic ritual of life, and it is only in so far as the constructivist succeeds, not only in constructing these platonic models of reality, but also in modifying the communal environment, that he acquires the full stature of the humanist.[65]

210

Read, who had once fought against Eric Gill's doctrines, had through the process of war come to agree with him: 'every man is a special kind of artist'.[66] Although Read obviously applied his new criterion to all works of art, Hepworth realized full well that her old friend had changed his mind about the perennially thorny issue of 'social relevance'.

Desperately afraid that Read was about to join ranks with the enemy, Hepworth wrote to him in April 1942 with scarcely concealed bitterness, maintaining that in an undigested way Read was shifting his ground.[67] Had he thought of the consequences? 'Dear Barbara,' Read scolded: 'Relax.' Their misunderstanding, he claimed, arose from no longer seeing each other frequently, but he firmly stood his ground: 'the gulf does exist between your art and the people at large, and the only question is how it can be bridged'.[68]

Earlier, in March, Read and Gabo had disagreed about the London Museum show. Gabo did not think art had to be placed in relation to 'current life', appreciating however Read's observation that the exhibition would seem 'dreamy' to a spectator wandering in off the street: 'But what else could we have expected? It represents on a small scale the pathetic picture of a spiritual world one half of which is dead.'[69] Gabo was obviously much more even-tempered about the *Horizon* piece (he had been singled out for the highest praise), and he tried to mollify Ben and Barbara: 'It took me quite a while to convince them that meals are not so hotly eaten as they are cooked. Ben seems to take it reasonably enough. Barbara is tired, poor girl: With all the 5 children (Ben included) on her hands it is not easy to keep a cool mind.'[70]

Barbara and Ben had obviously been irked by the unstinting praise given to Gabo at what they perceived to be their expense. Gabo informed Read: 'You have committed a major crime by allowing yourself the preference for somebody-else's work . . . which is not tolerated here on this side of the river.'[71] Gabo concluded with the particularly rueful observation: 'No, Herbert, an art critic shall have no friends if he has opinions; or he shall have no opinions if he has friends – but he *may not* have both.'[72] Sadly, Read responded that he had found – and then abandoned – the perfect formula in *Art Now*: 'theorize & mention nobody; illustrate everybody'.[73] Read was disgusted with Nash and Hepworth, as he confided to Treece: 'My Horizon article has caused much perturbation among my "art" friends. It was meant as a declaration of independence, but from all sides they accuse me of

211

desertion. They can't see that it is the world that will desert them unless they wake out of their egocentrism.'[74]

When the precocious Alex Comfort, twenty-two years old and two years short of qualifying as a doctor, sent him a small selection of his verse in May 1942, Read told him on 5 May that he did not have any anthologies in production, was going ahead with four volumes in his New Poets series, and would therefore like to see Comfort's poems again when he had enough to make up a volume of 32–48 pages. Comfort responded at once, for Read wrote a letter accepting *A Wreath for the Living* on 12 May – a week later. Another young writer to whom Read immediately warmed was Denton Welch, whose *Maiden Voyage* Comfort called to his attention.

By turns reclusive and exhibitionistic, Denton Welch, badly crippled by a bicycle accident, was twenty-seven when he approached Herbert Read with *Maiden Voyage*. In that strange, jewel-like book – part *Bildungsroman*, part memoir, part travel book – Welch attempted to write about, among other things, his early life in China and his homosexuality. Although the book is frank, its eroticism is subdued. Nevertheless, it had previously been rejected by Jonathan Cape and Chapman & Hall when Comfort offered to thrust it down Read's throat.[75] Soon after he received the book, Read invited Welch to lunch at the Reform, entertaining the sophisticated but bumptious young man with a variety of anecdotes about literary London. Welch was fascinated when Read, following his lead, did not have a draught of ale. Was this 'true politeness, lack of energy or love of simplicity, or even kindness for the waitress'?[76] Even after they had left the dining room, no mention had been made of Welch's book. Nervously, Welch alluded to Edith Sitwell's admiration of his work. Read replied: 'I used to make omelettes for her.' Eventually, almost as an afterthought, they got back to *Maiden Voyage*.

'Some people might call it precious,' Read began tentatively.

'But then I suppose that's my personality.'

'Exactly,' Read responded. 'It struck me in some odd way as very contemporary, or of your generation.' He then revealed to Welch that he had not yet come to a firm decision.

Read's hesitation was due to objections by two Routledge directors, to whom he had painstakingly explained the merits of the book. Finally, he informed Welch that he would do the book if it was vetted by his firm's libel lawyers. Really, he had wanted to have lunch to discuss terms.

'I know nothing about terms,' the young man confessed.

'What a good thing I'm a poet as well as a publisher,' Read proclaimed. Then he offered an advance of £50.

Welch was buoyed up by the experience. He realized that, as far as Read was concerned, the sections of his book which were frank were simply that. He did not have to feel guilty about his sexuality or writing about it. As he later announced, 'Tongues down throats and other things don't seem to worry Edith and Herbert Read.' Welch gleefully revealed to Comfort that Read subsequently authorized him to decorate 'endpapers, frontispiece, title-page, dedication page, full-length decorations to the three parts and an end piece. I think the production will really be quite *lavish* for wartime!'[77] He was a bit disappointed, however, when the promised advance turned out to be £30, not £50 – and not until ten days after the publication of the book did Read inform him that he was to be paid for his drawings.

Read's life at Broom House remained happy and uneventful. There were frequent forays to the 'Kitchen Front' to fix broken appliances, and Broom House really needed four servants 'for any sort of comfort'.[78] In March 1942, he wearily joked: 'We are all very well – house full of howling healthy children & no help. Ludo lives in a rubber apron & washing up is a social event. But we survive.'[79] Four months later, Read was happy to be off to Yorkshire for ten days: 'it is my first break for over two years & I am ready for it'.[80] True happiness would be a 'one-job life' and yet at least half the happiness of life, he realized, was 'busyness'.[81]

George Höllering, the surrealist cinema-owner, was making a documentary (*Message of Canterbury*) for the British Council, and Read asked him to take John on as a camera assistant. In turn, the wily Austrian persuaded the Archbishop of Canterbury to appear in his film, the sermon having been written by Read, who realized that with a little more zeal he might have become a bishop.[82]

Throughout May and June, Read was frantically trying to complete *Education Through Art*. On 14 May he emphasized to Treece that the book needed his 'utmost concentration': 'I am neglecting letters wholesale.'[83] A month later, he looked forward to being 'a free man – as free as I am ever likely to be'. He had only the preface, bibliography and 'some sort of peroration' to worry about.[84]

Read, concerned with his own role in a new society, agreed to become head of Design Research Unit, which was set up on 1 January 1943. The

213

impetus for this new organization had largely arisen as a response to Read's *Art and Industry*, published nine years earlier. In the summer of 1942, Marcus Brumwell, Chairman and Managing Director of Stuart's advertising agency – a member of the Advertising Services Guild, which was a conglomeration of agencies which had banded together to share resources in bombed-out London – held a ration-restricted dinner at his house in Surrey, at which he and Read conceived the idea of a service which would expand the role of design in British industry.

Brumwell and Read discussed their ideas with Cecil Notley, who, in turn, asked Milner Gray to devise a detailed plan. Gray, at that time head of the Exhibition Design Department at the Ministry of Information, contended that a skeleton group had to be formed which would be in a position at the end of the war to supervise the anticipated increase in the demand for first-rate design.[85] He envisioned a three-part structure, incorporating design, research and administration.

An early leaflet announced the group's aim in idealistic terms: 'Like every aspect of modern industry, design should be a co-operative activity, and the function of DRU is to focus on every project it undertakes the combined knowledge and experience of several creative minds since it believes that only by pooling the talents of a team of designers is it possible to offer a service capable of meeting every demand from the wide and varied field of present-day activity.'[86] As Misha Black recalled, despite the fact that he was fully aware of divided feelings within industry, Read's public statements revealed a very limited practical understanding of the frequently bitter struggles between manufacturers and designers: 'We thought we really could change the world, particularly through the design of low-cost products. . . . However, the things which Herbert wanted to have made and sold were in fact not the things (and still aren't the things) that most people want.'[87] Read felt that starting the Unit in 1943 was a 'little like setting out to make omelettes on a wartime egg ration'.[88]

Read's DRU office was a small one in Kingsway, where from 1 March 1943 he was director with 'a bare table & a blank sheet of paper'.[89] From the outset, he was able to give this new venture only two days a week. When it became apparent within a year that a full-time manager was needed, Bernard Hollowood, an economist who was then teaching at Loughborough College, took the job. Hollowood, later the editor of *Punch*, left after three months when he was offered the assistant editorship of *The Economist*. Although Hollowood had up to that time known Read only through his writings, he was stirred: 'It was like God

214

descending.' However, he realized, it 'was always an effort for him to become a man of the world'.[90]

As at Routledge, Read was an 'ideas man', not really comfortable with the hard-boiled businessmen who had to be convinced that industrial design had any relevance to commercial success. Read and Hollowood undertook one trip to the Midlands, where they were welcomed without enthusiasm at virtually every factory. There were many other problems. Notley and Brumwell's 'dangerous ambition'[91] made them 'unscrupulous' when dealing with fellow designers, with whom they frequently fought. On such occasions, Read would be caught in the middle.

By May 1944, Brumwell had made everyone at DRU restless: the secretary was quitting, Hollowood was nervously trying to make the operation more cost-efficient, and Read was convinced that Notley 'wanted to get rid of' him and that Brumwell was 'fighting all out' to save him.[92] But being supported by Brumwell was a dubious distinction: he was tactless, fussy and interfering. Then, the designers wanted their independence from the Advertising Services Guild. As Read observed, Brumwell had made the 'baby kick by his clumsy nursing'.[93] Quite soon, Read decided that 'administrative machinery' was the true enemy of good design.[94]

Working with an old friend also proved an arduous experience. When Jowett of Bradford wanted a design for a post-war car, loosely based on the 'wasp-tailed' line of the Lincoln Zephyr, Read asked for Gabo's assistance. Brumwell and Notley were eager that this project should lead to a successful outcome, since they envisioned this commission as a showcase for the Unit's talent. The contract could also have been lucrative (£6,000 over six years), and Read attempted a sales pitch.

> I spent three hours trying to persuade a motorcar manufacturer to employ Gabo to design his postwar cars. Succeeded up to a point, and then comes the dirty business. They are willing to pay the man who designs a new gearbox thousands and thousands, but they still think of the artist as somebody they can buy for tuppence-halfpenny. BUT for the first time in history we have got them by the balls.[95]

Read spoke too soon. Gabo, whom Read also asked to design vacuum tin packs for tobacco, proved to be pernickety in his dealings with Jowett and DRU, Read warning him in October 1943 that he was tending to be too legalistic. Exasperated by Gabo's tardiness in delivering detailed plans and models, Jowett exercised the escape clause in the contract in January 1945. Gabo's design, an early hard-top concept incorporating an all-Perspex canopy over the passenger compartment, was breathtakingly revolutionary: this may have been the real reason for rejection.

One of DRU's later, post-war efforts to sell itself was a display conceived by Misha Black and Milner Gray at the Britain Can Make It Exhibition: 'Birth of an Egg-Cup: What Shall the Egg-Cup Look Like?' A multitude of answers – ranging from a ceramic Humpty-Dumpty children's cup to a streamlined piece of international modernism – confronted the spectator in profuse, surrealistic splendour: only the size of the egg – determined by the hen – and the inventiveness of the designer could circumscribe the egg cup.

Read remained as Director until the end of the war, although he maintained a life-long interest in the Unit, into the running of which he instilled democratic principles, so that there was supposedly no 'boss' who handed out the work and told other people what to do.[96]

The interest in practicality which the war had induced in Read found its most valuable outlet in *Education Through Art*. In the late twenties, Evelyn Read, a former teacher, had carefully examined the early drawings of her son, asked him about them and kept a detailed scrapbook of the pictures together with John's comments and her own often psychological explications. Read's interest in children's art was largely influenced by his ex-wife's fascination with the significance of John's drawings, of how they revealed the unconscious world of his fantasies and conflicts.[97]

From the late twenties, Read had become obsessed with the inner landscape of his own early childhood, recreating the first stirrings of a love of literature and art in *The Innocent Eye*. He had also become intrigued by the separate worlds of innocence and experience. Like Blake, he increasingly realized that the world of simple innocence is often destroyed by experience; in order for society to have any chance of reconstituting itself in a meaningful way, a higher innocence had to be brought into being. Such feelings found full expression in his new book. No longer could children be corrupted – as he felt he had been at Crossley and Porter – by harsh, unfeeling, bureaucratic educational systems.

In addition, Read experienced 'something in the nature of an apocalyptic experience' when, while researching the book, he came across 'Snake around the World and a Boat', an image drawn by a five-year-old girl. He immediately recognized a mandala – a primordial

216

The mandala by the young girl which moved Read when he was writing
Education through Art.

symbol of psychic unity – in her circular, segmented image. Although
Read had been moving in the direction of Jung for years, this epiphanic
moment convinced him that the Swiss psychoanalyst understood better
than anyone else the forces which bind all mankind together.

If individuals and nations could build upon a common heritage of
symbols and dreams, perhaps there was a glimmer of hope for
civilization. In order for the world of the archetypes to find positive
expression, every child had to become an artist, and art had to be moved
to the centre of the educational curriculum, a place which it had never
occupied in most educational philosophies. Previously – as Barbara
Hepworth realized – Read had seen the artist as an outsider, who had no
social function. Now, in the forties, Read took up the political
implications of surrealism which he had once neglected, and applied
them to children's art. Art, he now insisted, had the power to transform
society. Hepworth imparted a modicum of praise, but she lamented that
no sculptural forms were reproduced in *Education Through Art.*

217

In 1943 Read authored six books. This left him in a mental weariness such as he had never experienced before. 'I deserve to be put into mental quarantine of some sort,' he complained to Treece.[98] Hepworth suggested that he and Ludo take in 'a P.G.' to alleviate financial stress. She also commiserated with him on the flak which he seemed to take for all manifestations of modernism: 'You are the mouthpiece, the infamous encourager (perhaps conjurer) of all this nonsense. . . . You are in the middle of things & I am outside it, but I get just as strongly as you the sense of the reaction setting in, & perhaps stronger than you the feeling of real danger.'[99]

Other friends were openly critical. Eliot made a series of minor complaints about *Education Through Art*.[100] This led Read to tell Richard Church that he and Eliot had never 'exchanged anything but . . . pedantic criticisms of each other's work'.[101] Dobrée confessed that 'A World Within a War' made him uneasy: he felt that Read was being 'true only to a self that isn't completely integrated with the you which represents what you really stand for: you are a happy warrior, not a hunted prey. Nor, I hope, are your children terrified little dormice just loving each other. I'm sure they scrap and bicker, and momentarily hate like any other healthy young animals.'[102]

A modicum of praise came from an unexpected source when H. G. Wells wrote to express his admiration for *The Politics of the Unpolitical*. Bluntly, Read told the novelist that, although they shared some views, he found Wells' anti-clericalism out of date: 'Not that I have a word to say in defence of priests and churches, and perhaps they are still active enough and powerful enough in countries like Spain to justify your invective. But here, and in most parts of the world, they seem to me to be as harmless as the rats and crows which also inhabit their historic monuments. They will be automatically cleared as we rebuild.'[103]

Read was quietly happy in November 1943 when he received a copy of the page proofs of the book on himself edited by Treece, which was published by Faber and Faber the following year. The production standards of the book were even pre-war. 'But I am getting into trouble over the frontispiece [a pencil sketch by Gregorio Prieto], which Ludo & all the ladies unite in condemning as an outrage on my poor old face. But most men agree with me that, like the essays in the book, it is to be regarded as an *interpretation* of a somewhat obscure subject, & as such is justified.'[104] Wistfully, he confided in Treece: 'It is a queer sensation to read all this about oneself & I hope it won't have a bad effect on me. It would be heady stuff if I had any inclination to be conceited.'[105]

218

13   Freedom: Is It a Crime?

In March 1944, the war hovered like a heavy cloud, dark and unmoving, above Read's head: 'I hate it so much & hatred breeds frustration.'[1] In January, the 'middle passage' had been broken by the 'Little Blitz'. Once again, London was silent and empty at night. Rumour had it that the invasion of France was imminent, this bit of news seeming to be confirmed when ten miles of coast were placed out of bounds from 1 April. When the bombing suddenly ceased that month, there was talk of secret weapons. All of a sudden, the Americans vanished. London was silent, anxiously awaiting news, when the landing at Normandy took place on 6 June. A week later came the first flying bombs, the V1s. George Orwell reported this new phenomenon to the American readers of the *Partisan Review*: 'After the wail of the siren comes the zoom–zoom–zoom of the bomb, and as it draws nearer you get up from your table and squeeze yourself into some corner that flying glass is not likely to reach. Then BOOM! the windows rattle in their sockets, and you go back to work.'

Despite the liberation of Paris on 25 August, London remained under siege, the first, silent V2 striking there on 8 September. Although the black-out was replaced by the dim-out nine days later, the ever increasing certainty of an Allied victory nevertheless left London resolutely depressed. In that month's *Horizon* Connolly reflected on the effect of the flying-bomb campaign: 'they have made London more dirty, more unsociable, more plague-stricken than ever. The civilians who remain grow more and more hunted and disagreeable, like toads each sweating and palpitating under his particular stone.' On 24 June Eliot cancelled lunch with Read because Faber and Faber had been blasted. No windows remained, the ceilings were down, and all the doors had flown off their hinges. Now, he had nowhere to sleep. Nevertheless, since he was a member of the fire watch, he would be camping out in the office on Tuesdays.[2]

The map of London was slightly different each day, as streets took

219

their turn to be pounded. Although he often had to navigate round streets filled with debris, Read continued to make his way to Routledge and the DRU. Like most Londoners, he found work a tiresome, unheroic relief from the frightening mysteries hovering in the night. The trains were so badly lit that reading was impossible. So Read's ride home in the evening was like a journey through 'one of the circles of the Inferno'.[3]

That January, Read told Denton Welch that he liked *In Youth Is Pleasure* but warned him that the picture of the hero he presented was one most people would find perverse or even unpleasant.[4] For his part, Read was happy to publish the book, so long as Welch realized the risks he was taking. Cooper had pressed on Read Connolly's *The Unquiet Grave*, which appeared under the pseudonym Palinurus. This volume, a book of aphorisms by Connolly and his favourite writers, irritated him:

> He is good on writing & on the position of the artist in modern society; but his moralisings on life in general are rather superficial, and clumsy in comparison with the quotations in which they are embedded. It is a fallacy to imagine that one enhances one's own jewels . . . by setting them in other people's gold.[5]

Barbara Hepworth, sometimes a difficult friend, liked the expression 'a life of forms' in Read's catalogue of Moore sculpture and drawings, but she objected to Read's association of abstract art with the machine. Also, she was dismissive about Moore's overly intellectual – for her – ideas about sculpture.[6] If there was disunity in the avant-garde, such bickering was not evident to the outside. Edward Bawden recalled Coldstream giving 'a wicked imitation of a prayer-meeting led by Herbert Read and Ben and Barbara praying with Salvation Army gusto, confessing their sins of representation, and asking the good Lord to make them abstract and advanced'.[7]

One bright spot as the war slowly began to wind down came in November 1944 when the Reads finally had Broom House to themselves.[8] Joe Ackerley ordered Read to free himself 'from the clutches of the businessmen, where you have become so lamentably buried away'; a 'nervous breakdown' was called for.[9] But Read carried on with his relentless round of tasks, including a speech given at the Areopagitica conference in London in August.

With unswerving zeal, Read rededicated himself to anarchism, which is fundamental to the schemes proposed in *Education Through Art*. There Read advocated a reformation of the senses which could lead to a gradual, peaceful transformation of society. In addition to *To Hell with Culture*, his full-length political publications in those years were *The Philosophy of Anarchism* (1940), a selection of Kropotkin's writings (1942), *The Politics of the Unpolitical* (1943) and *The Education of Free Men* (1944).

Throughout the war, Read clung to the 'insurrectionary passion' annunciated in *The Philosophy*. Towards the end of that conflict, however, he became concerned about a split between proletarian anarchists and intellectuals such as himself. Although saddened by this rift, he thought it inevitable: 'sooner or later a separate organization for the intelligentsia of the movement is inevitable. It is the same old story: the proletarian distrust of anything they don't understand & can't appreciate: their hatred of the artist.'[10] Also, Read's own position became increasingly concerned with anarchism as an ideal, rather than a programme with clear-cut political goals.

During the First World War, anarchist journals in England had been suppressed, and the movement did not revive until the Spanish Civil War, with the first number of *Spain and the World* in 1936 (it was succeeded by *Revolt* in 1939; in turn, *War Commentary* soon replaced it and was superseded by *Freedom* in 1945). Vernon Richards, an engineer, and his wife, the alluring Marie Louise Berneri, daughter of Camilio Berneri, the Italian anarchist, spearheaded the movement in England in the thirties and early forties. They were at the centre of the Freedom Group, which operated Freedom Press and published *War Commentary*. The Richards–Berneri circle was, in 1939, joined by the militant pacifists of the Forward Movement.

Deep divisions within the movement surfaced when, at the outset of the war, a clandestine Anarchist Federation of Britain was founded. Five years later, a group of syndicalists gained control of that Federation. Eventually, this led to a rupture with the Freedom Group, who withdrew the use of their press from the dissidents. Such breaks, Read was sure, could only lead to total eradication of the anarchist movement. Although he did not want to paper over quarrels, he felt a united front was the best opposition to any clamp-down from the government. Thus, he argued for concessions to the distrusting proletarian and advocated 'sounding-board' anarchy. Any hopes that Read had for quiet diplomacy were shattered when the Special Branch of Scotland Yard raided the offices of *War Commentary* at the end of 1944, seizing membership and subscription lists.

Like many other anarchist–pacifists, Read was outraged by this attack on the Freedom Group. His first response was to circulate a

221

protest letter, signed by, among others, Orwell, Eliot, Spender and Forster. The next move was the government's in early 1945 when the Director of Public Prosecutions charged Berneri, Richards, Christopher Hewetson, a doctor, and Philip Sansom, a commercial artist, with conspiracy to 'seduce from duty persons in the Forces and to cause disaffection'.[11] The government's evidence rested on a poem in a leaflet, two verses of which read:

> Your country, who says you've a country?
>   You live in another man's flat.
> You haven't even a backyard.
>   So why should you murder for that?
>
> You haven't a hut or a building,
>   No flowers, no garden, it's true;
> The landlords have grabbed all the country;
>   Let them do the fighting – not you.[12]

The prosecution was seen by left-wing intellectuals as a signal from the government that the same stringent control of speech exercised in the war would continue into the indefinite future. Probably, the government gave so much time and effort to this case because of its determination to carry on with conscription in peacetime.

The Freedom Defence Committee, a group which lasted until 1949, came into being not only to support the four defendants but also to guard the right of free speech in a supposedly democratic society. The Civil Liberties Association, which had been infiltrated by Stalinists, refused to help. As chairman of FDC, Read made two speeches (published jointly as *Freedom: Is It a Crime?*). Specifically, he claimed that the use of Defence Regulation 39A was being prolonged – despite the fact that the war was virtually over – in order that distasteful opinion might be suppressed.

In his first speech Read lambasted the government's conduct of the war and called for active opposition to its aims:

Our statesmen have made a chaos and call it victory. Millions of men are dead, and their silence is called peace. . . . Comrades, the time for doubts and hesitations is past. Those who waited for the war to bring about a revolution must now repent their mistake. The situation is unequivocal. There will be no revolution – just yet. But from this moment we move into active resistance. The front line of the Resistance Movement is now here, in England, and we, *alone* if necessary, will continue the fight against fascism.

Read's outrage is even more boldly expressed in a letter of 6 April 1945 to Henry Miller:

> though I may have been thrown a bit off my balance in 1940, under the imminent threat of invasion, I never, God be thanked, got entangled in the dirty mess, either as propagandist or as militant. The most I did was walk the Buckinghamshire lanes under the stars to watch for a falling bomb, which never fell. And of course one occasionally had to suffer the alarms and agitations of London. But I took an oath at the end of the last war that I would never fight again, and though my age has secured me against the compulsion to fight this time, it is my hatred of war which has kept me out of it.
>
> Now the real fight is on. Four of my anarchist friends have been arrested by the police (after an investigation conducted with the usual insolence by our Special Branch or Gestapo) and are to be tried at the Old Bailey later this month on a charge of 'attempting to cause disaffection among His Majesty's Forces'. We have organised a Defence Fund and are going to fight the case to the bitter end, with the best forensic aid we can command. It will be an interesting showdown for our fascist government, but incidentally it has been a wonderful stimulus for our movement, and hundreds of people who have hitherto been cynical or indifferent are rallying behind us.[13]

The trial began on 23 April. When Read attempted to enter the court, he was able to get in only as a press representative. He claimed to be writing for *Horizon*, the police subsequently telephoning Connolly to verify the story. The anarchists, who had previously espoused their doctrines in magazines of inconsequential circulation, now, in a fine bit of irony, had their propaganda hawked to millions by the newspapers and tabloids of Lord Rothermere and Lord Beaverbrook. The public benches were filled with a 'peacock array'[14] of the denizens of Bohemian pubs and Soho and Bloomsbury clubs. Police witnesses became confused and managed to invent a non-existent Surrealist Party. The glamorous appearance of Marie Berneri, the real professional revolutionary, made her into a tragedy queen who quickly won the hearts of the all-male jury.

On 27 April, three of the four defendants were found guilty and imprisoned for nine months. To no one's surprise, Marie Berneri was acquitted on the technicality that a wife could not conspire with her husband. This event brought Read an even greater sense of anxiety than the previous six years: was the government of his country, having subdued the fascists, now going to take on their attributes?

The Freedom trial had provided only a momentary break in Read's

223

daily existence. He had, for example, to deal with Samuel Beckett, who, upon learning that the 782 unsold copies remaining (out of a print-run of 1,500) of *Murphy* had been remaindered in 1942, wrote a vituperative letter to Routledge asking why they had not honoured a clause in his contract which allowed him to buy unsold copies before they were disposed of cheaply. No one at the firm had heard from Beckett since 1940, but he did not accept that explanation. However, he asked Read if Routledge wanted *Watt*, his new novel. Read was enthusiastic, but – as was to happen with increasing frequency over the years – his fellow directors did not want to take on a book which could not find its feet in the marketplace. Thus Read had the unpleasant task of saying no to Beckett.[15]

George Orwell, a fellow member of the FDC, asked Read in April 1943 to speak on modern English verse on the BBC's Indian programme. Read turned him down. He was very busy at DRU and, in any event, he had always made it a rule not to criticize fellow poets.[16] Also, the suggested poets (they have not been identified) were a 'particular bunch' towards which he felt only diffidence.

Spender, a supporter of the Freedom Defence Committee, renewed his attack on Read's poetry. In a review of *A World Within a War* (1944), Spender hit out again at the vagaries and woolliness of romantic verse in a world which had to face up to war and its aftermath: 'If Mr Read believes that the realisation of the intrinsic nature of the self and of nature and of poetic beauty is the answer to destruction, it is not quite easy to see why he often argues so ideologically.'[17] What Spender fails – or does not want – to see is that Read refuses to accept the world on its own sordid terms. He envisions the possibility of a new, democratic order, uncorrupted by the past. Spender's classical view is of an evil world which must be saved from itself. Read sees man as essentially good, capable of salvaging what has become an increasingly self-destructive universe.

When Read presented Eliot with a copy of *The Education of Free Men* at Christmas, he knew full well that his old friend would be hostile to that pamphlet, which is a summation of many of the arguments mounted in *Education Through Art*. Eliot made many marginal notations on his copy, indicating his displeasure. Read asserts: 'It is only onto a stock of goodness that knowledge can be safely grafted: by grafting it onto stocks that are unbalanced, undeveloped, neurotic, we merely give power to impulses that may in themselves be evil or corrupted.' Did that, Eliot asked, mean anything more than that we want children to be healthy? When Read casually refers to the 'classical buildings of our own time', Eliot sarcastically quipped that he was not claiming much.[18]

Despite the largely enthusiastic response to *Education Through Art*, Read was frequently upbraided for not having laid down a precise curriculum. He refused to do this, not wanting to substitute one bureaucracy for another. As was often the case, Read sought to stimulate discussions within small groups, discussions which could lead to changes within those groups. He informed Richard Church: 'Education is like life – you kill it if you try to plan it too systematically.'[19]

In February 1945, Read was delighted when his post as head of DRU led one of his business contacts, who had recently begun to collect modern painting, to ask him to approach Paul Nash on his behalf. This fellow was 'pathetically helpless' and Read appealed to Nash for mercy: 'Well, there you are, dear Paul, the bird is sitting pretty.'[20] Gabo, displeased that his design for Jowett Cars had been rejected, was extremely lonely, since he was not getting on with Ben and Barbara.[21] In March 1945, Herbert and Ludo were expecting their fourth child. He wished Henry Treece could see the children: 'Thomas's eyes are much better – he has lost his squint & no longer needs glasses. Sophie has grown into a beautiful child & Piers is a bright little clown.'[22]

That summer, Gabo heard that Read was to be in Paris: 'I understand you will be seeing Picasso & Co. Tell them from me that they are nuts.'[23] Douglas Cooper suggested that Read organize an exhibition of contemporary art for the British Council. John Rothenstein wanted the Council, while the Tate was closed, to allow him to shunt 'his mouldy collection round Europe, himself as itinerant showman'. Read opposed this, wanting something 'strong and fresh' as opposed to the New English group.[24] When Orwell sent him a copy of *Animal Farm* Read galloped through it in a sitting; then Thomas, aged seven and a half, spotted the book and insisted that his father read it to him. Read reported to Orwell: 'I tried Chapter I on him. He insisted on my reading it, chapter by chapter, every evening since, and he enjoys it innocently as much as I enjoy it maliciously.'[25] Read modified his praise of the book to his fellow anarchist, George Woodcock: 'After all I had been led to expect, I too was surprised by its comparative mildness.'[26] Herbert, Ludo and the children had a 'terrific' holiday in Scotland that August, despite the complicated transportation arrangements involving three separate trains, fourteen pieces of luggage, four lots of double taxis, and heavy tips to understandably reluctant porters.

The autumn of 1945 brought the first of a series of long, sententious and frequently bombastic and abusive letters from the American poet and critic Edward Dahlberg, whom Read had briefly praised in *Politics of the Unpolitical*. Although they had not met Dahlberg recalled seeing Read in Chelsea. Eager for a sounding board for his quasi-mystical pronouncements, the American got in touch with Read, who was seven years older. The surprising thing – even to Read himself – is that he maintained this friendship until the end of his life.

The American was a strange combination of William Blake and D. H. Lawrence. Like Blake, he believed that apparently villainous figures such as Satan and Judas were the real heroes of the Bible: these characters had had the courage to say no to those who would organize and lead them. Lawrence's indictment of the machine and of puritanism also found favour with Dahlberg, who increasingly saw himself as an Old Testament prophet shunned by the cowardly denizens of the United States. The paradox of Dahlberg's literary life was that he expected his victims to thank him for calling them knaves.

Dahlberg wanted, like Read, to reject the mediocrity to which he felt modern culture had sunk. What is not readily obvious is why Read was willing to accept abuse from Dahlberg for so many years. By temperament, the two men were completely unalike. The strange bond between them arose – and continued – because at some level Read saw in Dahlberg a wry, dark image of himself.

As his autobiography *Because I Was Flesh* makes clear, Dahlberg had also been deeply wounded by a possessive mother. The two men had had few advantages in embarking on literary careers, both being 'self-made' men. Read, who in Kneeshaw, for example, had explored other sides of himself, was brought face to face with alienated aspects of his character in Dahlberg. Read was kind, gentle, phlegmatic whereas Dahlberg was often cruel, harsh and manic. But Read was always aware of *what he could have become*, and he looked into a mirror, although a distorted one, in his dealings with Dahlberg. Read tried to make Dahlberg a more tolerant person, in the process perhaps trying to assuage the aggressive instincts within himself. Also, Dahlberg – in his perverse way – prodded Read with unanswerable questions: why bother, in an increasingly uninterested world, to defend art and literature? was 'culture' worth saving? In the mid-forties, Read was caught up in a whirlwind of public events which distanced him from private concerns. For better or worse, Dahlberg forced him to think about his inner life.

Like Read, Dahlberg had lost his father at an early age (in fact, he did not know with any certainty who his father was), and he had been placed in an orphanage by his mother, a barber named Lizzie, who wanted to live in peace with her lover. When he read Dahlberg's autobiography in 1962, Read told him that the orphanage chapter had intrigued him because 'I too spent five years in an "orphan home", a New Testament, non-conformist version of your Jewish one. Mine was perhaps a milder place, less cindery, but not essentially different. I had not realized we had this kind of experience in common: it is perhaps one explanation of our mutual sympathy.'[27]

Outwardly, Dahlberg remained very different from Read. In 1947, Dahlberg's wife Winifred left him, afraid that he would subject further physical abuse on her and their sons. A year later, he was fired from a teaching post at New York University when he improbably claimed that a student had threatened to shoot him. Dahlberg's flamboyant histrionics led others to treat him in the same way. When he chose the title for his 1941 book, *Do These Bones Live?*, he had ignored the King James translation. One day, as he was sauntering around Greenwich Village, Djuna Barnes accosted him: 'It's "Can," Mr Dahlberg! "Can"! "Can"!'[28]

Another of Read's American correspondents, Peggy Guggenheim, had opened a gallery in New York. Her chief function, she revealed to Read, was to give unknown artists a chance. Of those she was in touch with, Jackson Pollock was clearly the best – she thought he would one day be as well known as Miró: 'His painting is rather wild and frightening and difficult to sell.' Robert Motherwell, who was 'much weaker', had such perfect taste that he sold 'much more readily'.[29] Peggy herself was attracted to the work of Clyfford Still: 'there is a melancholy, almost a tragic sense incorporated in the paintings which makes them seem particularly near to me now.'[30]

Read and Gabo persisted in their bickering over Picasso. Read divulged to Gabo that, like him, he had serious reservations about the Spanish artist, but he did not wish to voice these doubts in public for fear that 'any qualification could be interpreted as a confession of weakness'.[31] Read also had serious doubts about the emergence of existentialism in the guise of Sartre and Camus: 'It is a bit of a racket, I am convinced, being a pretentious name for something quite commonplace.'[32] Later, somewhat more generously, he pointed out that the main concepts of this 'new' movement – angst, the abyss, immediacy, the priority of existence to essence – are to be found in Coleridge, who 'no doubt got them from Schelling'.[33]

The end of the war brought a series of new problems with Evelyn. Read made several trips to Scotland that autumn to make arrangements for the institutionalization of his ex-wife, who could no longer live on her own. As John recalled, Read undertook this task in a cold, businesslike manner. Later, in November, Read visited Switzerland, which seemed untouched by the war. In contrast, he always found in the French a 'sensation of simple physical decadence',[34] being appalled by their flourishing black market. Only the communists seemed to have any moral strength.

Read had gone to Switzerland to meet with Jung at Küsnacht, in order to broach the scheme for a collected edition of the seventy-year-old psychoanalyst's work. Beginning with *Psychology of the Unconscious*, Routledge had been Jung's English-language publisher since 1916. Because he was a great admirer of Jung, Read became the emissary who had to employ all the diplomatic skills at his disposal to persuade him to consent to this huge project. Another major undertaking for Read was his first visit in March 1946 to the United States in order to deliver the Woodward and Trowbridge Lectures at Yale.

These four lectures, published in *The Grass Roots of Art*, manifest the increasing utilitarianism of Read's aesthetic values, interconnections being made among politics, sociology, education, design and culture. Read no longer views the artist as the outsider; all men are capable of becoming artists but society has hampered them in that pursuit. Art is not a product of civilization but is, rather, a spontaneous, private activity in which all men could be made proficient. Read's feeling that the aftermath of war had led to another series of blind alleys is kept at bay, especially when he envisions the necessary conditions for rebuilding the world.

1.   The reconstruction of our physical environment to secure the most favourable framework of a vital culture.
2.   A social system without the wide diversity of personal wealth.
3.   An industrial system that gives the worker a direct responsibility for the quality of his work.
4.   An educational system that preserves and matures the innate aesthetic sensibility of man.[35]

However, only in small groups is any kind of reconstruction possible. When trade unions – in which Read fervently believes – become intermixed with politics, the result is chaos: 'In Great Britain, as is well known, it was found necessary to establish a separate body for political action, the Labour Party. The fate of this party, however, has always been dependent on the financial support of the trade unions, and its policy has been controlled by the materialistic aims of those unions.'[36]

Read did not have a specific prescription for post-war society, but he remained convinced that capitalism and socialism were ineffectual. He clung to anarchy not because it had solutions but because it had, at the very least, the courage to ask some interesting questions.

Excited at the prospect of his friend's trip, Gabo, who had visited the United States in 1938, beseeched Read to help him emigrate there.[37] During his stay, Read met Mary Mellon and John Barrett about the Bollingen Foundation's competing interest in publishing a complete translation of Jung. Earlier, Paul and Mary Mellon had become ardent disciples of Jung, Mrs Mellon in particular being devoted to the Swiss psychoanalyst. Convinced that Jung's teachings were of inestimable value to the weary soul of post-war mankind, she wanted, as a philanthropic gesture, to make his writings available in the English-speaking world. When Read met with Mrs Mellon and Barrett that March, he made it clear, as he wrote back to Routledge, 'that we had had the same bright idea before we had ever heard of Mellon, and the fact that I had already been to Zurich to see Jung was immensely impressive'. They had 'struck oil':[38] the agreement reached at that meeting was that Bollingen would pay all editorial and translation costs; Michael Fordham – Read's and Jung's choice – was to be general editor, and R. F. C. Hull was to be the translator.

As early as 1939, Read had flirted with the idea of emigrating to the States, but he realized that he would be no happier there than in a South Sea island.[39] That March, he was almost seduced by the high standard of living, much higher than he had been led to expect. Despite this, he was disdainful: 'the general standard of intelligence is obviously lower than the one we are accustomed to in Europe'. Although he could admire the naivety of his hosts, he felt that they could never really understand the artist or intellectual. 'So [they] in such a country remain terribly lonely.'[40] There was certainly no real interest in contemporary art at Yale. New York was most inhuman – it was a place where 'the machine & all its values has conquered man'.[41]

> But I do not despise America in general. I could live somewhere on this Continent & throw myself into its struggle for form, for values. But perhaps I do not estimate the difficulties at their true dimensions. The power belongs to men who have ruthlessly eliminated all their competitors, who are continually threatened by usurpers, who have completely divorced private & public morality. One of the most curious characteristics of this people is their complete misunderstanding of democracy. They do not believe in *equality*, but in 'equality of *opportunity*'. They confess that again & again, with pride, without

229

realising that 'equality of opportunity' is merely the law of the jungle, that they are not egalitarians, but opportunists, and that logically their faith leads to a struggle for existence in which the fittest who survives is merely the most unscrupulous.[42]

In April, Read spent Easter at the Moholy-Nagy farm in the mid-West, eighty miles west of Chicago, where he had flown the previous day on a Constellation plane, which, he gleefully reported to Ragg, 'did the trip of more than 1000 miles in four hours. It was very comfortable, indeed luxurious, with lunch on board served by stewardesses who looked like film stars.'[43] He found Chicago 'indescribable': 'the vitality, the vulgarity, the wealth *and* the poverty'. In the midst of attempting to get a berth on the *Queen Mary*, which was sailing from New York on 12 May, he forewarned directors' wives and secretaries: 'THERE ARE NO SILK STOCKINGS IN THE U.S.A. It is the only thing they haven't got, and they never stop complaining about it.'[44]

Kurt Wolff of Pantheon Books, who had arranged the meeting with Mellon and Barrett, had shown Read the drawings for a children's book on poodles. Wolff wanted Pantheon and Routledge to do 30,000 copies each, a prospect which Read found tempting, since he found the book the 'most delightful juvenile' he had ever seen. 'It is about seven French poodles who regret they cannot be distinguished one from the other, & go to a barber and are clipped until they resemble, one a horse, another a monkey, another a bear, another a hedgehog, &c, one only remaining a poodle.'[45]

While he was in the States, Read wrote to Aldington, who was living on Sunset Boulevard in Hollywood. He received back a starchy reply: 'I have thought that you gave up far too much time and energy to public works. You should cut them off. They just use your brains and good nature and organizing ability, and they're not really grateful.'[46] Aldington was convinced that Read was much too generous in his view of Americans. He reminded him that he had not had time to make a proper assessment: he was a guest and his hosts had been on their best behaviour. Such people were 'degenerate on acquaintance, when they are no longer out to impress the distinguished foreign visitor'.[47] In his missing letter to Aldington, Read claimed that he did not think Americans were very interested in sex. Aldington retorted: 'As to American sex, they have 153 babies born every second, so I guess they get around to it somehow.'[48] While Read was at Yale, Peggy Guggenheim sent him a copy of her autobiography, to which he sent a barbed compliment: 'You have outrivalled Rousseau and Casanova. . . . I found it quite fascinating as a document – an historical

230

document – and it is only the lack of introspection and self analysis which prevents it from being a masterpiece.'[49]

Awaiting Read upon his return to London in the late spring of 1946 was a peremptory letter from Jung, who reminded him that other publishers were interested in his collected works. Read replied on 23 May, setting forth the agreement reached with Bollingen and suggesting that they discuss things further that summer at the Eranos conference. Those meetings took place at Ascona, a village at the northern end of Lake Maggiore, on the slope of Monte Verità, a few miles below Locarno. Since the late nineteenth century, that place had attracted freethinkers, intellectuals, nudists and gurus, including Lenin, Trotsky, Bakunin, Kropotkin, Hesse, Isadora Duncan, Paul Klee and Erich Maria Remarque. Olga Froebe established the School of Spiritual Research at Casa Gabriella, her Ascona estate, in 1930; when Froebe quarrelled with Alice A. Bailey, who had come over from the States to assist her, she closed the doors to the school. Two years later, Froebe approached Rudolf Otto, who was also deeply interested in the connections between Eastern and Western religion. He responded warmly to her ideas about a lecture programme, suggesting the name Eranos, which in Greek means shared feast. Jung was among the speakers at the first Eranos conference in August 1933.

At a business meeting at Casa Gabriella in the autumn of 1946 Jung, Fordham, Barrett and Read came to an agreement in line with the accord reached in New York earlier that year. Mary Mellon did not travel to Europe that summer and died suddenly on 11 October, the work of the foundation subsequently being overseen by her husband. Eranos summers soon became a way of life for Read, who enjoyed the sublime beauty of the setting and the Jungian discussions, although he referred to the people at the Ascona café tables and Eranos veranda as 'wasps of every hue and size'.[50]

Back in London that autumn, Read and Clive Bell were actively buying pictures for the British Council, £1,000 a year having been allotted the previous May for the purchase of contemporary British art for the decoration of British institutes abroad.[51] A Nicholson, a Pasmore and a Matthew Smith were among their first joint purchases; later, Bell, without consulting Read, bought a Coldstream and a Gowing. Ben Nicholson was in a ruminative frame of mind when he wrote Read a stirring letter late that August: 'I suppose the urge to discover new things instead of repeating oneself is merely an urge towards life instead of death & that's about the biggest known urge? . . .

The excitement of discovering a new ptg "idea" is terrific – rather particularly because it's something *beyond oneself* – a kind of transformation – as much beyond oneself as being in love.'[52] The shared aims of critic and painter are movingly captured in this vivid passage – both wanted an art which reached 'beyond' the self in a way appropriate to the mid-twentieth century. During the Hampstead years, they had thought such a 'transformation' within their grasp.

The painter also confided in Read that the 'severity' of his work was due to his immense sympathy with his mother: 'She gave up her promising painting & put all her creative powers' into raising her children; '*I owe absolutely everything* to her'.[53] He also told Read that he felt that Moore needed to 'resolve' his sculptures more: 'Harry's are interesting as ideas *but* more or *less meaningless as enduring ideas*';[54] Ben also claimed that he and Barbara wanted to dissociate themselves from 'Constructiv*ism*. Constructive is a different matter, not a label but covering all the things one likes in all arts past & present.'[55] Meanwhile, Naum, Miriam and Nina Gabo, after a wretched crossing, arrived in the United States that December.

The last month of 1946 brought a new dispute with Ben and Barbara. In 1937, the Revd Walter Hussey had taken over St Matthew's, a large Victorian church in Northampton. The Anglican priest felt that contemporary music and art should be used in the modern church and seized upon St Matthew's fiftieth anniversary in 1943 to do something about this. Benjamin Britten and Michael Tippett were given commissions, and Kirsten Flagstad sang there twice. Through Harold Williamson, Principal of the Chelsea School of Art, which had been evacuated to Northampton during the war, Hussey approached Moore, who agreed to do a *Madonna and Child* for him. The sculpture was unfavourably received by Hussey's parishioners, some of whom claimed that the madonna had elephantiasis and wore jackboots.[56] Things did not go much better for Graham Sutherland on 16 November 1946, when his *Crucifixion*, inspired by Grünewald and Francis Bacon, was unveiled. Read admired the Moore but hated the Sutherland, as he confessed to his friends in Cornwall. Read, who detested Bacon's work but was careful not to say so in print, informed Ben and Barbara that Sutherland had been too much inspired by the Irish-born painter. For him, the Sutherland was uncompromisingly grim.

Read intensely disliked paintings or sculptures which he felt showed only the evil or hatred of which man was so readily capable.

232

Great artists avoided such subject matter – or transcended it. In his opinion, Sutherland had been defeated by his *Crucifixion*. Hepworth, who was always on the defensive as far as Moore was concerned, insisted that Read had got things backwards. Henry Moore's sculpture was the real failure.

> I don't think it's true H.M., it's a bad carving – both from construction & stone point of view & I don't think it's religious. To me it feels smug & smooth & de-vitalised. . . . On seeing Graham's Crucifixion I felt . . . that it was a genuine achievement. I was moved by the (to me) religious feeling – the uncompromising attitude he has held over the subject & his own sensibility; & the fact that it is contemporary painting in terms which I understand. I imagine the colours to be bitter & 'sadistic'? Wasn't the Crucifixion sadistic? . . . I don't know Francis Bacon's work so cannot sense the influence whether good or bad – it feels good to me. You suggest that they were wrong to do the work for the Church – or do you mean that it was not wrong for Henry because he compromised (for the first time in his life!) & was wrong for Graham who did not compromise? . . . If contemporary forms do not suit religious subjects what then happens when a 'believer' is a contemporary painter?[57]

A bit more succinctly, Ben supported his wife's position: 'the G.S. "Crucifixion" seems to me a grand effort, the outcome of his R.C. conviction & an idea worked out on a considerable scale & with great courage – the H.M. madonna & child – is just bunk – it is a sickly-sweet & highly competent compromise between his own living idea & a dead (C. of E.?) idea which he does not believe in at all.'[58]

Although Read could sympathize with Ben's and Barbara's enthusiasm for the Sutherland, he fervently clung to the notion that great art avoided the horrors of life and did not seek to exploit them. The 'wilfulness' of certain details in *The Crucifixion*, 'above all the purple & black colour scheme taken straight from Fr. Bacon', offended him. Sutherland's Christ was, as far as he was concerned, a 'wreck'.[59] Just as he would not – or could not – support the realist aesthetic of man's evil advanced by Stephen Spender, Read could not accept what he felt was the depraved sensibility all too evident in Sutherland's *Crucifixion*.

Nevertheless, Read did not like to think of himself as lacking bite. He was irritated when Henry Treece wrote what he felt was an overly complimentary piece on him for a popular magazine. He said that Treece gave a false picture: 'It is *too* sweet. And I am not so sweet as all that.'[60] Like many of his friends, Read was suffering from what he called 'post-war depression': 'The only cure is to work & if possible

233

to work at some concrete task. . . . There is little oxygen in our intellectual air at present. We have to climb into another atmosphere.'[61]

A Home for
Contemporary Art

In January 1946, seven years after his failed attempt at a
Museum of Modern Art under Peggy Guggenheim's
feckless patronage, Read, together with Penrose and Mesens, who had
hovered on the fringes of the previous scheme, convened a meeting of
what was to become the Museum of Modern Art Organizing
Committee. Other members of that group included Douglas Cooper,
Peter Watson, Jacques Brunius, George Höllering, Peter Gregory,
Robert Melville, Geoffrey Grigson. In a nice surrealistic touch, twelve
Herbert Reads were voted on to the Preparatory Committee.

The original objective of this board was to find 500 subscribers at
£100 each in order to provide the initial financing for the opening of the
Museum of Modern Art in London by 1950; this enterprise, which
quickly became the Institute of Contemporary Arts, was to have
substantial premises to house exhibitions, a theatre or concert hall and a
library. Read lamented that there was no organization in London which
provided 'a hearth round which the artist and his audience can gather in
unanimity, in fellowship'.[1] At the second meeting of the committee, the
first and second drafts of Cooper's proposed Statement of Policy were
considered too inflammatory. In his report Cooper acknowledged the
work of the Tate, the BBC and the Arts Council but claimed that there
was a serious gap in the way such national institutions presented the arts
to the public; not a single one, according to him, gave a comprehensive
picture of the evolution of art during the twentieth century. Cooper's
surliness this time round may well have had its roots in a conviction that
cubism would, if Roland Penrose had his way, play a lowly second
fiddle to surrealism in the new museum. He also loathed New York's
Museum of Modern Art and did not wish it to be used, as Penrose did,
as the model for the ICA: such an approach would only lead 'to a growth
of textiles, design, arts and crafts etc. The Museum of Modern Art of
New York has swamped itself by indulging in this sort of overgeared
cartel of modernism.'[2]

What Cooper really wanted to do was make the Tate and the British Council 'look as silly as they are – and this does not mean compromise, but making modern things clear to the ordinary person by giving him the necessary fodder'.[3] Cooper clearly desired an institute which would pugnaciously challenge all other competing bodies. When it became obvious to him that Read and the other members of the committee would not support such haphazard politics, Cooper resigned in October 1946, claiming that he no longer could support a 'wildly impracticable harebrained scheme'.[4] His aggressiveness would certainly have alienated the Arts Council, which eventually gave the ICA a subsidy of £500 late in 1947.

After a stint in the RAF, Cooper had become after the war Deputy Director of the Monuments and Fine Arts Division of the Allied Control Commission for Germany. In 1949 he published books on Klee, Gris and Léger; he also prepared the catalogue of the Courtauld Collection and eventually became Slade Professor at Oxford. By any reckoning, he was – as Read had learned in 1939 – a formidable, dangerous opponent, his anonymous reviews in the *Times Literary Supplement* usually identifiable because of their barking tone.

When he returned from the United States in the spring of 1946, Read felt strongly that the proposed museum should not have a permanent collection or rely on wealthy trustees. Earlier, he had been badly burned by Peggy Guggenheim; also, Alfred Barr had probably told him how difficult the wealthy members of the Museum of Modern Art's Board could be. That spring, the committee accepted a statement of policy, much milder than Cooper's, by Geoffrey Grigson, with a preface by Read. In November, Read told Cooper that the 'whole scheme must stand or fall on the enthusiasm & energy of one person, & unless that person comes forward, the thing will trickle out, money or no money'. He sadly realized that it was the 'foreigners' who were the most enthusiastic members of the committee. 'Perhaps they have a missionary zeal to convert the English to culture.'[5]

By February 1947, the Organizing Committee had increased to fifteen, the new members including Alex Comfort, Peggy Ashcroft, Jack Beddington and Michel St Denis, Director of the Old Vic. The first public announcement of the existence of the Institute of Contemporary Arts was made by Read in a letter of 26 June 1947 to *The Times*. He invited those interested to write for a copy of the Statement of Policy; he received three hundred requests. Not quite as successful was his appeal for at least 500 donations of £100 each. In his usual curmudgeonly way, George Bernard Shaw wrote to *The Times* asserting that since hygiene, rather than art, was the cause of the marked improvement in health in England in the past 100 years, the proposed Institute might be better off if it devoted itself to cleanliness rather than such shibboleths as artistic small talk and fine art scholarship. Francis Howard also attacked the proposal, claiming that the ICA would hardly attract the support of a representative public. And, he warned, if Read's common ground for a progressive movement in the arts existed – or could be brought into being – he hoped it would not fly 'only a left wing, with unauthorised pilots, and charts of abstraction'.[6]

Peggy Guggenheim wrote to Penrose from New York: 'The day before I got your letter I decided to send you the minimum modest sum of £100. Sorry to disappoint you but I can't do £1000 now as you had hoped.' She added a nice piece of distortion: 'I have my own baby here – to console me for the one you stole in London.'[7] Zwemmer promised £100–£500 when the organization was really off the ground; Henry Moore gave ten guineas. By September, only a disappointing £500 had been raised, but Read's suggestion that the ICA collaborate with the Arts Council or Anglo-French Centre was turned down by the Organizing Committee. He was also worried that the ICA might become a 'hole and corner affair': substantial premises had to be found. In 1949, Ewan Phillips, the ICA's Managing Director, and his staff of two worked on an enormous table in a dusty, book-lined room in the Fitzroy Street flat of Edward Clark, a member of the Managing Committee.

During 1947, Read lectured in France, Belgium, Czechoslovakia, Denmark and Sweden. He informed Richard Church that these trips left him with a pervasive feeling of disillusionment rather than any sense of exhilaration. He added: 'I have become a sort of Wandering Jew of British Culture.'[8] As far as Read was concerned, Clement Attlee and the Labour Party were no improvement on Churchill. In particular, the fuel crisis of 1947 made him realize just how run down a civilization England had become: 'completely finished because now based on assumptions which deprive social life of incentive. . . . I begin to think that the Americans are right to keep to a capitalist economy until a better alternative than state socialism becomes evident.'[9] He also characterized the Labour ministers as well meaning but stupid.

At the end of December 1947, Herbert and Ludo were worried about their youngest son Benedict, who had diabetes. Earlier, husband and wife had disagreed about the possibility of more children: in April 1945, Ludo was in 'good form & already looking forward to the next!' Read told her it was 'time to call a halt'.[10]

237

*

1948 was exceptionally frantic. Read was very much involved in setting up the first national exhibition of children's art; he wrote the introductory remarks on Gabo for the Gabo–Pevsner exhibition at the Museum of Modern Art in New York; he contributed an essay to the memorial volume for Paul Nash; he published books on Klee and Nicholson; he wrote the introduction to the section on Henry Moore in the catalogue to the Venice Biennale. Read had been on the British Council's selection committee, which had chosen thirty-three sculptures and thirty-three drawings by Moore. Read also sat on a selection committee in September to choose the pieces for the Moore exhibition which travelled to Paris, Brussels and Amsterdam in 1949–50.

Early that year, Read was subjected to an interview about the ICA. The reporter dubbed him the 'dean of highbrow art critics', described his white-panelled office at Routledge as decorated with 'ultra-modern' pictures and a 'gaily patterned' carpet, and mentioned that D. S. MacColl had called him 'our most distinguished lover of bad painting'. When asked about his anarchism, Read assured the journalist that he was not of the bomb-throwing type. He blandly characterized the ICA as a 'social meeting ground'. Then, he 'paused nervously, brushed a dust speck from his dark, well-fitting suit, and added: "Plenty is being done to strengthen the 'consumer end', whereas we want to strengthen the production of art. Today there is not a sufficient flow of vital ideas." '[11] In an aside, Read admitted playing croquet occasionally.

The first ICA show ('Forty Years of Modern Art: A Selection from British Collections') was to be held at George Höllering's Academy Hall in Oxford Street from 5 February to 6 March. Although he had serious reservations about Douglas Cooper's volatile temper, Read suggested at the November meeting of the Executive that Cooper be invited to write the catalogue. Höllering declared that he had already had enough of him. Other members of the committee felt that Cooper would not be content merely to write a catalogue; he would try to take the whole thing over. Read rejoined that he had made the suggestion only because Cooper was very good at such work, and it would be awkward in the future if they did not have his co-operation.[12] At the ICA meeting in December, it was learned that Cooper had written to Freddy Mayor warning him against the new Institute and claiming (truthfully) that the first exhibition was to be held in the basement of a cinema. Now thoroughly irritated, Read suggested that Cooper be warned that legal action would be taken against him if he continued in his efforts to wreck the show. On 6 December, he tried a more diplomatic approach to his highly strung friend:

> I hear that you are trying to sabotage the i.c.a. exhibition. It is rather difficult to construe this as a friendly action. I can understand your refusal to lend your own pictures, since you do not approve of the policy of the committee. But why make such a fuss about it? The exhibition will be held – there are sufficient promises of loans already to ensure that. You only succeed in making it difficult for your friends to explain your actions. Be tolerant, dear Douglas, & learn to suffer fools, if not gladly, passively.[13]

When the show opened, the public could not help responding to F. E. McWilliam's large sculpture – a surrealist nude – on the adjacent bomb site; traffic was held up and the resulting captions in the newspapers read: 'Guess What', 'Warped Lady', 'The New Look?', 'Oh Dear! Is This Another New Look?' and 'You never know what's waiting for you round the corner'. The organizers were prosecuted because the entrance to the show was blocking the pavement; there was an ensuing scuffle at Marlborough Street Magistrates' Court where the ica's case was heard by an unsympathetic magistrate.[14] According to Penrose, there was even a group of colonels with top hats and umbrellas who went round the exhibition proclaiming their rage at 'disgusting' modern art.[15]

Penrose had canvassed fellow collectors – friends and enemies – and obtained 127 works, including three Braques, four De Chiricos, two Dalis, three Matisses as well as pieces by Bacon, Freud, Nash, Nicholson, Sutherland, Hepworth and Moore. The neo-romantics, who in many ways embodied in visual terms the mixture of nostalgia, surrealism and landscape of the new apocalyptics, were represented by Colquhoun, MacBryde and Craxton. Eduardo Paolozzi showed a pen-and-ink drawing, *Fisherman and Wife*. According to Penrose, this show was put on in an 'ambiguous' way because the ica wanted to ingratiate itself with the entire artistic community. 'We were starting from blank and without prostituting ourselves we needed to find some allies.'[16] In his opening speech, Read stressed the innovative aspects of the ica:

> Such is our ideal – not another museum, another bleak exhibition gallery, another classical building in which insulated and classified specimens of culture are displayed for instruction, but an adult play-centre, a workshop where work is joy, a source of vitality and daring experiment. We may be mocked for our naive idealism, but at least it will not be possible to say that an expiring civilisation perished without a creative protest.[17]

Eric Newton in the *Sunday Times* was enthusiastic: 'The best of modern art is eclectic. And this is merely a way of saying that the diverse streams are now beginning to amalgamate into a more or less recognizable mid-twentieth-century style. Perhaps this is the moment for the institute of contemporary arts to step in and lend a hand.'[18] Even the *Daily Worker* was duly impressed: 'it was by far the most interesting exhibition to visit. Open until 10.00 p.m. in the evening, including Sundays, it gave working people a chance to make it a part of an evening in town.'[19] The *Scotsman* was parochial: 'Out of 67 names in their notice, 42 are almost certainly foreigners.'[20] Read was treated to a vituperative letter from Wyndham Lewis, who was furious that his 'posterish' *Tyro* had been placed on display.[21] Despite the good press, the show attracted only 16,000 visitors, with no substantial increase in membership. Expenses had run to £2,500, while only £1,783 was taken in.

March 1948 for Read was even busier than usual because he was preparing to visit the States for a month. That February Margaret Gardiner had asked him to read her poems and give her a candid appraisal of them. 'I find it very difficult to say anything very positive about your poems. I would say that they do not pass Coleridge's test of *essential* poetry – they *could*, for the most part, be translated into alternative words without diminution of their significance.'[22] Despite his criticism, Read was sure that she enjoyed the 'game' of writing verse, and, that being the case, he urged her to persist. A poetry reading, in this sense, was like a football match: you won some and lost others. Then he remembered: 'I saw you at the last match – Chelsea Athletic v. Welsh Rangers – and wonder if you enjoyed it?'[23] Read was also concerned that all the Freedom Press papers were still in his loft; he was not sure that he could cope, in an emergency, with moving them to safety.[24]

The principal reason for Read's visit to the States was to lecture on Coleridge at the Johns Hopkins University in Baltimore, where a seminar was being held on the great critics of the past. John Crowe Ransom, Allen Tate, R. P. Blackmur and Benedetto Croce were among the other speakers. Before his flight on 28 March, Read had to submit to the 'final indignity' of a smallpox vaccination, prepare himself to find his way to his hotel when his plane landed at 5.30 a.m. at La Guardia in New York, and compose an extra lecture for the National Gallery in Washington. Wistfully, he told Allen Tate that he wished that someone had written a Guide to Audiences.[25]

Upon Read's return, there were still further problems at the ICA to be ironed out. Even more frequent and bitter quarrels had surfaced in his absence. Committee members realized that the ICA was at the crossroads: should they continue to support the experimental or should they attempt to steer a middle course which might result in more lucrative exhibition receipts? Increasingly, Penrose favoured the latter approach.

At the meeting on 5 May Read announced that John D. Rockefeller had given him an unsolicited gift of $2,500 for the Institute. He also called attention to a flattering article on the ICA which had appeared in the *New York Times*; he did not, however, refer to the American reporter's qualms about the first exhibition: 'will such displays antagonize and bewilder rather than attract the broad effective patronage which art (in London) so desperately needs?'[26] Read certainly feared that constant squabbling within the Management Committee would lead to the demise of the ICA and any high hopes expressed for it in the United States. He observed that a small management committee would offer a more streamlined and peaceful way of running the young organization. Eventually that proposal was accepted, with Read gaining the most votes for the new five-member committee.

But that evening at Roland Penrose's home was filled with further vituperation, most of it centred on Geoffrey Grigson, who was irritated that Cecil Day Lewis had been invited by Alex Comfort to give a reading. Peggy Ashcroft asked what the objection to Day Lewis was. Grigson replied that Day Lewis was not a modern poet, his verse being 'on a level with Duncan Grant's paintings'.[27] Jack Beddington, the advertising executive, who had been the butt of Grigson's insults at previous meetings, announced his resignation. In an attempt to dissuade him, Penrose contended that he had often been badly treated by Grigson – he had learned to live with his frequent barbs. He also pointed out that some of the complaints of the bad-tempered Grigson were based on ignorance, since he frequently skipped meetings.

Acrimonious exchanges were not encouraging to the hopes that Read held for his museum of modern art. Until 1950, when the ICA found a home in Dover Street, its various exhibitions, lectures and readings had to take place in borrowed space. A reading by Auden had, at the last minute, to be put on in a Salvation Army hall by Victoria Station.[28] Such shuffling put a constant, wearying strain on the executive, who had only one paid employee. There was also the constant, wearying stress of making ends meet when receipts fell below expenditure. The infancy of the ICA was one in which various kinds of bandages were being affixed to keep it precariously alive.

*

Barbara Hepworth, who was having an exhibition of paintings at the Lefevre Gallery, was anxious that Read purchase one he really liked, being quite willing to meet him on the question of price. Her husband was grateful to Read for having buttonholed Kenneth Clark to demand that a book on him be included in the Penguin Modern Artists series. Barbara, Ben informed him, had very much enjoyed her recent stay with the Reads, particularly Herbert's evening readings to the children and Ludo's 'tall stories'.[29]

Read was in Paris in May to speak at a UNESCO conference on art in education. Late that summer, the entire family – except Benedict – went to Switzerland for four weeks. Upon his arrival back in England, one of the many letters awaiting him was from a young painter, Eric Finlay, who asked if he could send him some of his work for criticism. Read was reluctantly willing to do this. 'You could send me examples . . . and I could tell you how it strikes someone who is considerably older – but I have often given that sort of advice or criticism, & it has never, as far as I can see, made much difference (or even been acknowledged with thanks).'[30] At about the same time, Nicholson upbraided Read, whose Epilogue to the 1947 edition of *Art Now* he found thin-blooded. Artists, he reminded him, feel and then theorize; they do not set out to be revolutionary. 'An artist has an urge, that urge in a real artist is so terrific that it is all he can see or feel & he follows it until he's satisfied (& there is a particular glow inside when he has dug deep enough or built high enough to find something fresh).'[31]

Frequently, Read felt the temptation to abandon the steady stream of requests, meetings, letters which threatened to overwhelm his own creative urges. In 1946, he had attempted to put off would-be correspondents with a postcard containing a forbidding printed injunction: 'Herbert Read begs to thank you for your letter, but has to inform you that he has retired from all unsolicited correspondence . . . submitted to him through the post, and generally from all those activities which render his present existence fragmentary and futile.'[32] He informed Dahlberg that an invitation to join the Sociedad Fraternal Hutteriana in Paraguay had momentarily tempted him. 'I found it difficult to give reasons why I should not make such a permanent escape. I gave old age, and devotion to the unregenerate. But theirs is the true solution – to go out into the wilderness and begin a new civilization, slowly, from the sod upwards. . . . Our weakness is that we are appealing to a corrupt civilization.'[33] Meanwhile, the Read family was coping with Sophie's bout of chicken pox.

Barbara Hepworth's *The Poet Reading to his Children*. Left to right are
Thomas, Herbert, Sophie and Piers.

The next ICA exhibition was '40,000 Years of Modern Art', which
opened on 21 December 1948. In a speech given a week before, Read
assured his audience that the title was not meant to be frivolous, since
the aim of the organizers was to juxtapose primitive and modern art.
'We do not intend to show superficial comparisons but rather to point
out and make clear to the public some of the sources of inspiration in the
most important trends in painting and sculpture since the beginning of
this century.' The 1936 International Surrealist Exhibition had
included sixteen Oceanic objects whereas the ICA show was to have a
total of 126 such artefacts from Melanesia, Australia, Africa and
prehistoric Europe. Alongside these were to be sixty-four modern
works by thirty-two artists, many of whom had been represented in the
'Forty Years' show.

Roland Penrose wanted the poster advertising the exhibition to
show one of the Cyladic statues from the Ashmolean next to a great
Giacometti nude, a tall thin sculpture which he thought resembled the
ancient one. However, the curators at Oxford claimed that 'they would
rather see themselves dead than their beautiful Cyladic sculpture
compared to a piece of modern nonsense'.[34] Further complications
arose when the Museum of Modern Art agreed to lend Picasso's *Les*

243

Demoiselles d'Avignon. (Penrose was on especially good terms with that museum: he had stored the most important items from his collection there during the war.) Alfred Barr was embarrassed because he had been forbidden to send the painting by air: one of his trustees was an aeroplane executive, who pointed out that the risk of loss or damage by air was fourteen times greater than by ship. After the painting had made the slow crossing by sea, there were more complications. No one had thought to take measurements for getting the huge canvas down the curved concrete staircase at the Academy Cinema. As Penrose recalled, this was almost a disaster. 'The only way to get it in was to make a hole in the wall, which we did by making it from the bombed site outside.'[35]

Robert Melville in the *Studio* was favourably impressed by the confrontation between primitive and modern: 'The restraint of the modern work contrasted sharply with the barbaric violence of the primitive carvings but shared their power to convey invisible forces.' He was also fascinated by the deep pools of shadow which fell across the avenues between objects, giving the viewer a sense of descending into an initiation chamber. Generously, he did not mention that visitors were constantly walking on to the pebbles which had been packed in front of the uncased exhibits to prevent touching and pilfering. As a result, the room was filled with an unnerving crunching sound.

David Sylvester in the *New Statesman* was dismissive: he believed that it was extremely difficult to prove an affinity between fears that are childlike – as expressed in primitive art – and those that are self-conscious as in modern art. Eric Newton in *The Times* did not think that any genuine connections between primitive and modern had been made:

> Where then lies the connection between this urgent magic and the fascinating formal discoveries of a Picasso or a Henry Moore? A psychologist, presumably, could answer, but I am no psychologist.
>
> Footnote: Quite soon I hope to receive an invitation from the Gold Coast to attend the opening of an exhibition showing the influence of Landseer and Alma Tadema on West African sculpture.[36]

In the *Observer*, Douglas Cooper was, not surprisingly, damning: 'In terms of quality the so-called "primitives" are outstandingly higher, for the modern works have been unintelligently selected.'[37] The Arts Council had given £400 towards the cost of the show and, upon learning this, Cooper exploded: 'If the Institute of Contemporary Arts (a dilettante body) hopes for generous support it must begin to cultivate seriousness. Once again it has made a mock of the British public and

Henry Moore with 'Reclining Figure', 1929

On holiday at Happisburgh, Norfolk, 1931: (left to right) Ivon Hitchens, Irina Moore, Henry Moore, Barbara Hepworth, Ben Nicholson and Mary Jenkins.

Barbara Hepworth and Ben
Nicholson, 1932

BELOW: Interior of the Mall Studios,
Hampstead. Over the fireplace is
Ben Nicholson's 'Painting 1933';
above it is the red disc placed
there by Nicholson. The other
furnishings include Hepworth's
'Reclining Figure 1932' on the
table to the right of the fireplace,
and, on top of the bookcase, a
linocut by Nicholson and an
Alfred Wallis painting. The chair
between Ludo's piano and the
desk designed by Read is by Mies
van der Rohe.

 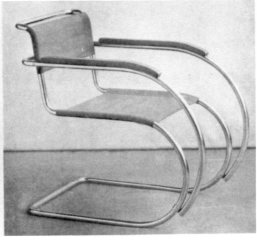

Mies van der Rohe's tubular steel chair

The Surrealist exhibitors, 1936. Back row, left to right: Rupert Lee, Ruthven Todd, Salvador Dali, Paul Eluard, Roland Penrose, Herbert Read, E. L. T. Mesens, George Reavey, Hugh Sykes-Davies. Front row: Diana Lee, Nusch Eluard, Eileen Agar, Sheila Legge, and friend.

Naum Gabo at work on a Construction, 1938

Naum Gabo's prototype design for Jowett Cars Ltd, 1943

ABOVE: André Raffalovich by
Eric Gill, *c.* 1920

RIGHT: Douglas Cooper by
Graham Sutherland, 1966

ABOVE: Canon John Gray by
Eric Gill, *c.* 1928

RIGHT: Edward Dahlberg, 1969

Read and Jung at Küssnacht, *c.*1930

ABOVE: Graham Sutherland's 'Crucifixion', 1946

LEFT: Henry Moore's 'Mother and Child', 1943–4

Herbert Read with Peggy Guggenheim and Ruth Francken, *c.* 1953

Read with Karl Appel's portrait of him, 1962

ABOVE: Read asleep, Venice, c. 1955

LEFT: Stonegrave

BELOW: Read in his study at Stonegrave, c. 1960

modern art.'[38] At the Private View, Peter Watson, 'with his habitually harrowed look', painstakingly removed the drinking glasses which had been placed in the open spaces of the Moore sculptures.

Just after the opening of the ICA show, Read lectured in Germany, and he was back there again in early January. His feeling that the aftermath of war had left Western society with a numb desolation became further ingrained when he visited Hamburg and Berlin: 'No one can have any conception of the reality – the subhuman unreality – of Germany today who has not been there. That sensitive human beings should be condemned to live like half-starved rats among the ruins of their pride is perhaps a just visitation of fate. . . . They feel like pariah-dogs and seek a hand to lick.'[39]

Constantly Read wondered why he agreed to speak on such a wide scale. And when Dahlberg accused him of pursuing fame, he felt compelled to defend himself.

> What drives me out into the world is not the desire for fame (to which I am as indifferent as anyone could honestly and humanly be), nor the desire for lucre (my journeys to Germany, for example, were a dead loss of time and money), but simply a missionary zeal, which may be vain in itself, but is surely not despicable. I know that in the end all that matters is the creation of concrete works of art, and that these are the only permanent witnesses to the truth.[40]

Read also answered Dahlberg 'out of weariness and despair. I have too many burdens (you do not know how many). You must forgive me if I stumble occasionally.'[41]

What were these burdens? Earlier, Read's discontents had been focused on his mother, on Evelyn and on a host of opponents such as Eliot and Lewis. Hampstead in the mid-thirties had been a pleasant idyll, when his career had seemed back on track. Then, that bubble had burst – he had had to face the fact that he had become a public man, famous for what he considered the wrong reasons. After the second war, he found it increasingly difficult to blame others for his misfortunes. Deeply wounded since childhood, he now realized how lonely and isolated a person he had become. In addition, he felt that he had not lived up to the goals he had set himself as a young man. A wearying sense of emptiness filled him. He was at war with himself.

Previously, Read had reminded Treece of the difficult patches which any writer or artist must live through. Obviously, he was attempting to following his own advice in the winter of 1949, but Dahlberg's relentless accusations only made him feel worse. In a

245

moment of anger, he turned on Dahlberg, upbraiding him for living a lie: 'There is a patent paradox in rejecting the world and yet continuing to address it, even if only to revile it. Would not silence in such circumstances be more dignified?'[42]

An additional obstacle that winter was a letter from Eliot telling him that Geoffrey Faber did not want to publish *Education for Peace*, which had appeared in the United States early in 1949. This volume contained the text of *The Education of Free Men*, which Eliot disliked. Faber's refusal was on the grounds that the new book merely repeated the premises of *Education Through Art*: the real reason for the rejection may have been Eliot and Faber's disdain for their author's idealistic politics.

That February Read became peripherally involved in yet another controversy in the art world. Since 1946, there had been considerable differences of opinion in St Ives between 'traditional' and 'advanced' artists. Borlase Smart, himself a traditionalist, had been drawn to the works of the more innovative artists and used his position as Secretary of the St Ives Society of Arts to protect them. Nevertheless, Hepworth, Nicholson and their followers – who were far from blameless – often found their work placed in darkly lit corners when the Society held an exhibition. In July 1946, Peter Lanyon, a pupil of Nicholson's, organized a separate show in the crypt of the Mariners' Chapel. The 'Crypt Group' – Sven Berlin, John Wells, Bryan Wynter, Guido Morris and Lanyon – brought the word 'CATALO' into vogue in St Ives when Morris, who designed the catalogue, found that the word 'catalogue' was too wide to fit his narrow pages, so he set 'CATALO' in large capitals with 'gue of an exhibition' following in smaller type below.[43]

After Smart's death in 1947, friction between the two camps increased considerably, and matters went from bad to worse when Alfred Munnings, President of the Royal Academy, became President of the St Ives Society in 1948. At the RA's annual dinner, he asserted that he 'would rather have a damned bad failure, a bad muddy old picture where somebody has tried to do something, to set down what they have seen, than all this affected juggling, this following of what shall we call it – of the School of Paris'.[44] He also vilified Picasso and Matisse – and labelled Moore's Northampton *Madonna* 'disgusting' (an opinion he shared with Hepworth and Nicholson).[45]

Spurred on by their new President's strong opinions, an extraordinary general meeting of the St Ives Society was called by ten of the 'traditionalists' in February 1949. The 'moderns' were roundly castigated and when a motion of no confidence split the assemblage, the entire modern section resigned. Three days later, the Penwith Society of Arts in Cornwall was founded. Read agreed to become President, his position in the art world obviously being in diametric opposition to Alfred Munnings'.

The next major controversy at the ICA focused on its contribution to the Festival of Britain. At the meeting of 13 April 1949, Penrose suggested that the ICA contribution be devoted to D'Arcy Wentworth Thompson's *Growth and Form*, a book which claimed that the causal relationship between things was 'ephemeral and accidental'. Although Thompson's thesis contradicted the teleological assumptions upon which much of Read's ever increasing interest in 'eternal forms' was based, Read was not opposed in principle to such an exhibition (that autumn, he supported Richard Hamilton's plans for a 'Growth and Form' show – mounted in 1950). He did point out, however, that the Festival was to be devoted to 100 years of British achievement and that the proposed topic did not really fit such a billing. Since he had been a member of the Arts Council's Art Panel since 1937, Read had up-to-date information on the long-term plans for the Festival, which was to celebrate the centenary of the Great Exhibition of 1851. Symbolically, the Festival – centred on the South Bank – was supposed to herald Britain's recovery from the havoc of war.

Because it was restricted to British art for its contribution and because the Arts Council sponsored the '60 [modern British artists] for 51' show, the ICA organized its only – up to that time – purely historical show, 'Ten Decades of British Taste', to which the Arts Council gave a grant of £1,500. This exhibition was essentially an assemblage of fusty kitsch. Despite a disclaimer by Geoffrey Grigson, the items on display provided a hilarious, ironic commentary on the persistence of philistinism. As such, 'Ten Decades' poked fun at a time when the proud history of Britain's contribution to art over the past 100 years was one of the major themes of the Festival. The reviewer in *The Times* was infuriated: 'the exhibition resembles nothing so much as a large provincial art gallery the successive directors of which have not been allowed to relegate any of their predecessors' purchases to the cellars'.[46] In a more contemporary vein than most other Festival activities, the ICA also exhibited the work of Matta and Picasso and showed surrealist films such as *Un Chien Andalou* and *The Seashell and the Clergyman*.

Although no public occasion arose in the late forties for Read to champion the neo-romantics, he was a great admirer of their work. In a preliminary discussion about the Festival, Read reported to Philip

James that he was favourably disposed to a scheme to commission five pictures for £500 each: 'I feel that the choice should be broadly representative – it would not do, on an occasion like this, to confine ourselves to the one school we might think the best. I would personally prefer say Sutherland, Colquhoun, MacBryde, Craxton and Nicholson.'[47] The wealthy collector and fervent ICA supporter Peter Watson, at various times the object of the affections of Igor Markevitch and Cecil Beaton, numbered works by all the neo-romantics in his collection. His obvious enthusiasm was contagious.

On 15 June, Read was busy preparing for yet another trip to the United States, where he would be lecturing at Kenyon College from 26 June until 6 July. Although he had been greatly saddened by Marie Louise Berneri's sudden death on 13 April caused by a blood syncope, following a still-birth a few weeks earlier, the scattering of the ashes in a small secluded glen at Kenwood was for him a heartless ceremony: 'it showed that there is some wisdom in traditional ritual, which enables such experiences to take significant shape'.[48] Just before leaving for the States, Read and Basil Taylor chose the paintings for the British section of the international exhibitions at the Musée d'Art Moderne and Salon des Realités Nouvelles.

Earlier that month, Read had acquired the house in Yorkshire he had been eyeing since the summer of 1948, although he could vaguely recall attending a tea party there as a child: 'Only 7 acres, but a nice old parsonage to live in, with stables and pigsties.'[49] Stonegrave, two and a half miles south-east of Muscoates, was at long last to restore Read to the landscape from which he had been abruptly separated as a child.

The rectory, Queen Anne in style but Georgian in date, was built about 1750 by the then incumbent James Worsley. Apart from the church and rectory, there were in the village three farmsteads and fourteen cottages in 1949, a total of sixty inhabitants. 'Grave', derive from the Saxon 'griff', refers to the village's setting in a dingle or narrow valley. The long honey-coloured house, covered with crimson pantiles, nestles comfortably in that landscape. The northern aspect of the house, as Read said, was regular and severe: the southern side is broken by twenty windows, irregular in shape and design. Although Read sometimes appeared quietly austere, he had, like his new house, another side which was warmer, touched by the quixotic.

The acquisition of Stonegrave was a symbolic act of renewal: Read had mastered the ways of the world to the extent of returning in triumph to his native land. Although she had never liked Broom House, Ludo had no desire to live in Yorkshire. Only the proximity to Ampleforth, the Benedictine monastery, induced her to agree to the move.

Read's great expectations were not completely met, however. Although he did not wish to admit it, he had become a Londoner. Conflicting loyalties can be discerned in a letter of October 1949 to Kathleen Raine: 'It is lovely to be back here, in the landscape that is part of me, and from which I have been separated forty years. The house is old & gracious, and though we have been here only three weeks, we have already fallen into place & feel, all of us, very happy to be here. But I shall be in London quite often.'[50]

15 Moon's Farm

All too quickly, Read became bored with life in Yorkshire. He relished the landscape but would no sooner arrive home than he had a hankering to be in London. The same uneasy process would take over when he was in London: he wanted to be back at Stonegrave. He was on a two-week cycle: one week in London at Routledge's, the other in Yorkshire. Quite soon, he became tired, as he told Eileen Agar, of sleeping *between* Yorkshire and London. Stonegrave was supposed to be a retreat – an alternative to London. But Read had merely created a very uneasy conflict between two opposing ways of life which – for him – did not mesh. The enormous expenses of the new house meant that he had to rely even more heavily on the kind of hack work from which he had hoped to free himself. Rather than taking advantage of his rustic retreat, Read spent enormous amounts of time walled up in his study.

Domestic tensions occasionally bubbled to the surface. The Reads were now closer to Ludo's relatives in Scotland, and Herbert resented the frequent descent of the Ludwig 'locusts'. Read's anti-Catholicism was stirred by the visits of the inhabitants of Ampleforth. He would sometimes joke that the house was 'awash with monks'. Once, when friends from London came to visit, they brought with them some Belgian chocolates. Graciously, Ludo accepted them, but, a few hours later after lunch, the children asked for some. All eyes in the room turned expectantly to Ludo, who calmly announced that she had given them to some monks who had popped in for a visit. Read, worried about the enormous costs of running Stonegrave, inclined towards moderation. Ludo would not stand for this. If he put out two bottles of wine, she would quickly fetch two more. Sometimes Read was simply irritable. On one occasion, one of the children called him a 'bloody bugger' whereupon he chased the offending youngster through the house with a riding crop.

Joe Ackerley, who was invited up to Stonegrave in March 1950, provided an amusing diversion when he became excessively concerned about the travel arrangements for Queenie, his Alsatian: 'your plan does not look as simple to me as it does to you. Is not your Fri. afternoon train pretty packed – what class do you travel – and do you expect to eat a meal on it? I like (I mean Queenie likes) an empty-ish train and a first class carriage.'[1]

Quite soon, Read uncomfortably realized that he was now one of the local squires and must be prepared to do a great deal of entertaining. Read's excessively quiet manner on such occasions tended to redound in his favour. Ludo, who was a loquacious and careful hostess, would receive little or no credit, but ladies who sat through dinner next to Read, who often said not a word, thought him extraordinarily charming. A sort of queuing system was in operation: Read would never answer a question right away. It might take minutes to receive a peremptory answer. A Frenchman, who sat next to him at lunch, asked him his opinion of Miró. Many minutes later, Read replied, 'Et vous?' Read's naivety also became legendary among the Yorkshire locals. A man appeared yearly at the gates of Stonegrave claiming that his truck and its full load of logs had broken down there. Read always bought the firewood. He also acquired some Chinese geese after being told (incorrectly) that they could subsist only on grass.

Socially, the Reads remained in a tenuous, vulnerable position. They had little in common with the local farmers, and the higher reaches of the squirearchy and aristocracy were closed to them. This fact was painfully brought home to Read when he received a dinner invitation from Lord Feversham, the owner of the Duncombe Park Estate. When he arrived at Nauton Tower, Read was received by the butler and waited for an almost an hour for his host and his house guests, who were dressing, to descend. Feversham, who vaguely knew that Read was someone in the art world, had a guest who was supposedly interested in such matters. Read had been invited to entertain this person, but Feversham had forgotten that he had invited Read at an unsuitable time. Although outraged at his apparent rudeness, Read patiently waited for his host.

Eventually, the Reads became friendly with Sir William Worsley and his family. Nevertheless, Tom and Piers felt that the move to Yorkshire had 'undermined' them: under trying circumstances, they had to acquire a new set of friends. Ludo expended much of her spare time in organizing musical events. There were some compensations. Occasionally, Read would rouse the children early in the morning and insist that they accompany him on a walk.

251

*

In the verse drama, *Moon's Farm*, broadcast in June 1951, Read wrote
of his return to the landscape of his youth. In the guise of the Second
Voice he recalls, in the poem's conclusion, a timeless moment:

> As boys we used to come here
> to gather wild daffodils.
> At Moon's Farm the pump was in the kitchen
> a well of clean crystal water.
> And there was an old clock
> standing opposite the kitchen door.
> It had a robin
> or perhaps it was a wren
> painted on its white face
> but the fingers never moved.
> It was always 12.25 at Moon's Farm.
> 12.25 is God's time.

But the Second Voice has never been able since childhood to live in
God's time.

> The truth is
> I have never been able to worship anything
> not even myself.
> Worship is an act of adoration
> the complete surrender of the self to some Other
> to some Otherness.
> It must be a great relief
> to get rid of that burden sometimes
> to feel utterly empty
> like a room that has been swept and made bright
> ready for a new occupant
> to return to a body that has been renewed in ecstasy!
> It is an illusion, of course
> but one of the desirable illusions.

As time went on, Read would see religious belief as desirable. In 1951,
he tried to purge himself of undue reliance on pent-up notions of an
ideal childhood past from which he had been unceremoniously
snatched, but his sufferings had their origins in that early loss of father
and home.

Read had certainly been separated from the easeful life of his valley
since the age of nine. The First Voice (feminine) and the Third Voice
(masculine), the two other characters in the play, have always resided in
the landscape to which the Second Voice wishes to return. They are
sceptical of his wishes and question him about his motives. The Second

Voice increasingly realizes that he has lived a life of illusions, one of the most central being the conviction that he could – or should – return to the place of his birth. But that landscape was the place where he came into being as a person aware of 'some perfect form' and it is here that if at the moment of death he 'could at the last moment / see some bright image / [he] should die without fear and trembling'.

The First and Third Voices remind the Second Voice that he must die to 'the day and its trivialities', 'the sense of time' and the 'place of generation and birth'. But the point of the poem is that one must have a place in which to come to an end, and the First Voice assures the returned native that she will, in the darkness, lead him to his bed.

In this sombre poem, Read attempted to dramatize his increasing awareness that he could not really go home again. And yet, he knew, he had had to return to his native Yorkshire. Like Oliver in *The Green Child*, he might come to the realization that he no longer belonged, but he had to undergo such an unrewarding quest. The anguish brought by that insight deeply bothered Read quite soon after his return, but, at the same time, he had to make some attempt to integrate the two strands of his existence. He had been born on a farm but devoted his life to things which had seemingly little to do with the tilling of the soil. Increasingly came an awareness of how much the pastoral landscape of youth had been the ideal towards which much of his writing moved.

The London to which Read commuted every other week was caught between the extremes of Cold War and national renewal. Read's nemesis, Winston Churchill, was returned to power in 1951, and Julius and Ethel Rosenberg were sentenced to death in the United States for espionage. In that same year, Graham Greene's *The End of the Affair* poignantly evoked the terminal stages of a relationship which defied convention, and J. D. Salinger in *The Catcher in the Eye* attacked the conventional hypocrisies underlying most adult behaviour. Coffee bars, jazz clubs and duffel coats were in fashion. Soho was now filled with spluttering *espresso* machines.

The Korean War, the new arena of military activity, was, as far as Read was concerned, pointless: 'The whole idea that we can *fight* communism with firearms is an illusion: it merely blows the smouldering embers to a flame.'[2] Communism, he maintained, could 'only be beaten by a better kind of communism, and we cannot create that better kind of communism so long as we are wasting our substance on armaments'.[3]

For Read, the Cold War was a daily experience in London. As a poet and publisher of poetry, Read increasingly found the England of 1951 a totally unreceptive place.

> Nothing could be so dead as the publication of poetry in this country, and my own efforts at Routledges are now at an end. I have never counted the losses, but others have, and they run into hundreds, possibly thousands of pounds. I am now met by an absolutely blank refusal to consider the publication of any poetry. . . . The publication of poetry, of all but the most vulgar, has become a secret activity, carried out in catacombs. But one must live in the catacombs. . . . The exceptions, Pound and Eliot, have floated on the Zeitgeist for non-poetic reasons: scandal, snobbery, above all: grist for the academic mills.[4]

Still, Read carried on with his work as a secret agent, although his fellow 'mole', Tom Eliot, often tried his patience.

Read was bitter when Eliot, who was supposed to provide him with tickets to *The Cocktail Party*, called to tell him that the seats were needed for a visiting sultan. A year later, in the autumn of 1950, Read had the unpleasant task of chairing a reading at the ICA by Emmanuel Litvinoff, one of his Routledge poets, who decided to read his acerbic 'To T. S. Eliot', perhaps unaware that Eliot was in the audience.

> I am not accepted in your parish,
> Bleistein is my relative and I share
> the protozoic slime of Shylock, a page
> in Stürmer, and, underneath the cities,
> a billet lower than the rats.

Most of the audience clapped at the conclusion of the poem, but Stephen Spender angrily shouted out that Litvinoff had grossly insulted Eliot. 'As a poet I'm as much a Jew as Litvinoff,' he also declared. Eliot muttered under his breath, 'It's a good poem, it's a very good poem.' When Litvinoff attempted to answer Spender, Read violently struck his gavel on the table. He refused Litvinoff's further pleadings; the young Jewish poet, pale-faced and exhausted, strode to the back of the hall and left shortly thereafter. An eyewitness to this intellectual carnage, Dannie Abse, discerned that Read because of ' "good taste" and genuine feelings of loyalty to Eliot tyrannically censored all further dissension'.[5] Read, who was obviously unsympathetic to his old friend's anti-democratic tendencies, had bent over backwards not to have him even more vilified.

An old antagonism was revived in 1950 by Wyndham Lewis' carping attacks on *Education Through Art*. Lewis felt that Read's suggestions in that book were too formulaic and rigid; he also maintained that Read did not defend art teachers who might have intuitively anticipated many of his notions about curricular reform. In November 1950, Read made a peace offering to the caustic artist: 'I always try to please you, but I don't always succeed! Here goes again. I am preparing, for those purveyors of mass culture, Penguin Books, a Pelican or King Penguin or some other bird-book, on Contemporary British Art.' He asked Lewis for permission to reproduce *The Armada* (1937) and commented on their differences regarding 'child art'. 'I did not reply to your remarks . . . because in the main I agreed with them. You are wrong, however, in assuming that Willy Wiggins of Wigan, *or his teacher*, has ever seen a Rouault, Dufy, etc. Most of these teachers are rather dumb creatures, and generally reactionary in so far as they are conscious of modern art.'[6] Lewis, however, was not about to accept any scraps from Read's table: 'You tell me that you always endeavour to please me, but alas without success. A pretty little self-portrait, I must say, of a blameless and self-effacing man.'[7]

Douglas Cooper, another enemy–friend, was interfering with Benedict Nicolson's attempts to edit the *Burlington Magazine*. In despair, Nicolson turned to his predecessor; Read told him to be firm with Cooper, who, he felt, was consumed by envy: 'Sooner or later someone will have to take legal action against Douglas.'[8]

At times, Read correctly saw his life as consisting of petty fights and meaningless travel. In July 1950, he had been 'wandering again', tempted by having his fare paid by the British Council and being offered hospitality by Peggy Guggenheim, who had now settled in Venice. All this was enjoyable, apart from the official events in which he had to participate. He was angry and frightened by a Congress of Cultural Freedom in Berlin at which the Americans shouted 'for bigger and better bombs to defend – what? Nothing that I could recognize as culture.'[9]

A year after arriving at Stonegrave, Read felt 'rootless . . . like dogs, we must rotate a little before we settle down'.[10] Christmas 1950 at Stonegrave was full of 'medieval junketings', and a Nativity play in the barn, written, produced and acted by the village children. Piers was Herod, Ben a Shepherd and 'Sophie very beautiful as the angel. They all acted with great verve.'[11] Still, the weather was excessively cold, making travel difficult. Read continued to feel immured in a continuous struggle against decay.[12]

Behind the public façade of frequent compromise, Read's resolute hatred of any kind of totalitarian regime persisted. In February 1951, he and Alex Comfort wrote a letter to the *New Statesman* directed against the Conservative government's willingness to rearm Britain according to the American government's rabid anti-Red dictates: 'Either the Soviet Government now intends to overrun Europe or it does not. If it does not, we are going the best way to provoke it to do so. If it does, then, however serious the threat, we do not believe that it approaches in gravity the threat, not merely of atomic war, but of the consequences of mass rearmament and of prolonged artificial war-hysteria.' According to Read and Comfort, an occupied Britain might paradoxically be able to influence a general movement towards disarmament on the part of the superpowers. 'A totally devastated Britain could not. . . . We therefore state not only our belief in the necessity of immediate disarmament, but our personal intention to refuse any participation, moral or physical, in war between East and West.'[13] Joe Ackerley asked Read what purpose such a letter served. Joining the Communist Party was, he thought, the only logical conclusion to such a protest. Meanwhile, Read's hostility towards the Americans had been fuelled by some nefarious activities at the ICA.

Lord Harewood officiated at the inauguration of the new ICA premises at 17 Dover Street on 12 December 1950. Well before that, in May, there had been an exhibition devoted to James Joyce which Eliot had reluctantly opened.[14] The official first exhibition, '1950, Aspects of British Art', displayed a range of works in which three kinds of art were prominent: realism (a style of art earlier advocated by the AIA), neo-romanticism (strongly supported by the Arts Council) and international art with a decided surrealist bent (the kind of art which Read and Penrose had supported since the thirties). Despite obvious differences of opinion on the direction in which English art should be moving, the opening exhibition was resolutely nationalistic.

The *Evening Standard* sarcastically called the new headquarters, designed by Jane Drew with curtains by Terence Conran, 'Advance Guard H.Q.' A year later, the *Glasgow Herald* claimed that 'the too-too arty air of the Institute of Contemporary Arts has often an unhappy effect on anything shown there, infecting quite blameless matter with the contagion of hi-falutin' nonsense'.[15] The cliquish atmosphere of the ICA fuelled the public suspicion about recherché activities: member-ships remained difficult to sell, and the funding from the Arts Council did not go very far (the annual maintenance of Dover Street was expected to run £3,000 a year over income from subscriptions). From its outset, the ICA had been welcoming of American art – and money. Before the official opening of Dover Street, the balletomane Lincoln

Kirstein paid for the catalogues for the exhibition, 'American Symbolic Realism', which was provided free of charge in July–August 1950.

One of the by-products of the Cold War was the interest in the United States in launching a form of art which could be seen as markedly superior to Soviet realism. Abstract expressionism was the answer, and that stylistic form had to be propagandized in Europe. The Americans soon decided that the ICA would be the perfect location in England from which to market this new form of cultural imperialism. In January 1951, Charles Howard, an American visitor to London, wrote to the *San Francisco Art Association Bulletin* to say that he was amazed that more exhibits were not sent from the States to Europe; to him, it seemed a 'first-class opportunity to demonstrate that there is more to America than ill-tempered soldiers and gold-plated bathrooms'. In his first visit to the States, Read had been an uneasy witness to the effects on art of corporate sponsorship, but Roland Penrose, desperate for the survival of the fledgling Institute, saw no real conflict between American money and British culture.

Early in 1951, an American public relations expert volunteered his services to improve the 'image' of the ICA. Funds could be raised, he claimed, by using a royal personage, possibly the Princess Elizabeth, as a fund-raising figurehead. In a letter to Philip James of the Arts Council, Read vented his fury.

> Roland will tell you of the approaches that have been made to us by a certain Pat Dolan – the smoothest operator I have ever come across. He has offered, on terms, to get us all the money we need, and is confident that he can raise half a million for a British equivalent of the Museum of Modern Art. I don't want to raise the question of his bona fides – we have been into that, and though there is a violent difference of opinion among the people we have consulted, it is a world full of prejudice, and anyhow if you sup with the devil you must use a long spoon. Dolan's scheme involves, as a preliminary, securing Royal patronage (and he doesn't regard Harewood as quite royal enough), and a whole façade of bankers and big business men, not only here, but in USA. . . . He also hints that of course our policy will not have to be too offensive to such people. . . . Roland is somewhat sold to the idea. I *am* very sceptical – indeed, I see the beginning of the end of any ideals I ever had for the ICA. . . . I do not believe that we could possibly maintain any degree of independence if we became a charitable dependency of Big Business. . . . it makes me all the less confident that we should be allowed to conduct the Institute as an outpost for experimental art. They might buy us up to make us socially harmless, but I don't see a lot of cunning tycoons such as Dolan associates giving immense sums of money to support an activity which they would rightly suspect of being 'subversive'.[16]

After a great deal of acrimonious wrangling, Dolan's scheme was accepted in March 1951. As an inducement to reluctant colleagues, Penrose threw in £1,000; substantial funding was not available from any other body such as, Read hoped, the Arts Council. As part of a package deal, Penrose proposed to the Management Committee of the ICA that Anthony Kloman, 'not at all the aggressive type of American' and the brother-in-law of the architect Philip Johnson, become their Director of Public Relations, a position he took up the following month.

Read's increasing dismay was justified. In 1952 there were shows of Saul Steinberg drawings, photographs from *Life* (sponsored by Time-Life) and photographs by Derek Knight, 'The Old and New in South-East Asia' (sponsored by Shell); Jackson Pollock was shown for the first time in England by the ICA in the 1953 'Opposing Forces' exhibition; there was a Mark Tobey retrospective in 1955. Before, ICA openings had been attended by 'bearded artists in duffel coats . . . sculptors in overalls and successful playwrights wearing white gardenias'.[17] The Shell-sponsored show was attended by Lord Latham, Lady Gent, Lord Milverton and the Petroleum Attaché at the American Embassy.

Kloman was the moving force behind the 'Unknown Political Prisoner' competition, an idea he had brought back from the States in May 1951.[18] Covertly – in a celebration of those persons who rebelled against totalitarian regimes – the 'open' society of the West was to be contrasted to Soviet repression. At first the suggestion was rebuffed, but the tempting offer of £16,000 from the United States – £1,000 of which was to go to the ICA as a management fee – was accepted a month later. The funds were donated by Jock Whitney, publisher of the *International Herald Tribune*, an honorary trustee of the Museum of Modern Art in New York, and later, in 1957, Ambassador to the Court of St James. It is probable, but not certain, that Whitney donated the money at the instigation of the CIA.

What is certain is that by 1952 Soviet artists and speakers were not welcome at the ICA because their presence would make it unlikely that any financial help would be forthcoming from American sources.[19] Earlier, the Soviets had been intrigued by the various projects coming to fruition in Dover Street. Late in 1951, they had even offered to exhibit contemporary English work in Moscow if Russian work was exhibited in London.[20]

Guy Burgess and Donald Maclean joined the ICA at some point between Maclean's return from the Egyptian Embassy in May 1950 and Burgess's departure for Washington in October of that year. They may have been reporting to Moscow on the growing American infiltration at the ICA. Later, in June 1951, the name of the ICA was dragged in the mud of political scandal when Donald Seaman, a *Daily Express* reporter, interviewed W. H. Auden, who mentioned that Burgess and Maclean – who had just been exposed as Soviet operatives – were ICA members. This fact, which linked the hi-falutin' activities of the ICA with communism, appeared in virtually every national and provincial newspaper. As Read feared, the ICA had become a puppet caught in the struggles between the two totalitarianisms he despised.

Read was further convinced that politics and arts did not mix when he glanced at the edition of Pound's letters published in 1951: 'He based his philosophy of life on Confucius, and yet no man had less of the Confucian spirit.'[21] Also, Read had become even more certain that he had spent far too much time on art criticism, at the expense of poetry, his 'natural muse'. In April 1951, he was trying to make a 'final collection' of his writings on art, although he regretted that he seemed to be forsaking many friends, whose reputations he had helped to make.[22]

The year before, Read had obtained an invitation for Barbara Hepworth to represent Britain at the Venice Biennale. Later that year, he was distressed to hear that she and Ben had separated: he had been 'vaguely aware that Ben was a bit "queer" in Venice, but put it down to a not unnatural attack of professional jealousy. Perhaps even now there is something of that in it – he feels he must have his compensations!'[23] In July 1951, Read opened Hepworth's retrospective at Wakefield, her native town. In his introduction to the catalogue, he claimed that she had not sacrificed 'her social or domestic instincts, her feminine graces or sympathies, to some hard notion of a career'.[24] However, Read told Gabo that Barbara was in a 'highly nervous state; you know, no doubt, that Ben has left her, gone off with another woman (some local St Ives lady)'.[25]

When R. P. Blackmur invited him to lecture at Princeton in the autumn of 1951, Read, mindful of his 'natural muse', said yes only on condition that he went as poet and literary critic (the first portion of *The True Voice of Feeling: Studies in English Romantic Poetry* was delivered there). In those talks and in *The Tenth Muse*, he asserted that what was revolutionary in romanticism 'was the recognition of sensibility itself as the raw material of literature and painting'.

Eliot told Read that the Princeton stipend ($1,500) was good enough for five or six lectures, but that the travelling expenses ($600) which he would have to pay out of that sum cut too deeply into the resulting profit. He suggested that Read 'peddle' himself at some other places nearby.[26] At the same time, Read's most recent work, *The Parliament of Women*, another verse drama, was being unfavourably reviewed at the BBC, where it was perceived as uncommonly prosy. 'A great deal of the early part of the play suggests excerpts from an obscure history book shoved somehow into oratio recta.'[27] Although he disdained Eliot's verse dramas, Read was, perhaps unconsciously, competing with *Murder in the Cathedral*. Read's play, not published until 1960, deals with political morality by contrasting the wily Machiavellianism of William Villehardouin, Prince of Achasia, to his wife's intuitive pursuit of virtue. As is usual with Read, political bureaucracies are shown to be evil when juxtaposed to small, anarchist assemblages.

By June, Read had formally accepted the offer from Princeton, being pleased by an extra $1,000 from the Bollingen to help defray the funding needed for the trip. This meant that he could concentrate, while there, on last-minute preparations for the first volume of the Jung edition and would not have to scour about for speaking engagements. Cecil Franklin was not amused. He icily congratulated Read on the 'large' payment but hoped that this did not mean that he would prolong his visit 'as long as the money lasts'.[28]

But Read had no real desire to protract his stay, which was his fourth visit to the United States. No longer was he excited by 'skyscrapers, American women, or even American automobiles. The enduring satisfactions are American plumbing, unlimited supplies of orange juice and the telephone operators.' According to him, the 'new horror' was the 'undergraduate in tight jeans, with "crew-cropped" head and ape-like slouch'.[29] Read found the lack of an office at Princeton an impediment. He was assigned to a ' "carrel", an underground steel cubicle, such as might exist in a modern prison'. The university's Firestone Library could only have been invented by Kafka, he told Edward Dahlberg. He retreated to his room at the Nassau Tavern Hotel, 'much to the distress of the negro chamber maid, who cannot get in to make the bed'.[30] Despite his disdain, Read was a celebrity at Princeton, being pressed almost every day to attend a cocktail party or give a lecture. He stayed with Huntington Cairns at Kitty Hawk, North Carolina, and Paul Mellon and his second wife invited him to their Virginia estate at Upperville, where he reluctantly admired their good taste. But he was not completely comfortable with the 'miscellaneous' assemblage: 'a Degas drawing, a Matisse, some modern primitives, 18th century equine paintings'.[31]

Edward Dahlberg, jealous of the attentions given by his fellow Americans to his English friend, wrote him, as had now become usual, a letter of venomous castigation. Read was stung.

> You accuse me of consorting with publicans and sinners – with the bankers of art and letters. You do not go so far as suggesting that I have been defiled by these contacts, but you obviously think I am in that danger. In this waste land we inhabit I go where the spirit calls me. . . . It was to these people that you now revile that you asked me to appeal on your behalf. . . . Besides, I do not find these people as evil as you do. . . . One more personal retort. If I am a money-changer of literature, a Barabbas, a Pharisee, a Pilate and much else that is reprehensible, remember too that you too receive your mite from the same tainted sources. . . . Why should I hate when there is no hatred in my soul? Why should I scourge and attack when it is not in my nature to kill a fly?[32]

Despite his exceedingly mild manner, Read increasingly found himself at the receiving end of ungenerous barbs. In August 1952, he had to put up with a public reproach from Jung, whom he had long revered but with whom he had had an extended quarrel about modern art. In the midst of his lecture at Eranos, Read became aware of a growling noise which emanated from the middle of the hall. Then, he became more and more conscious of what sounded like rolls of thunder. Someone began screaming (in German), 'That's mine!' and 'That's yours!' The voice belonged to Jung, who obviously felt that Read was in some way borrowing, and at the same time misrepresenting, his work. Suddenly, the psychoanalyst stood up and stormed out of the hall. A few minutes later, there were loud footsteps coming from the floor above the hall. Then, the barrage of sound came to a merciful end.

Although he attempted to divest himself of his own role as pundit, Read found that artists would not allow him to abandon them. Painters or sculptors of varying qualities (Jankel Adler, Alberto Burri, Austin Cooper, Hubert Dalwood, Jean Fautrier, Rupprecht Geiger, Iqbal Geoffrey, Louis Le Brocquy, Ernst Van Leyden, Desmond Morris on behalf of Congo the Chimp) would approach Read, who was usually too polite to say no. As a result, Read wrote on a number of artists of little distinction. Artists of the first rank, like David Bomberg, who were overlooked were usually not persistent or resourceful enough in soliciting Read's attention.

He also felt hemmed in by the low standard of living in England.

261

By 1952, Read was convinced that his country was hopelessly bankrupt, its standard of living reduced to one of the lowest in Europe. His nation had become a 'slave population producing luxuries . . . for the emporiums of New York and Buenos Ayres'. In a sardonic mood, he remarked that England, having saved the world from the tyranny of the Germans, was now far worse off than Germany.[33] Still, Read persisted in his attempts to make the world slightly better. In March 1952, he asked Moore, Forster, Britten and Greene, among others, to take part in a demonstration against political murders in Spain. Somewhat crossly, Greene refused, telling Read that in such protests 'the intellectuals were clearing their consciences in an awfully easy way and helping to increase the tortures on the prisoners they were defending. . . . If an intellectual really wants to protest and not simply to clear his conscience I do feel that the old Victorian method of throwing a bomb is more respectable.'[34]

When Douglas Cooper, who had added Benjamin Britten and Peter Pears to the 'same dust-bin with Moore, Sutherland, Piper, Sitwell',[35] persevered with his relentless complaints, Read told him that, although he agreed that the modern scene was fragmentary and feeble, he would 'rather adopt an attitude of sympathy, even of compromise, on the chance that some good will come out of evil, some order out of chaos'.[36] Read also tried to interest the Tate's John Rothenstein in an exhibition devoted to Gabo's work.

In the summer of 1952, Herbert and Ludo were in Paris 'to celebrate the xxe Siècle, meet Mr Stravinsky, & hear Billy Budd'.[37] Then Read went on alone to the Biennale where he was on a jury awarding the 'big prize' for painting. The choice was between Dufy and Léger: 'the one a salon painter, a manufacturer of confections for ladies' boudoirs; the other an honest but unimaginative inventor of contemporary symbols, but a communist by conviction'. Read wanted to submit a blank vote, but he decided in favour of Léger. However, Dufy got the prize: 'He is an old man, pushed round in a bath-chair, and I do not grudge him such a solace, so late in life.'[38]

Eight English sculptors (Adams, Armitage, Butler, Chadwick, Clarke, Meadows, Paolozzi, Turnbull) had been chosen for the British pavilion that year. A double version of Moore's *Standing Figure* was placed at the entrance, and Read approvingly commented on this in his introduction to the catalogue. Moore was 'the parent of them all'. The images of the younger generation, he claimed, belonged to the 'iconography of despair, or of defiance . . . here are images of flight . . . of excoriated flesh, frustrated sex, the geometry of fear'. In these works, monumentality – such as practised by Moore – was avoided. These young persons had 'seized Eliot's image of the Hollow Men . . . and people the Waste Land with their iron or bronze waifs'.

Although the Biennale had been devoted to her sculpture the previous time, Hepworth was furious in December 1951 that a sculpture by Moore was to be given patriarchal pride of place at the entrance to the show. Read assured Hepworth that her contribution to modern British sculpture was not being overlooked. An 'exception' had been made for Moore because he happened to have a 'big new bronze available'. Read guaranteed 'equal representation' for her if she had a suitable sculpture available to balance Henry's. Failing this, he did not want the lay-out of the show wrecked.[39] Hepworth might well have been further irritated by this sentence in Read's printed Introduction, when he spoke of the eight young sculptors: 'No doubt they have been inspired by the successes of the immediately preceding generation, above all by Henry Moore.'[40]

Another – milder – dispute with Barbara arose in July 1952 when Read wrote the Introduction to *Barbara Hepworth: Carvings and Drawings*. Although she agreed in the main with his sympathetic treatment of her career, Barbara asked Herbert to remove a comparison of herself to Kandinsky, whose work revolted her. She was also displeased that he did not like the naturalistic detail (a facial profile) which had been introduced into *Rock Form*. As far as Read was concerned, this sculpture revealed a confusion between representational and abstract forms. He reminded Barbara that he had to be allowed the opportunity to express a modicum of 'critical independence'. Also, she had asked him, was it difficult being impartial because she was a woman or because she was a close friend? In any event, she did not want her work penalized because of her sex.[41] Tactfully, Read reminded Barbara that he had a tendency 'to be severe just to show how objective' he could be: 'It is a question of keeping everything in focus.'[42]

Read was understandably filled with a pervasive emotional weariness when he reached Venice late that summer. Although he enjoyed Peggy's company, she could be tiresome. She also had 'gassy little dogs' who frequently made messes in the bedrooms. At Peggy's palazzo, a blend of the beautiful and the grotesque, including a statue with a removable penis, Read met the beautiful and alluring artist Ruth Francken, twenty-eight years old in contrast to his fifty-nine. She had been born of Jewish parents in Prague, but her family had moved to

Vienna when she was an infant. In 1936, the family settled in Paris. During the middle of the war in 1942, Ruth emigrated to the United States, where she became a naturalized American. From 1950 to 1952, unable to find an affordable studio in Paris, she lived in Venice. Even after she settled in Paris in 1952, she spent her summers in Venice until 1964. Although she did not feel at home in any of the cities to which she drifted, Ruth was already steadfast in her determination to become an artist when she was introduced to Read.

Rapidly, Read became intrigued with Ruth's Jewishness. He told her that Jews were obsessed with death wishes; he urged her to reject angst in her paintings; he implored her to bypass anxiety in her work in order to reach a state of resolution beyond such puny feelings. Of course, Read told her things that he had long believed in but simply had not been able, in recent years, to put into practice in his own life and work. So entranced was he with this radiant young woman that he was able to forget momentarily the tribulations which had beset him since the end of the war. Sexually attracted to her, he made a pass, but Ruth told him that she thought of him only as a father. Somewhat relieved by not having to worry about having an affair, Read was able to transmute physical passion into a passionate friendship.

Since Read helped her to hold steadfastly to her determination to become an artist, 'Anchor' became her nickname for him. Because her own father, a wealthy banker, had renounced her when she decided to become a painter, Read's paternal affection for Ruth became crucial. When she was discouraged, he would try to point the way forward. He recounted Moore's struggle for recognition, prodded her to read Jung, and insisted that her devotion to art would ultimately prevail. In February 1955 he told her, 'You are a living experiment, one who is dedicated to a research into the Self such as few artists or poets have dared to undertake.' Like Henry Moore, Ruth was exploring the archetypes buried within herself: 'But there is a complication in your case because you are a woman! (But not, I guess, a normal woman!)'[43]

Peggy, who was still attracted to Read, felt that Ruth was foolish not to sleep with him. Obnoxiously, she called Herbert 'Ruth's boyfriend', reminding her of the real ways of worldly success. The winds of gossip certainly intertwined the names of Herbert and Ruth: Paul Éluard informed Eileen Agar that Ruth was Herbert's mistress. Later that summer, Ludo was understandably furious when Herbert told her that he had propositioned Ruth. At first, she threatened to go to a convent. Later, whenever she saw Ruth, she was excessively polite to her, her cordiality being a barometer of underlying enmity. Later, Ludo would refer to any young woman who showed an interest in Herbert as 'one of the Ruthies'. Once, when Ruth visited Stonegrave, she was placed at dinner next to a local baronet who, upon being told that she was a painter, remarked: 'She looks like someone in a picture, not one who makes them!'

If Herbert's friendship with Ruth had been adulterous, it would have been less threatening to Ludo. A physical relationship might eventually have dissipated itself. As it was, Ludo had to face the fact that her husband had formed a close friendship, the circumstances of which bore an uncanny resemblance to her own affair with Herbert in the early thirties. Now, she was the wronged wife, whose claims to intimacy were being subtly undermined by a younger woman.

For Ruth, Herbert embodied an innocence which had not been corrupted by worldly success. One evening, she, Herbert and a group of young artists went to the Crazy Horse Saloon, where the dancers in the floor show eventually removed all their clothes. Ruth asked him which one he preferred. He looked up slowly at the assemblage of flesh and pointed to one: 'Her. She has such a pretty face.'

In 1952 Read clung to the illusion that it was 'not yet too late / for any of [his] illusions to be re-established'. But, he increasingly realized, he had been very much alone emotionally since the time of his father's death. His melancholia persisted, as he felt the full force of his struggles. Unfortunately, the return to Yorkshire had been a largely unsuccessful attempt to turn back the clock to the green world of youth: the 'wild daffodils' existed only in time past.

16 Not Art, Not Now: The Glimmerings of Post-Modernism

Nineteen-fifty-two came to an end with a piece of disturbing news: a letter of 3 December from the Palace offering Read a knighthood 'for services to literature'. As far as he was concerned, this was a dubious distinction. Such honours, he knew, often made the recipients into the pawns of officialdom. Such largesse meant that he was now considered 'safe'.

More crucially, Read had spent a considerable amount of time attacking governmental bureaucracy, in the process advocating the disbandment of any and all forms of government. How could he accept a mark of distinction which loudly proclaimed that he had valiantly served such a system?

As far as Read was concerned, his writings on art had been a double-edged sword – they brought in a modicum of money while distracting him from his genuine interests. Read always felt that his art criticism was of the left hand, his poetry and literary writings being his real loves. The knighthood was being given to him for work of which he was deeply proud. If the proposed honour had been for his contribution to art, he might have summarily rejected it. Read was not a vain man, but his vanity was touched by the terms under which the offer was made.

Ludo had no doubt that Herbert had to accept the Palace's invitation – she was not enthusiastic about any other distinction which might come her husband's way. She told William and Flora Read: 'Darlings, what's the use of being Mrs o.m.?' Ludo, who still felt branded as an outcast because she had abandoned Edinburgh with Herbert, hankered after the public recognition of private virtue which, she felt, being Lady Read would bring her. She was still deeply hurt by Herbert's involvement with Ruth Francken, and, in turn, Herbert was doubtless guilty about his behaviour the previous summer in Venice. Finally, Read succumbed to Ludo's considerable powers of persuasion. A bit mendaciously, he told Geoffrey Grigson, 'I didn't feel important enough to refuse.'[1]

266

Wyndham Lewis secretly enjoyed the discomfiture the knighthood brought his old enemy, as his sarcastic remarks to Michael Ayrton reveal: 'When you said, by the way, that you would like *to mother* Herbert Read, I ought to have told you that someone else had that idea about twenty years ago (a musical lady) and she has mothered him along into the total eminence that you see. But perhaps you feel she has overdone it. (I saw Lady Herbert for the first time at a party not long ago, in a coral red garment. I studied her with interest.)'[2] Like Virginia Woolf years earlier, Lewis was a persistent, hostile witness to Read's shortcomings.

Not surprisingly, Read's anarchist colleagues were furious. Ethel Mannin revealed to him that there was now a joke in her circle about 'a broken reed'.[3] She also told him: 'to accept an honour from the State is surely to honour the State, and an anarchist cannot wish to do that'.[4] Somewhat illogically, Read argued to Vernon Richards that the 'recognition now given to me personally I take as an official recognition of the causes which I have represented'. Perversely, he also claimed that the knighthood was given for 'public services' and, in reality, was a wound to his 'most intimate pride'.[5] Read mounted a strong, if not completely convincing, defence of his position:

> I would ask my accusing comrades to examine their own consciences before condemning me. Daily and continually, almost everyone of you accepts an order of living which is integrally bourgeois and from which you cannot escape, unless you are prepared to go and live on a desert island. . . . Every glass of beer you drink, every cigarette you smoke, helps to sustain the bourgeois society which (in theory) you so rightly despise. . . . My convictions have not changed and will not change. I regard war as the curse of humanity, and governments as the instruments of war. I shall as always work unceasingly to abolish those social and economic institutions which exclude love and foster hatred.[6]

But his decision was made on domestic, not philosophical, grounds. To Caroline Gordon he joked that the award was 'not for sitting on committees. I . . . can only suppose that my loyalty to the House of Windsor was not in question.'[7] All too sadly, Read saw that he now had the 'same status as jockeys, actors, music-hall comedians'.[8] He also realized the sheer stupidity of what had occurred: 'that Winston Churchill should make the offer to an anarchist is a comedy that could only take place in England'.[9]

Shortly afterwards, when he lunched at the Savile with Stephen Spender at the end of January 1953, Read mentioned his precarious financial condition. He was fifty-nine but had no prospect of being able to retire. Correctly, Spender felt that such complaints were metaphoric of deeper, psychic distresses. Nevertheless, Stonegrave was expensive to run, especially when the monks from Ampleforth descended upon the house. 'The monks', Read informed Spender, 'love eating and drinking . . . because this is their substitute for sex.'[10] Read also complained about the minimalist art that was on display at the ICA. And he confessed that Eliot's reputation had overshadowed him all his life: 'He said he thought Eliot did not want to see anyone, was curiously lacking in affection for "perhaps everyone", and that all Eliot wanted to do now was to "slink away into some corner and die".'[11] Despondently, Read told Spender: 'Everything is dead.'

In turn, Eliot thought that Read's anarchist pamphlets sounded like the pronouncements of an old-fashioned nineteenth-century liberal.[12] At their lunch, however, Spender's overwhelming impression was of Read as a person 'of great sensibility and beauty of personality' who, in order to survive, had been forced to

> produce a far too large quantity of generalizations, very carefully reasoned, about art, literature, education, etc., etc., in order to live. The creative side of his talent has gradually been submerged, and the more this has happened the more depressed he feels about the arts in general. He has a line which is to support nearly everything that is experimental and he therefore gives his readers the impression of being in the vanguard, and someone in the vanguard is supposed of course to have burning faith and vitality: qualities which, in reality, H.R. lacks.[13]

Spender also criticized Read for being a 'Recognizer',[14] one who witnesses and then promotes literary and artistic trends.

Read would certainly have accepted some of these strictures: he felt that he had moved drastically away from his interest in literature when he took up art criticism. He had been forced into the position of defending the 'new' in a *seemingly* uncritical way because he felt England was so reprehensively suspicious of anything modern. In the face of philistine indifference, he considered it best to close ranks. He realized that he had written far too much, 'without sufficient premeditation. But I do not think I have ever written falsely, against my inner light.'[15] What Spender did not see was the 'burning faith and vitality' that Read still held in the power of art and literature to transform his life and that of his nation. During the war, he had told Gabo: 'You know as well as I do what I must retain: the revolutionary element, the romantic renewal, the Dionysian fervour.'[16] In the early 1950s, Read found it difficult to get himself back on track, but he ardently believed that the path, although hidden, still existed.

268

Meanwhile, Read saw himself as 'consumed by other people'.[17] His own views certainly tended to get swallowed up at the ICA where they were either in the minority or under increasingly hostile scrutiny. 'The Unknown Political Prisoner' competition had, as Read feared, brought dubious distinction to the ICA when well-known sculptors (Lipchitz, Epstein, Zadkine, Marini and Moore) did not submit work. Naum Gabo unsuccessfully pressured Read, who was on the panel of judges, to help him win.

In March 1953, Read told Gabo that the symmetry in his sculpture had, ironically, worked against him.[18] Its idealism had been recognized, but its lack of humanism had defeated it in the eyes of the majority of the jury, who 'yearned for [an] element of suffering'.[19] The maquette by Reg Butler which did garner the £4,525 top prize was an assemblage of cage, scaffold, guillotine, cross and watchtower. (Barbara Hepworth won second prize.) The insularity of the ICA became a major focus of public outrage when a stateless Hungarian refugee, László Szilvassy, smashed the Butler maquette when it was displayed at the Tate. A casual suggestion by Butler that he would like to erect a large version of his entry on the cliffs of Dover led to a stormy scene in Parliament.

From 1950, Read's anarchism was assaulted at the ICA by involving him in Cold War art politics, but he was also the object of belligerent resentment by a group of young artists and critics (Eduardo Paolozzi, Nigel Henderson, William Turnbull, Toni del Renzio, Richard Hamilton, Rayner Banham and, later, Lawrence Alloway) who, in Oedipal fashion, wanted to overthrow his patriarchal authority. Alloway later recalled: 'There was nobody much else to attack. He was always interested in the visual arts in England. . . . Herbert was really all there was.'[20] Gradually, by November 1952, this Young Group had become the Independent Group – 'independent' in the sense that they were affiliated with the avant-garde and not committed to a 'received' history of art. The name popped into the head of Dorothy Morland, now Co-Director of the ICA, when she had to write down a booking in her diary.

Early in January 1952 'a Committee of young members' suggested the names of those who might be invited to lecture. The one person who accepted was A. J. Ayer, whose rejection of metaphysical statements as unverifiable spurred the group to realize how antagonistic they were to the neo-Platonic, neo-Aristotelian stances taken by most art critics, chief among such reactionaries being Herbert Read. An influence, which accorded fully with Ayer, remained D'Arcy Wentworth Thompson's book on morphology, *Growth and Form*, which Penrose had championed a few years earlier and which Hamilton, with Read's support, had used as the central focus of an exhibition in 1950. However, Thompson's thesis, as we have seen, was completely antithetical to everything in which Read believed. For Thompson, there were no eternal or universal forms.

Not surprisingly, the mice felt free to play when father cat was away: the Independent Group's first full-fledged event was the lecture series, 'Aesthetic Problems of Contemporary Art', given while Read was again in the United States. These talks were ripostes to Read's 1953 lectures at the ICA, 'The Aesthetics of Sculpture', where he had claimed that vitality 'in organic objects is an effect of movements – either the immediate movements of muscles, or the slow movement of growth'.[21] In direct contrast, Ayer, Thompson and the Independent Group rejected a quasi-religious, Jungian, archetypal, symbolic order. For Toni del Renzio, Read 'was seen as compromising and compromised. Banham and myself, particularly, used to say we needed a new book, *Not Art, Not Now*. Our objections were primarily concerned with a certain academicising "purism" which somehow separated art from life and spoke about "harmony".'[22] Alloway did not like the way in which Read used the geometric principles of abstraction as 'a means to a higher world'.[23] Another member of the Group, William Turnbull, felt that Read 'brood[ed] over everything'. He called him 'the Great White Whale, the Moby Dick of English letters'.[24]

Since Read found post-war Britain incredibly humdrum, he retreated back to the ideal world of symbolic forms. The members of the Independent Group also found England dreary, but they had no belief in an ideal world beyond the present one. Unlike Read, they decided to make do with the actual physical world which presented itself to them, gradually becoming convinced that American culture presented the most satisfactory material world extant. Their eyes, as Banham recalled, were drawn to American magazines.

> We goggled at the graphics and the colour-work in adverts for appliances that were almost inconceivable in power-short Britain, and food ads so luscious you wanted to eat them. Remember we had spent our teenage years surviving the horrors and deprivations of a six-year war. For us, the fruits of peace had to be tangible, preferably edible. Those ads . . . looked like Paradise Regained.[25]

The notion of art as something to be 'consumed' led to the

Expendable Aesthetic, according to which previously disreputable objects – magazine ads, television commercials, B-movies – became worthy of serious investigation. The problem Read had with such a theory lay in the redefined role of the artist, who no longer attempted to exert any kind of control on his inner symbolic world. Since the Expendable Aesthetic rejected such notions, the domain of art had been redefined – there were thousands of new rooms in the palace of art, if that palace existed at all.

Although Read had a limited admiration for the vitality in Jackson Pollock's drip paintings and saw him as a type of romantic artist, he did not, like Lawrence Alloway, respond favourably to the disorder in those canvases. Read maintained that a poet or artist had to exert control over his material – he did not believe that one could passively absorb any and all phenomena on equal terms into one's art. For example, the vogue in the United States in 1954 for calligraphic or '*doodling*' art confirmed Read's mounting suspicion that America was simply an offshoot of European decadence.[26]

What Read did share with the Independent Group was an interest in the process of art: he was not concerned with paintings or sculptures as products but, rather, with the mental and physical means which brought them into being. More and more, he came to believe that artists had to lure images out of that area of the unconscious which was pre-verbal.

In 1942, Read had been profoundly moved by Gabo's *Spiral Theme* because he saw it as a work of art concerned with moving the emerging form of the unconscious into an articulate shape; it was, moreover, a work of art which proudly displayed its dual status. For Read, the work of art was not an 'analogy – it is the essential act of transformation; not merely the *pattern* of mental evolution, but the vital process itself'.[27] Read differed sharply from the Independent Group as to what the concern with process signified. For Read, it was a means of discovering residual, archetypal meaning in the artist's psyche; for the Independent Group, process was an end in itself.

Read had earlier sought to displace Fry as the primary spokesman for art in England. Now his authority was under attack. Read's modernism was tied to the thirties and his close friendships with Moore, Hepworth, Nicholson and Gabo. Although he very much wanted to remain sympathetic to young artists, whose theories might veer wildly from his own, he could not redefine his aesthetics in terms of the Independent Group. Hampstead of the 1930s remained his ideal. Read even found it difficult to keep up with the work of young painters and

271

sculptors with whom he was in substantial agreement: he could only judge by the standards he had grappled with and annunciated in *Art Now*. For him, modernism was not an evolving aesthetic; it had stopped before the second war.

When Tooth's held its second 'Critic's Choice' in 1956, Read was asked to make the selection: the paintings had to be by living English painters; there were to be no less than three and no more than five by each; one artist was to be under thirty, one between thirty and forty-five, and one over forty-five; there could be from five to nine artists, the maximum number of canvases being restricted to twenty-seven. At least, those were the printed regulations. Read accepted the challenge but then panicked after he had settled on Nicholson (seven paintings) and Pasmore (five). He telephoned Patrick Heron, whom he had first met in 1944 at the Café Royal with his father Tom: 'Who should I use?' Heron gave him some names, including Terry Frost (three) and Alan Davies (three). Eventually, Read, dependent on yet further pieces of advice, added three Herons and four Peter Kinleys. Heron later joked with him about the fact that he had been given only three spots: 'I see what my function is. I am the pilot, and the pilot has been discarded.'

In his comments in the Tooth's pamphlet, Read resolutely defended what he knew many considered to be an antiquated modernism. Although it was no longer as fashionable as before, he 'liked' abstract art because it gave him a 'directly sensuous and profound enjoyment'.[28] However, he did not want this exhibition to be yet another milestone in the bitter struggle between abstraction and realism. Read also pondered his own role in the art world: 'am I a critic in the accepted meaning of the word?' There was some justice, Read concluded, in the accusation that he was 'an intellectualist without any sensuous response to aesthetic values'. However, Read asserted that he had 'lived' among artists and witnessed first-hand 'the miracle of transformation that takes place in the *process* of creation'. But he had been a party to such activities twenty years before.

In 1953 Read continued to be besieged. He had an unpleasant interchange with the irascible F. R. Leavis, when he chaired the Cambridge don's sharp, tense, aggressive and venomous lecture at the ICA. When Read posed a question, Leavis became even more strident, as if he had never learned the basic social conventions which apply when discussion involves more than hectoring.[29] On this occasion, Read was outdone by his own decency. Another major ego whom Read had to placate was Carl Jung, who wrote to express in the most vehement terms his dissatisfaction with the progress in the publication of the Collected Works. In fact, he accused his publishers of suppressing his work. On 3 January, Jung, in a paranoid frame of mind, asked the Bollingen's John Barrett: 'What is the name of the evil genius that keeps on interfering? Or is there any bad human will behind this tiresome performance?'[30]

Read continued to feel that he had 'sacrificed' his career to his artist friends, some of whom had now become wealthy. He felt compelled to answer the three- or four-inch-high pile of letters which routinely descended upon him each week. The correspondence devoted to education through art, he claimed, could 'alone occupy the time and energy of any other man'.[31] Read could also be sharp when he became irritated with those antagonistic to himself, as when Dorothy Morland announced that Le Corbusier would be in London on 12 May and was willing to meet 'useful people' during the afternoon. She said that she was certain that many young architects and members of the Independent Group would like to meet him. Acidly, Read observed that Corb had probably met enough architects. Once again, the Group only became more involved in the running of the ICA when Read left for the United States in the autumn.

That summer, Read, in his capacity as President of the Penwith Society, fought with Peter Lanyon, who accused the Society of trying to purge 'traditional' artists. Read felt compelled to defend what were in reality the policies of the Barbara Hepworth circle, policies which smack of earlier Seven and Five tactics. A bit complacently, Read assured Lanyon that the Penwith Society had 'set an admirable example in developing a regionalism in art which is, in my view, the only art politics that matters in the long run.' Lanyon, who had voiced a similar complaint to Read in 1950,[32] would have none of this: 'I should not blame you because you have always been remote but surely you have known that these two [Hepworth and Nicholson] would capture everything?'[33]

Domestic politics could also be arduous. In the summer, Read frequently travelled alone to Switzerland. Often, Ludo and the children would join him there for a motoring holiday. Frequently, Ludo's companion on the outward journey was a tall, amiable monk, Austin Rennick, whom, because of his slouching walk, the children nick-named 'King Kong' or, more simply, 'Kong'. One day in the Po Valley, when the family car was giving trouble, Read wondered aloud why he was 'stuck in such a tin box place'. After such outbursts, Ludo would refuse to speak to Herbert, who would, in turn, be reduced to sheepishness.

*

In late September 1953, Herbert, accompanied by Ludo and Ben, left for a seven-month visit to the United States, where they stayed with Francis and Maymay Cooke in Lexington, Massachusetts. (Thomas, Sophie and Piers were at their boarding schools.) Read had been named Charles Eliot Norton Professor of Poetry at Harvard: 'the plum of all such appointments' he gleefully informed Gabo.[34] Earlier, Read had agreed to give the Andrew Mellon Lectures in the Fine Arts at the National Gallery in Washington during 1955–6, but his talks were brought forward to early 1954 when the scheduled speaker, Aldous Huxley, became ill. The sea-crossing was the roughest Read had ever endured: they reached New York forty-eight hours late.

Read's first task upon arrival was to attempt to placate Georges Simenon, who was accusing his English publishers of not being aggressive enough in marketing him. The Belgian wanted Routledge to release many more of his novels on the cavalier assumption 'that the more you publish the more you sell – the principle of throwing on more fuel to feed the flames'.[35] Read was delighted when Rudolf Bing invited him and Ludo to share his box at the Metropolitan Opera on the same evening that the King and Queen of Greece were there. In early December, Read and Alfred Barr travelled together to Brazil, where they were members of the jury of the second São Paulo Biennale, at which Moore won the sculpture prize and Alfred Manessier and Rufino Tamayo shared the painting award. For Read this was another time-wasting expedition at which prizes were given to 'undeserving artists'. He found 'one or two honest people even in that jungle, which is otherwise like a caricature of these United States'.[36]

Despite the fact that he forged an alliance with another visitor from England, Isaiah Berlin, Harvard was for Read a 'treadmill' where there was a complete absence of leisure. He spoke to 'about a thousand anonymous faces', feeling and conducting himself like an actor.[37] Nevertheless, he was happy to dine with the 'ghosts of Emerson and James' and to be inducted into the Signet and the Saturday Club. Mischievously, he publicly criticized the custom of drinking milk at High Table in dinner jackets.

His lectures, later published as *Icon and Idea*, were, Read maintained, 'difficult, and would be disturbing if I was understood. I am trying to show that the image comes before the idea, and that there would have been – there has been – no awareness or intelligence that was not first a visual or sensuous symbol in the experience of the poet or image-maker.'[38] According to Read, in the beginning was the image –

not the logos. Words, usually accorded pride of place in all histories of culture, came after images. In these essays, Read blends his twin interests in poetry and painting: both are derived from 'sensuous' icons which can be unleashed only by a poet or artist who can unlock their inner, symbolic meanings in a correspondingly 'feeling' manner. Read had now found a new way to justify his much earlier rebellion against Eliot, who had no pictorial sensitivity.

Both the Norton and Mellon lectures were pivotal in other ways. In the latter, published as *The Art of Sculpture*, dedicated to Gabo, Hepworth and Moore, Read reflected back on the Hampstead years, but he had also come to realize that he much preferred sculpture to painting. Perhaps as a result of his return to the fecund landscape of Yorkshire and probably as a result of his distaste for many of the developments in painting, he began to respond in a markedly more enthusiastic way to dimensional form. He was also intrigued by the relationship of actual physical existence to sculpture: like men, sculptures occupy horizontal or vertical space; like the imaginations of men, constructive sculpture attempts to create forms filled with transcendent significance.

What *The Art of Sculpture* and *Icon and Idea* also share is a concern with the origins of images – whether they be two- or three-dimensional. Previously, much of Read's art criticism had been concerned with how to interpret, respond to and utilize modern art, although he had frequently drawn examples from the entire history of art. By 1953–4, Read was disgusted with much of contemporary painting and sculpture, which reflected the angst of post-war man. By shifting his emphasis to its origins, Read was trying – as he had in the thirties – to demonstrate the possibilities of renewal of which art, as far as he was concerned, was the messenger.

Before, Read had, following Worringer, made a sharp differentiation between the organic and the geometric; in *Icon and Idea* he makes a similar distinction between the realistic style of Palaeolithic wall paintings and the geometrical style of the Neolithic in order to talk of two different, equally valid aesthetic processes: 'one tending to an emphasis on *vitality*, the other discovering the still centre, the balance and harmony of beauty'. The history of Western art can be divided along these lines: the first leads to an exploration of the self as unique – surrealism, expressionism, automatic art are some of its manifestations in the twentieth century; the second, which seeks images of harmony, is more societal and, ultimately, transcendental – cubism and abstraction are some of its descendants. However, both forms of art find their fullest

275

expression in subjective emotion and intuition, as in the case of Cézanne, whose 'agonized career as a painter is to be understood as an attempt to realize an objective world without abandoning the sensuous basis of his aesthetic experience. . . . Art is its own reality: it is the revelation or creation of an objective world, not the representation of one.' Read now asserts that an artist like Cézanne achieves a 'pure state of consciousness before the natural object'. The artist discovers the real form lying dormant behind the world of appearances. In so doing, he literally uncovers something hidden from his fellow men and which he shares with them. Like Ruskin, Read believed that only the artist can recover the hidden world of the image, and, again in a manner remarkably similar to Ruskin, Read held that the redemption of man could be achieved only by artists. Although built upon the foundation of Read's other writings, *Icon and Idea* has a new messianic zeal.

Read was both fascinated and terrified that autumn in the States by the menacing spectacle on television of Senator Joe McCarthy interrogating supposed communists: 'Feeling runs very high, especially at Harvard!'[39] Also, concerned about Routledge's grudging attitude towards the Bollingen Foundation, he warned Cecil Franklin: 'If we drop out of this close collaboration . . . another publisher will quickly step in. We shall have then lost our only valuable connection in the United States.'[40] Among other places, he lectured at Chicago, Ann Arbor, Smith, Yale and Mount Holyoke, 'an overheated seminary for American virgins'.[41] When Read complained about *The Confidential Clerk*, which he saw in Boston, Eliot agreed: he had not been able to find that 'damned' objective correlative, a phrase which the inventor now wished had never been invented.[42] Read told Dahlberg that the play was an intricate comedy, smooth on the ear, 'but one can only ask why a man of his intelligence should spend his time on such trivialities. . . . I think he tries to compensate for fading fires, of emotion and inspiration, but that too is a form of heroism.' Read realized that he himself was involved in a multiplicity of 'frenzied labours'.[43] When he asked Kathleen Raine about her anxieties he could have been questioning himself: 'What is the real trouble – just finance, or some deeper despair?'[44]

The Reads travelled to Washington in March for the first of the Mellon lectures. On the way back to Boston, Read put Ludo and Ben on a plane to England. He stayed back for the five remaining lectures and the exhausting commute by train. John then arrived to visit his father in Washington. During a reception at the Phillips Collection, Herbert spilled some sherry on a cushion, looked about to see if anyone had seen him, and then, satisfied that he was unobserved, turned the cushion over so that his misdemeanour would not be noticed. For John, this small incident displayed his father's continuing, deep-seated insecurity and overweening concern for the worldly honours he pretended to despise.

The last six weeks of his American sojourn completely depleted Read, who was thankful that the children's education could be paid for, as a result of his labours, for the next two years. He hoped to be able, at last, to do 'something nearer to the heart & imagination'.[45] What did surprise Read upon his return was how much he had missed the intimacy of England: 'after eight months in the wilderness, I nearly wept'. He even returned to London 'with subtle pleasure': 'This country is like a walled garden, *hortus inclusus*, and it has a quality of *freshness* that one does not appreciate until one has been away from it for a long time.'[46] During this stay in the United States, Read had been bothered by the superficiality of his American friendships: 'the warmth is glowing, but only skin-deep. . . . Sentiments are as fluid as the cash.'[47]

Read arrived back in England to many of the conflicts which had long dominated him. In *The Demon of Progress in the Arts*, Wyndham Lewis claimed Read had been knighted for being too contemporary: 'for having been for years ready to plug to the hilt, to trumpet, to expound, any movement in painting or sculpture — sometimes of the most contradictory kind – which was obviously hurrying along a path as opposite as possible from what had appealed to civilized man through the ages'.[48] Here, Lewis seemed to have forgotten his earlier revolution-. ary stance as a vorticist. In the same piece, Lewis took the opportunity to attack the ICA, 'Sir Herbert's dream'.[49]

When John Berger complained to him that the ICA had become little more than a jazz club, Read became agitated. Dorothy Morland was irritated by his immediate assumption that Berger had to be right. She icily explained that the purpose of the Institute was to present contemporary work in the arts. Read frostily rejoined: as far as he was concerned 'contemporary' had become an imprecise adjective covering a multitude of sins.[50]

Throughout 1955, Read and Dahlberg planned, at the American's instigation, a joint book. *Truth Is More Sacred* was to be a series of epistolary exchanges on the great modernist writers. Throughout the long-drawn-out process, Read had to curb some of Dahlberg's wilder excesses and, ultimately, he found himself defending certain positions only because his friend veered in such nonsensical directions. Read, who had never been a great admirer of D. H. Lawrence, now came to 'forgive him his crudities because they were loaded with pagan beauty'.[51] Read also did not want the proposed book to be used as a launching pad for invective against old friends, particularly Eliot. He vetoed Dahlberg's proposed title: *The New Dunciad*.[52]

Anti-Catholic sentiments on Read's part surfaced in July 1955, leading to a squabble with another friend, Graham Greene. In a review in the *New Statesman* of Jacob Epstein's autobiography, Read claimed that a 'campaign' to discredit the sculptor had been instigated, in part, by the Catholic Church. Greene angrily rejected this in the Letters section of the same periodical: 'Is there some encyclical letter from the Pope directed against Sir Jacob? . . . Have there been any fulminations from the Vatican?'[53] The novelist pointed out that the Convent of the Holy Child Jesus in Cavendish Square had unveiled in May 1953 a Mother and Child by the sculptor. He neglected to mention, however, that the nuns had initially approved a maquette by an unnamed sculptor. When they were congratulated on having hired a Jew, they panicked. Only after some skilful negotiations – and alterations to the Madonna's face – was this commission saved.

Read refused to budge. 'No doubt,' he shrewdly claimed, the Catholic enemies of Epstein spoke as individuals, 'but judging from the kind of art the Church does generally encourage, they are representative enough'.[54] As far as *all* institutionalized religions were concerned, Read gleefully observed, there was usually a choice between bad art and no art. On 9 August, he wrote to Greene: 'No ill-will, I hope, about the little tiff.'[55]

Earlier, on 27 January 1955, the Reads, Ben Nicholson and Barbara Hepworth attended the first production of Michael Tippett's *The Midsummer Marriage* at Covent Garden, for which Hepworth had made the designs. At the time she accepted this commission, Read told her that Tippett was 'rather "woollily" mystical, but you would correct that tendency'.[56] During an interval, a woman rushed into the box where Nicholson sat: 'Excuse me, Sir Herbert, but I have always wanted to meet you.' Ben: 'Tell me, would you be interested in meeting Ben Nicholson?' Lady: 'Oh, yes, I would!' Ben: 'Oh, he's in the adjoining box.'

Read was stung that February by Eliot's defence of Wyndham Lewis in the winter issue of the *Hudson Review*:[57] 'I have read this with a sense of betrayal, and believe it to be a monstrously insincere piece of criticism.' Read particularly disliked this loaded sentence: Lewis is 'the greatest prose master of my generation – perhaps the only one to have invented a new style'. When Read lunched with him the following month, Eliot admitted that he was not 'proud' of the essay, which, he confessed, had been written out of 'kind feelings towards a blind and embittered old friend'. In a manner typical of their constricted dealings with each other, Read did not press his objections.[58]

Although Read did not feel that Eliot was mounting a furtive attack on him, he was hurt that Eliot was, by implication, endorsing Lewis' attack on him the previous year:

> The poignancy of the event (for me) comes from the fact that it is I who am accused (by Lewis) of betraying aesthetic standards (though all I have done is to refuse to put him among the great masters of modern painting and modern literature). He was a good draughtsman; but he never had either the sense of colour or the vision to make him a good painter; and he was a good satirist and keen critic, but never had the sensibility or the humanity to make him a great writer.[59]

Read is being completely open here: Lewis' intense dislike of him dates from the mid-thirties, when he realized that Read regarded him as talented but second-rate. In turn, Lewis saw Read as someone who used the system as a series of building blocks to worldly success. These two enormously talented men simply did not appreciate each other's strengths, and they were certainly intimately aware of each other's weaknesses.

Eliot lunched with Lewis as well as Read and – according to Lewis – Eliot expressed to him his misgivings for having, in effect, given Herbert Read his 'start . . . saying that there was no one whose ideas he considered more pernicious'.[60] In his sly way, Eliot was agreeing with both men. He was fully aware of how disturbed Lewis was but greatly admired the pure classicalness of his work. On the other hand, Eliot, as much as he treasured anyone's friendship, valued Read's companionship; undoubtedly, he considered his romantic doctrines 'pernicious'.

Irritation with Eliot and Lewis led Read to perform a slightly dishonourable act. When he answered Lewis' attack in a pamphlet published by the ICA, he asserted: 'Reactionaryism is a negative doctrine. It vigorously denounces an existing trend – the historical present – and seeks to establish a contrary trend. It is revolution in reverse.' This squib was also published in the *Sewanee Review*, where Read inserted a note, at the insistence of the editor: 'It may be no accident that these thoughts came to me after reading *The Demon of Progress in the Arts*, an attack on the contemporary movement in art by

Wyndham Lewis. It should be obvious, however, for reasons given in the course of my essay, that my observations have no application to Mr. Lewis himself.'

On 10 November, Eliot asked Read: was he dreaming, or had he inadvertently been led up a garden path?[61] Read had given him to understand that the ICA pamphlet was a rejoinder to Lewis. Why, then, did he have the disclaimer in the American version? Read assured Eliot that the American editor had insisted upon the note, but he then ingenuously and somewhat untruthfully defended his action:

> To you, privately, and to any others who read between the lines, I can suggest the possibility that Lewis is a similar case, but I don't know enough about his private life to make a public assertion; and in any case, such an assertion, about a living man, might be libellous. Lewis's statements about me are perhaps also libellous, but I don't wish to emulate him in that direction. I only find it difficult to explain why a man for whom I have always had friendly and loyal feelings should turn on me with bitterness and resentment. Having explained the matter to my own satisfaction, I now prefer to forget, and to try to forgive.[62]

Eliot sometimes enjoyed playing the role of injured martyr, but he did not like his friends to emulate him. Read's letter gave him a new shock:[63] why had Read bothered to publish the piece in America with a note which possibly opened him to the libel he claimed that he wanted to avoid? In a subsequent letter, he asked for frankness.[64] Read responded by telling Eliot that his conscience had been clear until he began to question it: 'Even now I am not sure what is the nature of the crime I have committed.'[65] Again, Read claimed that he had previously regarded Lewis as a friend, was surprised by the attack and had really intended the essay as a psychological evaluation of a certain type of art. 'Then, in order to earn some badly needed dollars, I sent the lecture to the Sewanee Review, explaining its origins to Monroe Spears. He accepted it for publication, but suggested that its point would be lost on his readers unless there was some more direct reference to Lewis's pamphlet.' But, Read asked, what real harm had been done to Lewis, who was excluded from implication by the note? He concluded: 'The harm is that I have shocked you, and there is no one in the world for whose good opinion I have more respect.'[66] Rightly, Eliot remained dubious about this extremely illogical explanation. He wondered if they were looking at the same object with different eyes, or whether they were looking at different objects.[67]

All too desperately, Read tried to conceal the truth from Eliot. Despite profound disagreement with him on a wide variety of subjects, he venerated Eliot. His jealousy had surfaced when he thought (probably correctly) that Eliot favoured Lewis over him. By slamming Lewis in the ICA pamphlet and the article in *Sewanee*, Read attempted to garner Eliot's approval, but that ploy backfired. Naively, he branded Lewis a reactionary when he knew full well that Eliot endorsed 'revolution in reverse'.

At one of their last meetings, Eliot 'confessed' to Read that in his life there had been few people whom he had found it impossible to like, 'but Lewis was one of them'.[68] Was Read telling the truth? Very likely he recorded what Eliot told him. The incidents of 1955 display how Eliot attempted to keep feuding friends in tow: he told each man exactly what he wanted to hear. He remained a distant father, who allowed his sons to vie for the affection which was never forthcoming.

The Cold War of the 1950s led Read to experience a cold war within himself. Increasingly, he found it difficult to have faith in any external system of belief. Although he distrusted Eliot's religiosity, Read desperately wanted his friend's benediction. When that was withheld, Read's insecurity was heightened. All he had left was a strong intuitive feeling that the truths of human experience were contained in the images lurking in the murky depths of the unconscious. Only in the excavation of that terrain was any hope left.

17   Blind Drift of Annihilation

'We are at the beginning of a new Dark Age,' Read warned Edward Dahlberg, 'and it is impossible to see beyond it.'[1] Read was forlorn, feeling trapped in a world in which he no longer belonged:

> as slowly as the yellow leaves
> as softly as the silken sleeves
>   discarded by a bridal bed
> now the bright day is dead
>   is dead
> and we must sleep
>   or die

Read envied Tom Eliot his religious beliefs, but he was quite sure that self-interest rather than faith was the motivating force in his Anglo-Catholicism. Commenting on the possibility that Eliot was insecure because of his Americanness, he disdainfully observed: 'I doubt if Eliot has ever worried very much about the future of America: he is interested only in the future of his own soul.'[2]

Read's continuing sense of the degenerate, decayed values of contemporary existence led to the bitter realization that his generation had not lived up to its determination, in the twenties and thirties, to transform England. Partially out of a sense of his own failure, Read carelessly wrote in January 1956 of Siegfried Sassoon, in an anonymous review for the *Listener*: 'During the Second World War he writes exactly like the people he satirized in the First World War – "the spiritual horror of what the Allies are contending against . . . we must defeat these powers of darkness . . . Germany must expiate the crimes committed by the Nazis", etc. Is this the man who wrote *Counter-Attack?*'[3] Sassoon was furious, not only because he was characterized as a 'bellicose non-combatant' but also because the citations Read quoted were lifted out of context: his grief-stricken reaction to the death of his friend, the artist Rex Whistler.

Sassoon, in two separate letters, threatened to take legal action against the BBC: 'So you'd better make up your little minds, whether you wish to fight an action for damages.'[4] Although he realized that he had made a tactical error, Read did not express any remorse for his words, feeling, as he told the BBC, that it was he who had been betrayed: 'Sassoon was my idol in 1917–18, and my own war poems were influenced by his. I knew, of course, that he had not kept up his fervours of that time, but it came as a painful shock to find him using the journalistic phrases which he had satirised in *Counter-Attack*.'[5] Read prepared a pugnacious disclaimer for publication, but the BBC chose, wisely, to send Sassoon Read's letter of apology, conveniently drafted at the same time. Even here the undiplomatic side of Read is readily visible: 'you were my hero. . . . The man who wrote *Counter-Attack* must know that the powers of darkness are not defeated with the instruments of darkness; and that to lose that knowledge is to lose all faith in goodness. But I write not to arraign you, but to ask for your forgiveness.'[6] Sassoon did not pursue the matter. Blithely, Read did not think that Sassoon should have been annoyed by the accusation of 'having lost his earlier ideals, and of writing like one of the people he had satirised in his early poems. I used no rough words: I merely quietly spoke the truth.'[7]

Later that year, Read narrowly stuck to his pacifist principles when Arthur Koestler and Stephen Spender asked him to join them in a protest against the brutal suppression of the Hungarian revolutionaries by the Soviets. He refused: 'I feel as you feel: a monstrous injustice has been done. . . . But these people resisted force by force: they defended themselves with lethal weapons, and they were defeated by stronger and more numerous lethal weapons . . . the only way to end war is to refuse to fight, under any provocation.'[8]

Although he was overruled, Read vigorously opposed an exhibition at the ICA of the work of Georges Mathieu, whom he considered neo-fascist. Lawrence Alloway defended the French artist, who, clad in a fencing costume, painted some of his rapidly recorded 'psychic impressions' in the gallery at Dover Street. Read was also disturbed by the rumour that a member of the staff was receiving fees for the buying and selling of works exhibited at the ICA.[9]

When Read mentioned his brush with a possible libel action to Ruth Francken, he warned her in February 1956 of the dangers of becoming involved in the confused and confusing mysticisms of the theosophists, Madame Blavatsky and 'Californian buddhists'. If one had to resort to such beliefs, he preferred the clear and objective doctrines of St John of the Cross, Pascal and Simone Weil: 'The others are bad mystics because they never *see* their ideas as clear images – they live in clouds, in vague emotional stews. They begin at the wrong end – with ideas and not with experiences.'[10] Read also cautioned Ruth against taking any ideas for works of art from books: he told her that she had many rich images in her psyche.[11] In her reply, Ruth – to whom he had given the nickname 'Moor' (she was his second Henry Moore) – told him that she had acted badly in her dealings with some friends. He playfully responded: 'So the Moor grows into a Monster – and the more monstrous she becomes, the more I shall love her.'[12]

Regardless of his affection for Ruth, Read hated her adopted city, Paris: 'I think I am more a stranger in Paris than in any other European city . . . to me it always seems a dead city, a city of dreadful despair.'[13] German metropolises were places of 'selfish satisfaction – no petrol rationing, no bombs, no guns – plenty of butter'.[14] New York 'revolted' him;[15] London was only intermittently acceptable. As he became older, urban landscapes symbolized for Read the failure of twentieth-century man to reach any kind of accord with himself. In order to make his forays into London slightly more comfortable, Read, who had usually stayed with Leonie Cohn, now a BBC producer, and her husband in Hampstead, in the late fifties took a studio room at the top of a house at 76 Charlotte Street; after he slipped a disc, he moved to a flat on the ground floor in the same building. Although the furnishings at Stonegrave were a pleasant mix of Herbert's modernistic impulses with Ludo's more baroque taste, the flats in Charlotte Street were resolutely contemporary. In the early sixties, the Bollingen Foundation acquired for his use a small flat at 81 Southampton Row, overlooking the British Museum.

Despite his façade of calm assurance, Read felt saddled with a reputation that he could easily do without: 'I have no great influence in the world of letters: I am universally regarded (and sometimes respected) as an art pundit . . . the public has a single-track mind in these matters.'[16] Meanwhile, the ICA continued to be a never-ending source of vexation. Roland Penrose wanted Churchill, whom Read loathed, to open a Picasso exhibition. Read thought that that would result in a riot rather than an opening: 'I think we are in a terrible danger . . . in our desperate need to raise money, of compromising ourselves. Churchill really hates all we stand for. . . . And his own paintings! As for the money we need, I don't mind where it comes from so long as it doesn't stink.'[17] At last, Read was willing to approach American foundations: 'The ICA is really the London branch of an international movement – one can write quite a song on these lines.'[18]

Read was also grappling with his own attitude towards abstract expressionism, which he began to perceive as apocalyptic in intent. In De Kooning he saw 'some kind of titanic struggle with the Shadow, the dark aspects of the mind', such 'fanatical' faith appealing to him.[19] Sam Francis was an artist who searched for forms 'behind the veil of consciousness, for forms irrespective of any representational significance, that can be teased out of the seething cauldron of psychic particles'. With passionate honesty he was trying to uncover the ' "objective correlative" of his most inward awareness'.[20] Read linked Ruth Francken's work with the American abstract expressionists when he praised the indeterminate forms with which she covered a canvas before allowing more definite forms to emerge. In this manner a 'unifying precept' was 'wrested from the mist in which the previously unorganized forms had swirled'.[21]

Although Read had become by 1956 a hardened, professional student of art, there were times when he simply surrendered to the beauty of a painting or sculpture, as when he was bowled over by Rembrandt's *The Slaughtered Ox* that August in Amsterdam:

> Nothing 'human' in this eviscerated carcase, nothing for pity or admiration. Nothing revolting, no smell of blood. Nothing didactic, no direct attack on our emotions. Whence, then, the fascination of this painting? *In the paint*. The carcase, the blood-stained wall, the pelt on the floor – all these are intricate surfaces of colour, of colour manipulated for its richness and harmony, its scintillation and unity.[22]

Earlier that summer, Read had been in Vancouver where he lectured on children's art at the University of British Columbia. That summer turned into a nightmare when Ludo, whom Read was to meet up with in Switzerland, broke her leg in a motoring accident and had to be hospitalized for nearly a month in Lucerne. Read flew to Switzerland to drive her home, but disaster followed disaster when the back-axle of their car broke just as they reached London.

Yet another quarrel was brewing for Read in the autumn of 1956. When he approached Ivon Hitchens to ask if he could reproduce a painting of his in colour for a revised edition of *Contemporary British Art*, he received a surly letter of complaint, similar to the one from Wyndham Lewis in 1951: Hitchens felt that Read had always neglected him. Read responded by saying that he was a philosopher, not a broker. He also made the point that he himself had never been able to afford to collect – except on a casual basis.

285

Read's own collection at Stonegrave included sculptures by Hepworth and Gabo, paintings by Nicholson, Delvaux, Tanguy, Miró, Ernst, Hélion, Schwitters and Heron and drawings by Moore, Nash, Magritte and Klee. Most of these were gifts of the artists, although Penrose provided him with a small Picasso, and Read purchased one of the two Herons. Before the outbreak of the Second World War, Alexander Calder had given Read a large mobile, which, because he did not have room for it, he placed in a large bag. After the war, Read opened the sack, discovered that the mobile was rusty and threw it out. Despite frequent financial anxiety, it never occurred to him that he should sell off any of his works of art.

Read reminded Hitchens that he had often insisted that his paintings be included in British Council exhibitions. Once, he had even tried unsuccessfully to persuade someone, who had taken a painting by Hitchens on approval, to purchase it. He was sorry that that scheme had not worked – all he could offer was the publicity to be generated by the Penguin book. This answer did not satisfy Hitchens, who moaned that the painting Read wanted to reproduce was not representative.[23] Read also made the telling point in reply to Hitchens that it was easy for the professional critic to have his feeling for an artist diminished when he had to come up with a precise examination of his work: 'I would say that Paul Nash's work, for example, has been completely spoiled for me by having had to make it a subject for *critical* appreciation. In the case of Henry Moore it is rather different, for there I have been able to confine myself to general issues.'[24]

In a similar vein, Read felt that his appreciation of modern literature was being corrupted by having to write responses to Edward Dahlberg's increasingly cranky pronouncements. Richard Aldington warned Read in general about Dahlberg's long-windedness and in particular about the possibility that he intended to make libellous remarks about Robert Graves. Read frequently lost patience with his American friend: 'when you call Emily Brontë a bore, you pass beyond my comprehension'.[25] He was furious with Dahlberg's attempt to ridicule Henry James's supposed homosexuality: 'it does not make a damn of difference'.[26] And he correctly observed that Dahlberg wrote vituperation, not criticism.[27]

Read could also be censorious of younger writers, as when he told Kathleen Raine that Colin Wilson's lecture at the ICA had been pathetic: 'He has broken his shell before his feathers have sprouted.'[28] To the celebrated author of *The Outsider*, he was brutally frank. He asked him why he ignored Gandhi, 'the one authentic holy man of our time'. He also suspected that Wilson wanted religious emotions without religious experience. 'I shy away too but I know I am not made for religion, or religion for me. My way must be the way of aesthetic discipline, of psychological integration, and this is the Other Way.'

Such fleeting asides betoken Read's own flirtations with religious belief. Kathleen Raine thought that he approached and then retreated from the acceptance of an Otherness, but she was convinced that he was looking for some form of creed. Read became fascinated by the fourteenth-century mystical treatise, *The Cloud of Unknowing*. In that work, the insoluble mystery of God lurks behind the cloud – Read thought that the secret of art was frequently obscured and emerged only in that moment when form was snatched from the 'unknowing' recesses of the mind. Read's aesthetic beliefs in the latter part of his life have an increasingly religious component. In particular, he clung to a passionate faith in the artist as the person who could, by the imposition of form, rescue his fellow human beings from the chaos of modern civilization.

Between moments of self-recrimination, Read had to fit in 'bread-and-butter work' to keep his 'expensive pot simmering'.[29] The year 1957 was a punishing one: Switzerland in August, then Italy as far south as Sicily in September, Canada and the States in November and December; he also lectured in St Ives, Birmingham and London. Read's journeys to the States were usually devoted to Routledge business, but he often filled up his spare time with lectures. In addition, he was quite willing, because of much-needed supplementary funds, to accept invitations elsewhere. At the age of sixty-four, the preparation of these lectures and the time spent travelling to them were exacting a heavy toll.

That autumn in New York, Jack Barrett suggested that Bollingen give Read a subsidy of $5,000 a year for six years. This money was given on the understanding that Read would relinquish most of the lecturing and administrative work which was inhibiting him. Read told Cecil Franklin of this proposal, suggested that his visits to London be every month rather than every two weeks, that his salary be reduced by £1,000 a year (his salary was £2,500 plus £250 as his share of profits and an expense allowance of £300), that another editor (preferably a woman) be appointed, that his prospects of a pension not be prejudiced, and that he reduce his commitments to Design Research Unit and the British Council. Since Read's income from all sources was £4,050, the loss of a thousand pounds plus £150 from DRU was

287

considerable. Franklin and the other Routledge directors did not like this scheme: he was told that the time he spent at the office was already at an absolute minimum and that he would have to resign if he planned to spend less time there. If he became a 'consultant director', he would be paid £500 a year, with no share of profits and no pension. Somewhat ingenuously, Read informed Barrett that he was 'chagrined' to discover that his fellow directors 'had such a contractual conception of my relationship to the firm'.[30] In order to comply with the terms that Barrett had outlined, Read decided to hire a secretary at Stonegrave and to stop lecturing. Barrett was agreeable to this, but the stipend was reduced to $4,000.[31]

Although Read had to undertake some minor duties for Bollingen, he was now freed from the necessity of performing a vast array of chores which had for years been assailing him. But there was to be little peace. T. S. Eliot petulantly resigned from a sub-committee of the ICA when he concluded that his name was being used in what he considered a carte-blanche way.[32] Read felt called upon to defend Jung when he was accused, in the letters column of the *New Statesman*, of having been pro-Nazi and anti-Semitic.[33] And there were difficult days at the office, such as the time Arnold Hauser, the Marxist critic, stormed into Routledge demanding an audience with his editor. Read instructed Margaret Selley, his secretary, to tell Hauser that he was not in. He would wait, Hauser insisted, thus trapping Read in his office. Hours went by. Finally, Read escaped by a back door.

Contemporary trends in both literature and art continued to baffle Read. In March 1958, he told Dahlberg that J. D. Salinger had been highly recommended to him. However, he was angry, in general, at the younger generation: 'they are ignorant, they no longer read anything, they no longer know how to write. And yet they are full of conceit and their "anger" . . . is the froth of empty minds.'[34] 'A poet called Betjeman', he told Dahlberg, 'is hailed as a new Byron; his trivial verses are selling 1,000 copies a day.' Intrigued by a novel by a 'philosophical donness . . . which is greeted as a work of genius, comparable to Flaubert or Proust', Read purchased a copy of Iris Murdoch's *The Bell*: he found it 'quite unreadable – crude uninspired English, primitive structure, banal symbolism, unreal characters'.[35] Read knew that he now sounded like a 'disgruntled reactionary' but he still felt capable of recognizing an authentic 'new genius'. For Read, the literature of the 1950s was merely pushing the clock backwards; in his view, Betjeman had returned to the 'tepid sentiments and wordy diction against which the imagists revolted in 1910'.[36]

288

When he published in 1958 an essay on art in England since 1945, Read devoted most of his twenty pages to Moore, Hepworth and Nicholson. He also wrote with great sensitivity of Reg Butler, Lynn Chadwick, Kenneth Armitage, Victor Pasmore, Graham Sutherland and Francis Bacon – the principal satellites of the big three; when he came to the painters who were emerging after the war, Read provided birth years and pigeon-holes. The essay ends in a perfunctory vein: 'In general, British art since 1945 has kept to the tradition of individualism or eccentricity that has characterized its history since the Middle Ages.'[37] As in the case of his selection of canvases for Tooth's two years before, Read was deeply unsure of the younger generation. And yet he genuinely wanted to promote the new and the misunderstood: he, together with Frank Kermode, Rosamond Lehmann, Iris Murdoch and Stephen Spender among others, signed a letter to *The Times* in January 1959 in opposition to the government's claim that Nabokov's *Lolita* was obscene.

At the same time, Read was overwhelmed by the megalomania of the persons he assisted. During a trip to Italy in the spring of 1959, he saw many artists: 'but *as artists* they weary me. Have you noticed how egotistical these artists are? They fight for their existence, of course, as we all do, but they have no love for or conception of other arts, and would use poets as their publicity agents.'[38] Of course, as Read realized all too well, he continually placed himself in vulnerable positions because he was apt to respond favourably to 'an old friend, or a pretty woman. One is lost before one knows what one has done.' And, as far as Read was concerned, the art world, always sordid, was now one of complete venality and corruption, due to the combination of Latin (French and Italian) dishonesty with American wealth and vulgarity'.[39]

Although they had not been close friends, Edwin Muir's death affected Read profoundly. The son of crofter folk, the Scotsman had migrated from Orkney to Glasgow in 1901 when he was fourteen, spent much of his time performing menial tasks and reading Nietzsche, Shaw and Ibsen, and became devoted to left-wing causes. Like Read, Muir was a person whose early literary career had come into being only because of strong inner drives. As Read said, Muir 'spent much of his life in mean employments, and it was a forceful wife that rescued him from a Glasgow bone factory and brought him to London, where he continued to hide his light under a bushel'.[40]

In a manner similar to Read's, much of Muir's later life was spent in a succession of hand-to-mouth public employments: the British

Council, the British Institute in Rome, the adult education college at Newbattle Abbey, Midlothian. Read helped Muir to obtain Bollingen funding and suggested his name for the Norton Professorship at Harvard. The two men were fascinated by the landscape of childhood experience and its relationship to an archetypal world of the imagination. Muir's struggles were for Read a mirror of his own turmoils, although for Muir a belief in immortality had been the steadying influence upon his life, despite the fact that 'it makes whatever is unstable in this life seem even more unstable'.[41]

Peter Gregory, who had long been a mainstay of the ICA, died in February. Although Read, who had never owned a sculpture by Moore, was supposed to obtain one from Gregory's estate, he had to settle for a nude by Maillol when it was decided that the Moores should be sold to endow a literary fund. 'The Two Cultures and the Scientific Revolution', C. P. Snow's Rede Lectures at Cambridge, provided yet another acerbic diversion, when Read challenged Snow's advocacy of technology. Snow might consider him a Luddite, Read conceded, but he was really a man of feeling who believed that the technological revolution would lead to the extermination of humanity. Without sensibility, men become robots whose only needs are physical.

> Only by ruthless, urgent, massive industrialization can the native's mud-hut become an air-conditioned apartment, his daily bowl of rice a succulent steak, his loin-cloth a decent two-piece Terylene suit. . . . That he will exchange the peace and poverty, the languor and cow-shit of his present village for the noise and lethal fumes of internal-combustion engines, the nervous anxiety and stomach ulcers of the industrialized city, is possibly regarded as a small price to pay for the material progress he has achieved.[42]

Read's astringent words brought equally harsh ones from Snow, who accused Read of being intellectually irresponsible. He told him to tell the poor of the world that food and health were inessential trivialities.[43]

Read's only sense of stability in 1959 came from his wife, children and Stonegrave. Although he had a propensity to record only complaints – happier moments going unchronicled – the homelife of Stonegrave, created by husband and wife, provided a much needed retreat. Despite the enormous costs the house entailed, city life, he realized, would be a living death: 'So I shall try to defend my crazy castle to the last breath.'[44]

Much too desperately, Read tried to find his bearings in a new series of poems, 'Vocal Avowals', which are uneasy efforts to

290

incorporate abstract expressionism into verbal form. As a much younger man, Read had striven to find the poetical equivalent of vorticism in his imagist poems. Now, he was attempting to respond to the vigour of artists like Rothko and De Kooning, as in 'little war':

> geometric my alkahest
> migrant fists passion vale
> flash high o paraclete
> all violet vast
> eyelashes entelechy
> stone water-swords
> white shock

This poem, like its companions, does not work because its few touches of colour and the violence of its verbs do not create any sort of unity of impression. Confusion – rather than abstraction – is the result. Nevertheless, these poems were honourable failures, attempts on Read's part to get himself back on the track of the then prevalent modernisms.

Throughout 1959 and 1960, Read struggled 'like a drowning man for air'. Ironically, he realized, he had created the fame that destroyed him.[45] His health was usually good, although he now suffered from varicose veins. Read's despair at the self-destructiveness of Cold War Europe and North America was the illness, he felt, which threatened to exterminate him. Then, suddenly, he saw a new way forward when, as the head of a Cultural Exchange, he visited China for three weeks in September 1959. That trip, by way of Moscow, did not start well. There were long queues to get into the exhibitions, the Kremlin and Lenin's Tomb. The Tretyakov Museum, each of its fifty-three galleries crammed with Russian paintings, was a 'mistake', but the Renoirs, Gauguins and Matisses at the Pushkin were ample compensation.

Modified pleasure gave way to rapture when Read arrived in Peking on 8 September. New buildings rose 'like mushrooms, with incredible speed', reflecting the enthusiastic pride of the builders. Despite the hodge-podge of styles and the resulting architectural muddle, the sheer energy of Peking overwhelmed him. The emperor's palace in the Forbidden City, with its patterned stones, white pines, pomegranates, lotus plants and beautifully shaped rocks was like an immense abstract sculpture. A night visit to the Yangs, who were Cambridge graduates, led to a magical moon-lit promenade through a maze of narrow lanes, with no street lighting.

Even more appealing to Read than the physical beauty of Peking was the 'innocent, intense, and intolerant' attitude of the Chinese. Each street was ruled by a committee, and Read's anarchist eye was instantly charmed by the fact that government control was meted out in such small units. Not surprisingly, given Read's love of land, he was moved by a visit to an agricultural commune, where he eagerly jotted down seven and a half pages of statistics: 'the most important fact is that these communes are *autonomous*'. His enjoyment increased as he went from day nursery to irrigation system to canteens to compost heaps to living quarters. 'I forgot to ask what had happened to *their* wicked landlord – no doubt he was in charge of one of the five piggeries.' For Read, this was 'a dream come true'. Although he managed to avoid such delicacies as sliced intestines and sea slugs, he relished his new diet.

The Summer Palace, fifteen miles from Peking, was in the worst possible taste: 'Betjeman would love it – rather like the Brighton Pavilion.' Although he had initially been daunted by the prospect of a National Day of Sports, Read responded exultantly to the large crowd dressed in white and blue who filled a large stadium, brilliantly coloured flags being placed on the perimeters. Then battalions of athletes poured into the arena. A signal was given and thousands of doves were released; a few minutes later, an equal number of balloons floated into the sky. Soon afterwards, masses of little girls rushed over to where Mao was seated, heaping flowers around him. Only then did the show begin.

Read's party went to Chengtu, the capital city of Szechuan, on the 15th. Here was a China much more primitive than Peking, with crowded little shops: 'the general atmosphere rather like Naples, but not so sinister'. When Read noticed that there were no policemen, he was told that none had been needed since the Liberation. Read was also moved to see that the life of the whole place spilled over into the streets.

Although Read remained impressed with the Chinese commitment to achieve a more productive economy, he thought that the resulting changes would rob his new friends of the small units of government which stirred him. Progress, he thought, would be exacted at too high a price:

> it all fills me with horror – another country committed to technological doom – the destruction of natural beauty, congested roadways & death on the roads, lethal fumes, lung cancer & juvenile delinquency. I warn some of them, but they smile & say it will be different with us – our workers will be educated, they will want beauty & leisure & we shall not repeat the mistakes of the capitalist world.

One of the final events of Read's visit was a reception at the People's

Assembly Hall in Peking: 'seats 8000, all marble & plush, and built in ten months – waiting for Mao to speak'. There was also a meeting at the Writers' Union with four leading novelists and critics who were evasive on the touchy issue of freedom of speech.[46]

Despite some minor reservations, Read was so infused with a new vitality that he wished to return in another life as a Chinese lens polisher – if there were such a thing as reincarnation. China had renewed his sense of inner harmony. 'I never felt so well. Spiritually, too. There is a spirit there such as we do not know in the decadent West.' The Chinese determination to create a new way of life brought back to Read a sense of the youthful vigour which had infused him at the end of the First World War, when he had thought that modernism could remake the world in a better image.[47]

Upon his return to Stonegrave, Read's newly buoyant spirits were crushed when he saw the two hundred letters awaiting him. He was worried as well, he told Penrose, by yet another financial crisis at the ICA:

> Briefly: although we still have a nominal membership of 1500, I do not believe there is any vitality left. We lost on *all* our activities last month. The audiences for lectures & discussions have dropped to a handful. The bar is deserted most evenings & is a dead loss. The barmen are demoralized & have robbed us of large sums of money. . . . The only purpose we serve now is that of a cheap lunch club & perhaps a gallery for artists who cannot get a show in a commercial gallery.[48]

At about the same time, Douglas Cooper, now characterized as a 'wealthy pederast who nurses his social frustrations in a chateau in the south of France', had launched yet another attack on Read in the *Times Literary Supplement*. Also, Read was appalled at the prospect of yet another speaking engagement in Washington, but his financial needs remained acute.[49] He had to be careful with the excessively thin-skinned Edward Dahlberg. Since the American wanted to speak freely about Pound and Eliot, Faber would probably not be a good publisher for their epistles; they would have to fall back on Routledge.[50]

Read's trip to the United States that spring involved him in a frenzy of appearances: Yale, Harvard, Duke, North Carolina, New York, Richmond and Minneapolis. He was 'hustled from post to post' in infernal aeroplanes, simply to be met by 'men as mechanical if not so infernal, who drink milk at midday & poison themselves with raw spirits in the evening'.[51] As soon as he left, Read felt that any spiritual sustenance he had to offer was quickly forgotten. He also realized that he had been tricked: under the guise of an 'International Cultural Exchange' he had been forced to make far too many appearances for very little money.

Back in London, the Australian painter Sidney Nolan was convinced that Read was telling everyone of his hatred for his Leda and Swan pictures.[52] Read also travelled to Munich to open a Moore show and in June spoke at the Europa-Cespräch, a conference held in Vienna. In July 1960 he launched the British Society of Aesthetics, in part a ploy to allow him to attend and claim expenses for the 4th International Congress of Aesthetics in Athens that September. Two years earlier, the Bollingen funds had been given to relieve Read of the necessity of such lecturing. The truth was that he had a great many expenses and still a comparatively small salary. More importantly, travelling, as he increasingly realized, was a manic defence against the depressive feelings which tended to invade him at Stonegrave and in London. In addition, Read firmly believed in the central role of art in human life: he wanted to proselytize. Nevertheless, he increasingly felt that he was casting pearls before swine.

Read's quarrel with Jung about modern art came to a head in September 1960. Increasingly, Jung saw Picasso's enormous success as a symptom of the failure of contemporary art. Although he did not diagnose Picasso a schizophrenic, he felt that his art manifested the schizophrenia of modern life:

> Picasso is ruthless strength, seizing the unconscious urge and voicing it resoundingly, even using it for monetary reasons. By this regrettable regression he shows how little he understands the primordial urge, which does not mean a field of ever so attractive looking and alluring shards, but a new world, after the whole has crumpled up. Nature has a horror vacui and does not believe in shard heaps and decay, but grass and flowers. . . . The great problem of our time is the fact, that we don't understand, what is happening to the world. We are confronted with the darkness of our soul, the Unconscious. It sends up its dark and unrecognizable urges.[53]

Despite his own lack of enthusiasm for Picasso, Read could not accept Jung's interpretation of his work. To a large degree, artists such as Picasso reproduced the world as they experienced it. In addition, there was a danger in exploring new ways of expression. To be revolutionary was to subject oneself to inner turmoil and possible annihilation:

> The whole process of fragmentation, as you rightly call it, is not, in my opinion, wilfully destructive: the motive has always been (since the

294

beginning of this century) to destroy the conscious image of perfection (the classical ideal of objectivity) in order to release new forces from the unconscious. This 'turning inwards' . . . is precisely a longing to be put in touch with the Dream, that is to say (as you say) the future. But in the attempt the artist has his 'dark and unrecognizable urges', and they have overwhelmed him. He struggles like a man overwhelmed by a flood. He clutches at fragments, at driftwood and floating rubbish of all kinds. But he had to release this flood, in order to get nearer to the Dream. My defence of modern art has always been based on this realization: art must die in order to live, that new sources of life must be tapped under the parched crust of tradition.[54]

Experimentation, Read argues, always exposes the artist to the possibility of discovering the horrible as well as the beautiful within himself. The process, despite the attendant pain, is worthwhile if new forms of beauty come into being, each age having an obligation to make its mark. Despite his own increasing trepidations about the directions that modern art and literature were taking and despite his own overpowering sense of being excluded from the new battle stations, Read chose to defend 'new sources of life'. For him, this was the only way in which the parched crust of the Wasteland could once again be made fertile. He agreed with Jung that many of the great writers and artists of the century – Joyce, Picasso, Eliot, Pound, Brecht, Kandinsky and Klee – were 'rootless and restless'. But in contrast, he pointed out, Moore's work was not fragmentary: he 'buys land, digs himself in, respects the genius loci'.[55] Of course, Read had tried to engage himself in a similar, largely unsuccessful, process by returning to Yorkshire.

The honest acrimony of their disagreements led to a revitalization in the friendship of Read and Jung, both of whom saw themselves as outcasts. Saddened by Jung's increasingly morbid bitterness, he confided in him: 'I am not unfamiliar with such things myself, and it will not surprise you to learn that the generally hostile reviews of my last book attribute some of my shortcomings to your influence. I am proud to share your enemies.'[56] In turn, Jung was shocked by Lawrence Alloway's hostile review in the *Listener* of *The Forms of Things Unknown*. In that notice, Alloway had attacked Read's conviction that society could achieve salvation only through art. Alloway's counter-vailing opinion was that the artist was of negligible social importance: 'It is by means of Jung's theory of archetypes that Sir Herbert invests the unique product of the artist with this high general significance.'[57] Since Read could not scientifically prove the existence of the archetypes, he was relying, Alloway pointed out, on that which was only 'wordlessly known'. On 27 October, Read told Jung: 'I know the author of the review quite well – he is a young and very opinionated journalist, and I am quite sure he has never taken any trouble to read your works or to understand what you mean by the term "archetypes".'[58] Read was not bothered by Alloway's hostility to his new book, but he was hurt by Eliot's indifference. Read had 'struggled through to some kind of enlightenment. It is a little discouraging. Not a word from Tom on it. I had lunch with him last week: his bliss [in his second marriage], it seems to me, is apathetic.'[59]

What Read had grasped for in *The Forms of Things Unknown* was a kind of religious belief, building upon the ideas in *Icon and Idea*. Again, despite the despair that invaded him, he was trying to see an underlying causality to life by examining the way in which forms emerged from the shadowy world of the unconscious.

A trip to Greece in September was restorative. At Olympia and at the Temple of Apollo at Bassae, Read felt once again in touch with the origins of Western art. Back in London, he had to face up once again to a host of chores, including the incessant planning for *Truth Is More Sacred*. 'The "Epistles" were rather forced out of me by persistence,' he told Richard Hull, 'and I was perhaps driven by the violence of Dahlberg's opinions to defend some positions which I would have been happier to attack.'[60] Read alerted Moore to the fact that the United Nations Secretary-General Dag Hammarskjöld, if approached correctly, might like to commission a sculpture for the UN building in New York. To his protégé, the artist Eric Finlay, Read vented his irritation with the art historian Ernst Gombrich and his followers' 'Viennese pastry approach to art; they are afraid of the senses. Perhaps they are also afraid of their unconscious. Since they are *dissectors* they must first murder the living forms of art.'[61] No one at Faber liked the sequel to *The Innocent Eye*, and Read also had to face up to the fact that he could not write a continuation which would in any way be of the same quality as the earlier work. The only benefit of such a task was to rid himself of his 'tiresome ego'. Read also tried to place Dahlberg's autobiography with Routledge, but, not surprisingly, they found the book repulsive.

Read's own insecure place at Routledge menacingly surfaced at a directors' meeting in April 1961, shortly after Cecil Franklin's death early that year. In a letter to *The Times*, Read made the point that publishing had never been for Franklin a 'romantic profession'; he was a realist who maintained the high standards of a university press rather than a commercial business: 'As a man he often gave the impression of curtness, but at heart he was very kind and generous.'[62] For Read, any semblance of kindness and generosity at Routledge disappeared after Cecil Franklin's death.

Although some 'tactful periphrasis' was used, it was 'made pretty clear to me', Read told Barrett, 'that my services were no longer considered essential to the company, and that if I would like to retire I might receive a pension of £1,000 per annum (somewhat less than the pension awarded to Mr Franklin's widow)'.[63] A higher pension was possible if Read 'lent' his name to the firm.[64] As he told Barrett, he had never found the position a congenial one. Now, his contributions to the firm – the publication of people such as Jung, Buber and Weil – were dismissed by the younger generation.[65] A pension of £1,000 a year was totally inadequate: Stonegrave cost 'at least £2,000 *not* to keep up'.[66] However, even a pension of £1,000 was not assured, he soon found out.

An enlarged treadmill of even more frequent lecturing and travelling was a horrible prospect. Read even considered leaving England for a country with more liberal tax laws. His fellow director, Jack Carter, whom he implored for help, was sympathetic but the outcome was that the Board had decided by 23 May that they wanted to retain Read's services and 'above all his name for as long as possible'. Nevertheless, they did not intend to give him any pension.[67] So Read had to stay with a firm which did not want him but which would not allow him a graceful exit.

Read's bitter struggle with Routledge in 1961 reminded him of just how much outside the prevailing modernities he was perceived to be by younger colleagues. And he had struggled for years to obtain some sort of financial equilibrium but had never quite managed to reach that elusive goal. However, the most harrowing aspect of the trauma was the nightmarish possibility that he might have to sell Stonegrave to which he had become more and more attached. He thought of 'its dozen rooms, thousands of books, scores of pictures, intimate associations, and those deep deep roots in the landscape'.[68]

For Read, the possible loss of Stonegrave recalled the wounds which had been inflicted upon him when as a boy of nine he had been expelled from the paradisal beauty of Muscoates. In 1961, he was forced to face the possibility of reliving that tragedy all over again. Although the quarrel with Routledge was soon papered over, he realized that he was, in many ways, still as vulnerable as he had been as a boy those long years before. Read was able as an older man to undertake a passionate search for 'the forms of things unknown' because he retained a childlike wonder at the beauty of a world which wanted to destroy itself. And yet that innocence never really made him a man of the world.

18 The Forms of Things Unknown

If Read had been irritated not to hear from Eliot about *The Forms of Things Unknown*, he was certainly not pleased by his friend's icy but justified response in June 1961 to the dubiously named *Truth Is More Sacred*. Since Read had not bothered with a rebuttal to Dahlberg's claim that Eliot was anti-Semitic, Eliot assumed that Read now believed that such was the case.[1] He sarcastically observed that he was gratified to find himself a fallen idol side by side with Robert Graves, who considered taking legal action against Dahlberg but let the matter drop, dubbing the attack 'a dirty damp squib left over from last year's wet Guy Fawkes night'.[2]

Read and John Berger had been friendly enemies for a number of years, ever since Berger, an aspiring poet of fifteen, had written to ask the older man's advice. The teenager was so touched by the sensitive lack of condescension that Read bestowed upon him that he carried the letter on his person until it disintegrated. Since Berger's Marxist bent led him to enthuse about paintings and sculptures which displayed the sordidness of capitalist society or proclaimed the glories of socialism, Read politely distanced himself from the younger critic's 'realism'. In order for their friendship to survive, the two men usually agreed to disagree. However, when Berger sent him his novel, *The Foot of Clive*, Read did not hesitate to voice serious reservations. He was disturbed by the 'little minds and alienated sensibilities' of Berger's characters; and he did not like Berger's assumption, in his fiction and criticism, that 'the groping sensibility of the man in the street is intrinsically more valuable than the refined sensibility of the aristocrat'.[3]

A minor point – the coarseness is sometimes a little aggressive. Now that the censor allows us to use words like arse and cunt, we should use them with discretion. I don't know what to think of the climax on pages 154–5. It is true enough and beautiful enough, but I don't feel that prick and cunt are dream-words: they destroy the poetic unity of the narrative. My only objection to pornography in general is the aesthetic one: it can grate on the ear like a wrong note in a sonata. . . . I would not have written at such length if I had not been impressed – and if I had not had so much faith in your perversity.[4]

Despite their differing attitudes towards art and literature, both Read and Berger were united in their opposition in December 1961 to the belligerent tactics being employed by the peace movement.

The Campaign for Nuclear Disarmament was formed largely as a result of the uproar caused by a 1957 article by J. B. Priestley in the *New Statesman*, which had severely criticized the development of a British hydrogen bomb. CND itself was launched on 17 February 1958 at a mass meeting at Central Hall in Westminster. The Direct Action Committee, started by Pat Arrowsmith in the same year, organized pickets, sit-downs and trespasses at nuclear stations in England. Two years later, the Committee of 100 came into being: this was a collection of prominent citizens ('the names') who were opposed to nuclear war. Although Read usually avoided direct political action, he joined the Committee because it 'got in touch with' him and because he sympathized with its aims.[5] He also agreed to approach a 'select' number of artists and writers who might be willing to swell the ranks.[6]

Mass demonstrations of at least 10,000 'reliable adherents' were favoured by Read. Nevertheless, he added one important caveat: 'All the history of civil disobedience points to the necessity of discipline and a quasi-military planning of strategy and tactics.'[7] What he discerned from the outset was a confusion between civil disobedience and hostile confrontation. He told Michael Randle and Bertrand Russell in December 1960: 'I am not convinced of either the practicability or the effectiveness of the Whitehall sit-down. As it has been decided that the time and place cannot be kept secret, the police will be able to frustrate the plans without difficulty. An abortive demonstration will do more harm than good.'[8]

Although he was suffering from a bout of cystitis and an enlarged prostate, Read, despite Ludo's objections, took part in the demonstration at Trafalgar Square on 17 September 1961 (earlier, he had participated in the sit-down at the Ministry of Defence in February). Ludo and Sophie accompanied him, but Ludo insisted upon leaving as soon as reporters descended upon her husband, whom, resisting her, she pushed into a taxi.

By the end of 1961, however, Read had become disillusioned by the violence he saw rising to the surface in CND:

There can be no doubt that recourse to civil disobedience and direct action has now taken a direction that is increasingly masochistic in its manifestations. Some of the leaders of the movement are quite explicit in their revelations of this tendency to self-punishment. For example, I notice that in an interview which Pat Arrowsmith gave to the press on her recent release from nine weeks' imprisonment, she said: 'I am campaigning against violence in all forms. Therefore I must provoke violence. Violence must be *seen* to be done to me.' We all admire the immense courage of Pat Arrowsmith, and consciously she is motivated by the same respect for life that is the rational ground for our hatred of war. But there is a fundamental difference between an attitude or a policy that is *passive* in its resistance and one which, for all its pacific motivations, is *provocative*.[9]

In Read's view, one could not fight fire with fire: 'We cannot use the instruments of Death or lift menacing hands against the powers of darkness; if we are motivated by love all our actions should be gentle.'[10] The demonstrations at Wethersfield Air Base, a few days later on 9 December, persuaded him that the Committee had used tactics reminiscent of 'Mosley fascists and Empire Loyalists': 'We have become a public spectacle, a group isolated from the general body of public opinion and feeling, a rowdy show to be televised and reported in the press for the interest and amusement of a majority who are not with us. We provide entertainment and not enlightenment to the man in the street.'[11] In a slightly more unguarded fashion, he disgustedly told Berger that the actions of the peace movement were those of rebellious teenagers.[12] Despite Berger's advice not to leave the Committee, Read resigned.

Frequently, Read was worried about Ruth Francken's rebellious determination to combat the art world on her own. In his opinion her existence was too resolutely urban: 'I sometimes think that there are not enough old pine trees & wild birds in your life. You are shut into yourself & that is the prison where one becomes lonely & afraid.'[13] As he confided to Ruth, Read's admiration for the American abstract expressionists had now become more fervent: he was especially attracted to Clyfford Still and Mark Rothko, although he insisted that André Masson was the catalyst for radical American art.

In December 1962, Read finally made his much desired purchase of a Moore maquette from the artist himself. He had been shown several things while visiting Much Hadham and had finally decided on a two-piece bronze, which he bought at a reduced price. When he returned to Stonegrave, he realized that he did not really like the maquette. John told him to telephone Moore and arrange for a trade, but the possibility of a fight with Moore was too much for Read, who ignored his son's advice. Moore, who had sensed that Herbert might be making a mistake, wrote on 21 December offering an exchange. This incident displays the remarkable constraint which existed in a close friendship. Moore was reluctant, under any circumstances, to give away pieces of sculpture: payment and praise were essential in any transaction. Well aware of this, Read did not want to rock the boat by suggesting that anything by Moore could be the wrong piece.

Read's problems with the ICA's younger generation continued throughout the sixties. He found pop art 'tedious',[14] and the prospect of the ICA playing host to 'prank' events filled him with trepidation. At a meeting of the Tate Trustees – to which he had been appointed the year before – in November 1966, he was furious when he and his fellow trustee, Barbara Hepworth, could not garner enough votes to block the purchase of Roy Lichtenstein's *Whaam!*: 'I refuse to believe that I am getting reactionary in my old age. This sort of thing is just nonsense. A

'WHAAM!' Read and Hepworth were among the Tate trustees who objected in 1967 to the purchase of Roy Lichtenstein's oil painting.

302

little nonsense is amusing from time to time, but not at the price of £5000.'[15] Certainly he did not want the ICA to have a membership 'predominantly of hippies and diggies': 'For good or for bad we have emerged from "the underground", and the image we have to present has more in common with the Museum of Modern Art than a forum for "happenings".' What Read really wanted was a serious modernism, not 'sheer silliness'.[16] Read also disliked geometricism: 'Amusing for a moment, especially if a transparent plastic sheet is provided to jiggle in front of the basic pattern. But basically non-vital, therefore deadly.'[17]

For Read, the parodic nature of pop art meant that it whole-heartedly accepted the civilization of which it was a part; he did not think that it contained any strands of ironical or satirical commentary of the society with which it seemed too lovingly involved. In pop art – and to a lesser degree in geometricism and minimalism – Read detected a view of the role of the artist which he found reprehensible. Those movements were not concerned with an inner symbolic world to which the artist seeks to give plastic expression. That humanistic view of art was, for them, dead. Rather, these young artists were attempting to discover new ways of making art through magazine illustrations, optical illusions or a seeming absence of draughtsmanship or painterliness. For Read, such processes were alchemical, attempts to transmute base materials into gold. He upbraided his young artist friend Eric Finlay when he toyed with such approaches: 'the tiger's stripes don't make a work of art – or if they do, we need a new philosophy of art which resigns the creative act to some force outside ourselves'.[18] Read reminded Finlay that Kandinsky's early abstractions were the product not of chance but of the transformation of natural motifs into art of enduring beauty.

Also a cause for concern was the state of design in England. Read felt that design was being infected with the 'adolescent pruriency' and 'beatnikery' of the art schools, as he warned Misha Black.[19] For Read, design was supposed to be at the service of the artist. 'Confusion arises, from the fact that it is now the ideal of some young artists to de-personalize their works. They create functionless industrial designs. Not, in my opinion, works of art.'[20]

Although he had been a resolute defender of expressionism in art and poetry, Read began to see a link between that movement and violence. He told the poet Vernon Watkins that it was no accident that such art had been most prevalent in fascist countries. With Igor Stravinsky, he wanted a *cool* art: 'the lava flows but must set before it can assume a permanent form'.[21]

Read had himself experimented with literary equivalents to abstract expressionism and minimalism in 'Vocal Avowals'. Unfortunately, he soon found himself the victim of strictures similar to those he was pronouncing against many young artists. In March 1962, Eliot informed him that Faber and Faber would not allow these experimental poems to appear at the end of his new collection of verse. For one thing, Eliot could not make head or tail of them. Nor did they mesh with the other poems in the volume. Above all, the poems simply did not fit into any recognizable Faber category: Read was welcome to market these poems elsewhere, perhaps with a small imprint specializing in such new verse.[22] The poems were published later that year in St Gallen by Tschudy-Verlag; 'Vocal Avowals' ultimately appeared under the Faber imprint in 1966 in Read's *Collected Poems*.

More Faberish in 1962 was *Daphne*, a sequence of twelve sonnet-like stanzas, in which the possibility of metamorphosis is examined:

> By love deceived or men rejected
> we may frequent this sheltered grove
> and listen to the canticles
> about us and above
>
> and some who well distinguish
> Daphne's argent voice
> may then decide that love is vain
> in loveless life rejoice
>
> Beyond the reach of sickly lust
> and fretful strife
> there is a stillness of the flesh
> another mode of life
>
> in which the still inquiring mind
> a recompense for love may find

These poems were written during a three-week holiday in Venice and show the 'inquiring mind' of the poet very much at work in an attempt to find a 'recompense' for the years of devotion to literature and art.

The years 1962 and 1963 brought a new series of gruelling trips: South America in the summer of 1962; the United States that autumn. Why did he travel yet again to North America, Dahlberg asked. 'The answer is $2,000. . . . I also want to disabuse American poets of certain pretensions to uniqueness.'[23] New Zealand and Australia followed in the spring of 1963. Not unexpectedly, Read was disappointed in the Antipodes:

Australia was one of those ambiguous nightmares – nothing to complain of, except the prevailing ugliness, but nothing to explain why one was there, except the large and enthusiastic audiences. It is America without the negroes, and without the South – a country without social complexes. Very dull! But very energetic, and with all kinds of possibilities in the dim future (including disaster).[24]

He joked with Edward Dahlberg that like Jules Verne's hero, he was going round the world in eighty days, 'but with no sense of wonder'.[25] London for Read remained cataclysmic. That summer he was thrown headlong from a London bus, sustaining a few bruises and a hole in his jacket. His conviction – acquired in 1914–18 – that he led a charmed life was reconfirmed, but he insisted that the conductress was at fault and made London Transport replace the jacket.[26] Summer 1963 meant a series of lectures in Canada.

Now that their joint book had been published, Dahlberg pestered Read to advance his name and revise his poems. Disgustedly, Read told his American friend: 'I cannot bring your name into every book I write, nor can I relinquish my friendships with other writers simply because you disapprove of their style.'[27] The prospect of reworking Dahlberg's poems also revolted him: 'I cannot butcher another man's flesh.'[28]

On 4 December a dinner was held at the Arts Club to celebrate Read's seventieth birthday. Although he claimed to be mildly annoyed by this (and by another dinner held in Leeds), Read was secretly pleased by this tribute, not least because Stephen Spender, Joe Ackerley and Allen Tate were among those present. Sophie playfully asked her uncle William: 'Doesn't Daddy love to be loved?' Later that evening, Henry Moore took William aside and made him promise to inform him if Herbert and Ludo ever needed anything.

Trouble at Routledge blew up again shortly after Read's birthday. Suddenly, it seemed to him, a clause was discovered in the firm's regulations to the effect that directors retired upon reaching the age of seventy or were re-elected by a special resolution of the board. This new controversy had been ignited by Read's proposal to spend four months in the United States. An acrimonious discussion ensued, as Read told Jack Barrett: 'It was proposed that I should retire but remain as a consultant of the firm for a fee exactly half the minimum wage of an agricultural labourer. This offer I refused and after some rather painful discussions it was agreed that I should be pensioned off with a £1,000 a year and no further obligations to the firm. So be it! Life begins again at seventy, and I am a free man.'[29] Read told another friend, Stanley Burnshaw, that he had been in effect dismissed from the firm.

The Bollingen Foundation renewed its annual grant, but, as Read reported to Alex Comfort, there was no 'sleepy corner for this Gerontion'.[30] For the first time since he had left school at the age of fifteen,[31] he felt a 'free & independent being'. Kindly, Eliot assured him that he had acquired all the titles worth publishing which bore the Routledge imprint.[32]

During his 1964 trip to the States Read was a Fellow of the Center for Advanced Studies at Wesleyan University, where there were minimal duties. However, as usual, Read filled his diary with speaking engagements, this time in North Carolina, Georgia and Ohio. Ludo was 'fully converted to "the American way of life" ', but her husband hankered after Yorkshire.[33] In August, he was in Switzerland and visited Ben Nicholson at his home in Ticino. He told the painter's ex-wife that the studio was 'more like a fortress than ever'. The entrance was electrified, and he had had to telephone from outside. If one was 'approved', a button opened the gates.[34] Wasn't marble awfully expensive to use for the entrance way, he asked. Ben assured him that marble 'lasted longer'.

Early that autumn, Herbert and Ludo spent a weekend with the Moores at Much Hadham, where Herbert had not been for a while. Moore remained simple and unspoilt, although Read noticed a few signs of luxury: a Cézanne, two Rodins, a Courbet. But 'the way of life is still very modest', he reassured Barbara Hepworth.[35] Read was supposed to visit Japan that November but the trip had to be abruptly cancelled.

In the midst of a routine check-up in 1961, Read's dentist had discovered a growth on his tongue and urged him to get in touch with a doctor immediately. The surgeon whom Read consulted told him that 'everyone' had such lumps and that he should see him again only if the growth got bigger. The tumour was considerably larger on 23 October 1964 when Read went again to see the same doctor, who insisted on operating the following day.[36] The tumour (an epithelium), which was removed, was malignant, but the surgeon was cautiously optimistic.

Nevertheless, Read, furious that the physician had offhandedly allowed the growth to remain in place for three years, knew that the seriousness of the symptoms could not be disguised. 'It is just one of those things one has to expect at my age,' he told Dorothy Morland.[37] Radiotherapy and further hospitalization had to be endured in November and December, this time under the supervision of Sir Stanford Cade. With radium needles firmly affixed in his mouth, Read wrote to the *Times Literary Supplement* in December 1964 to attack Donald Davie, 'a poet turned Universal Academic Woolf' who had snarled at 'the still-unburied carcase of Shelley'.[38]

That autumn, Sophie became engaged to Nicholas Hare – 'charming, serious and kind', his future father-in-law called him. Ludo had ambitious plans for the January wedding in Yorkshire, which Read feared would 'exhaust' them 'financially and emotionally'.[39]

Less than a month after Read arrived home from hospital, T. S. Eliot died on 4 January 1965. For Read, fully aware that he might not have long to live, Eliot's passing was more than the loss of a man whom he had loved and with whom he had vigorously struggled. He also had a profound sense that he was now one of the last of the moderns, one of the final defenders of a view of literature and art that seemed to have reached its end. Richard Church told him: 'You and I have known each other for forty-four years, both silently eloquent, I think – two "cats who walk alone" in this ghastly, overcrowded' world.[40]

Read's retirement and his increased sense of mortality led him to prepare a collected edition of his poems; he also published eight other books during his last three years. These final works were often – as his son, Piers Paul Read, has pointed out – hack work, betraying the haste in which they had been conceived. Read was desperate for money, and he traded on his name. Thus, as his health worsened, Read had the painful experience of being subjected to justifiably harsh notices from reviewers such as Hilton Kramer and David Sylvester.

When he was appointed a trustee of the Tate in 1965, Read was suspicious that the invitation had been proffered because he was a good friend of Peggy Guggenheim, whose collection the Tate was eyeing enviously. Laughingly, he told her that he had been appointed to 'look after "her" interests'.[41]

Herbert and Ludo returned to Wesleyan for the spring term of 1965. 'I don't intend to give any lectures,' he claimed, 'but just to drink martinis & meditate.'[42] The crossing was rough: it 'nearly killed poor Ludo, who is not a good sailor'.[43] However, he managed to read *Paradise Lost*: that poem still held some surprises for him but the poet was 'a monster of some sort'. Also entertaining was Saul Bellow's *Herzog*, although Read thought the novel a 'shapeless mass of unleavened dough & I can't believe that it will survive as a significant work of art. Perhaps I'm prejudiced – I have no sympathy for the wail of the alienated Jew – sympathy perhaps, but no patience with it.'[44] Jean Stafford, Martin D'Arcy and Edmund Wilson were his 'fellow Fellows'.[45] Naughtily, Read decided to 'try out' his memoir of Eliot on

307

his companions in order to irritate Wilson, renowned for his hatred of Eliot's work. True to expected form, 'the "Curmudgeon" walked out, mumbling something about TSE's unamericanness'. Read assured Allen Tate – contrary to some nasty gossip that had come his way – that Eliot had not habitually referred to him as 'little' Allen: Tom, he told him, 'was certainly no saint, but I am sure he was neither cruel nor malicious – perhaps ruthless in affairs of the heart'.[46]

Edward Dahlberg arrived for a weekend and managed to insult everyone whom the Reads 'produced to pay him homage'.[47] Dahlberg's 'relentless blackmail' had led him, Read told Tate, to bestow unqualified praise on everything he wrote: would Father D'Arcy give him absolution for such rank dishonesty?[48] Before he returned to England, there was the usual round of lectures, including Yale, Virginia and Berkeley. He received an honorary doctorate at Boston University on 6 June: 'I don't want such meaningless decorations, but I don't want to offend the kind people who think me worthy of them.'[49] During July and August, Read continued well but frequently exhausted. As he told Ackerley, he had lost his zest for life.

On the way back from Switzerland at the end of August, Herbert and Ludo had a slapstick adventure in Antibes when they attempted to enter the flat there of a Yorkshire neighbour who had lent it to them. They arrived at nine in the evening to discover that three keys – not two as they had been given – were necessary to gain entry. They dashed into the countryside to find the *femme de ménage*, who was away. Then, they went to a locksmith, who would only open the door in the presence of the police. The police would not co-operate unless the owner was contacted – and he was on a fishing holiday at an unknown location in Scotland. Finally, the distraught couple had to settle for a hotel.[50]

In October, Read, accompanied by Piers Paul, took an all-expenses-paid trip to Japan, the 'fantastic reward' for writing the introduction to the catalogue of a collection of paintings by the Zen Buddhist painter Sengai. Unknown to Read, the owner, Sazo Idemitsu, was supposedly the richest man in Tokyo.[51]

Read's stay in Tokyo was impeded by a slipped disc, but a giggling masseuse relieved his pain. In direct contrast to China, Read found Japan a wasteland, exceeding 'in horror any other industrialised nation'.

> It is a vast unplanned mechanized chaos. There are some beautiful works of art, of course, and some gracious customs and people, but they will be

308

submerged and what will remain will not differ from Manhattan or Chicago. The American influence is everywhere in the Far East, ruthless and ugly . . . this madness will destroy the world – the madness of a rootless, deeply alienated technocracy.[52]

In addition, Tokyo was a 'strenuous town' which could only be survived by drinking numerous cups of saké. At Hiroshima, Read saw no sign of *the* bomb, except in a museum.

At this time, Read had also become increasingly upset at the American presence in Vietnam, where, he said, 'democracy is completely irrelevant to their way of life'.

These vast millions of peasants can only live in communes and if the western world will leave them alone they will be content to stay in their paddy-fields. Communism? Why not? They are communists by tradition and all their troubles have come from western infiltration. I have really got to the state of mind in which I don't want to come to the States again so long as this bloody aggression goes on.[53]

As usual, Read opposed any sort of military intervention: 'It never solves anything – it merely drives the poison deeper into the social system, to erupt again sooner or later.'[54] Late in 1965 Read heard that he had been awarded the Erasmus Prize (shared with René Huyghe); he also became one of the first Honorary Doctors of York University and accepted an honorary membership in the American Academy of Arts and Letters.

In January 1966, Read quarrelled with Kathleen Raine about their differing, mystical theories of poetry. Although Read did not believe in a pre-existing Platonic order of things, he thought the poet's function was to unleash the secrets implanted in words.[55] People, he also reminded her, were not atheist because they 'have chosen *not* to believe in the beautiful, the true, the holy'. For him, art was the answer. The logos could only really be distilled in 'new & unexpected forms, into untarnished images or icons'. He was not sure, however, if such a renewal would take place 'this side of universal catastrophe, & that I more & more doubt'.[56] Moreover, Read could not write any new poems. In March 1966, he was awaiting publication of his *Collected Poems*: 'impossible to conceive while one is pregnant'.[57] He felt like a 'scarred battlefield . . . but even a battlefield', he remembered, 'is quickly covered with new growth'.[58]

As he reflected upon his time as a literary modernist, George Orwell, who had died in 1950, rose 'like some ghost to admonish' him.

Despite Orwell's proletarian affectations, his narrow range of interests, his insensitivity to the visual, Read felt nearer to him than to any other English writer of his time.[59] What he had probably come to realize was that he and Orwell had undertaken similar missions as prose writers: both had written romances – rather than novels – and both had used the essay to proselytize a largely unreceptive nation. Read also became more poignantly aware of the greatness of W. B. Yeats and Wallace Stevens, twentieth-century inheritors of the romantic tradition. Particularly, he saw Yeats not only as a great poet, 'but a great teacher of poets, in a deeper sense than Pound or Eliot'.[60]

October 1966 brought a recurrence of the cancer and another operation on his tongue, this time at the London Clinic. This was followed by six weeks of radiotherapy: he was in London from Monday to Friday and travelled up to Yorkshire at the weekends. Despite the fact that he lived in 'Damoclean suspense', he tried to remain calm. 'But I have no energy left for creative tasks: all is consumed in the will to live.'[61] In January 1967, he went into hospital yet again for surgery and doses of radium. The pain was not great, he claimed – he suffered only 'a certain amount of toothless humiliation'.[62] His mouth, however, had become a 'fiery furnace of radio-activity'.[63] In addition, the insertion of the radium needles into his mouth left behind a burned taste, and in consequence his appetite dwindled. He had reached a stoical serenity, 'intimately linked with Nature, in Wordsworth's sense'.[64] He wanted to write poems on this new turn, but inspiration again evaded him.

Like a condemned criminal, Read waited for his specialist's verdict. Not unexpectedly, he kept busy. Plans for the removal of the ICA to the Mall were well in hand under the supervision of Desmond Morris, the 'secret surrealist' handpicked by Read and Penrose as Director of the ICA; then, Morris resigned when his book *The Naked Ape* became an overnight success. Read told Roland Penrose: 'It . . . shows that it pays to write on Apes rather than Art!'[65] Graham Greene discussed with Read the possibility of a massive withdrawal of foreign members from the American Academy of Arts and Letters in protest against the Vietnam War, but, since only Read and Bertrand Russell were willing to join him, Greene eventually resigned alone.

Read also worried about the alimony payments to Evelyn, who obviously would survive him. During her father's stay in the Far East, Sophie had given birth to a daughter – Eliza – Read's first grandchild. 1967 brought some other happy events: the marriages of Thomas in January and Piers in July. In October he told Margaret Gardiner: 'Now

310

that three of them are married & are beginning to "breed", the family becomes a problem. By a rare chance they all love each other & love coming here, which they still regard as their home.'[66] An attempt to garner some sun in Portugal that March was a failure. The cancer again made its presence known in June, when he had a haemorrhage and had to be taken to York Hospital in the middle of the night. He also suffered from the radiotherapy. 'I am like one of those Hiroshima victims,' he confided to Kathleen Raine.[67]

Hospitals began to obsess Read that July: 'the absence of *visual* sustenance – always the same blank walls, the same dull routine, the feeling that one is in a condemned cell. . . . How lucky people are who die asleep in their own beds, as Joe Ackerley did the other day!'[68] Although Read went to Switzerland in August, he left after four days. The discomfort he experienced was simply not touched by the pills supplied by his new specialist, Stanley Lee:

> The pain continues but there is nothing to be done about it. It accumulates during the night, like a battery being charged, and is hell when I wake up. Then gradually during the day it abates and by the time one can decently take a strong martini it has almost vanished. But it leaves me exhausted and irritable.[69]

By October Read was better, hoping against hope that the malignancy had been eradicated. Allen Tate informed him that he was praying for him, to which Read made the riposte: 'if it succeeds it will disturb my spiritual complacency!'[70]

Weary and often depressed, Read still welcomed a challenge. Therefore, he decided to attend the International Cultural Congress in Havana from 4 to 11 January 1968. Read's hope was that he would be revitalized once again, just as he had been by China almost ten years before. He wanted 'to see what kind of a new world they are making. It cannot be worse than ours & may be much better.'[71] When Read applied at the American Embassy in London for a visa to enter Puerto Rico, he did not 'think it any of their business' that he was also visiting Cuba. A dossier was produced which detailed Read's support of cultural co-operation with China. He was even accused of being an active communist. Although he felt like throwing the 'beastly' visas in the face of the vice-consul who interrogated him, he spent an hour convincing the reluctant American that he was 'merely a well-meaning intellectual who had been seduced' by the wicked Chinese.[72] Read could not avoid flying to Cuba by way of Madrid: he was irritated at the prospect of having to spend even a few hours in Franco's Spain.

Read was stirred by Cuban socialism, by Castro's intuition and intelligence, and by a country where ideals of justice, equality and decency had been put into practice: 'No robberies, no prostitution, no bribery – impossible to tip anyone.'[73] He was also 'glad to see hundreds of Leyland buses from England!'[74] As Read told Graham Greene, even Ludo, 'who has the usual Catholic attitude towards communism, came away quite converted and is all for going back to wield a machete in the sugar plantations'.[75]

Through Graham Greene, Read met the Cuban artists Millian and Portocarrero. Millian was a recluse who put a sheet over his head when his companion had visitors, particularly women. But the Cuban trip was not a total success, Read being offended by the demagogy and brutality of many of the third-world participants. Finally, one afternoon at a round-table discussion, he stood up and proclaimed: 'I shall say only one sentence. The revolutionary ideal of the nineteenth century was internationalist; in the twentieth century it became enclosed in nationalism and the only internationalists left today are the artists.' A resounding silence followed this declaration, the only pronouncement during the entire conference which was not applauded.

Herbert and Ludo travelled home by way of Puerto Rico and Haiti. While in Port au Prince, Read was somewhat disappointed, he told Graham Greene, not to see the sinister side of the island à la *The Comedians*, but he did hear the distant sound of drums at night and was reassured when told they were voodoo.

By the time the Reads reached England in early March, Herbert was desperately ill once again. He had a further operation – an 'excavation' he called it – from which he never recovered, although the surgeon was trying to 'root out' the problem once and for all. The floor of the left side of the mouth, a slice of tongue, a piece of jawbone and several glands were removed. Even six weeks after the operation, Read could tolerate only liquids. Alcohol tasted like poison, though rum punch – purchased in Cuba – was tolerable. His weight was reduced to about nine stone, and he had to grow a beard to hide the sutures: 'shaving would be painful – & look fearsome'.[76] He did not look 'marvellous', he assured Hepworth: 'rather like one of Francis Bacon's worst nightmares'.[77] Nevertheless – once he was back at home – he felt far from paralysed: 'I get up every day, keep the correspondence in reasonable control, air myself in the garden & slowly put on weight.' Although 'bloody but unbowed',[78] he was haunted by the thought of Freud, whose cancer was identical to his own.

Graham Greene offered Herbert and Ludo the loan of his cottage on Anacapri. During April, May and early June Read assiduously planned this trip: the Alitalia flight from London to Naples was booked, the *vaporetto* service was scratched in favour of a helicopter, a small liquifying machine was purchased. By 2 June, ten days before he died, Read was so weak that he knew there was no hope of leaving Stonegrave. Resolute in his anti-Catholicism, he jokingly told his old friend: 'It is such a bore – I had built up the Lourdes spirit and there was going to be a miraculous cure.'[79] Despite intermittent high spirits, the wavy, irregular lines of his handwriting show that his strength was almost completely gone. He also abandoned the idea of attending the opening of the ICA's new premises. Henry Moore drove up to Stonegrave. Characteristically, they sat together in calm silence.

Read's strength did not return. Desperately, he tried to work. He demanded his 'tools' – spectacles, pencils, pens – but could use them only intermittently. He remained up for only short periods of time. Occasionally, he teased, as when he told Graham Greene that he was reduced to a liquid diet: 'but what is wrong with that, except the price of drink, which will probably again go up after the Budget?'[80] And he had moments of railing against death. In the middle of the night, he often roamed the passages of Stonegrave, his bearded face a mask of utter despair.[81] He was not a good patient, frequently rejecting Ludo's instructions and complaining bitterly when he could find no relief from the sheer physical agony he endured. Although he never discussed Evelyn, he agonized about his abandonment of John in 1933.

Eventually the calm bravery of Read's young manhood reasserted itself, although he tended to dismiss it: 'I am perhaps *stoical*: I acquired that attitude (or aptitude) in the First World War.'[82] He squarely faced the oblivion he thought would soon overtake him: 'I believe in my unbelief – would not force / One fibre of my being to bend in the wind / Of determinate doctrine.' At last, the tiredness overtook him in his sleep on 12 June 1968.

At the very end, dreams were for Read a form of creativity, 'akin to art . . . not explained by analysis'.[83] A bit earlier, he had found sustenance in the 'work of those who bear witness to the reality of a living God rather than in the work of those who deny God. . . . In that state of suspense, "waiting on God", I still live and shall probably die.' Perhaps in his final moments, Read dreamed, as he wished, of 'some bright image', 'some perfect form': 'the gold disc that blurs all hard distinctions'.

Notes

Principal sources are listed at the beginning of each set of chapter notes. In the main, these consist of references to Read's major books and information gained in interviews with Read's relatives and friends. The notes cite other manuscript and printed sources.

Herbert Read: Major Writings

Ambush. London: Faber & Faber, 1930.

Art and Industry: The Principles of Industrial Design. London: Faber & Faber, 1934.

Art and Society. London: William Heinemann, 1937.

Art Now: An Introduction to the Theory of Modern Painting and Sculpture. London: Faber & Faber, 1933.

Collected Poems. London: Faber & Faber, 1946. Revised edition, 1966.

The Contrary Experience: Autobiographies. London: Faber & Faber, 1963.

The Cult of Sincerity. London: Faber & Faber, 1968.

Eclogues: A Book of Poems. London: C. W. Beaumont, 1919.

The Education of Free Men. London: Freedom Press, 1944.

Education Through Art. London: Faber & Faber, 1943.

The End of a War. London: Faber & Faber, 1933.

English Prose Style. London: G. Bell, 1928.

English Stained Glass. London and New York: G. P. Putnam, 1926.

Essential Communism. London: S. Nott, 1935.

Form in Modern Poetry. London: Sheed & Ward, 1932.

The Forms of Things Unknown: Essays Towards an Aesthetic Philosophy. London: Faber & Faber, 1960.

Freedom: Is It a Crime? London: Freedom Press, 1945.

The Grass Roots of Art. London: Drummond, 1947.

The Green Child: A Romance. London: William Heinemann, 1935.

Henry Moore, Sculptor: An Appreciation. London: Zwemmer: 1934.

Icon and Idea: The Function of Art in the Development of Human Consciousness. London: Faber & Faber, 1935.

315

In Defence of Shelley and Other Essays. London: William Heinemann, 1936.

The Innocent Eye. London: Faber & Faber, 1933.

In Retreat. London: The Hogarth Press, 1925.

Julian Benda and the New Humanism. Seattle: University of Washington, 1930.

The Meaning of Art. London: Faber & Faber, 1931.

Moon's Farm and Poems Mainly Elegiac. London: Faber & Faber, 1955.

Mutations of the Phoenix. London: The Hogarth Press, 1923.

Naked Warriors. London: Art and Letters, 1919.

'A Nest of Gentle Artists', *Apollo* 67, no. 7 (September 1962), 536–8.

The Origins of Form in Art. London: Thames & Hudson, 1965.

Paul Nash. London: Soho Gallery, 1937.

Phases of English Poetry. London: The Hogarth Press, 1928.

The Philosophy of Anarchism. London: Freedom Press, 1940.

The Place of Art in a University. Edinburgh: Oliver & Boyd, 1931.

Poetry and Anarchism. London: Faber & Faber, 1938.

Reason and Romanticism. London: Faber & Gwyer, 1926.

The Sense of Glory: Essays in Criticism. Cambridge: University Press, 1929.

Songs of Chaos. London: Elkin Mathews, 1915.

Staffordshire Pottery Figures. London: Duckworth, 1929.

Surrealism. (Edited with an introduction by Read.) London: Faber & Faber, 1936.

To Hell with Culture. London: Kegan Paul, 1941.

Truth Is More Sacred (with Edward Dahlberg). London: Routledge & Kegan Paul, 1961.

The True Voice of Feeling: Studies in English Romantic Poetry. London: Faber & Faber, 1953.

T.S.E. – A Memoir. Middletown: Center for Advanced Studies, Wesleyan University, 1967.

Vocal Avowals. St Gallen: Tschudy-Verlag, 1962.

Wordsworth. London: Jonathan Cape, 1930.

A World Within a War. London: Faber & Faber, 1944.

Short Titles and Abbreviations

HR — Herbert Read
BBC Radio Programme — BBC Radio Programme, produced by Leonie Cohn c. 1969

Manuscripts

Arts Council — Arts Council Archive, London
BBC — BBC Written Archives

316

Black	Misha Black Archive, Victoria and Albert Museum
Burlington	*Burlington Magazine* Archive
Calgary	The Library, University of Calgary
Cornell	Cornell University Library
Francken	Ruth Francken, Paris
Gardiner	Margaret Gardiner, London
Getty	Getty Museum and Art Gallery
Greene	Graham Greene, Paris
Harvard	Houghton Library, Harvard
ICA	Archive of the Institute of Contemporary Arts, London
Leeds	Brotherton Library, The University of Leeds
Morland	Dorothy Morland, London
Nottingham	Library, University of Nottingham
Penrose	The Roland Penrose Archive
Princeton	Firestone Library, Princeton University
Queen's	Queen's University, Kingston, Ontario
Ray	Paul Ray, New York City
Read Family	Manuscripts in the possession of the Read Family
John Read	John Read, London
Routledge	Routledge Archive, Library, University of Reading
Russell	Bertrand Russell Archive, McMaster University, Hamilton, Ontario
Spark	Muriel Spark
Tate	Tate Gallery Archive
Texas	Harry Ransom Humanities Research Centre, The University of Texas
UCLA	Library, The University of California at Los Angeles
Victoria	The Read Archive, McPherson Library, The University of Victoria
V & A	Victoria and Albert Museum
Yale	Yale University Library

Chapter 1: The Leaf and the Stream
1893–1903

Principal sources: *The Contrary Experience*, *Eclogues*, *The Innocent Eye*, *Songs of Experience*; Robert Parrington Jackson, 'Herbert Read – The Yorkshire Background' in *Tribute*; interviews with William and Flora Read, Sir Martyn Beckett.

1. G. Bernard Wood, *Yorkshire Villages* (London: Robert Hale, 1971), p. 173.
2. Marie Hartley and Joan Ingilby, *Life in the Moorlands of North East Yorkshire* (London: J. M. Dent, 1972), p. 124.
3. HR to Edward Dahlberg, 9 December 1962. MS Texas.
4. HR to Edward Dahlberg, 6 October 1951. MS Texas.
5. *Historia Riavellensis* (London: 1824), pp. 160–1.
6. HR to Naum Gabo, 27 March 1955. MS Yale.
7. HR to Richard Church, 18 March 1968. MS Texas.
8. HR to Edward Dahlberg, 6 October 1951. MS Texas.
9. HR to Naum Gabo, 4 August 1941. MS Yale.
10. HR to Edward Dahlberg, 8 April 1962. MS Texas.
11. HR to Naum Gabo, 25 March 1968. MS Yale.
12. Logbook of John Essex as cited by Robert Parrington Jackson in *Tribute*, p. 62.
13. Ibid.
14. HR to Louis Adeane, 18 April 1949. MS Victoria.

Chapter 2: Paradise Lost 1903–1910

Principal sources: *The Contrary Experience*; interview with William Read.

1. *Education Through Art*, pp. 168–9.
2. Information from 'A History of the Crossley and Porter Schools', *Centenary Souvenir* (1964).
3. Ibid., p. 3.
4. F. Leach to Geoffrey Hargreaves, 26 October 1970. MS Victoria.

Chapter 3: Awakenings 1911–1914

Principal sources: *The Contrary Experience*, *Eclogues*, *Songs of Chaos*; interviews with John Read, William Read.

1. *Studies in the History of a University, 1874–1974*, ed. P. H. J. H. Godsen and A. J. Taylor (Leeds: E. J. Arnold & Son, 1975), p. 4.
2. *The Contrary Experience.*, p. 165.
3. *Storm Jameson, Journey from the North*, vol. I (London: Collins & Harvill Press, 1969), pp. 51–2.
4. Ibid., p. 52.
5. *Studies in the History of a University*, p. 21.
6. Ibid.
7. Michael Sadleir, *Michael Ernest Sadler* (London: Constable, 1949), p. 237.
8. Ibid., p. 239.
9. *The Meaning of Art*, p. 148.
10. As cited by Richard Cork, *Vorticism and Abstract Art in the First Machine Age*, vol. I (London: Gordon Fraser, 1976), p. 39.
11. Frank Rutter, *Since I Was Twenty-Five* (Boston and New York: Houghton Mifflin, 1927), p. 204.
12. Gerald Cumberland, *Set Down in Malice* (New York: Brentano, 1919), pp. 131–2.
13. Holbrook Jackson, obituary notice for Orage, *New English Weekly* (15 November 1934), 114.
14. A. R. Orage, *Friedrich Nietzsche, The Dionysian Spirit of the Age* (London and Edinburgh: T. N. Foulis, 1906), pp. 74–5.
15. Ibid., 34–5.
16. As cited by Noel Stock, *The Life of*

Ezra Pound (Harmondsworth: Penguin Books, 1974), pp. 82–3.
17. Leeds Arts Club brochure, 10 December 1909.
18. Holbrook Jackson, *Bernard Shaw: A Monograph* (London: Grant Richards, 1907).
19. Holbrook Jackson, obituary notice for Orage.
20. BBC Radio Programme.
21. *The Letters of Roger Fry*, ed. Denys Sutton (London: Chatto & Windus, 1972), vol. II, p. 531.
22. Jeffrey Meyers, *The Enemy: A Biography of Wyndham Lewis* (Boston and London: Routledge & Kegan Paul, 1980), p. 125.
23. Robin Skelton, *Memoirs of a Literary Blockhead* (Toronto: Macmillan, 1988), p. 66.
24. Jacob Kramer to HR, 10 March 1918. MS Victoria.
25. *New Age*, 1 January 1914, 271.
26. HR to Jacob Kramer, 6 April 1918. MS Leeds.
27. 'August Strindberg,' *Gryphon* XVII (1914), 5.
28. *The Death of a Hero* (New York: Covici, Friede, 1929), p. 159.

Chapter 4: The Contrary Experience 1914–1918

Principal sources: *Ambush, Collected Poems, The Contrary Experience, Eclogues, In Retreat*, 'A Soldier's Diary' (*New Age*, 10 October 1916), *Songs of Chaos*; typescript of HR's letters to Evelyn Roff at the Read Archive (University of Victoria); interview with John Read.

1. *Collected Letters*, ed. Harold Owen and John Bell (London: Oxford University Press, 1967), p. 427.
2. As a child, John Read discovered – and read through – this group of letters.
3. *Margin Released* (1962), p. 89.
4. *Memoirs of an Infantry Officer* (London: Faber & Faber, 1930), pp. 107–8.
5. *Art and Letters* I (1917), 26, 28, 30.
6. MS Dedication to 'A Journal of the Retreat'. Victoria.

Chapter 5: Killing the Nineteenth Century 1918–1923

Principal sources: *The Cult of Sincerity; T. S. E. – A Memoir*; interview with John Read.

1. As cited by Peter Ackroyd, *T. S. Eliot* (London: Hamish Hamilton, 1984), p. 73.
2. *Blasting and Bombardiering* (London: Eyre & Spottiswoode, 1937), p. 273.
3. As cited by Jeffrey Meyers, *The Enemy: A Biography of Wyndham Lewis* (Boston and London: Routledge & Kegan Paul, 1980), p. 38.
4. *Pound/Ford: The Story of a Literary Friendship*, ed. Brita Lindberg-Seyersted (London: Faber & Faber, 1982), pp. 36, 57.
5. *The Letters of Wyndham Lewis*, ed. W. K. Rose (London: Methuen, 1963), pp. 101–2.
6. Ibid., p. 102.
7. HR to Wyndham Lewis, 31 March 1920. MS Cornell.
8. Osbert Sitwell, *Laughter in the Next Room* (London: Macmillan, 1949), p. 30.
9. Ibid., p. 154.
10. Edith Sitwell's letter is cited in Michael De-la-Noy, *Denton Welch: The Making of a Writer* (Harmondsworth: Penguin, 1986), p. 147; *The Journals of Denton Welch*, ed. Michael De-la-Noy (London: Allison & Busby, 1984), p. 15.
11. HR to Wyndham Lewis, 31 March 1920. MS Cornell.
12. 2 September 1919. MS Victoria.
13. *The Diary of Virginia Woolf*, ed. Anne Olivier Bell, vol. II (London: The Hogarth Press, 1978), p. 326.

14. Richard Aldington to HR, 13 January 1919. MS Victoria.
15. Richard Aldington to HR, 28 August 1919. MS Victoria.
16. *Arts Gazette*, 13 September 1919, 392.
17. Ibid., 391.
18. A. R. Orage to HR, 9 February 1920. MS Victoria.
19. Ford Madox Ford to HR, 13 June 1920. MS Victoria.
20. Ford Madox Ford to HR, 19 September 1920. MS Victoria.
21. Ibid.
22. Cited in Philip Mairet, *A. R. Orage: A Memoir* (London: Dent, 1936), p. 59.
23. HR to Henry Miller, 8 June 1958. MS UCLA.
24. Ford Madox Ford to HR, 25 June 1921. MS Victoria.
25. HR to Edward Dahlberg, 15 October 1965. MS Texas.
26. A. R. Orage to HR, 26 August 1921. MS Victoria.
27. Michael Roberts, *T. E. Hulme* (New York: Haskell House, 1971; reprint of the 1938 edition), p. 19.
28. As cited by Richard Cork, *Vorticism and Abstract Art in the First Machine Age*, vol. I (London: Gordon Fraser, 1976), p. 144.
29. J. Meyers, *The Enemy*, p. 53.
30. HR to Allen Tate, 22 March 1927. MS Princeton.
31. A.R. Orage to HR, 12 December 1921. MS Victoria.
32. HR to Wyndham Lewis, 18 April 1931. MS Cornell.
33. *Art and Letters* I (1917), 30.
34. 'Lone Wolf', *New Statesman* 53 (16 March 1957), 337.
35. *The Question of Things Happening: The Letters of Virginia Woolf* (vol. II), ed. Nigel Nicolson (London: The Hogarth Press, 1976), pp. 572–3.
36. Richard Aldington to Ford Madox Ford, 29 March 1922. MS Victoria.
37. Ibid.
38. Ford Madox Ford to HR, 3 May 1921. MS Victoria.

Chapter 6: Reviving the Nineteenth Century 1923–1929

Principal sources: *English Stained Glass, Phases of English Poetry, Reason and Romanticism, Staffordshire Pottery Figures, The True Voice of Feeling, Truth Is More Sacred, T. S. E. – A Memoir, Wordsworth.*

1. HR to Richard Church, 26 April 1943, MS Texas.
2. HR to Richard Aldington, 4 October 1921. MS Texas.
3. *Criterion* 2 (1924), 232.
4. Richard Aldington, *Life for Life's Sake* (New York: Viking Press, 1941), p. 220.
5. T. S. Eliot to HR, c. 1924. MS Victoria.
6. Richard Aldington to HR, 19 June 1925. MS Victoria.
7. HR to H. W. Häusermann, 6 August 1937. MS Victoria.
8. *The Journals of Denton Welch*, ed. Michael De-la-Noy (London: Allison & Busby, 1984), p. 15.
9. *Criterion* 3 (1924–5), 214–30.
10. Ibid. 4 (1926), 756.
11. Richard Aldington to HR, 9 January 1925. MS Victoria.
12. Richard Aldington to HR, 23 June 1925. MS Victoria.
13. *The Diary of Virginia Woolf*, ed. Anne Olivier Bell, vol. III (London: The Hogarth Press, 1980), pp. 41, 45.
14. T. S. Eliot to HR, 27 October 1925. MS Victoria.
15. HR to Richard Aldington, 22 December 1925. MS Texas.
16. HR to Richard Aldington, 30 January 1926. MS Texas.
17. Ibid.
18. MS Texas.
19. MS Texas.
20. Richard Aldington to HR, 9 June 1926. MS Victoria.
21. 'Spain–1926': unpublished manuscript diary owned by Thomas Read.

22. *Punch*, 2 June 1926, 588.
23. Richard Aldington to HR, 16 June 1925. MS Victoria.
24. T. S. Matthews, *Great Tom* (New York: Harper & Row, 1974), p. 85.
25. Frank Morley, 'A Few Recollections of Eliot', in Allen Tate (ed.), *T. S. Eliot: The Man and His Work* (New York: Delacorte Press, 1966), pp. 100–1.
26. T. S. Eliot, 'The Idea of a Literary Review', *Criterion* 4 (April 1926), 4–6.
27. Ibid.
28. Ibid., 5.
29. John Gould Fletcher, *Life Is My Song* (New York: Farrar & Rinehart, 1937), pp. 308–9.
30. *The Bibliophile's Almanack*.
31. HR to Wyndham Lewis, 8 January 1928. MS Cornell.
32. 'Time and Mr Wyndham Lewis', *Nation and Athenaeum* XLII (1927), 282, 284.
33. Richard Aldington to HR, 29 November 1926. MS Victoria.
34. T. S. Eliot to HR, 18 January 1927. MS Victoria.
35. HR to Allen Tate, 22 March 1927. MS Princeton.
36. HR to Richard Aldington, 12 May 1927. MS Texas.
37. T. S. Eliot to HR, c. 1927. MS Victoria.
38. Graham Greene, *Ways of Escape* (Toronto: Lester & Orpen Dennys, 1980), p. 28.
39. 'Potted Ruskin', *Nation and Athenaeum* XLII (1927), 158–9.
40. Richard Aldington to HR, 2 February 1926. MS Victoria.
41. *The Letters of Roger Fry*, ed. Denys Sutton (London: Chatto & Windus, 1972), vol. II, p. 632.
42. *A Change of Perspective: The Letters of Virginia Woolf*, vol. III, ed. Nigel Nicolson (London: The Hogarth Press, 1977), p. 561.
43. *Literary Correspondence of Donald Davidson and Allen Tate* (Athens: University of Georgia Press, 1974), p. 218.

44. T. E. Lawrence to HR, 19 March 1929. MS Victoria.
45. MS Victoria.
46. Bonamy Dobrée to HR, 9 April 1929. MS Victoria.
47. Richard Aldington to HR, 15 July 1929. MS Victoria.
48. 28 July 1929. MS Texas.
49. 18 December 1930, 1073.
50. HR to Allen Tate, 7 May 1927. MS Princeton.

Chapter 7: Time Regained 1929–1933

Principal sources: *The Contrary Experience, Julian Benda and the New Humanism, The Meaning of Art, The Place of Art in a University*; 'Proposals for a Scottish Philanthropist' (MS Victoria); interviews with A. C. Davis, Nigel McIsaac, John Read, Lady Read, William and Flora Read.

1. 'A Lost Generation', *Nation and Athenaeum* XLV (1929), 116.
2. F. R. Leavis to HR, 6 July 1930. MS Victoria.
3. MS Leeds.
4. HR to J. T. Boulton, 20 September 1967. MS Nottingham.
5. HR to Edward Dahlberg, 10 February 1966. MS Texas.
6. HR to Edward Dahlberg, 27 March 1966. MS Texas.
7. R. S. Lambert to HR, 18 December 1929. MS Victoria.
8. *The Times*, 21 January 1928.
9. As cited by Roger Berthoud, *The Life of Henry Moore* (London: Faber & Faber, 1987), p. 113.
10. 11 April 1931.
11. T. S. Eliot to HR, 12 August 1929. MS Victoria.
12. Richard Aldington to HR, 27 November 1930. MS Victoria.
13. HR to William Rothenstein, 2 June 1931. MS Harvard.

14. D. S. MacColl to HR, 18 January 1931. MS Victoria.
15. MS Victoria.
16. HR to J. Middleton Murry, 22 September 1931. MS Calgary.
17. HR to Richard Church, 7 March 1932. MS Texas.
18. HR to David Bomberg, 28 October 1931. MS Tate.
19. HR to William Rothenstein, 2 June 1931. MS Harvard.
20. *Student* XXX, no. 2 (25 October 1933), 41.
21. Geoffrey Grigson, *Recollections: Mainly of Writers and Artists* (London: Chatto & Windus, 1984), p. 58.
22. Bonamy Dobrée to HR, 15 August 1932. MS Victoria.
23. David Daiches to James King, 1 March 1988.
24. As cited by Richard Ellmann, *Oscar Wilde* (London: Viking, 1987), p. 369.
25. Margaret Gardiner, *Barbara Hepworth: A Memoir* (Edinburgh: Salamander Press, 1982), p. 31.
26. Margaret Read to Caroline Gordon, 23 January 1962. MS Princeton.
27. MS Victoria.
28. *The Journals of Denton Welch*, ed. Michael De-la-Noy (London: Allison & Busby, 1984), p. 349.
29. Ibid., p. 350.
30. *The Master Eccentric: The Journals of Rayner Heppenstall*, ed. Jonathan Goodman (London: Allison & Busby, 1986), pp. 10–11.
31. HR to Franklin Gary, 2 March 1932. MS Victoria.
32. HR to Muriel Spark, 4 February 1962. MS Spark.
33. Arthur Wheen to HR, undated but 1933. MS Victoria.
34. HR to William Rothenstein, 19 June 1933. MS Harvard.
35. Henry Miller to HR, 11 October 1935. MS UCLA.
36. Frank Morley to HR, undated but 1932–3. MS Victoria.
37. MS Victoria.
38. David Daiches to James King, 1 March 1988.
39. HR to Eric Finlay, Whit Monday 1966. MS V & A.
40. Richard Aldington to HR, 14 January 1933. MS Victoria.
41. HR to Richard Church, 25 January 1933. MS Texas.
42. Frank Morley to HR, 7 February 1933. MS Victoria.
43. Collection: John Read.
44. HR's letter of resignation to Sir Thomas Holland, the Principal of the University, is dated 28 June 1933 (MS Read Family). When I interviewed her, Lady Read felt that she and Herbert might have gone to Germany in the summer of 1932 – rather than in 1933 before settling in London – but the evidence seems to go against such a trip having taken place in 1932.
45. HR to Sir Thomas Holland, undated draft of a letter. MS Read Family.
46. *Student* XXX, no. 2 (25 October 1933), 41.
47. MS Victoria.
48. Charles Ludwig to HR, 5 July 1933. MS Read Family.
49. David Daiches to James King, 1 March 1988.
50. Eric Maclagan to HR, 13 August 1933. MS Read Family.
51. William Read to HR, 27 July 1933. MS Read Family.
52. HR to Edward Dahlberg, 8 April 1962. MS Texas.
53. HR to Muriel Spark, 8 November 1961. MS Spark.

Chapter 8: *Art Now* 1933–1934

Principal sources: *Art Now*; *English Prose Style*, *Henry Moore*, 'A Nest of Gentle Artists', *Unit One*; Evelyn Read's annotated copy of *Art Now* (Collection: John Read); interviews with Leonie Cohn, John Read, Lady Read.

1. *The Letters of Roger Fry*, ed. Denys Sutton (London: Chatto & Windus, 1972), vol. II, p. 683.
2. *Criterion* 3 (1924–5), 471–2.
3. Roger Fry to HR, 30 August 1933. Ms Victoria.
4. Margaret Read, 'Moving into the Mall Studios', *Belsize Park, A Living Suburb* (London: Belsize Park Conservation Area Publication, n.d.), p. 47.
5. David Higham, *Literary Gent* (London: Jonathan Cape, 1978), p. 268.
6. Margaret Read, Op. cit. p. 49.
7. Statement for *Unit One* book: as cited by Charles Harrison, *English Art and Modernism 1900–1939* (London: Allen Lane, 1981), p. 260.
8. John Skeaping, *Drawn from Life: An Autobiography* (London: Collins, 1977), p. 90.
9. Ibid., p. 93.
10. Margaret Gardiner, *Barbara Hepworth: A Memoir* (Edinburgh: Salamander Press, 1982), p. 10.
11. Skeaping, p. 82.
12. Ibid., p. 85.
13. Basil Taylor, obituary for Read, *Burlington Magazine* CX (August 1968), 463.
14. Geoffrey Grigson, *Recollections: Mainly of Writers and Artists* (London: Chatto & Windus, 1984), p. 12.
15. This anecdote is given in Jeffrey Meyers, *The Enemy: A Biography of Wyndham Lewis* (Boston and London: Routledge & Kegan Paul, 1980), p. 213.
16. P. N. Furbank, *E. M. Forster: A Life*, vol. II (London: Secker & Warburg, 1978), pp. 178–9.
17. Margaret Read, 'Moving into the Mall Studios', in *Belsize Park, A Living Suburb* (London: Belsize Park Conservation Area Publication, n.d.), p. 47.
18. Gardiner, *Barbara Hepworth*, pp. 21–2.
19. *Spectator*, 3 November 1933.
20. *Cambridge Review*, 3 February 1933.
21. HR to Rayner Heppenstall, 21 April 1938. MS Texas.
22. Piers Paul Read, 'Upon This Rock', in *Why I am Still a Catholic*, ed. Robert Nowell (London: Collins, 1982), p. 61.
23. Margaret Read, 'Moving into the Mall Studios', p. 51.
24. Grigson, *Recollections*, pp. 56–7.
25. Ibid., p. 57.
26. Early Autumn Book Supplement (11 October 1933), xii.
27. *Architectural Review*, June 1935, 269.
28. HR to Wyndham Lewis, 9 December 1934. MS Cornell.
29. Ibid.
30. T. S. Eliot to HR, 31 October 1933. MS Victoria.
31. Daniel Farson, *Soho in the Fifties* (London: Michael Joseph, 1987), p. 35.
32. As cited by Harrison, *English Art and Modernism*, p. 164.
33. MS Victoria.
34. MS Yale.
35. HR to Rayner Heppenstall, 10 January 1936. MS Texas. Robert Barker in two articles in *Notes and Queries* (October 1977 and December 1980) has shown that HR made extensive use of J. P. Robertson's *Letters on Paraguay* (London, 1838) and Plato's *Phaedo*.
36. HR to C. G. Jung, 25 October 1948. MS Victoria.
37. HR to Richard Church, 13 November 1935. MS Texas.
38. HR to Rayner Heppenstall, 10 January 1936. MS Texas.
39. Wyndham Lewis to HR, 29 January 1938. MS Cornell.
40. Joshua Hannah to HR, 3 June 1934. MS Victoria.

Chapter 9: Brave, New Machine World 1934–1936

Principal sources: *Art and Industry, Collected Poems, The Cult of Sincerity, Essential Communism, In Defence of*

Shelley, Paul Nash; interviews with Lady Read, Thomas Read, Sir Stephen Spender.

1. Wells Coates, *Listener*, 24 May 1933.
2. Margaret Read, 'Moving to the Mall Studios', in *Belsize Park, A Living Suburb* (London: Belsize Park Conservation Area Publication, n.d.), p. 49.
3. As cited in Gwen Finkel Chavzit, *Herbert Bayer and Modernist Design in America* (Ann Arbor: UMI Research Press, 1987), p. 108.
4. MS Victoria.
5. *Listener*, 28 November 1934.
6. V (1933), 379.
7. Stephen Spender to HR, 5 September 1934. MS Victoria.
8. Stephen Spender to HR, undated but 1935. MS Victoria.
9. Frank Morley to HR, 12 December 1934. MS Victoria.
10. Richard Aldington to HR, 22 December 1934. MS Victoria.
11. A. S. Frere-Reeves to HR, 13 November 1936. MS Read Family.
12. Josiah Wedgwood to HR, 15 December 1934. MS Victoria.
13. *The Journals of Denton Welch*, ed. Michael De-la-Noy (London: Allison & Busby, 1984), p. 15.
14. HR to Rayner Heppenstall, 10 January 1936. MS Texas.
15. Victor Gollancz to HR, 15 October 1934. MS Victoria.
16. XXXI (1934–5), 335–6, 340.
17. Victor Gollancz to HR, 6 April 1935. MS Victoria.
18. Leonard Woolf to HR, 3 February 1935. MS Victoria.
19. *Spectator*, 2 August 1940, 124.
20. *The Diary of Virginia Woolf*, ed. Anne Olivier Bell, vol. IV (London: The Hogarth Press, 1982), pp. 280–1.
21. Ibid., p. 288.
22. Ibid., p. 324.
23. HR to Rayner Heppenstall, 1 March 1935. MS Victoria.
24. HR to Rayner Heppenstall, 4 September and c. September 1935. MSS Texas.
25. Stephen Spender to HR, 20 June 1935. MS Victoria.
26. As cited in Jay Martin, *Always Merry and Bright: A Life of Henry Miller* (Santa Barbara: Capra Press, 1978), p. 317.
27. Henry Miller to HR, 5 September 1935. MS Victoria.
28. Henry Miller to HR, c. 1935. MS Victoria.
29. HR to Wyndham Lewis, 9 December 1934. MS Cornell.
30. HR to Rayner Heppenstall, postmark 24 October 1935. MS Texas.
31. HR to Allen Tate, 28 December 1965. MS Princeton.
32. MS Read Family.
33. Richard Aldington to HR, 25 February 1936. MS Victoria.
34. MS Texas.
35. Ibid.
36. *The Use of Poetry and the Use of Criticism* (London: Faber & Faber, 1933), pp. 101, 84.

Chapter 10: Surrealism and Spain 1936–1939

Principal sources: *Art and Society*, *Collected Poems*, 'A Nest of Gentle Artists', *Paul Nash*, *Poetry and Anarchism*; interviews with Eileen Agar, Margaret Gardiner, Graham Greene, Lady Read, Thomas Read.

1. Geoffrey Grigson, *Recollections: Mainly of Writers and Artists* (London: Chatto & Windus, 1984), p. 58.
2. HR to Häusermann, 6 August 1937. MS Victoria.
3. See Charles Harrison, *English Art and Modernism 1900–1939* (London: Allen Lane, 1981), p. 285.
4. Margaret Gardiner, *Barbara Hepworth: A Memoir* (Edinburgh: Salamander Press, 1982), pp. 44–5.
5. Roland Penrose, *Scrap Book 1900–*

1981 (London: Thames & Hudson, 1981), p. 16.

6. BBC Radio Programme.

7. Ibid.

8. HR to Paul Ray, 10 June 1964. MS Ray.

9. Meryle Secrest, *Kenneth Clark: A Biography* (London: Weidenfeld & Nicolson, 1984), p. 111.

10. Ibid.

11. Roger Berthoud, *The Life of Henry Moore* (London: Faber & Faber, 1987), p. 157.

12. Cited in ibid., p. 120.

13. Robert Radford, *Art for a Purpose, The Artists' International Association, 1933–1953* (Winchester: Winchester School of Art Press, 1978), p. 22.

14. XXX (1934), 574–5.

15. Cited by Radford, *Art for a Purpose,* pp. 70–1.

16. HR to Douglas Cooper, 21 February 1938. MS Getty.

17. Cited by Radford, *Art for a Purpose,* p. 45.

18. *Surrealism in Britain in the Thirties* (Leeds: Leeds City Art Galleries, 1986), p. 26.

19. BBC Radio Programme.

20. William Anderson, *Cecil Collins: The Quest for the Great Happiness* (London: Barrie & Jenkins, 1988), p. 42.

21. Eileen Agar, *A Look at My Life* (London: Methuen, 1988), p. 117.

22. Paul C. Ray, *The Surrealist Movement in England* (Ithaca and London: Cornell University Press, 1971), p. 139.

23. Anthony Penrose, *The Lives of Lee Miller* (London: Thames & Hudson, 1985), p. 75.

24. Whitney Chadwick, *Women Artists and the Surrealist Movement* (London: Thames & Hudson, 1985), p. 106.

25. *New English Weekly* IX (1936), 252.

26. *The Crest on the Silver* (London: The Cresset Press, 1950), p. 164.

27. *New English Weekly* IX (1936), 280.

28. *Surrealism in Britain in the Thirties,* pp. 28–9.

29. Ibid., p. 28.

30. *Left Review,* July 1936, as cited by Radford, *Art for a Purpose,* p. 89.

31. Cited by Radford, *Art for a Purpose,* p. 51.

32. Gardiner, *Barbara Hepworth,* p. 46.

33. Naum Gabo to HR, 14 July 1941. MS Victoria.

34. BBC Radio Programme.

35. Read made this remark to Eileen Agar.

36. W. H. Auden, *The Critical Heritage* (London and Boston: Routledge & Kegan Paul, 1983), pp. 272–3.

37. HR to Tom Ragg, 3 August 1937. MS Routledge.

38. HR to Tom Ragg, 2 January 1938. MS Reading. At about the same time, HR recommended Jack B. Yeats' *The Charmed Life* to Heinemann; when that firm decided against the book, HR showed his enthusiastic report to Ragg, who acquired the book for Routledge's list.

39. Deirdre Bair, *Samuel Beckett* (New York: Harcourt, Brace, Jovanovich, 1978), p. 270.

40. HR to Mrs Gray of the BBC, 27 November 1937. MS BBC.

41. Undated. MS Greene.

42. 12 August 1937.

43. 23 December 1937.

44. 23 September 1937.

45. HR to Graham Greene, 3 September 1937. MS Greene.

46. Whitsun 1936. MS Victoria.

47. *London Bulletin* (April 1938).

48. HR to Heppenstall, 2 July 1939. MS Texas.

49. HR to Ian Cox, 22 June 1938. MS BBC.

50. Guy Burgess, internal memo of 24 June 1938. MS BBC.

51. HR to Douglas Cooper, 20 August 1988. MS Getty.

52. Radford, *Art for a Purpose,* p. 90.

53. 'Picasso's Guernica', *London Bulletin* no. 6 (October 1938), 6.
54. Blunt, 'From Bloomsbury to Marxism', in *Studio International* (November 1973).
55. HR to Douglas Cooper, 27 November 1937. MS Getty.
56. HR to Douglas Cooper, 15 January 1938. MS Getty.
57. HR to Rayner Heppenstall, 21 April 1938. MS Texas.
58. HR to Rayner Heppenstall, 19 June 1938. MS Texas.
59. Undated letter to HR. MS Victoria.
60. Bernard Crick, *George Orwell* (London: Secker & Warburg, 1980), p. 245.
61. Ethel Mannin to HR, 1 July 1938. MS Victoria.
62. Robert Payne to HR, 11 December 1938. MS Victoria.
63. HR to Copyright Section, BBC, 27 November 1937. MS BBC.
64. Joe Ackerley memorandum of 14 October 1938. MS BBC.
65. HR to Rayner Heppenstall, undated but autumn 1938. MS Texas.

Chapter 11: World Within a War 1939–1941

Principal sources: *Collected Poems*; interviews with Leonie Cohn, Graham Greene, Sophie Read Hare, Lady Read, Sir Stephen Spender.

1. George Orwell to HR, 4 January 1939. MS Victoria.
2. *England's Hour* (London: Macmillan, 1941).
3. HR to Douglas Cooper, 2 November 1939. MS Getty.
4. Bernard Crick, *George Orwell: A Biography* (London: Secker & Warburg, 1980), p. 247.
5. George Orwell to HR, 5 March 1939. MS Victoria.
6. Roland Penrose to HR, 27 January 1939. MS Victoria.
7. HR to Louis Adeane, 7 August 1949. MS Victoria.
8. Ibid.
9. HR to Barbara Hepworth, 24 May 1940. MS Tate Gallery Archive.
10. HR to Douglas Cooper, 2 November 1939. MS Getty.
11. Paul Nash to HR, 21 January 1939. MS Victoria.
12. Nigel Henderson as quoted by Jacqueline Bograd Weld, *Peggy, the Wayward Guggenheim* (New York: Dutton, 1986), p. 132.
13. See ibid., p. 172.
14. Peggy Guggenheim, *Out of This Century* (London: André Deutsch, 1980), p. 197.
15. Ibid., p. 198.
16. Ibid., p. 199.
17. Ibid.
18. MS Victoria.
19. Guggenheim, *Out of This Century*, p. 206.
20. MS Getty.
21. See Dorothy M. Kosinski. *Douglas Cooper and the Masters of Cubism* (Basel and London: Kunstmuseum and the Tate Gallery, 1988).
22. Douglas Cooper to HR, 5 April 1939. MS Victoria. 'Do you believe that a museum – a Modern Museum – should contain representative examples of every living painter whose name is known? Obviously not since you talk of excluding Euston Road.'
23. Douglas Cooper to HR, 5 April 1939. MS Victoria.
24. Douglas Cooper to HR, 3 July 1939. MS Victoria.
25. HR to Douglas Cooper, 15 April 1939. MS Getty.
26. Ben Nicholson to HR, c. April 1939. MS Victoria.
27. See HR to Tom Ragg, 19 April 1939, and Tom Ragg to HR, 20 April and 23 May 1939. MSS Reading.
28. Guggenheim, *Out of This Century*, p. 206.
29. Peggy's reference is to *Annals of Innocence and Experience*, which was

published late in 1940. This book contains *The Innocent Eye*, *The Raid* and parts 3 and 4 of what became *The Contrary Experience*.

30. Edwin Muir to HR, 25 October 1939. MS Victoria.

31. HR to Naum Gabo, 2 December 1939. MS Yale.

32. Ibid.

33. HR memo of 27 July 1939. MS Routledge.

34. Memo, 26 December 1939. MS Routledge.

35. HR to Douglas Cooper, 24 June 1939. MS Getty.

36. Ibid.

37. Margaret Gardiner, *Barbara Hepworth: A Memoir* (Edinburgh: Salamander Press, 1982), p. 61.

38. Ben Nicholson to HR, August? 1939. MS Victoria.

39. Ben Nicholson to HR, 17 August 1940. MS Victoria.

40. Ben Nicholson to HR, 14 January 1940. MS Victoria.

41. HR to Barbara Hepworth, 30 April 1944. MS Tate.

42. See HR's letter to Douglas Cooper, 10 May 1940. MS Getty.

43. MS Texas. Postmarked 9 October.

44. MS Texas.

45. *Kingdom Come* III, no. 10 (1942), 19.

46. HR to Douglas Cooper, 25 June 1941. MS Getty.

47. HR to Barbara Hepworth, 4 April 1942. MS Tate.

48. HR to Rayner Heppenstall, 18 April 1940. MS Texas.

49. T. S. Eliot to HR, 2 August [1940?]. MS Victoria.

50. Ibid.

51. Joe Ackerley to HR, undated but c. 1940–1. MS Victoria.

52. HR to Dylan Thomas, 25 October 1939. MS Victoria.

53. 'Herbert Read: A Memoir' in *Herbert Read: A Memorial Symposium*, ed. Robin Skelton (London: Methuen, 1970), p. 10.

54. Ibid., p. 11.

55. *Spectator*, 2 August 1940, 124.

56. Ibid.

57. Eric Gill, *Letters* (London: Jonathan Cape, 1947), pp. 464–5.

58. Fiona MacCarthy, *Eric Gill* (London: Faber & Faber, 1989), p. 274.

59. 18 January 1941, p. 67.

60. Ibid., p. 68.

61. HR to Henry Treece, c. 1942. MS Texas.

62. HR to Henry Treece, 29 November 1943. MS Texas.

63. III, no. 15, 214, 218.

64. Ibid., 215.

65. Ibid., 216.

66. Cited on p. 217 of the *Horizon* article.

67. Graham Greene to HR, 31 March 1941. MS Victoria.

68. HR to Henry Treece, 23 March 1941. MS Texas.

69. HR to Rayner Heppenstall, 18 April 1940. MS Texas.

70. Read has sometimes been said to have advocated Official War Poets (see Brian Gardner (ed.), *The Terrible Rain: The War Poets 1939–1945* (London: Methuen, 1966), xix), but this is incorrect.

71. *Studio*, April/May 1943.

72. HR to Rayner Heppenstall, 2 March 1941. MS Texas.

73. Ibid.

74. HR to Rayner Heppenstall, 20 December 1941. MS Texas.

75. See Robert Hewison, *Under Siege: Literary Life in London, 1939–45* (London: Quartet Books, 1979), p. 35.

76. 'Art in an Electric Atmosphere', *Horizon*, vol. III, no. 17 (May 1941), 308.

77. Ibid., 313.

Chapter 12: To Hell with Culture 1941–1943

Principal sources: *The Cult of Sincerity*, *Education Through Art*, *Essential*

Communism, To Hell with Culture;
interview with George Woodcock.

1. See Robert Hewison, *Under Siege:
Literary Life in London, 1939–45*
(London: Quartet Books, 1979), p. 54.
2. *View*, April 1943. See Hewison,
Under Siege, p. 55.
3. HR to Richard Church, 18 February
1941. MS Texas.
4. *How I See Apocalypse* (London:
Lindsay Drummond, 1946).
5. Ibid., p. 21.
6. Introduction to *Lyra*, ed. Alex
Comfort and Robert Graecen (Billericay:
Grey Walls Press, 1942), pp. 9–11.
7. 'The Youngest Poets', *New
Statesman* 22 (23 August 1941), 186.
8. HR to Henry Treece, 29 August
1940. MS Texas.
9. Henry Treece to HR, 4 September
1940. MS Victoria.
10. HR to Henry Treece, 9 September
1940. MS Texas.
11. Ibid.
12. HR to Henry Treece, 30 October
1940. MS Texas.
13. Henry Treece to HR, 10 November
1940. MS Victoria.
14. HR to Henry Treece, 15 April
1941. MS Texas.
15. HR to Henry Treece, 28 April
1941. MS Texas.
16. HR to Henry Treece, 20 May 1941.
MS Texas; Henry Treece to HR, 24 May
1941. MS Victoria.
17. T. S. Eliot to HR, 10 May 1941. MS
Victoria.
18. T. S. Eliot to HR, 27 June 1941.
MS Victoria.
19. John Guenther, *Sidney Keyes, A
Biographical Inquiry* (London: London
Magazine Editions, 1967), p. 59.
20. Ibid., p. 96.
21. Ibid., p. 113.
22. Ibid., p. 34.
23. Herbert Read, 'Publishing Keyes',
London Magazine (November 1967),
53–4.
24. Guenther, *Sidney Keyes*, p. 184.

25. Cited in ibid., p. 214. HR's
statement was made in the preface to the
American edition (1947) of Keyes'
Collected Poems.
26. Henry Treece to HR, 3 July 1941.
MS Victoria.
27. Henry Treece to HR, 29 June 1941.
MS Victoria.
28. Henry Treece to HR, 14 September
1941. MS Victoria.
29. HR to Henry Treece, 4 December
1941. MS Texas.
30. HR to Henry Treece, 22 December
1941. MS Texas.
31. HR to Henry Treece, 16 January
1942. MS Texas.
32. HR to Henry Treece, 7 November
1941. MS Texas.
33. Ibid.
34. The reaction of the anonymous
woman was relayed to HR by Henry
Treece in a letter of 8 November 1941
(MS Texas).
35. HR to Mr Salmon, 21 April 1941.
MS BBC.
36. Ibid.
37. HR to Henry Treece, 26 November
1941. MS Texas.
38. *Listener*, 30 October 1941, 603.
39. See Roger Berthoud, *The Life of
Henry Moore* (London: Faber & Faber,
1987), p. 178.
40. Page 532.
41. HR to Naum Gabo, 4 August 1941.
MS Yale.
42. HR to Douglas Cooper, 25 June
1941. MS Getty.
43. HR to Naum Gabo, 12 July 1942.
MS Yale.
44. Ibid.
45. John Russell to James King, 12
November 1988.
46. III, no. 17 (May 1941), 310.
47. Ibid., 312.
48. Ibid., 312–13.
49. MS Victoria.
50. Ibid.
51. Ibid.
52. HR to Douglas Cooper, 25 June
1941. MS Getty.

53. Douglas Cooper to HR, 6 June 1941. MS Victoria.

54. HR to Douglas Cooper, 25 June 1941. MS Getty.

55. HR to Henry Treece, 26 November 1941. MS Texas.

56. HR to Henry Treece, 29 November 1941. MS Texas.

57. IV, no. 23 (November 1941), 299.

58. HR to Douglas Cooper, 12 November 1941. MS Getty.

59. Ibid.

60. Ibid.

61. V, no. 28 (April 1942), 220.

62. 'Vulgarity and Impotence: Speculations on the Present State of the Arts', *Horizon* V, no. 28 (1942), 269.

63. Citation from Gabo's diary in Christina Lodder, 'Naum Gabo in England', *Art Monthly* (March 1987), 4.

64. Paul Nash to HR, undated. MS Victoria.

65. V, no. 28 (April 1942), 275.

66. Ibid.

67. Barbara Hepworth to HR, c. April 1942. MS Victoria.

68. HR to Barbara Hepworth, 4 April 1942. MS Tate.

69. Naum Gabo to HR, 14 March 1942. MS Victoria.

70. Naum Gabo to IIR, 9 April 1942. MS Victoria.

71. Naum Gabo to HR, 10 May 1942. MS Victoria.

72. Ibid.

73. HR to Naum Gabo, 12 July 1942. MS Yale.

74. HR to Henry Treece, 14 May 1942. MS Texas.

75. Michael De-la-Noy, *Denton Welch: The Making of a Writer* (Harmondsworth: Penguin, 1986), p. 142.

76. *The Journals of Denton Welch*, ed. Michael De-la-Noy (London: Allison & Busby, 1984), p. 14.

77. De-la-Noy, *Denton Welch*, pp. 185, 150.

78. HR to Barbara Hepworth, 14 August 1945. MS Tate.

79. HR to Flora?, 2 March 1942. MS Victoria.

80. HR to Henry Treece, 5 August 1942. MS Texas.

81. HR to Barbara Hepworth, 3 January 1943. MS Tate.

82. HR to Henry Treece, 4 October 1942. MS Texas.

83. HR to Henry Treece, 14 May 1942. MS Texas.

84. HR to Henry Treece, 15 June 1942. MS Texas.

85. John and Avril Blake, *The Practical Idealists: Twenty-five Years of Designing for Industry* (London: Lund Humphries, 1969), pp. 8–9.

86. Quoted by Fiona MacCarthy, *British Design Since 1880* (London: Lund Humphries, 1982), p. 46.

87. BBC Radio Programme.

88. HR to Barbara Hepworth, 3 January 1943. MS Tate.

89. Ibid.

90. *The Practical Idealists*, p. 27.

91. HR to Naum Gabo, 12 November 1943. MS Yale.

92. HR to Naum Gabo, 19 May 1944. MS Yale.

93. HR to Naum Gabo, 4 July 1944. MS Yale.

94. Ibid.

95. HR to Rayner Heppenstall, 3 May 1943. MS Texas.

96. Ibid., p. 34.

97. These scrapbooks are in the collection of John Read.

98. HR to Henry Treece, 7 March 1943. MS Texas.

99. Barbara Hepworth to HR, 7 February 1943. MS Victoria.

100. T. S. Eliot to HR, 7 January 1943. MS Victoria.

101. HR to Richard Church, 26 April 1943. MS Texas.

102. Bonamy Dobrée to HR, 2 May 1943. MS Victoria.

103. HR to H. G. Wells, 27 August 1943. MS Victoria.

104. HR to Henry Treece, 16 March 1944. MS Texas.

105. HR to Henry Treece, 2 November 1943. MS Texas.

Chapter 13: Freedom: Is It a Crime? 1944–1946

Principal sources: *The Education of Free Men*, *Education Through Art*, *Freedom: Is It a Crime?*, *The Grass Roots of Art*; interviews with John Read, Sir Stephen Spender, George Woodcock.

1. HR to Henry Treece, 16 March 1944. MS Texas.
2. T. S. Eliot to HR, 24 June 1944. MS Victoria.
3. HR to Douglas Cooper, 5 January 1945. MS Getty.
4. Michael De-la-Noy, *Denton Welch: The Making of a Writer* (Harmondsworth: Penguin, 1986), p. 193.
5. HR to Douglas Cooper, 29 January 1945. MS Getty.
6. Barbara Hepworth to HR, 14 May [1944]. MS Victoria.
7. Alan Ross, *Colours of War: War Art 1939–1945* (London: Jonathan Cape, 1983), p. 139.
8. HR to Alex Comfort, 25 November 1944. MS Victoria.
9. Joe Ackerley to HR, November? 1944. MS Victoria.
10. HR to Alex Comfort, 1 September 1944. MS Victoria.
11. *News Chronicle*, 24 April 1935.
12. Ibid.
13. MS UCLA.
14. George Woodcock, 'Big Ben and the Anarchists', *Tamarack Review* 83 and 84 (Winter 1982), 79.
15. See Deirdre Bair, *Samuel Beckett* (New York: Harcourt, Brace, Jovanovich, 1978), p. 336.
16. HR to George Orwell, 18 April 1943. MS BBC.
17. 'Four Poets', *New Statesman* xxix (1944) 29.
18. Eliot's copy of the pamphlet is now in the Read Archive at the University of Victoria.
19. HR to Richard Church, 4 February 1945. MS Texas.
20. HR to Paul Nash, 20 February 1945. MS Tate.
21. Naum Gabo to HR, 12 March 1945. MS Victoria.
22. HR to Henry Treece, 21 March 1945. MS Texas.
23. Naum Gabo to HR, 9 July 1945. MS Victoria.
24. HR to Douglas Cooper, 7 August 1945. MS Getty.
25. HR to George Orwell, 13 August 1945. Cited by Bernard Crick, *George Orwell* (London: Secker & Warburg, 1980), pp. 339–40.
26. HR to George Woodcock, 17 August 1945. MS Queen's.
27. HR to Edward Dahlberg, 22 July 1962. MS Texas.
28. Charles L. DeFanti, *The Wages of Expectation: A Biography of Edward Dahlberg* (New York: New York University Press, 1978), p. 148.
29. Peggy Guggenheim to HR, 12 November 1945. MS Victoria.
30. Peggy Guggenheim to HR, 2 February 1946. MS Victoria.
31. Naum Gabo to HR, 15 January 1946. MS Victoria.
32. HR to Henry Treece, 2 December 1945. MS Texas.
33. 'Existentialism, Marxism and Anarchism', in Howard Zinn (ed.), *Anarchy and Order, Essays in Politics* (Boston: Beacon Press, 1971), p. 141.
34. HR to Henry Treece, 2 December 1945. MS Texas.
35. *The Grass Roots of Art* (London: Faber & Faber, 1955), p. 47.
36. Ibid., p. 40.
37. Naum Gabo to HR, 15 January 1946. MS Victoria.
38. HR to Tom Ragg, 19 April 1946. MS Routledge.
39. HR to Naum Gabo, 2 December 1939. MS Yale.

40. HR to Naum Gabo, 28 March 1946. MS Yale.
41. Ibid.
42. Ibid.
43. HR to Tom Ragg, 19 April 1946. MS Routledge.
44. Ibid.
45. Ibid.
46. Richard Aldington to HR, 7 March 1946. MS Victoria.
47. Richard Aldington to HR, 17 May 1946. MS Victoria.
48. Ibid.
49. Jacqueline Bograd Weld, *Peggy, the Wayward Guggenheim* (New York: Dutton, 1986), p. 347.
50. William McGuire, *Bollingen: An Adventure in Collecting the Past* (Princeton: Princeton University Press, 1982), p. 148.
51. Minutes of the Fine Arts Advisory Committee Meeting of 29 May 1946. HR had become a member of this committee in September 1941. MSS British Council Archives.
52. Ben Nicholson to HR, 21 August [1946]. MS Victoria.
53. Ben Nicholson to HR, 25 September 1946. MS Victoria.
54. Ben Nicholson to HR, 28 October [1946]. MS Victoria.
55. Ben Nicholson to HR, 6 September [1946]. MS Victoria.
56. Roger Berthoud, *The Life of Henry Moore* (London: Faber & Faber, 1987), p. 188.
57. Barbara Hepworth to HR, December 1946. MS Victoria. Hepworth had only seen a black and white reproduction of the Sutherland.
58. Ben Nicholson to HR, 31 December 1946. MS Victoria.
59. HR to Barbara Hepworth, 6 February 1947. MS Tate.
60. HR to Henry Treece, 23 October 1946. MS Texas.
61. HR to Henry Treece, 30 October 1946. MS Texas.

Chapter 14: A Home for Contemporary Art 1947–1949

Principal sources: interviews with Margaret Gardiner, Dorothy Morland.

1. Minutes. MS ICA.
2. Douglas Cooper to HR, 22 February 1946. MS ICA.
3. Ibid.
4. Douglas Cooper to HR, October 1946. MS ICA.
5. HR to Douglas Cooper, 23 November 1946. MS Getty.
6. *Listener*, 31 July 1947.
7. As cited in 'Contemporary Arts Museum: Statement of Policy' (1946), p. 2. ICA.
8. HR to Richard Church, 24 January 1948. MS Texas.
9. HR to Naum Gabo, 28 February 1947. MS Yale.
10. HR to Rayner Heppenstall, 7 April 1945. MS Texas.
11. *News Review*, 22 January 1948.
12. Minutes, 19 November 1947. MS ICA.
13. HR to Douglas Cooper, 6 December 1947. MS Getty.
14. Roland Penrose interview with Dorothy Morland, October 1976. MS ICA.
15. Ibid.
16. As cited by John Sharkey in his unpublished history of the ICA, p. 13. MS ICA.
17. ICA.
18. 10 February 1948.
19. February 1948.
20. 19 February 1948.
21. Wyndham Lewis to HR, 5 February 1948. MS Victoria.
22. HR to Margaret Gardiner, 20 February 1948. MS Gardiner.
23. Ibid.
24. HR to George Woodcock, 20 February 1948. MS Queen's.
25. HR to Allen Tate, 14 March 1948. MS Princeton.
26. Sharkey, unpublished history of the

ICA, p. 15. The article in the *New York Times* appeared on 4 April 1948.
27. Minutes, 5 May 1948. MS ICA.
28. Penrose interview with Dorothy Morland, October 1976. MS ICA.
29. Ben Nicholson to HR, c. 1948. MS Victoria.
30. HR to Eric Finlay, 13 September 1948. MS V & A.
31. Ben Nicholson to HR, 8 October 1948. MS Victoria.
32. A sample accompanied HR's letter to Naum Gabo of 20 August 1946. MS Yale.
33. HR to Edward Dahlberg, 25 October 1948. MS Texas.
34. Penrose interview with Dorothy Morland, October 1976. MS ICA.
35. Ibid.
36. 2 January 1949.
37. *Observer*, 2 January 1949.
38. 'London Paris', *Eidos* no. 1 (May/June 1950), 46.
39. HR to Edward Dahlberg, 16 January 1949. MS Texas.
40. HR to Edward Dahlberg, 13 February 1949. MS Texas.
41. Ibid.
42. HR to Edward Dahlberg, 8 March 1949. MS Texas.
43. Tom Cross, *Painting the Warmth of the Sun* (Penzance and Guildford: Alison Hodge and Lutterworth, 1984), p. 85.
44. 28 April 1949. Reprinted in A. J. Munnings. *An Artist's Life* (London: Museum Press, 1950).
45. Ibid.
46. As cited in *Studio*, February 1950, p. 62.
47. HR to Philip James, 9 November 1949. MS Arts Council.
48. HR to George Woodcock, 15 June 1949. MS Queen's.
49. Ibid.
50. HR to Kathleen Raine, 12 October 1949. MS Victoria.

Chapter 15: Moon's Farm 1950–1952

Principal sources: *Collected Poems, The Tenth Muse*; interviews with Eileen Agar, Ruth Francken, Patrick Heron, Dorothy Morland, Piers Paul Read.

1. J. R. Ackerley to HR, undated but March 1950. MS Victoria.
2. HR to Naum Gabo, 21 December 1950. MS Yale.
3. Ibid.
4. HR to Edward Dahlberg, 3 June 1951. MS Texas.
5. Dannie Abse, *A Poet in the Family* (London: Hutchinson, 1974), p. 132.
6. HR to Wyndham Lewis, 10 November 1950. MS Cornell.
7. Wyndham Lewis to HR, 17 November 1950. MS Victoria.
8. HR to Benedict Nicolson, 23 May 1950. MS *Burlington*.
9. HR to Edward Dahlberg, 15 July 1950. MS Texas.
10. HR to Edward Dahlberg, 17 September 1950. MS Texas.
11. HR to Edward Dahlberg, 31 December 1950. MS Texas.
12. HR to Allen Tate, 12 January 1951. MS Princeton.
13. *New Statesman*, 10 November 1951, 158.
14. T. S. Eliot to HR, 15 May 1950. MS Victoria.
15. 12 April 1951, p. 3.
16. HR to Philip James, 21 January 1951. MS Arts Council.
17. *Daily Telegraph*, 5 December 1950.
18. ICA Managing Committee Minutes, 23 May 1951. MS ICA.
19. ICA Managing Committee Minutes, 29 October 1953. MS ICA.
20. HR to Naum Gabo, 7 December 1951. MS Yale.
21. HR to Edward Dahlberg, 1 April 1951. MS Texas.
22. Ibid.
23. HR to Barbara Hepworth, 3 December 1950. MS Tate.

24. *Barbara Hepworth: Carvings and Drawings* (London: Lund Humphries, 1952), p. xii.
25. HR to Naum Gabo, 16 June 1951. MS Yale.
26. T. S. Eliot to HR, 14 April 1951. MS Victoria.
27. MS BBC.
28. C. A. Franklin to HR, 27 June 1951. MS Routledge.
29. HR to Mr Newby, 24 October 1951. MS BBC.
30. HR to Edward Dahlberg, 6 October [1951]. MS Texas.
31. HR to Naum Gabo, 7 December 1951. MS Yale.
32. HR to Edward Dahlberg, 19 November 1951. MS Texas.
33. HR to Edward Dahlberg, 13 January 1952. MS Texas.
34. Graham Greene to HR, 6 March 1952. MS Victoria.
35. Douglas Cooper to HR, 23 September 1952. MS Victoria.
36. HR to Douglas Cooper, 10 November 1952. MS Getty.
37. HR to Douglas Cooper, c. July 1952. MS Getty.
38. HR to Edward Dahlberg, 22 June 1952. MS Texas.
39. HR to Barbara Hepworth, 6 December 1951. MS Tate.
40. MS Victoria: Introduction to the XXVI Biennale.
41. Barbara Hepworth to HR, 19 July 1952. MS Victoria.
42. HR to Barbara Hepworth, 21 July 1952. MS Tate.
43. HR to Ruth Francken, 16 February 1955. MS Francken.

Chapter 16: Not Art, Not Now 1953–1955

Principal sources: *Icon and Idea*, *T. S. E. – A Memoir*; interviews with Patrick Heron, Dorothy Morland, William and Flora Read, Sir Stephen Spender.

1. Geoffrey Grigson, *Recollections: Mainly of Writers and Artists* (London: Chatto & Windus, 1984), p. 59.
2. Wyndham Lewis to Michael Ayrton, 4 April 1953. MS transcribed by Benedict Read.
3. Ethel Mannin to HR, 6 January 1953. MS Read Family.
4. Ethel Mannin to HR, 3 January 1953. MS Read Family.
5. HR to Vernon Richards, 31 December 1952. MS Read Family.
6. 'A Statement', *Freedom*, 17 January 1953, 2. The same issue of *Freedom* contained an editorial denouncing Read's action, and letters of protest were published in the 24 January, 31 January and 7 February issues of that magazine.
7. HR to Caroline Gordon, 27 January 1953. MS Princeton.
8. HR to Edward Dahlberg, 3 January 1954. MS Texas.
9. HR to Naum Gabo, 24 December 1952. MS Yale.
10. Stephen Spender, *The Thirties and After* (London: Methuen, 1978), p. 174.
11. Ibid., p. 175.
12. Ibid., p. 251.
13. Ibid., p. 174.
14. *The Struggle of the Modern* (London: Hamish Hamilton, 1963), pp. 177–85.
15. HR to Edward Dahlberg, 23 February 1954. MS Texas.
16. HR to Naum Gabo, 4 August 1941. MS Yale.
17. HR to Edward Dahlberg, 3 May 1953. MS Texas.
18. HR to Gabo, 19 March 1953. However, Gabo did receive $2000.
19. Ibid.
20. Lawrence Alloway interviewed by Rayner Banham, 25 May 1977. MS ICA.
21. MS ICA.
22. As cited by Anne Massey, 'The Independent Group: Towards a Redefinition' (doctoral dissertation: Newcastle upon Tyne Polytechnic, 1984), p. 223.
23. Ibid.

24. Ibid.
25. Ibid., p. 246.
26. HR to Naum Gabo, 16 October 1954. MS Yale.
27. *Art and the Evolution of Man* (London: Freedom Press, 1951), pp. 38–9.
28. Folio page 2.
29. Geoffrey Summerfield to James King, 23 April 1988.
30. C. G. Jung to John Barrett, 3 January 1953. MS Routledge.
31. HR to Edward Dahlberg, 3 May 1953. MS Texas.
32. Peter Lanyon to HR, undated but December 1950. MS Victoria.
33. Peter Lanyon to HR, 11 May 1959. MS Victoria.
34. HR to Naum Gabo, 19 March 1953. MS Victoria.
35. HR to C. A. Franklin, 1 October 1953. MS Routledge.
36. HR to Edward Dahlberg, 3 January 1954. MS Texas.
37. Ibid.
38. Ibid.
39. HR to Colin Franklin, 18 January 1954. MS Routledge.
40. Ibid.
41. HR to Edward Dahlberg, 8 February 1954. MS Texas.
42. T. S. Eliot to HR, 28 May 1954. MS Victoria.
43. HR to Edward Dahlberg, 31 January 1954. MS Texas.
44. HR to Kathleen Raine, undated but late 1953 or early 1954. MS Victoria.
45. HR to Edward Dahlberg, 30 April 1954. MS Texas.
46. HR to Edward Dahlberg, 24 May 1954. MS Texas.
47. HR to Edwin Muir, 3 March 1956. MS Victoria.
48. *The Demon of Progress in the Arts* (London: Methuen, 1954), p. 53.
49. Ibid., p. 54.
50. ICA Managing Committee Minutes, 15 December 1954. MS ICA.
51. HR to Edward Dahlberg, 23 February 1954. MS Texas.

52. HR to Edward Dahlberg, 13 March 1955. MS Victoria.
53. *New Statesman*, 16 July 1955, 72.
54. *New Statesman*, 23 July 1955, 104.
55. MS Greene.
56. HR to Barbara Hepworth, 16 October 1954. MS Tate.
57. 10 (1957), 167–70.
58. HR to Edward Dahlberg, 27 March 1955. MS Texas.
59. HR to Edward Dahlberg, 13 March 1955. MS Texas.
60. John Rothenstein, *Time's Thievish Progress* (London: Cassell, 1970), p. 40.
61. T. S. Eliot to HR, 10 November 1955. MS Victoria.
62. HR to T. S. Eliot, 12 November 1955. MS Victoria.
63. T. S. Eliot to HR, 14 November 1955. MS Victoria.
64. T. S. Eliot to HR, 19 November 1955. MS Victoria.
65. HR to T. S. Eliot, 21 November 1955. MS Victoria.
66. Ibid.
67. T. S. Eliot to HR, 23 November 1955. MS Victoria.
68. Lewis' biographer, Jeffrey Meyers, thinks that Read was lying (see *The Enemy: A Biography of Wyndham Lewis* (Boston and London: Routledge & Kegan Paul, 1980), p. 312). This is unlikely. The probability is that Eliot made contradictory statements to both men.

Chapter 17: Blind Drift of Annihilation 1956–1961

Principal sources: *Collected Poems*; interviews with John Berger, Ruth Francken, Kathleen Raine, Piers Paul Read, Margaret Selley.

1. HR to Edward Dahlberg, 29 June 1958. MS Texas.

2. HR to Edward Dahlberg, undated but August 1958. MS Texas.

3. *Listener*, 2 February 1956.

4. Ibid.

5. HR to A. E. W. Thomas of the BBC, 9 February 1956. MS Victoria.

6. HR to Siegfried Sassoon, 9 February 1956. MS Victoria.

7. HR to Edward Dahlberg, 10 February 1956. MS Texas.

8. MS Victoria.

9. HR to Roland Penrose, 24 June 1959. MS Penrose.

10. HR to Ruth Francken, 19 February [1956]. MS Francken.

11. Ibid.

12. Ibid.

13. HR to Edward Dahlberg, 17 March 1957. MS Texas.

14. HR to Alex Comfort, 10 December 1956. MS Victoria.

15. HR to Edward Dahlberg, 28 January 1956. MS Texas.

16. HR to Edward Dahlberg, 8 May 1956. MS Texas.

17. HR to Roland Penrose, 8 August 1956. MS Penrose.

18. Ibid.

19. HR to Edward Dahlberg, 24 March 1956. MS Texas.

20. 'Recent Tendencies in Abstract Painting', *Canadian Art* XV (August 1958), 200.

21. Ibid., 202.

22. HR to Edward Dahlberg, 5 August 1956. MS Texas.

23. HR to Ivon Hitchens, 16 October 1956. MS Victoria.

24. Ibid.

25. HR to Edward Dahlberg, 7 October 1957. MS Texas.

26. HR to Edward Dahlberg, 27 October 1957. MS Texas.

27. HR to Edward Dahlberg, 7 October 1957. MS Texas.

28. HR to Kathleen Raine, 13 October 1956. MS Victoria.

29. HR to Edward Dahlberg, 18 November 1956 and 27 July 1958. MSS Texas.

30. HR to John Barrett, 5 January 1958. MS Read Family.

31. John Barrett to HR, 18 April 1958. MS Read Family.

32. T. S. Eliot to HR, 1 April 1958. MS Victoria.

33. HR to *New Statesman*, 31 May 1958.

34. HR to Edward Dahlberg, 22 March 1958. MS Texas.

35. HR to Edward Dahlberg, 28 December 1958. MS Texas.

36. Ibid.

37. *Art Since 1945*, ed. Marcel Brion and others (London: Thames & Hudson, 1958), p. 250.

38. HR to Edward Dahlberg, 30 May 1959. MS Texas.

39. HR to Edward Dahlberg, 27 July 1960. MS Texas.

40. HR to Edward Dahlberg, 5 February 1959. MS Texas.

41. Edwin Muir to HR, 16 April 1941. MS Victoria.

42. 'Mood of the Month-x', *London Magazine* VI (August 1959).

43. VI (October 1959).

44. HR to Edward Dahlberg, 7 March 1959. MS Texas.

45. HR to Edward Dahlberg, 4 December 1960. MS Texas.

46. Citations are from Read's letters to his family of 8, 9, 10, 11, 14, 15, 16, 18, 19, 21, 24, 28 and 29 September. As printed on pp. 43–9 of *A Tribute to Herbert Read*.

47. HR to Edward Dahlberg, 11 October 1959. MS Texas.

48. HR to Roland Penrose, 5 December 1959. MS Penrose.

49. HR to Edward Dahlberg, 15 November 1959. MS Texas.

50. Ibid.

51. HR to Edward Dahlberg, 25 April 1960. MS Texas.

52. Brian Adams, *Sidney Nolan. Such Is Life* (London: Hutchinson, 1987), p. 146.

53. C. G. Jung to HR, 2 September 1960. MS Routledge.

54. HR to C. G. Jung, 19 October 1960. MS Victoria.
55. Ibid.
56. Ibid.
57. *Listener*, 22 September 1960, 479–80.
58. HR to C. G. Jung, 27 October 1960. MS Routledge.
59. HR to Allen Tate, 27 November 1960. MS Princeton.
60. HR to Richard Hull, 14 April 1961. MS Victoria.
61. HR to Eric Finlay, 25 March 1961. MS V & A.
62. 'Publisher of High Standards', *The Times*, 2 February 1961, 21.
63. HR to John Barrett, 15 April 1961. MS Read Family.
64. HR to Richard Hull, 20 April 1961. MS Victoria.
65. HR to Richard Hull, 20 April 1961. MS Victoria.
66. Ibid.
67. HR to Jack Barrett, 23 May 1961. MS Read Family.
68. HR to Richard Hull. 20 April 1961. MS Victoria.

Chapter 18: The Forms of Things Unknown 1961–1968

Principal sources: *Collected Poems*; interviews with Graham Greene, Benedict Read, Lady Read, Piers Paul Read, Thomas Read.

1. T. S. Eliot to HR, 1 June 1961. MS Victoria.
2. Martin Seymour-Smith, *Robert Graves: His Life and Work* (London: Hutchinson, 1982), p. 515.
3. HR to John Berger, 24 December 1961. MS Victoria.
4. Ibid.
5. Nicholas Walter, 'Remembering Herbert Read', *Anarchy* 91 (vol. 8, no. 9; September 1968), 288.
6. HR to Graham Greene, 1 January 1961. MS Greene.
7. HR to Mr Schoenman, 28 August 1960. MS Russell.
8. MS Russell.
9. 'An Appeal to Fellow-Members of the Committee of 100', c. 3 December 1961. MS Russell.
10. Ibid.
11. 'A Note on Policy Submitted to the Meeting of the Committee of 100 to be held on December 17, 1961'. MS Russell.
12. HR to John Berger, 10 December 1961. MS Victoria.
13. HR to Ruth Francken, 18 March 1962. MS Francken.
14. HR to Roland Penrose, 28 February 1965. MS Penrose.
15. HR to Barbara Hepworth, 27 November 1966. MS Tate.
16. HR to Roland Penrose, 30 October 1967. MS Penrose.
17. HR to Eric Finlay, 11 January 1964. MS V & A.
18. HR to Eric Finlay, 13 February 1965. MS V & A.
19. HR to Misha Black, 15 October 1965. MS Black.
20. HR to Misha Black, 27 March 1968. MS Black.
21. HR to Vernon Watkins, 2 June 1967. MS Victoria.
22. T. S. Eliot to HR, 30 March 1962. MS Victoria.
23. HR to Edward Dahlberg, 28 August 1962. MS Texas.
24. HR to Allen Tate, 20 July 1963. MS Princeton.
25. HR to Edward Dahlberg, 10 February 1963. MS Texas.
26. HR to T. S. Eliot, 29 July 1963. MS Victoria.
27. HR to Edward Dahlberg, 18 March 1962. MS Texas.
28. HR to Edward Dahlberg, 28 August 1962. MS Texas.
29. HR to Jack Barrett, 4 January 1964. MS Read Family.
30. HR to Alex Comfort, 9 January 1964. MS Victoria.

31. HR to Edward Dahlberg, 22 January 1963. MS Texas.

32. T. S. Eliot to HR, 20 May 1964. MS Victoria.

33. HR to Jack Barrett, 30 April 1964. MS Routledge.

34. HR to Barbara Hepworth, 30 August 1964. MS Tate.

35. HR to Barbara Hepworth, 1 November 1964. MS Tate.

36. Margaret Read to Miriam Gabo, c. November 1964. MS Yale.

37. HR to Dorothy Morland, 23 October 1964. MS Morland.

38. *Times Literary Supplement*, 11 December 1964.

39. HR to Naum Gabo, 10 December 1964. MS Yale.

40. Richard Church to HR, 31 January 1965. MS Victoria.

41. Jacqueline Bograd Weld, *Peggy, the Wayward Guggenheim* (New York: Dutton, 1986), p. 404.

42. HR to Eric Finlay, 18 March 1965. MS V & A.

43. HR to Allen Tate, 7 April 1965. MS Princeton.

44. HR to Allen Tate, 7 April 1965. MS Princeton.

45. HR to Edward Dahlberg, 7 March 1965. MS Texas.

46. HR to Allen Tate, 13 May 1965. MS Princeton.

47. Ibid.

48. Ibid.

49. HR to Allen Tate, 29 April 1965. MS Princeton.

50. HR to Graham Greene, 18 March 1968. MS Greene.

51. HR to Edward Dahlberg, 15 October 1965. MS Texas.

52. HR to Edward Dahlberg, 7 January 1966. MS Texas.

53. HR to Allen Tate, 28 December 1965. MS Princeton.

54. HR to Margaret Gardiner, 11 October 1967. MS Gardiner.

55. HR to Kathleen Raine, 9 January 1966. MS Victoria.

56. HR to Kathleen Raine, 17 January 1966. MS Victoria.

57. HR to Allen Tate, 22 March 1966. MS Princeton.

58. HR to Edward Dahlberg, 28 March 1966. MS Texas.

59. HR to George Woodcock, 3 August 1966. MS Queen's.

60. HR to Vernon Watkins, 26 January 1967. MS Victoria.

61. HR to Edward Dahlberg, 8 October 1966. MS Texas.

62. HR to Edward Dahlberg, 14 February 1967. MS Texas.

63. HR to Barbara Hepworth, 15 January 1967. MS Tate.

64. HR to Kathleen Raine, 28 February 1967. MS Victoria.

65. Undated letter to Roland Penrose. MS Morland.

66. HR to Margaret Gardiner, 16 October 1967. MS Gardiner.

67. HR to Kathleen Raine, 25 September 1967. MS Victoria.

68. HR to Barbara Hepworth, 1 July 1967. MS Tate.

69. HR to Barbara Hepworth, 11 August 1967. MS Tate.

70. HR to Allen Tate, 5 October 1967. MS Princeton.

71. HR to Kathleen Raine, 20 December 1967. MS Victoria.

72. HR to Graham Greene, 16 December 1967. MS Greene.

73. HR to Barbara Hepworth, 22 January 1968. MS Tate.

74. Ibid.

75. HR to Graham Greene, 22 February 1968. MS Greene.

76. HR to Naum Gabo, 25 March 1968. MS Yale.

77. HR to Barbara Hepworth, dated only 'Tuesday' but March 1968. MS Tate.

78. HR to Naum Gabo, 25 March 1968. MS Yale.

79. HR to Graham Greene, 2 June 1968. MS Greene.

80. HR to Graham Greene, 8 March 1968. MS Greene.

81. George Woodcock to James King, 19 December 1988.

82. HR to Barbara Hepworth, 20 September 1966. MS Tate.

83. HR to Kathleen Raine, 9 April 1968. MS Victoria.

Select Bibliography

ABSE, Dannie. *A Poet in the Family.* London: Hutchinson, 1974.

ACKROYD, Peter. *T. S. Eliot.* London: Hamish Hamilton, 1984.

AGAR, Eileen. *A Look at My Life.* London: Methuen, 1988.

ALDINGTON, Richard. *Death of a Hero.* New York: Covici, Friede, 1929.

ALI, Agha Shadid. *T. S. Eliot as Editor.* Ann Arbor: UMI Research Press, 1986.

ANDERSON, William. *Cecil Collins: The Quest for the Great Happiness.* London: Barrie & Jenkins, 1988.

BAIR, Deirdre. *Samuel Beckett.* New York: Harcourt, Brace, Jovanovich, 1978.

BERRY, Francis. *Herbert Read.* London: Longmans Green for the British Council, 1953.

BERTHOUD, Roger. *Graham Sutherland: A Biography.* London: Faber & Faber, 1982.

——. *The Life of Henry Moore.* London: Faber & Faber, 1987.

BLAKE, Avril. *Misha Black.* London: The Design Council, 1984.

BLAKE, John and Avril. *The Practical Idealists: Twenty-five Years of Designing for Industry.* London: Lund Humphries, 1969.

BROME, Vincent. *Jung.* London: Paladin Books, 1980.

——. *J. B. Priestley.* London: Hamish Hamilton, 1988.

CALDER, Angus. *The People's War: Britain 1939–1945.* London: Panther Books, 1971.

CARPENTER, Humphrey. *A Serious Character: The Life of Ezra Pound.* London: Faber & Faber, 1988.

CHAVZIT, Gwen Finkel. *Herbert Bayer and Modernist Design in America.* Ann Arbor: UMI Research Press, 1987.

COHN, Leonie, ed. *Belsize Park: A Living Suburb.* London: Belsize Park Conservation Area Publication, n.d.

CORK, Richard. *Vorticism and Abstract Art in the First Machine Age.* London: Gordon Fraser, 1976.

CRICK, Bernard. *George Orwell.* London: Secker & Warburg, 1980.

CROSS, Tom. *Painting the Warmth of the Sun.* Penzance and Guildford: Alison Hodge and Lutterworth, 1984.

CUMBERLAND, Gerald. *Set Down in Malice*. New York: Brentano, 1919.

DAVID, Hugh. *The Fitzrovians: A Portrait of Bohemian Society, 1900–55*. London: Michael Joseph, 1988.

DEFANTI, Charles. *The Wages of Expectation: A Biography of Edward Dahlberg*. New York: New York University Press, 1978.

DE-LA-NOY, Michael. *Denton Welch: The Making of a Writer*. Harmondsworth: Penguin, 1986.

FISHMAN, Solomon. *The Interpretation of Art*. Berkeley and Los Angeles: University of California Press, 1963.

FRY, Roger. *Letters*, ed. Denys Sutton. 2 vols. London: Chatto & Windus, 1972.

FURBANK, P. N. *E. M. Forster: A Life*. London: Secker & Warburg, 1977, 1978.

FUSSELL, Paul. *The Great War and Modern Memory*. New York and London: Oxford University Press, 1975.

GARDINER, Margaret. *Barbara Hepworth: A Memoir*. Edinburgh: Salamander Press, 1982.

GARDNER, Brian, ed. *The Terrible Rain: The War Poets 1939–1945*. London: Methuen, 1966.

GHANEM, Salma Mohammed. 'The Literary Criticism of Sir Herbert Read'. Doctoral dissertation: The University of Liverpool, 1963.

GILL, Eric. *Letters*, ed. Walter Shewring. London: Jonathan Cape, 1947.

GODSEN, P. H. J. H., and A. J. Taylor, eds. *Studies in the History of a University, 1874–1974*. Leeds: E. J. Arnold & Son, 1975.

GREENE, Graham. *Ways of Escape*. Toronto: Lester & Orpen Dennys, 1980.

GRIGSON, Geoffrey. *The Crest on the Silver*. London: The Cresset Press, 1950.

——*Recollections: Mainly of Writers and Artists*. London: Chatto & Windus, 1984.

GUENTHER, John. *Sidney Keyes, A Biographical Inquiry*. London: London Magazine Editions, 1967.

GUGGENHEIM, Peggy. *Out of This Century*. London: André Deutsch, 1980.

Hampstead in the Thirties: A Committed Decade. London: Camden Arts Centre, 1975.

HEALY, Philip. 'The Making of an Edinburgh *Salon*', *Journal of the Eighteen Nineties Society* 12–13 (1981–2), 25–39.

HEPPENSTALL, Rayner. *The Master Eccentric: The Journals of Rayner Heppenstall*, ed. Jonathan Goodman. London and New York: Allison & Busby, 1986.

HESLING, Bernard. *Little and Orphan*. London: Constable, 1954.

HEWISON, Robert. *Under Siege: Literary Life in London 1939–45*. London: Quartet Books, 1979.

HIGHAM, David. *Literary Gent*. London: Jonathan Cape, 1978.

HOFFMANN, Edith. 'The Magazine in War-time', *Burlington*

Magazine CXXVIII, no. 1000, 478–80.

JACKSON, Holbrook. *Bernard Shaw: A Monograph*. London: Grant Richards, 1907.

JAMESON, Storm. *Journey from the North*. Vol. I. London: Collins & Harvill Press, 1969.

KANDINSKY, Wassily. *Concerning the Spiritual in Art*. Translated by M. T. H. Sadler. New York: Dover Publications, 1977.

KOSINKI, Dorothy M. *Douglas Cooper and the Masters of Cubism*. Basel and London: Kunstmuseum and the Tate Gallery, 1988.

LEWIS, Wyndham. *The Letters of Wyndham Lewis*, ed. W. K. Rose. London: Methuen, 1963.
——*The Demon of Progress in the Arts*. London: Methuen, 1954.

LODDER, Christina. 'Naum Gabo in England', *Art Monthly* (March 1987).

MACCARTHY, Fiona. *British Design Since 1880*. London: Lund Humphries, 1982.
——. *Eric Gill*. London: Faber & Faber, 1989.

MCGUIRE, William. *Bollingen, An Adventure in Collecting the Past*. Princeton: Princeton University Press, 1982.

MARTIN, Jay. *Always Merry and Bright: The Life of Henry Miller*. Santa Barbara: Capra Press, 1978.

MASSEY, Anne. 'The Independent Group: Towards a Redefinition'. Doctoral dissertation: Newcastle upon Tyne Polytechnic, 1984.
——. 'The Independent Group: Towards a Redefinition',

Burlington Magazine CXXIX, no. 1009 (April 1987). 232–42.

MEYER, Michael. *Not Prince Hamlet: Literary and Theatrical Memoirs*. London: Secker & Warburg, 1989.

MEYERS, Jeffrey. *The Enemy: A Biography of Wyndham Lewis*. Boston and London: Routledge & Kegan Paul, 1980.

MUNNINGS, A. J. *An Artist's Life*. London: Museum Press, 1950.

NOWELL, Robert, ed. *Why I Am Still a Catholic*. London: Collins, 1982.

ORAGE, A. R. *Friedrich Nietzsche, The Dionysian Spirit of the Age*. London and Edinburgh: T. N. Foulis, 1906.

ORR, Peter. *The Poet Speaks*. London: Routledge & Kegan Paul, 1966.

PENROSE, Roland. *Scrap Book 1900–1981*. London: Thames & Hudson, 1981.

PERKINS, David. *A History of Modern Poetry*. 2 vols. Cambridge, Mass. and London: Harvard University Press, 1976 and 1987.

RADFORD, Robert. *Art for a Purpose: The Artists' International Association, 1933–1953*. Winchester: Winchester School of Art Press, 1987.

RAY, Paul C. *The Surrealist Movement in England*. Ithaca and London: Cornell University Press, 1971.

READ, Margaret. 'Moving into the Mall Studios', *Belsize Park: A Living Suburb*. London: Belsize Park Conservation Area, n.d. but c. 1984.

ROSS, Alan. *The Colours of War: War Art 1939–1945.* London: Jonathan Cape, 1983.

ROTHENSTEIN, John. *Time's Thievish Progress.* London: Cassell, 1970.

RUTTER, Frank. *Since I Was Twenty-Five.* Boston and New York: Houghton Mifflin, 1927.

SADLEIR, Michael. *Michael Ernest Sadler.* London: Constable, 1949.

SECREST, Meryle. *Kenneth Clark: A Biography.* London: Weidenfeld & Nicolson, 1984.

SEYMOUR-SMITH, Martin. *Robert Graves: His Life and Work.* London: Hutchinson, 1982.

SHELDEN, Michael. *Friends of Promise: Cyril Connolly and the World of Horizon.* London: Hamish Hamilton, 1989.

SILBER, Evelyn. *The Sculpture of Epstein.* Oxford: Phaidon, 1986.

SITWELL, Osbert. *Laughter in the Next Room.* London: Macmillan, 1949.

SKEAPING, John. *Drawn from Life: An Autobiography.* London: Collins, 1977.

SKELTON, Robin. *Herbert Read: A Memorial Symposium.* London: Methuen, 1970.

SPALDING, Frances. *Vanessa Bell.* London: Weidenfeld & Nicolson, 1983.

SPENDER, Stephen. *The Struggle of the Modern.* London: Hamish Hamilton, 1963.

SPENDER, Stephen. *The Thirties and After.* London: Methuen, 1978.

STOCK, Noel. *The Life of Ezra Pound.* Harmondsworth: Penguin, 1974.

THISTLEWOOD, David. *Herbert Read: Formlessness and Form, An Introduction to His Aesthetics.* London: Routledge & Kegan Paul, 1984.

THOMAS, Dylan. *Collected Letters.* London: J. M. Dent, 1985.

TOMALIN, Claire. *Katherine Mansfield: A Secret Life.* New York: Alfred A. Knopf, 1988.

TREECE, Henry, ed. *Herbert Read: An Introduction to His Work by Various Hands.* London: Faber & Faber, 1944.

A Tribute to Herbert Read. Bradford: City of Bradford Metropolitan Council Art Galleries and Museum, 1975.

WELCH, Denton. *Journals*, ed. Michael De-la-Noy. London: Allison & Busby, 1984.

WELD, Jacqueline Bograd. *Peggy, The Wayward Guggenheim.* New York: Dutton, 1986.

WELLEK, René. *A History of Modern Criticism, vol. 5: English Criticism, 1900–1950.* New Haven and London: Yale University Press, 1986.

WOODCOCK, George. *Herbert Read: The Stream and The Source.* London: Faber & Faber, 1972.

YORKE, Malcolm. *The Spirit of Place: Nine Neo-Romantic Artists and Their Times.* London: Constable, 1988.

Index

INDEX

Mathews, Elkin 38–9
Mathieu, Georges 283
Matisse 97–8, 180, 239, 246
Matta, Roberto 247
Maugham, Somerset 123
Maupassant, Guy de 46
Mayor, Freddy 126, 130–1, 238
McCarthy, Joe 276
McFadden, Roy 201
McIsaac, Nigel 100
McWilliam, F. E. 239
Meadows, Bernard 262
Mellis, Margaret 185–6
Mellon, Mary 229, 230, 231
Mellon, Paul 229, 231, 260
Melville, Robert 235, 244
Mendelsohn, Eric 139
Meninsky, Bernard 120
Meredith, George 46
Mesens, E. L. T. 120, 162, 180–1, 187,
   235
Meyer, Michael 204
Mies van der Rohe, Ludwig 119, 142
Miller, Henry 111, 148, 204; *Tropic of
   Cancer* 148
Miller, Lee 163
Millian 312
Milton 89; *Paradise Lost* 307
Milverton, Lord 258
minimalist art 303
Miró, Joan 162, 170, 190, 227, 251, 286
Moholy-Nagy, László 120, 139, 142,
   153, 230
Mondrian, Piet 120, 139, 153, 187
Montblanc fountain pens 142
Moore, Henry 7, 100, 105, 111, 114,
   117, 123, 125, 126, 129, 130, 134,
   145–6, 153, 158, 163, 179, 199,
   208–9, 220, 237, 238, 239, 244,
   246, 262, 264, 269, 271, 274, 275,
   284, 286, 289, 290, 294, 295, 301–
   2, 305, 306; early career 95–6;
   HR's identification with him and
   espousal of him in the *Listener* and
   The Meaning of Art 95–6; HR's
   first, influential book on him 118;
   his rivalry with Hepworth 121–2;
   and Unit One 130–2; alarmed by
   HR's promotion of Gabo and
   surrealism 165; HR suggests coal-
   mining as subject 206; HR defends

his *Madonna and Child* for St
   Matthew's, Northampton to
   Hepworth and Nicholson 232–3,
   246; *Standing Figure* at 1952
   Biennale 262–3; HR flustered when
   he purchases his first maquette by
   him 301–2; visits dying HR 313
Moore, Irina, *née* Radetzky 95, 125,
   145–6
Moore, Nicholas 199
Moorman, F. W. 24
Morison, Stanley 142
Morland, Dorothy 269, 273, 277
Morley, Frank 79, 80, 88, 108, 111,
   143, 144, 172
Morrell, Ottoline 57
Morris, Cedric 179
Morris, Desmond 261, 310; *The Naked
   Ape* 310
Morris, Guido 246
Morris, William 46, 47, 141
Mortimer, Raymond 208, 209
Mosley, Oswald 139, 164, 301
Motherwell, Robert 227
Mount Holyoke college 276
Much Hadham 301, 306
Muir, Edwin 46, 184, 289–90
Munnings, Alfred 246, 247
Munro, Harold 75, 79
Murdoch, Iris 288, 289; *The Bell* 288
Murray, Gilbert 46
Murray, Keith 144
Muscoates Grange 1, 2, 4–11, 12, 14,
   106, 248, 297
Museé d'Art Moderne 248
Museum of Living Art project 178
Museum of Modern Art, New York
   (MOMA) 180, 235, 236, 238, 243,
   257, 258, 302

Nabokov, Vladimir, *Lolita* 289
Nash, Paul 118, 120, 137, 158, 160,
   163, 164, 166, 225, 238, 239, 286;
   spearheads Unit One 130–2; his
   work castigated by Nicholson 131–
   2; his *Room and Book* and HR's *Art
   and Industry* share similar views on
   design in England 142; and
   surrealism 153, 157; affair with
   Eileen Agar 161, 162; gives pencil
   sketch of *Encounter on the Downs* to

352